Intercultural Lea

in Language Education
and Beyond

LANGUAGES FOR INTERCULTURAL COMMUNICATION AND EDUCATION

Series Editors: Michael Byram, *University of Durham, UK* and Anthony J. Liddicoat, *University of Warwick, UK*

The overall aim of this series is to publish books which will ultimately inform learning and teaching, but whose primary focus is on the analysis of intercultural relationships, whether in textual form or in people's experience. There will also be books which deal directly with pedagogy, with the relationships between language learning and cultural learning, between processes inside the classroom and beyond. They will all have in common a concern with the relationship between language and culture, and the development of intercultural communicative competence.

All books in this series are externally peer-reviewed.

Full details of all the books in this series and of all our other publications can be found on http://www.multilingual-matters.com, or by writing to Multilingual Matters, St Nicholas House, 31–34 High Street, Bristol, BS1 2AW, UK.

LANGUAGES FOR INTERCULTURAL COMMUNICATION AND
EDUCATION: 38

Intercultural Learning in Language Education and Beyond

Evolving Concepts, Perspectives and Practices

Edited by
**Troy McConachy, Irina Golubeva
and Manuela Wagner**

MULTILINGUAL MATTERS
Bristol • Jackson

DOI https://doi.org/10.21832/MCCONA2606

Names: McConachy, Troy, editor. | Golubeva, Irina, editor. | Wagner, Manuela (Educator), editor.

Title: Intercultural Learning in Language Education and Beyond: Evolving Concepts, Perspectives and Practices/Edited by Troy McConachy, Irina Golubeva and Manuela Wagner.

Description: Bristol; Jackson: Multilingual Matters, [2022] | Series: Languages for Intercultural Communication and Education: 38 | Includes bibliographical references and index. | Summary: "This book provides a contemporary and critical examination of the theoretical and pedagogical impact of Michael Byram's pioneering work on intercultural communicative competence and intercultural citizenship. The book offers comprehensive, up-to-date and accessible knowledge for researchers, teachers, teacher-trainers and students"—Provided by publisher.

Identifiers: LCCN 2021059012 (print) | LCCN 2021059013 (ebook) | ISBN 9781800412606 (hardback) | ISBN 9781800412590 (paperback) | ISBN 9781800412613 (adobe pdf) | ISBN 9781800412620 (epub)

Subjects: LCSH: Language and languages—Study and teaching. | Intercultural communication—Study and teaching. | Multicultural education. | Byram, Michael. Classification: LCC P53.45 .I566 2022 (print) | LCC P53.45 (ebook) | DDC 418.0071—dc23/eng/20220120 LC record available at https://lccn.loc.gov/2021059012
LC ebook record available at https://lccn.loc.gov/2021059013

Library of Congress Cataloging in Publication Data
A catalog record for this book is available from the Library of Congress.

British Library Cataloguing in Publication Data
A catalogue entry for this book is available from the British Library.

ISBN-13: 978-1-80041-260-6 (hbk)
ISBN-13: 978-1-80041-259-0 (pbk)

Multilingual Matters
UK: St Nicholas House, 31–34 High Street, Bristol, BS1 2AW, UK.
USA: Ingram, Jackson, TN, USA.

Website: www.multilingual-matters.com
Twitter: Multi_Ling_Mat
Facebook: https://www.facebook.com/multilingualmatters
Blog: www.channelviewpublications.wordpress.com

The policy of Multilingual Matters/Channel View Publications is to use papers that are natural, renewable and recyclable products, made from wood grown in sustainable forests. In the manufacturing process of our books, and to further support our policy, preference is given to printers that have FSC and PEFC Chain of Custody certification. The FSC and/or PEFC logos will appear on those books where full certification has been granted to the printer concerned.

Typeset by SAN Publishing Services.

To Mike Byram – inspiration, colleague, mentor and friend

Contents

Looking Back and Looking Forward

Tables and Figures

Acknowledgements

It has been an honour for us to have undertaken this project with the help and guidance of many colleagues, mentors and friends who shared our sentiment and vision. We are, first, very grateful to Multilingual Matters for supporting the concept and for always offering quick and helpful advice along the way. We also thank Tony Liddicoat as co-editor of the Languages for Intercultural Communication and Education (LICE) series for his enthusiasm towards the project and insightful suggestions.

As many will know, this book was completed during the COVID-19 pandemic, a time that continues to be very challenging for all. We wish to express our utmost respect and thanks to the authors for their commitment to the project, for being so responsive to feedback and for being resilient in the face of tight completion deadlines. Naturally, a book like this could not come to fruition without the wisdom and generosity of reviewers. We are deeply indebted to those who kindly provided feedback on the chapters in spite of various hardships. Their contributions have had a great impact on the book.

We are also indebted to Michael Fleming, who kindly contributed the Foreword to the volume, and to Marjukka Grover, Joe Sheils, Martyn Barrett and Prue Holmes, who generously agreed to share their reflections on getting to know and working with Mike in four final chapters. These chapters include not only interesting incidents from their professional collaborations but also reflections on Mike's exemplary personhood and dedication to the profession, as well as his magnanimous and selfless support for colleagues and ongoing contribution to the field.

Contributors

José Aldemar Álvarez Valencia
Professor, Universidad del Valle, Colombia

Martyn Barrett
Emeritus Professor of Psychology, University of Surrey, UK

Fabiana Cardetti
Professor of Mathematics, University of Connecticut, USA

Paloma Castro
Associate Professor, Universidad de Valladolid, Spain

Sin Yu Cherry Chan
Lecturer in English, The Chinese University of Hong Kong, China

Verónica Di Bin
Lecturer, Universidad Nacional de La Plata, Argentina

Mike Fleming
Emeritus Professor of Education, Durham University, UK

Irina Golubeva
Associate Professor of Intercultural Communication,
University of Maryland, Baltimore County, USA

Marjukka Grover
Co-Founder of Channel View Publications and Multilingual Matters, UK

Manuela Guilherme
Researcher, Universidade de Coimbra, Portugal

Prue Holmes
Professor in International and Intercultural Education, Durham
University, UK

Jane Jackson
Professor Emerita, The Chinese University of Hong Kong, China

Michelle Kohler
Senior Research Fellow, University of South Australia, Australia

Anthony J. Liddicoat
Professor of Applied Linguistics, University of Warwick, UK

Ulla Lundgren
Researcher, Jönköping University, Sweden

Troy McConachy
Associate Professor in Applied Linguistics, University of Warwick, UK

Aleidine J. Moeller
Edith S. Greer Professor, University of Nebraska – Lincoln, USA

Claudia Mustroph
Research Associate, Ludwig-Maximilians-Universität München, Germany

Rita A. Oleksak
Director of Foreign Language/ELL, Glastonbury Public Schools, Glastonbury, CT, USA

Beatriz Peña Dix
Associate Professor, Universidad de los Andes, Colombia

Alison Phipps
Professor of Languages and Intercultural Studies, University of Glasgow, UK

Melina Porto
Professor and Researcher, Universidad Nacional de La Plata; CONICET, Argentina

Shuoqian Qin
Associate Professor, Qingdao University, China

Petra Rauschert
Senior Lecturer, Ludwig-Maximilians-Universität München, Germany

Karen Risager
Professor Emerita, Roskilde University, Denmark

Angela Scarino
Associate Professor in Applied Linguistics, University of South Australia, Australia

Joe Sheils
Former Head of the Language Policy Division at the Council of Europe

Tongle Sun
Assistant Professor, The Chinese University of Hong Kong, China

Manuela Wagner
Professor of Language Education, University of Connecticut, USA

Lihong Wang
Dean of the School of Translation and Interpreting, Beijing Language and Culture University, China

Jane Woodin
Senior University Tutor, University of Sheffield, UK

External Reviewers

Ana Beaven
University of Bologna, Italy

Martin Cortazzi
University of Warwick, UK

Carolin Debray
University of Basel, Switzerland

Adriana Raquel Díaz
University of Queensland, Australia

Melinda Dooly
Universitat Autònoma de Barcelona, Spain

Paula Garrett-Rucks
Georgia State University, USA

Hild Elisabeth Hoff
University of Bergen, Norway

Adrian Holliday
Canterbury Christ Church University, UK

Erin Kearney
University at Buffalo, USA

Flavia Monceri
Università degli Studi del Molise, Italy

Ana Oskoz
University of Maryland, Baltimore County, USA

Lynne Parmenter
Nazarbayev University, Kazakhstan

Jan Van Maele
KU Leuven, Belgium

Foreword

When I joined the School of Education at Durham University in 1988, Mike Byram was already well-established within the Department. It was my good fortune to find in him a colleague and advisor who supported and encouraged me in many aspects of academic life: publication, grant applications, research, doctoral supervision and assessment. Just like many of his colleagues and students throughout the world, I benefitted from the qualities that make him such an outstanding mentor: a willingness to share his own expertise and experiences; the ability to advise gently without dominating; endless patience and empathy that never turned into indulgence. His generosity of spirit and kindness always infused his professional work. He was genuinely ambitious for fellow colleagues, taking pleasure in the successes they achieved. His capacity for hard work in the Department was legendary, but he never made others feel inadequate, nor did he allow work to get in the way of social activities; he was always an effective catalyst for getting people together to enjoy each other's company. The personal qualities he embodied in those earlier days have been present throughout his career right up to the present day, and his work is as prolific as ever.

This present volume does not aim to be a biography; it is primarily focused on the huge contribution Mike's academic work has made to the field of intercultural learning. However, it does not surprise me at all to read tributes to his personal qualities (not just in the Introduction and in the excellent contributions at the end of the book but embedded in several of the chapters) for the person and his work are, in his case, deeply interrelated.

The book is very successful in presenting not just the impact of Mike's work on language education and other fields, but also its development over time. It reflects, for example, the extension of intercultural learning and the notion of Intercultural Communicative Competence into other fields, the adoption of the notion of 'intercultural speaker', the inclusion of crucial ideas related to criticality and the foregrounding of the concept of intercultural citizenship. His work embodies the best sense of being 'academic' (theoretically informed, empirically rigorous, reflective) while avoiding its more negative associations (remote, unduly abstract, irrelevant). There is a deep sense of moral purpose at the heart of his research which is ultimately directed towards practice, towards developing social, moral and political responsibility in learners, enhancing pedagogy and making the world a better place. His own capacity to de-centre, to see issues from others' perspectives and question what may be taken for granted has imbued his scholarship with a flexibility and vitality that has ensured its growth and contemporary relevance. Mike's openness to other disciplines and his intellectual curiosity have always made him ready to embrace the benefits of collaboration. His leadership in Durham in the 1990s brought together scholars from a wide range of disciplines, including literature, psychology, business, arts and philosophy that resulted in fruitful dialogue and a number of publications over several years. The Cultnet network that Mike started always conducted in a spirit of openness and mutual support, quite rightly features in several chapters as an example of dialogue and collaboration at its best. Many groups of people, including those at the Council of Europe, have derived benefit from his skills at mediation and his ability to bring people together across countries, cultural groups and specialisms.

The chapters in the book reflect the wide reach of his work, with authors from a diverse range of countries, institutions and contexts. Many of his former students and mentees are now significant voices in the field in their own right, forging new ideas and providing academic leadership for others. The book combines a valuable retrospective examination of his contribution to the field with a look towards the future, pointing the way towards new pathways based on fresh insights. Examples of the practical application of his ideas to teaching in the description of concrete projects provide considerable inspiration. Mike Byram would be the first to acknowledge the importance of constructive criticism and dialogue in the growth of ideas; overall, the chapters provide a thoughtful account of how his ideas have evolved and been clarified in response to criticism and changing times.

The editors and contributors are to be congratulated on an impressive book that is both a fitting tribute to Mike Byram's contribution to the field and a work of original scholarship in its own right.

Mike Fleming
Durham University, UK

Introduction: Michael Byram's Contribution to Intercultural Learning in Language Education and Beyond

Irina Golubeva, Manuela Wagner and Troy McConachy

While the field of language education has had a longstanding interest in the notion of culture, it was Michael Byram's pioneering work on the cultural dimensions of language learning that called attention to the 'educational' value of foreign language learning and the need for learners to bring into relationship not only different linguistic conventions but also different values, beliefs, attitudes and behaviours. Byram and Zarate's (1994) notion of 'the intercultural speaker' challenged the assumption that language learners should model themselves after native speakers and emphasised the learner's ability to mediate between different cultural understandings of the world and decentre from their taken-for-granted worldview. Throughout his career, Michael Byram's work has served to highlight the potential for language learning to contribute to the humanistic development of the learner, facilitate intercultural dialogue and enable joint action towards improving societal conditions. It encourages language learners to see themselves as 'intercultural citizens' who have critical awareness of their own and other's societies and who can bridge cultural differences in order to collaborate for the common good.

This volume aims to pay tribute to Michael Byram's profound contribution to the theory and practice of intercultural learning within and beyond language education. It does so on a very noteworthy occasion – the 25th anniversary of the publication of his landmark monograph, *Teaching and Assessing Intercultural Communicative Competence* (1997), which presented a model of Intercultural Communicative Competence (ICC) that has since had a transformative impact on educational theory and practice not only in the field of language education but also in broader disciplinary and cross-disciplinary areas. Positioned in a theoretical universe that neglected the role of language in successful intercultural interactions, Byram's model of ICC aimed to provide a theoretically rigorous yet accessible model that would help language teachers conceptualise concrete objectives for intercultural learning that could be taught and assessed, particularly within the context of formal schooling. It thus took into account the reality that formal education is frequently situated within a curriculum oriented towards nation states and provided teachers with a theoretical and pedagogical foundation for developing the knowledge, skills and attitudes necessary for positive inter-cultural engagement with those within the same country and other countries.

Importantly, however, Byram (1997, 2021) points out that this need to take into consideration the typically 'national' orientation within which compulsory education is framed does not imply that culture should only be seen in terms of 'national culture', nor that nations themselves are cul-turally homogenous. Aiming to address misunderstandings of his orienta-tion towards culture, Byram (2021) has reiterated his view (also expressed in the 1997 monograph) that 'within one society there are many commu-nities and their associated cultures' (2021: 11). We note that such a posi-tion is already evident in Byram's earlier monograph – *Cultural Studies in Foreign Language Education* – published by Multilingual Matters in 1989. At the same time, Byram (2021) points out that many intercultural encounters do result in national group identity being brought into sali-ence, which means that individuals need to be able to engage with differ-ent representations of the relationship between culture and the nation held by the self and others. In fact, he argues that it is precisely because nations are heterogeneous that language learners need to be able to reflect on diversity between groups within and across nations. He explains that:

> Only if learners know and can critically analyse the dominant national culture can they challenge it, critique its values and take their own posi-tion in the exchange with those who benefit from it. It then becomes pos-sible for them to turn this critique back on their own society and become aware of power issues around them, as seen from the vantage point of analysing another society. (2021: 26)

Byram has taken many opportunities to underscore the centrality of this kind of critical engagement and critical cultural awareness to the learner's development as an intercultural communicator and responsible citizen. Taking further the ideas of *politische Bildung* ('political education') and *Demokratie Lernen* ('democracy-learning') (Himmelmann, 2001, 2006), and expanding on the concept of critical cultural awareness, Byram (2008) presented a vision for foreign language education that needed to do more than facilitate effective intercultural communication – it needed to pro-mote cooperation towards addressing important societal concerns, such as global environmental problems, international conflicts and so on. He captured this vision in the idea of 'intercultural citizenship' (Byram,

2008), suggesting how the 'disposition for engagement' transforms into actual engagement in the language classroom (Byram, 2008). Intercultural Citizenship, thus, extends the notion of critical cultural awareness and takes learners out of classrooms, taking the stance that language education ought to contribute to learners' ability to apply their ICC to take action in the world around them.

In his recent work, Byram (2021) argues that '[i]ntercultural citizenship need not be the responsibility only of language teachers, just as citizenship education or *Demokratie Lernen* is a cross-curricular endeavour' (2021: 122). These ideas have crystallised in various forms, including the co-authored volume, *Teaching Intercultural Citizenship Across the Curriculum: The Role of Language Education* (Wagner *et al.*, 2019), which presents concrete ideas for interdisciplinary units based on current societal problems. Byram has also facilitated and inspired a number of communities of practice to integrate ICC and intercultural citizenship (e.g. Byram *et al.*, 2017; Oleksak & Cardetti, this volume; Wagner *et al.*, 2018).

Byram's model of ICC and his work on intercultural citizenship have had a profound and far-reaching influence not only within language education but also within broader spheres of international, intercultural and cross-disciplinary education. It has helped shape trajectories of educational theory and practice in areas such as international student mobility, teacher education, intercultural service learning (ISL), intercultural assessment and more. His work has also impacted on the development of curriculum frameworks and educational practices within a wide range of institutions, language teaching organisations and among individual educators.

Whenever educational models and ideals developed in one particular context come to be influential on an international scale, it is natural and indeed healthy for them to be subject to critical evaluation both in terms of their theoretical tenets and ideological fit for the context as well as the practical opportunities and constraints associated with using them to inform pedagogical practices. This is particularly important in the case of models and conceptions of teaching and learning associated with the 'intercultural'. All models of intercultural competence implicitly or explicitly present particular ways of conceptualising 'self' and 'other' and the relational territory and forms of engagement within which specific types of knowledge, skills, attitudes, etc. are considered valuable. It is, thus, indispensable to acknowledge that models are inevitably associated with and shaped by the political structures, ideologies, power relations, educational discourses and institutional agendas dominant in the contexts in which they arise (see, in particular, Chapter 7 of this volume).

With respect to his own model of ICC, Byram has actively called for critique (see *Preface* Byram, 2021) and emphasised the importance of educators adapting the model as appropriate for their local contexts. Of course, this also includes the possibility that educators might decide not to use the model to inform their practice at all. We concur with Byram's position that no model of ICC, including his own, can just be transplanted into any context uncritically. And, indeed, no model can be expected to comprehensively capture the incredible complexity entailed in intercultural interaction and the negotiation of intercultural relations. In accordance with the increasing diversification of the epistemological landscape within the intercultural field, there is an ongoing need for dialogue between different understandings of 'the intercultural' shaped by epistemological traditions, material conditions and languages in different parts of the world. Indeed, there is evidence that such dialogue is already underway.

Aims and Organisation of the Volume

In addition to paying tribute to the legacy of Mike's work, this volume also aims to provide a contemporary and critical examination of how understandings of his notions of ICC, intercultural citizenship and related educational concepts have evolved within the field of intercultural language education, how they have informed research into intercultural development and how they have been creatively utilised or adapted for pedagogical purposes in a range of different contexts. We, thus, use the notion of 'intercultural learning' in a broad and non-exclusive sense to encapsulate this work. The volume is organised into two sections.

Part 1: Evolving Conceptual Foundations

Chapters in Part 1 of the book focus on key concepts in intercultural language education that have emanated from Michael Byram's work, or which provide synergy with his ideas, including ICC, language awareness, mediation, intercultural citizenship, intercultural dialogue and intercultural responsibility. Chapters discuss these concepts within their historical and theoretical context, considering how they inform understandings of intercultural learning and pedagogical practices within and beyond language education. Chapters make an effort to critically evaluate concepts in the context of the current epistemological landscape and consider future directions.

In Chapter 1, 'Intercultural Communicative Competence: Transnational and Decolonial Developments', Karen Risager considers the historical context and theoretical foundations of Byram's model of ICC and reflects on developments in Byram's thinking around intercultural citizenship and values in the 2021 'revisited' version of his 1997 monograph. The chapter then suggests a rethinking of the 'knowledge' dimension of ICC in connection to transnational and decolonial perspectives and what this could mean for pedagogical practice.

Chapter 2, 'Language Awareness and Intercultural Communicative Competence: Revisiting the Relationship', authored by Troy McConachy, takes Byram's work on language awareness as a starting point for considering the role of language awareness in ICC. It considers assumptions about the interrelationship between language and culture that underpin rationales for developing language awareness, discusses the nature of language awareness through the lens of analytical and reflective engagement and explores the implications of recent research for integrating language awareness within Byram's model of ICC.

In Chapter 3, 'Intercultural Mediation in Language Teaching and Learning', Anthony J. Liddicoat addresses the idea of the language learner as an intercultural mediator by examining the evolution of understandings of mediation within language education, from a focus on problem-solving to a focus on meaning-making and interpretation. The chapter considers what it means for language learners to be intercultural mediators and what is entailed in becoming a mediator.

In Chapter 4, 'From Intercultural Communicative Competence to Intercultural Citizenship: Preparing Young People for Citizenship in a Culturally Diverse Democratic World', Martyn Barrett and Irina Golubeva consider the theoretical tenets of Byram's model of ICC and how these have given shape to a number of important theoretical and pedagogical developments, including projects, resources and policy frameworks. This chapter also discusses the evolution of ideas within the context of the theory and practice of intercultural citizenship education, not only within foreign language education but also in a broader context, across the entire curriculum.

Chapter 5, 'Intercultural Dialogue and Values in Education', co-authored by Paloma Castro, Ulla Lundgren and Jane Woodin, addresses the concept of intercultural dialogue and how the meaning of this term has evolved historically, linguistically and socially. It considers points of synergy between the values underlying contemporary understandings of intercultural dialogue and the work of Michael Byram. The chapter offers a reflection on working with Michael Byram over a period of over 25 years, in particular through the Cultnet group, as an example of intercultural dialogue in action.

In Chapter 6, 'From Critical Cultural Awareness to Intercultural Responsibility: Language, Culture and Citizenship', Manuela Guilherme takes a close look at Byram's notion of 'critical cultural awareness' and explains how she has adopted and adapted this concept within the context of her own work informed by Freire's critical pedagogy. The author brings Byram's ideas into relationship with her own notions of 'critical intercultural awareness' and 'intercultural responsibility', which entail a decolonial, critical and inter-epistemic stance towards knowledge and cognitive and social justice.

The notion of critical cultural awareness is also under focus in Chapter 7, 'Conflict and the Cognitive Empire: Byram's Critical Cultural

Awareness', authored by Alison Phipps. This author urges recognition of the historical, regional, material and ideological context in which this notion was proposed, warning against the dangers of 'presentism' in theoretical critiques of Byram's work. The chapter reflects on the significance of critical cultural awareness against the backdrop of decolonial perspectives.

Part 2: Intercultural Development in Diverse Contexts: Perspectives and Practices

In Part 2, there are 10 chapters which consider the significance of Michael Byram's work and its contribution to shaping understandings of intercultural learning in different pedagogical contexts such as mobility, service learning, teacher education and assessment, as well as his impact on the work of professional organisations, communities of practice and individual teachers. The chapters provide accounts of different ways in which Michael Byram's ideas have been applied and adapted across a range of geographical and institutional contexts for the purposes of generating innovation and local impact. Importantly, the chapters demonstrate the power of collaborative work and professional activity designed to bring an intercultural perspective to language education in locally appropriate ways.

In Chapter 8, 'Intercultural Development in the Context of Mobility', Jane Jackson, Sin Yu Cherry Chan and Tongle Sun are calling for research-driven pedagogical interventions that draw on relevant models of intercultural competence development and recent advances in critical pedagogy and e-learning technology. Building on the seminal work of Byram (1997), this chapter offers concrete examples of possible ways to scaffold, deepen and extend the language and intercultural development of participants before, during and after academic mobility.

In Chapter 9, 'Intercultural Education Through Civic Engagement: Service Learning in the Foreign Language Classroom', Petra Rauschert and Claudia Mustroph link intercultural citizenship education, language education and service learning as community-engaged transformative action. They start with providing a theoretical perspective on ISL and related pedagogies, and then discuss a practical example of implementing ISL in foreign language education. The Global Peace Path project, carried out in Germany, illustrates how students develop intercultural competence during a peace campaign.

Chapter 10, 'Revisiting Intercultural Communicative Competence in Language Teacher Education: Perspectives from Colombia', written by Beatriz Peña Dix, discusses the role of ICC in language teacher education, pointing to the persistence of a gap between theory and practice and the need to find local solutions. The author reports on a study investigating how English language teachers in Colombia understand and approach their own interculturality and what issues need to be addressed.

In Chapter 11, 'Assessing Intercultural Capability: Insights from Processes of Eliciting and Judging Student Learning', Angela Scarino and Michelle Kohler address the current state of play with regard to assessing intercultural language learning, recognising the diverse conceptualisations of the nature and purposes of assessment that are drawn upon in relation to this kind of learning. The authors draw on a number of classroom-based studies that they have undertaken predominantly within the schooling sector, that have investigated language teachers' conceptions and practices in assessing intercultural language learning.

Chapter 12, 'The NCSSFL-ACTFL Can-Do Statements for Intercultural Communication: Cultivating Sojourners in the Language Classroom', authored by Aleidine J. Moeller, explores the impact of Michael Byram's (1997) work on ICC on the American Council on the Teaching of Foreign Languages (ACTFL) and the National Council of State Supervisors for Languages (NCSSFL). The author considers how Byram's model has helped inspire the NCSSFL/ACTFL *Can-Do Statements for Intercultural Communication* (2015) and the practice of teaching ICC in the US context.

In Chapter 13, 'Exploring a Pedagogy for Understanding and Developing Chinese EFL Students' Intercultural Communicative Competence', Shuoqian Qin and Prue Holmes report on a six-week pedagogical intervention carried out in a Chinese higher education context that was directly informed by Byram's model of ICC. The chapter details the key considerations and processes involved in integrating intercultural dimensions into the course and triangulates data from several sources to document important instances of learning engagement that correspond to learning objectives informed by the ICC model. The chapter also identifies a number of areas where learners' reflections on their own ICC reveal features distinct from the model.

In Chapter 14, 'Engaging Educators: Facilitating Interdisciplinary Communities of Practice in the USA', Rita A. Oleksak and Fabiana Cardetti highlight the impact of Michael Byram's scholarly contributions that deepen the work between language teachers and other educators across disciplines. The authors focus on advancing the understanding and perspectives of communities of practice working together to improve the learning experiences of students using the theories of ICC and citizenship as developed by Byram (1997, 2008) and illustrate projects at the elementary, high school and graduate levels in the Northeast of the USA.

Chapter 15, 'Developing Intercultural Citizenship and Intellectual Humility in High School German', authored by Manuela Wagner and José Aldemar Álvarez Valencia, explores the concept of Intellectual Humility (IH), which has been shown to have connections with certain components of intercultural competence. The authors share a case study of a high school German class in interaction with students from their partner school in Germany during their visit in America, in which they investigated how the teaching and learning of ICC and intercultural citizenship can be supported through applications of IH. Preliminary findings suggest that IH indeed can support components of students' ICC and increase engagement with those from different backgrounds.

In Chapter 16, 'When the Axiom of Supranational Communication in Intercultural Citizenship Theory is not Met: Expanding Theory and Pedagogy', co-authored by Melina Porto and Verónica Di Bin, aims to investigate whether intercultural citizenship is possible pedagogically in classrooms where transnational collaboration is not feasible. This chapter describes a project that challenged nationalist thinking in a way not identified in the theory. The case contributes perspectives from an under-researched region, South America, as well as a sub-represented educational context, public secondary school.

In the final chapter, Chapter 17, 'Towards a Shared Future: Michael Byram's Engagement with the Chinese Academic Community', Lihong Wang considers the impact of Michael Byram's intercultural work and his direct collaborations with scholars in China in the area of language education and higher education. The author reflects on key research findings from collaborative work with Michael Byram on Chinese practices of international doctoral student supervision and Chinese postgraduate students' learning belief development in an intercultural setting. Particular emphasis is given to insights derived from indigenous concepts linked to Chinese cultures of teaching and learning.

The volume ends with *Looking Back, Looking Forward*, a collection of reflections and *memoirs* shared by Marjukka Grover, Joe Sheils, Martyn Barrett and Prue Holmes.

For those who know Michael Byram, it is perhaps not surprising that an additional theme appears organically throughout the chapters in this volume: Michael Byram as mentor. Throughout the years, Mike has facilitated collaborations around research and teaching locally, nationally and internationally. Mike inspired emerging researchers and those who were already established. One of the most longstanding examples of such collaborations and networks is Cultnet which started as a small network consisting of Mike and a group of graduate students who met yearly and discussed their work in progress. Today, Cultnet – which also celebrates 25 years of existence in 2022 – is an international network with over 300 members that provides opportunities for all members to learn with and from each other. In this and every other collaborative context, Mike himself embodies and models for others the knowledge, skills, attitudes and actions of intercultural citizenship, thereby supporting numerous fruitful collaborations and communities of practice, some of which will be described in this volume.

As Editors, we realise that no one book could do justice to the scope, depth and impact of Mike Byram's work. We feel humbled to have had the opportunity to put together this volume as one part of the ongoing dialogue on the role of intercultural learning within and beyond language education. We hope that contributors and readers will be happy with the final product and that this volume serves as a deserving tribute to an outstanding scholar whose commitment to language learners, teachers and the scholarly community continues to have a momentous impact. We also hope that the critical discussion of different theoretical concepts and perspectives as well as the diverse accounts of pedagogical practice will be useful for researchers, language teachers, teacher-trainers, students and professional organisations. Needless to say, all typos, blemishes or inaccuracies are our own responsibility.

References

Byram, M. (1989) *Cultural Studies in Foreign Language Education*. Clevedon: Multilingual Matters.

Byram, M. (1997) *Teaching and Assessing Intercultural Communicative Competence*. Clevedon: Multilingual Matters.

Byram, M. (2008) *From Foreign Language Education to Education for Intercultural Citizenship: Essays and Reflections*. Clevedon: Multilingual Matters.

Byram, M. (2021) *Teaching and Assessing Intercultural Communicative Competence: Revisited*. Bristol: Multilingual Matters.

Byram, M., Golubeva, I. Han, H. and Wagner, M. (eds) (2017) *From Principles to Practice in Education for Intercultural Citizenship*. Bristol: Multilingual Matters.

Byram, M. and Zarate, G. (1994) *Définitions, objectifs et évaluation de la compétence socio-culturelle* [Definitions, Objectives and Evaluation of Socio-cultural Competence]. Strasbourg: Report for the Council of Europe.

Himmelmann, G. (2001) *Demokratie Lernen als Lebens-, Gesellschafts- und Herrschaftsform. Ein Lehr- und Studienbuch*. Schwalbach: Wochenschau Verlag.

Himmelmann, G. (2006) Concepts and issues in citizenship education. A comparative study of Germany, Britain and the USA. In G. Alred, M. Byram and M. Fleming (eds) *Education for Intercultural Citizenship: Concepts and Comparisons* (pp. 69–85). Clevedon: Multilingual Matters.

Wagner, M., Cardetti, F. and Byram, M. (2019) *Teaching Intercultural Citizenship Across the Curriculum: The Role of Language Education*. Alexandria, VA: ACTFL.

Wagner, M., Conlon Perugini, D. and Byram, M. (2018) *Teaching Intercultural Communicative Competence Across the Age Range: From Theory to Practice*. Bristol: Multilingual Matters.

Michael Byram:
A Biographical Sketch

Michael S. Byram was born in 1946 to a working-class family in Dewsbury, a small industrial town in the north of England. After attending grammar school where he focused on Latin, French and German, he spent a year teaching English as a foreign language in Algeria. It was during that year that Mike, as he is known by most, realised that he wanted to become a teacher. Upon return to the UK, he enrolled at King's College Cambridge to continue his study of literature and linguistics. Upon completion of his undergraduate studies, Mike decided to pursue a PhD, writing a thesis on the Danish contemporary writer Tom Kristensen. With PhD in hand, he began his career, teaching French and German at secondary school level and in adult education in an English comprehensive community school.

After six years working as a schoolteacher, including as Head of Languages, Mike joined the School of Education at Durham University as a lecturer in 1980. He was involved in initial teacher education and also began to do research on education in linguistic minorities education and then on the cultural dimension in language teaching. His first book on education, about the German minority in Denmark, was published with Multilingual Matters with whom he has had a close working relationship ever since. He also came to supervise Doctoral students from all over the world, later taking on the role of Director of Research Degrees. In the mid-1990s, Mike also began contributing to work at the Council of Europe on the *Common European Framework of Reference for Languages* (CEFR). This was the start of many great collaborations and lines of development in educational policy and practice (in particular in his time as Adviser to the Language Policy Division), most recently with his role as a member of the expert group designing the *Reference Framework of Competences for Democratic Culture* (RFCDC) (Council of Europe, 2018). In 1997, the same year that he published his landmark monograph, *Teaching and Assessing Intercultural Communicative Competence*, Mike also founded an intercultural collaborative network with the support of several doctoral students at the time – Cultnet (https://cultnetintercultural.wordpress.com/). Cultnet has since grown into a truly diverse, international and supportive community for researchers and teachers around the world. It has also spawned many new research collaborations and publications, some of which have been published in the *Languages for Intercultural Communication and Education* (Multilingual Matters) book series Mike established together with Alison Phipps in 1999 (currently co-edited with Tony Liddicoat).

Throughout this career, Mike has developed a rich and diverse research portfolio including, but not limited to, the education of linguistic minorities, foreign language education and student residence abroad, education for intercultural citizenship, ethics and education, international comparison of doctoral studies in social sciences and history of education. He has published many books and articles, including his most often cited publications, to list but a few:

1986:   *Minority Education and Ethnic Survival. Case Study of a German School in Denmark.* Multilingual Matters (Awarded annual prize of the British Association for Applied Linguistics, 1987).

1989:   *Cultural Studies in Foreign Language Education.* Multilingual Matters.

1991:   Joint author (with V. Esarte-Sarries and S. Taylor). *Cultural Studies and Language Learning: A Research Report.* Multilingual Matters.

1997:   *Teaching and Assessing Intercultural Communicative Competence.* Multilingual Matters.

1998:   Joint editor (with M. Fleming) and contributor. *Language Learning in Intercultural Perspective: Approaches through Drama and Ethnography.* Cambridge University Press.

1999:   Joint author (with K. Risager). *Language Teachers, Politics and Cultures.* Multilingual Matters.

2008:   *From Foreign Language Education to Education for Intercultural Citizenship: Essays and Reflections.* Multilingual Matters.

2013:   (with Adelheid Hu). *Routledge Encyclopedia of Language Teaching and Learning.* Routledge. Now translated into Chinese and Arabic.

2017:   (co-edited with Irina Golubeva, Han Hui and Manuela Wagner). *From Principles to Practice in Education for Intercultural Citizenship.* Multilingual Matters.

2019:   (co-authored with Manuela Wagner and Fabiana Cardetti). *Teaching Intercultural Citizenship across the Curriculum.* American Council on the Teaching of Foreign Languages (ACTFL).

2020:   (co-edited with Maria Stoicheva). *The Doctorate as Experience in Europe and Beyond: Supervision, Languages, Identities.* Routledge.

2021:   *Teaching and Assessing Intercultural Communicative Competence: Revisited.* Multilingual Matters.

His contribution to the field has been recognised by numerous invitations as keynote speaker internationally and through visiting or guest professorships at various universities across the continents, currently, for example, at Luxembourg University and Sofia University St Kliment Ohridski. In 1995, he was named *Chevalier des Palmes Académiques*, an honour awarded by the French Government to distinguished academics and teachers.

Since October 2008, Mike has been Professor Emeritus at Durham University. He continues to devote himself to supporting research supervision, mentoring emerging researchers, teaching, giving plenary talks and actively working on various international projects, including the Council of Europe initiative on the *Reference Framework of Competences for Democratic Culture*.

Part 1

Evolving Conceptual Foundations

1 Intercultural Communicative Competence: Transnational and Decolonial Developments

Karen Risager

Introduction

When it comes to intercultural communicative competence (ICC), and generally the field of intercultural language education, Michael Byram occupies a central position. In this chapter, which is a part of the *Festschrift* for Michael Byram, it is natural to use his work as a reference and baseline for some of the many developments that have seen the light in the field since the 1980s. Among the numerous influential works by Byram, I have chosen the monograph *Teaching and Assessing Intercultural Communicative Competence* (1997) as the now classical work, which has gained worldwide dissemination, and which has recently appeared in a revisited edition (Byram, 2021).

The chapter begins with an outline of the historical context and theoretical foundations of Byram's book from 1997 and the revisited edition from 2021, with special reference to the model of ICC. In this outline, there is – in anticipation of the topics dealt with in the rest of the chapter – a certain emphasis on the Knowledge dimension of ICC. This dimension in Byram's model refers to the cultural content of foreign and second language education: the representations of target-language countries and the learners' own countries that can be found in learning materials and in the choice of authentic materials, topics for collaborative projects, etc.

The rest of the chapter deals with further developments in the field of intercultural language education, especially since 2000, with a focus on *transnational and decolonial studies*. These developments primarily touch upon the Knowledge dimension of ICC and propose to widen the perspective both in geographical and historical respects. Transnational studies takes up the question of how we can transcend the traditional narrow focus on nations/states and include transnational processes and practices in a broader representation of the world as an interconnected entity. Decolonial studies focuses on how we can introduce some elements of history in the picture of the contemporary world in order to raise the awareness of the role of history, not least colonial history, for the understanding of global inequity, injustice and racism today.

These more recent developments, which are illustrated by a concrete example at the end of the chapter, try to reformulate the Knowledge dimension and thus the whole model of ICC. They point to the importance of considering what the learner should know about the world, in terms of discourses and perspectives, in order to become a competent intercultural speaker/reader who can use the target language in real-life settings often characterised by inequities and hierarchisations with regard to identity parameters as social class, ethnicity, language, race, gender, sexuality, religion, etc. They offer reflections on how we can transnationalise and decolonise intercultural language education.

Byram's Model of Intercultural Communicative Competence

Michael Byram was the first to publish a truly research-based monograph (*Cultural Studies in Foreign Language Education*, 1989) that aimed to develop the entire field of intercultural language education both theoretically and empirically, and thereby establish it as an academic discipline (see the historical chapters in Risager, 2007). Debates on what we may now call 'the cultural dimension' of language teaching had already started in the 1880s in Europe, particularly in the recently unified German Reich, and research interest in the field took its first steps in the 1970s. This development was intensified in the 1980s where the general interest in 'culture' and 'the intercultural' made its influence on many parts of the humanities, including foreign language teaching. In the mid-1980s, Byram led the first larger empirical project in the field, with a focus on the teaching and learning of French in Britain (The Durham Project). With Dieter Buttjes, he organised the first international European symposium in Durham in 1986 on the cultural content of language teaching (I was one of the participants), and as a result of that, they edited the book *Mediating Languages and Cultures: Towards an Intercultural Theory of Foreign Language Education*, 1991.

The concept of 'competence' (communicative competence, cultural competence, intercultural competence [IC]) was not prominent in discussions and publications in the 1980s, although it was present. But during the 1990s, 'competence' became a central concept in the field of education, including intercultural language education, and Byram's monograph: *Teaching and Assessing Intercultural Communicative Competence* (1997) was a part of this development.

	Skills interpret and relate (savoir comprendre)	
Knowledge of self and other; of interaction; individual and societal (savoirs)	Education political education critical cultural awareness (savoir s'engager)	Attitudes relativising self valuing other (savoir être)
	Skills discover and/or interact (savoir apprendre/faire)	

Figure 1.1 Intercultural competence

The general background was the increasing economic and cultural glo-balisation and, in Europe, the reunification of Germany in 1990, which in the educational sector led to a marked focus on internationalisation and study travel. This was especially the case within the European Common Market (from 1993 the EU), which had set up a series of major exchange programmes. Thus, language students, or at least some of them, gained greater opportunities of meeting students from other countries, either physically via student exchanges and school trips, or via email and other digital communication. This meant that the teaching of culture tended to become more oriented towards experienced culture and personal cultural encounters (Byram & Risager, 1999). In connection with this, there was a growing interest in assessment. Comprehensive projects were undertaken in both Europe and the USA on developing criteria for the assessment of cultural competence (see the overview in Byram, 2021, Chapter 5). The Council of Europe was very active in this field and among the central fig-ures were Byram and Geneviève Zarate. Together, they developed the con-cepts of 'intercultural speaker' and 'the four *savoirs*', i.e. the four aspects of sociocultural/intercultural competence, which in Byram's book became 'the five *savoirs*' as he added '*savoir s'engager*'.

Byram's well-known model of IC (or more precisely 'factors in inter-cultural communication', Byram, 1997: 34) is represented in Figure 1.1. (This graphical model is not changed in the 2021 edition.)

A Multidisciplinary Model Rooted in Several European and American Traditions

Many models of IC distinguish between attitudes, skills and knowl-edge, based on a very common approach within social psychology (see

Deardorff, 2009). The models tend to exhibit rather simplistic conceptions of knowledge as factual knowledge and do not usually pay attention to the role of language. Byram's model from 1997 stands out for a number of reasons:

It is research-based and theory-based. The theoretical foundation is not *one* theory but several theories originating in different disciplines in the humanities and social sciences. The theories, which are not spelt out in the book as it is primarily aimed at practitioners, are linked loosely together. This makes the whole model multidisciplinary (separate disciplines) more than interdisciplinary (integrated disciplines). This eclectic approach offers users and researchers possibilities of focusing on each of the widely different theories underlying the model. Thus, the model can serve both as a flexible tool for practitioners, and as an open research programme. The most important disciplines involved at this stage in 1997 are as follows:

Social psychology (Tajfel, 1981) and intercultural communication (Gudykunst, 1994) are the points of departure. They are the foundation of the structure of the whole model: attitudes, skills and knowledge, and they primarily emphasise the importance of the social-psychological dimension of IC, represented in the Attitudes dimension.

Interpretive anthropology (Geertz, 1975) is a significant addition that has its origin in Byram's studies of literature and interest in especially American anthropology. This addition emphasises the importance of perspective, interpretation and discovery in all intercultural relations. It is primarily present in the two Skills dimensions.

Social science education (Doyé, 1991) is an important addition rooted in the discussions in West Germany (the German Federal Republic) since the 1970s, concerning the content of *Landeskunde* (knowledge of a country) in language teaching in Germany. In these discussions, it was argued that language teaching should now stop the idealistic and at times Nazi-influenced approaches dominant since the First World War and move towards a more realistic and empirically valid knowledge about target-language countries (Risager, 2007). Language teaching should draw on knowledge developed by social science disciplines such as sociology, political science and geography. This is primarily present in the Knowledge dimension.

Political education (Gagel, 1983) is a central addition closely linked to social science education just mentioned. Both are related to Byram's educational focus as he is primarily thinking of the education of young people in general education. Political education was developed after the Second World War in West Germany, where there was a strong emphasis on education for democracy in schools. It is primarily present in the Education dimension.

The whole model of IC is finally supplemented with dimensions coming from (socio)linguistics, especially studies of communicative competence within the frames of the Council of Europe (van Ek, 1986). Byram describes communicative competence as consisting of linguistic competence, sociolinguistic competence and discourse competence. While IC does not necessarily incorporate a foreign language perspective, ICC – this concept was created by Byram – is described as a competence for those who are using a foreign language, i.e. for intercultural speakers (despite the fact that native speakers also use a language, namely their first language). In the comprehensive model (Byram, 1997: 73), IC is loosely attached to communicative competence, so the relationship between language and culture is unclear. This is a central challenge in the model that is still in need of further exploration, not least as regards possible consequences for practice (Liddicoat & Scarino, 2013; McConachy, 2018; Chapter 2, this volume; Risager, 2006).

The Epistemological Approach Underlying Byram's Model, and Alternative Approaches

Although Byram's model is not founded on *one* theory, it is characterised by a common epistemological approach that can be described as modernist (see, e.g. Risager, 2007: 163f). This lies behind his research and the very purpose of the model, namely, to categorise and list the *objectives* for the education of the intercultural speaker. One cannot do this without presupposing that there *is* something to know about and relate to, that there are groups in society to investigate, that there are conventions and rituals to learn and that there are prejudices out there to discuss.

There have been critiques of this approach from various (ideology-) critical and postmodernist positions, such as, e.g. Gray, 2010; Holliday, 2011; Guilherme, 2002; Kramsch and Whiteside, 2008; Risager, 2007 (see an overview of some of these critiques in Hoff, 2020). One example could be Kramsch' discourse approach, which usually involves the analysis of processes of interaction and learning, for instance, in order to investigate how identities and worldviews are constructed or emerge in the course of spontaneous conversations, classroom interactions, interviews, etc. Byram himself indirectly indicates that in the field of intercultural language education at large, he imagines a balance between modernist and postmodernist approaches (in the following quote, he actually speaks about structuralist and poststructuralist approaches, but there is a certain parallel between the two dichotomies). In his words: 'The way forward may be to have a balance of structuralist and post-structuralist approaches with a, not exclusive, emphasis on the former in the early stages of learning and on the latter in later stages' (Byram, 2021: 76).

My own position is oriented towards a critical postmodernist approach, by virtue of the transnational and decolonial theories I argue for (see below). But I want to retain some modernist and realist aspects, as I think knowledge, and the recognition of knowledge, is important in the contemporary world. At the same time, I stress that factual knowledge is always embedded in discourse. I have described my own position as 'modernism in postmodernism' (Risager, 2007: 164).

As far as the philosophy of education is concerned, Byram characterises his own position as representing *liberal education* (Byram, 2009: 326). This implies a concern for the education of the free and independent citizen having acquired a broad range of knowledge and skills, and having a strong sense of values, ethics and (critical) civic engagement. This may also be described as a modernist approach, as opposed to *postmodernist approaches* to education, which would put particular stress on cultural diversity and fluidity, and on the role of different discourses and worldviews in the classroom, and *critical pedagogy*, which would stress the critique of power and oppression, and the struggle for social justice concerning oneself and others.

The Revisited Edition

The second version entitled *Teaching and Assessing Intercultural Communicative Competence: Revisited* (Byram, 2021) does not change the central message of the first version. 'It re-visits and renews the first', as Byram writes in the Preface. The book contains many additions and explanations, in the form of extra codas, notes and revised conclusions. As such, it keeps the substantial core and the modernist approach, and at the same time refers to the importance of intercultural education in the contemporary global context and in the face of current social and political issues. I would like to point out two major elaborations: on intercultural citizenship and on values.

The sections on intercultural citizenship build on the Education dimension. They unfold the concept of the intercultural citizen, who is engaged in making use of the foreign language in, e.g. transnational projects on social and political issues in a target-language country and in one's own, or issues of a more global nature touching on several countries. They refer to some of the numerous innovative projects accomplished as a result of the increased focus on intercultural citizenship since the 1990s and especially in the 2010s (e.g. Byram, 2008; Byram *et al.*, 2017; Porto *et al.*, 2017; Porto & Yulita, 2017; Wagner *et al.*, 2018). In this connection, it should be noted that the definition of 'critical cultural awareness' has been changed from 'based on explicit criteria' to 'on the basis of a systematic process of reasoning', thereby making the rationalist (modernist) foundation even clearer.

In these years, there is an increased emphasis on values, due to the growing conflicts among the big powers. The Council of Europe is one of the important actors in relation to this issue and has tried to define the democratic values that should be a part of education in Europe. One of the results is the *Reference Framework of Competences for Democratic*

Culture (Council of Europe, 2018). Byram has been a part of this work, and in the revisited edition of his 1997 book, he has included an interesting coda on moral relativism, pluralism and human rights, inspired by the philosopher Isaiah Berlin, who speaks about values pluralism. Byram sums up: 'values pluralism is not relativism' (Byram, 2021: 75), meaning that we as teachers should not abandon the right to make a moral judgment, but on the other hand, we should seek to understand the variability of values, examine the context, the history and other relevant factors. In another section of the book, Byram discusses the ethical responsibilities of the teacher, including different meanings of 'political engagement' (Byram, 2021: 119).

It should be noted that Byram includes 'symbolic competence', as theorised by Kramsch and Whiteside (2008), among the objectives in the Knowledge dimension, explained by the words: 'knows how different languages position their speakers in different symbolic spaces; how languages evoke historic cultural memories; how language performance can create alternative realities' (Byram, 1997: 59). In view of the discussion of epistemologies above, this might be described as an instance of 'postmodernism in modernism'.

Finally, Byram comments on some of the critiques of his supposed focus on national cultures in the 1997 book (this is also discussed in Byram, 2009). Byram reminds us that he has often used the expression 'communities and countries', and he stresses that 'community' and 'society' are not synonymous (referring to the sociologist Tönnies). (I would add that Byram seems to use the words 'country' and 'society' as synonymous or co-terminous.) Byram emphasises that within one society, there are many communities and their associated cultures. So, he stresses that there is cultural diversity in any country and notes in passing that foreign language teaching tends to focus on the culture of the dominant elite (Byram, 1997: 19, with a reference to Bourdieu, 1990). When he mentions 'the national' several times among the objectives of the Knowledge dimension (Byram, 1997: 59), it is because it would be relevant to know what children in the target-language country are taught about their own country, such as national history.

So, Byram deals with the country, the state, the nation, as an entity that is *internally diverse*. But his approach, as represented in Byram (1997, 2021), is marked by the national paradigm (Risager, 2007) after all, because he does not deal in any systematic way with processes and practices that cut across national borders, such as language spread, transnational migration, spread of cultural products worldwide, spread of social movements, etc.

Transnational Studies

Byram has, however, raised serious questions about the national tradition in a recent article on internationalism (Byram, 2018). In this article, he refers to the historical role of nationalism in education and discusses the concept of internationalism, especially the idea of internationalism as a moral and political force. He argues that foreign language teaching has a particular role to play in prompting learners to take a different view on the world than the nationalist one and says about liberal internationalism that it 'has a vision of the world which goes beyond the national and is based on promoting a change for the better both in terms of the moral position taken and with respect to the actions which follow' (Byram, 2018: 77). As examples of ways forward, he mentions two projects of transnational collaboration, one between learners in Denmark and Argentina, focusing on environment education (Porto *et al.*, 2017) and one between learners in Argentina and the UK, focusing on peace education (Porto & Yulita, 2017). Several other projects (e.g. Golubeva *et al.*, 2017; Conlon Perugini, 2018; Silvey & Gräfnitz, 2018) are based on ideals of global citizenship.

But in spite of such ideals expressed in innovative projects and various curricula, it is still the case that much language teaching, and not least language textbooks (Risager, 2018, 2021), are too often bound to the national frame of thinking. Knowledge about the world too often stops at the national border. In my view, intercultural language education should orient itself more clearly towards a world that is characterised by a complex interplay of national and transnational processes (Risager, 2007).

A rethinking of the Knowledge dimension

This requires a rethinking of the Knowledge dimension, if we refer to Byram's model of ICC. As already mentioned, the Knowledge dimension stems from the German tradition of *Landeskunde* and may comprise many aspects of a country – geography and history; social, ethnic and linguistic diversity; education and other institutions; cultural production; politics; economy; etc. Thus, *Landeskunde* may be described as multidisciplinary area studies with a focus on a state or nation (the relationship between 'state' and 'nation' may be complicated). A transnational reorientation of the Knowledge dimension would break with this tradition and try to foreground the world as an interconnected entity, without disregarding that there are states, borders and (debates about) national identities. It should also, in my view, foreground some of the issues that characterise the world at large today (cf. the innovative projects mentioned above), such as the climate crisis, the biodiversity crisis, racism and sexism, political suppression, poverty, refugees, diseases and epidemics, problems of security, problems of tech power and many others (Risager, 1989), cf. the UN sustainable development goals from 2015.

There are many different theories on the transnational, as large parts of the social sciences and the humanities are beginning to direct their focus away from the traditional, national view of the world. My own primary inspiration is the Swedish anthropologist Hannerz (1992), and I have explained in Risager (2006) how his theory of cultural flows can be used to develop a view of transnational flows of languages (and languaculture) across cultural contexts. These flows are driven by transborder migrations and other kinds of mobility resulting in the formation of local complexity (e.g. in cities) characterised by interethnic communication, hierarchisation and other forms of power struggles among speakers of different languages. The flows are also driven by language learning in different contexts all over the world, where the languages in question spread to new learners as foreign or second languages. Modern digital communication makes it easy to maintain worldwide linguistic networks, both for speaking and for reading/writing. So, learning a language may give access to many places and spaces across the world, not only in the 'target-language countries'. This goes for many languages of the world, not only English.

In the following, I will list some aspects of the transnational that may be relevant to include in learning materials and teaching for global citizenship in intercultural language education (Risager & Svarstad, 2020). What is important to note here, is that – as in the *Landeskunde* tradition – it is not supposed that all these aspects should be included, or learned as such. But at least some of them should be present because they can *make transnational connections visible* for the learners and help them construct a realistic image of the interconnected world.

International relations – contributions from sociology, political science and economy: This could be exemplified with international organisations such as the UN, WHO, ASEAN (the Association of Southeast Asian Nations), AU (the African Union), the Commonwealth of Nations, OIF (*Organisation internationale de la Francophonie*) and the EU (which also has supranational traits). It can also be import-export relations considered at the national level, and many other kinds of multilateral or bilateral collaboration between state actors.

Transnational mobility – contributions from sociology and anthropology: People move around in the world for many reasons and with different purposes (tourism, family visits, education, discovery, sport, labor migration, pensioner migration, flight from war and environmental destruction, human trafficking); transnational networks and diasporas which are the results of migration, e.g. the Turkish diaspora in Europe, especially in Germany, and the Chinese diaspora in most countries, not least in Southeast Asia.

Transnational flows of ideas, discourses and practices – contributions from Cultural studies and sociology: Youth culture and music spreading all over the world; ideas and ideologies about democracy or capitalism; news and conspiracy theories spreading in the (social) media; various forms of activism in relation to climate change.

Transnational flows of languages – contributions from the sociology of language and sociolinguistics: The spread of languages (not only English) across the world and the formation of multilingual settings, where several languages are used and perhaps mixed (translanguaging, García & Li, 2014), and where people may use the particular languages as first language, or second or foreign language (as intercultural speakers).

Transnational organisations – contributions from sociology and political science: Transnational companies such as LEGO, Coca-Cola or the Tech Giants; nongovernmental organisation (NGOs) such as Greenpeace, Doctors Without Borders or Extinction Rebellion; world organisations such as the Roman Catholic Church; transnational networks of sustainable cities; transnational green movements.

Transnational infrastructure and communication – contributions from technology and geography: The technologies that make transnational processes possible, such as railways, roads and ports, e.g. the Chinese *Belt and Road Initiative* (BRI); communication lines across borders via ocean cables and satellites; more or less global communication and collaboration via mass media, the internet and social media.

Global/regional natural conditions – contributions from the natural sciences and others: Landscapes, animal and plant life, epidemics, weather, climate and natural disasters, and the complex interplay of nature with society and culture.

Transnational Developments: Consequences for ICC

These thoughts are primarily related to the Knowledge dimension in Byram's model, as already said. But steps towards a transnational paradigm (Risager, 2007) have implications for the whole area of competences covered by the model.

In the *Knowledge* dimension, the learners may still make comparisons between a certain country and their own country, and questions of national structures and national identities are still very relevant. But a transnational representation of the foreign country, for example, Scotland (focusing on what one could call 'Scotland in the world and the world in Scotland') would perhaps make learners aware of the transnational identity of their own country, and in this way, tendencies towards 'banal nationalism' (Billig, 1995) are diminished, both as regards target-language countries and the learners' own country.

In the *Skills* dimensions, the learners should develop their abilities to cope with local cultural and linguistic complexity (as they often do in their everyday life outside school): Interacting with people who have different life histories and perspectives (McConachy, 2018; Risager, 2009); reading and interpreting literature perhaps written by people who have experiences of migration and language shift (Matos, 2012); analysing images and videos that represent the complexity of life in reality or in virtual spaces (Chapelle, 2016); using the target language as a lingua franca in relation to different groups – or in reading; using it as a language for specific purposes, for example, reading simple texts in German about China.

In the *Attitudes and Education* dimensions, learners should become familiar with taking a global perspective in language learning (which some of them already do outside school), similar to Byram's proposals of internationalism and global citizenship. One can say that while the Skills dimensions focus on local complexity, as represented in particular interactions, texts and images, the other dimensions can combine the local and the global in more comprehensive cultural representations (textbooks, larger themes, etc.), and in visions of critical global citizenship – both as intercultural speakers and as intercultural readers/writers (Hoff, 2020).

Decolonial Studies

The different aspects of transnationality outlined above focus on contemporary society. They focus on transcontinental and global processes and practices that characterise our world today or the immediate past during the past three or four decades. This can be described as a geographical orientation as opposed to a more historical orientation.

Decolonial studies takes up the historical orientation and focuses on the legacy of world history, not least the role of European colonialism since the 15th century. Thus, decolonial studies are interested in furthering an awareness of inequity and injustice at local and global levels, and points at colonial history as one of the factors behind the contemporary situation.

What is important to note here is that – as it was said in relation to transnational aspects – it is not suggested that colonial histories and narratives should always be included in language teaching or learned as such. But at least some of these narratives should be present because they can *make global inequity and its historical roots visible* for the learners.

A second rethinking of the Knowledge dimension

This requires a second rethinking of the Knowledge dimension, in which countries, regions and continents are seen in a world-historical perspective, and which includes an awareness of global power relations and their reflection in local settings (such as racism and sexism).

Byram's model of ICC does contain a few references to history. The Knowledge dimension includes two objectives relating to history: 'Historical and contemporary relationships between one's own and one's interlocutor's countries' and 'The national memory of one's own country and how its events are related to and seen from the perspective of one's interlocutor's country' (Byram, 1997: 51). These formulations point to a binational, bilateral approach, and this is relevant to include. But they miss the wider structures of colonialism and imperialism.

Among the analyses in Risager (2018), there is an analysis of the textbook *A Piece of Cake* (Boesen & Rosendal, 2011). It is meant for the teaching of English in Denmark, in lower secondary, where the learners are 13–16 years old (they started English when they were about 9). The textbook was analysed from a number of different theoretical perspectives, among them a decolonial perspective, and it turned out that in the whole textbook (three volumes plus learner's and teacher's guides), there was hardly any mention of history at all (except stories of the fate of Native Americans). There was no mention of British colonialism or the British Empire or the Commonwealth, and this means that there was no explanation of, e.g. the selection and order of 'English-speaking countries' in the textbook (first Britain, then the USA, Canada, Ireland, Australia and at the end South Africa). There was no explanation either of the widespread use of English in the world, in some places as majority language, in some places as official language, minority language, elite language, etc. This is just a small example showing how important it is to include at least some information on the historical background of the contemporary world.

In *A Piece of Cake*, and many other learning materials for foreign language learning, one can see how the content is based on global hierarchies that contribute to power structures in the world (Risager, 2018): Certain countries are mentioned before certain others. Certain countries are always mentioned, others are never mentioned. In *A Piece of Cake*, for example, there is no treatment or mention of any other 'English-speaking countries' in Africa besides South Africa (and Zambia, which is very briefly mentioned in a text on the internet). Analyses may show similar hierarchisations in textbooks as regards race, religion or language, and it could be an important learning task to become aware of such hierarchisations and reflect upon them: Is it possible to rearrange these hierarchies? Is it possible to think without them?

The hierarchies are created by world history. This is especially the case with *racism*, which was institutionalised during the European colonisations: The exploitation by European colonisers of indigenous people in the Caribbean and the rest of America, the trade with enslaved people from Africa, the use of slaves as manual labor on a very large scale and the creation of racial hierarchies encompassing various mixtures of 'indigenous', 'black' and 'white'. People had been taken as slaves for long periods before European colonialism (the word 'slave' comes from the fact that very often, e.g. in the Viking Age, slaves were captured among the Slavonic peoples living north of the Black Sea), but it was not until the triangular trade that racism was fully systematised, and 'slave' came to be equated with 'black'.

Another hierarchy that should be mentioned here is *orientalism*, described by Said (1978). Said was one of the pioneers within postcolonial studies focusing on how literature and other forms of art deal with the difficult questions of identity in countries that have obtained independence and now try to define themselves (e.g. India or countries in Africa or the Middle East). Orientalism is the Western view of 'the East' as an exotic place where 'the Oriental', 'the Arab', 'the Moslem', 'the Asiatic' lives. It builds on a dichotomy between 'us' in the rational West and 'them' in the passionate and despotic East. Orientalism may also be used more generally to refer to the Eurocentric and exotising view of the West of everything that is not part of the West. One can say that recently independent countries have had to struggle against orientalism.

An even broader critique of colonialism comes from representatives of decolonial studies, who point to links between all dimensions of colonialism: economic oppression, political oppression, cultural oppression, linguistic oppression, etc. They are working particularly in relation to Latin America, which was colonised in an earlier phase than the others (Mignolo, 2011). But decolonial studies is relevant for all countries and areas in the world, both former colonies and former colonial powers. Decolonial studies is a (multidisciplinary) field that is engaged in the general decolonisation of the world, i.e. it aims to obtain a situation where both objective and subjective consequences of colonialism, including racialisation and racism, have disappeared or at least been diminished. One focus point of decolonial studies is the diversity of worldviews. For example, worldviews of indigenous peoples have been investigated (epistemologies of the South, de Sousa Santos, 2014) in order to elucidate their insights and experiences concerning the relationship between nature and human beings. Such studies are important in the light of ongoing destructions of natural resources and the climate balance.

Therefore, it is important that intercultural language education includes voices from many different places in the world and from many different contexts, also people who have been most marginalised. It is important to listen to as many different voices as possible in order to understand, interact and perhaps collaborate. This is a form of decentering: turning the attention away from the usual center in most foreign language teaching: white middle-class Western society, and direct it towards other narratives and perspectives that might teach us something more, or something different, about the world (Guilherme, 2002, 2015; Kramsch & Vinall, 2015; Risager, 2018; Risager & Svarstad, 2020; Risager, forthcoming).

Decolonial Developments: Consequences for ICC

These thoughts about the importance of including historical aspects in intercultural education, relate in the first place to the Knowledge dimension. But they are actually just as relevant for the Education dimension as they put particular weight on the awareness of power relations and on – not only the competence but – the responsibility of the global citizen (Guilherme, 2015). The intercultural speaker/reader is supposed not only to communicate, mediate and collaborate, using the target language, but also to reflect on questions concerning their position in the historically created hierarchies of the world: Race? Ethnicity? Nationality? Gender? Sexuality? Religion? Language? For example, is the target language one of the colonial languages, and what does that mean in relation to local language hierarchies?

As already mentioned, Byram suggests categorising symbolic competence (Kramsch & Whiteside, 2008) as one of the objectives of the *Knowledge* dimension, and this is an important inclusion of decolonial interpretations of language choice and language use in multilingual settings, interpretations that require some knowledge of the larger historical context.

In the *Skills* dimensions, the learners should develop their ability to understand and manage power relations in interaction and collaboration and to analyse texts and images drawing on critical (media) literacy and an awareness of identities and positions involved in the communication process. The learners should have some time and resources to try to make real, small-scale changes, perhaps via (transnational) digital media.

In the *Attitudes* dimension, the decolonial developments presuppose even more openness and curiosity towards people with different perspectives and perhaps epistemologies – an ability to decenter, not only at the (micro) personal level (looking at things with the other person's eyes) but also at the (macro) global level (looking at things with the eyes of people living in another corner of the Earth).

An example of contextualisation of a teaching theme

The following is an imagined example of a larger theme that might be explored in the teaching of French, concretely in Denmark, for young people or adults: *Senegal and the Great Green Wall for the Sahara and the Sahel*.

In *Français Formidable*, which is a textbook used in Denmark for the teaching of French in lower secondary (learners are about 14 years of age), several francophone countries in the world are briefly described, among them Senegal (Brandelius *et al.*, 2011, Vol. 2, analysed in Risager, 2018). There is one page with a green map of Africa without any names except Sénégal and Dakar, and with two photos: one showing a fishing boat on a beach with fishermen, and one showing a smiling boy called Abdoulaye. Abdoulaye explains (in a short text in French) that he is from Senegal in West Africa and that Senegal was colonised by the French at the end of the

19th century and became independent in 1960. He tells us that he helps his father with the fishing and that his mother goes to the island of Gorée, near Dakar, every day in order to sell nuts at the museum about the history of African slaves: La Maison des Esclaves. He says that it is difficult to get a job in Senegal, so his brother lives in Marseille, and as for himself, he is dreaming of playing football in Europe.

In the *Teacher's guide*, there is a longer text in Danish (about 230 words) offering some more information about Senegal: Its poverty with respect to gross domestic product (GDP) per capita (the very first piece of information), its area, its geographical position in West Africa (Gambia is mentioned), the triangular trade, St. Louis on UN's World Heritage List, Senegal influenced by the North African countries with Arab background, the Paris-Dakar rally, and export of fish, especially tuna. Concerning languages, it is said that the official language is French and that several 'local languages' are recognised and widely used, including Wolof as the most common.

These very short glimpses of life, and encyclopaedic notes, focus on the nation, but there are also some references to neighboring countries and to France. How could we contextualise this theme in order to open up for further transnational and decolonial perspectives?

Senegal is a country that is unknown to most Danes. Very few Danes travel to Senegal, and there is next to nothing about real, contemporary Senegal in the common Danish media. The dominant image of Africa as a whole is characterised by ideas of poverty, unemployment, emigration (for example, to Europe/Denmark) and conflict. So, there are innumerable aspects of Senegal that would be new and interesting to focus on in the teaching.

One aspect could be information about the great ethnic and linguistic diversity of the country, a situation that is much more prominent than the situation in Denmark, where the question of national identity is somewhat easier. Apart from immigrants from Lebanon, Mauritania, Morocco, Europe and China, there are a number of (indigenous) ethnic groups, among them the Wolof, the Fula (Peuls), the Toucouleur, the Serer, the Mandinka (Malinkés) and the Jola (Diolas). They all identify more or less strongly with different regions, have different histories in the past (most of them formed kingdoms and empires at various times), have different modes of living (various types of agriculture, degrees of nomadism), different social and political structures, different religions (mostly Sunni Islam) and different languages (more than 30). Most of them belong to ethnic groups that are represented in several neighboring countries. It should be noted that essentialisation of the ethnic groups should be avoided as the country is also culturally complex and dynamic. It could be added that the Senegalese (multiethnic) diaspora is large, especially in Europe, and plays an important part in Senegal's economy and general development.

The above-mentioned Fula is a very widely dispersed ethnic group in the Sahel region (i.e. the belt between Sahara and the tropical rain forests) stretching from Senegal in the west to regions near the Red Sea in the east. Some of the Fula are pastoralists and lead a more or less nomadic life with grazing herds (cattle, goats and sheep). The Fula people are involved in issues concerning 'the Great Green Wall for the Sahara and the Sahel' (*la Grande muraille verte pour le Sahara et le Sahel*). This is a grand project of rural development involving Senegal and 10 other states in the Sahel region: Mauritania, Mali, Burkina Faso, Niger, Nigeria, Chad, Sudan, Ethiopia, Eritrea and Djibouti. The initial idea was to plant a belt of trees, primarily acacias, from west to east, bordering the Saharan Desert in order to combat increasing desertification and climate change, a belt about 15 kilometres deep and 7600 kilometres long. This idea developed into a broader project aiming to create a mosaic of green and productive landscapes in the whole region. The project started in 2005 and is one of the most important collaboration projects of the AU. (There is also a Green Wall of China, south of the Gobi Desert, which started in 1978.) The project is already advancing; in Senegal, for example, over 11 million trees have been planted. There are, however, many kinds of difficulties in implementing the project. Populations have to be relocated, and conflicts may arise between sedentary farmers and pastoralists (e.g. the Fula) concerning grazing areas. There are also increasing problems of security in politically unstable areas, e.g. Mauritania, Niger, Chad and Sudan, including terrorist activities.

The learners who work with this theme while developing their communicative competence in French will become aware that Senegal is not an isolated country. It is deeply integrated in the whole region because of its ethnic composition and because its national border cuts across a number of ethnic areas each with their separate identity and history. They will become aware of transnational collaboration in the Sahel region, including the role of the AU – an institution based on ideas somewhat similar to those of the EU. They also get an impression of linguistic diversity in Senegal and neighboring countries and learn that French is (only) the official language, whereas there are several national languages, among them Wolof as the most common. An important decolonial strategy in relation to the theme is to move learners away from the usual (Danish) colonial stereotypes of a poor and weak Africa to a focus on regional collaboration on visionary projects for the future – although hampered by difficult circumstances. The learners in Denmark may begin to reflect on their own positions, perspectives and resources in relation to the people concerned in the Sahel. They may also have opportunities to act, perhaps by way of asking people from mainstream Danish media why they do not write about this project, or by way of setting up a dialogue in French (and maybe English) about climate change with a school or community in Senegal that is involved in the project.

Conclusion

This chapter has presented Michael Byram's very influential work on intercultural language education since the 1980s, put it in historical perspective and discussed its theoretical and epistemological foundations. It has noted that Byram's model of ICC is multidisciplinary and rooted in several European and American traditions, and this open structure has made it possible for a great variety of scholars and researchers to develop and/or critique different parts of the model without having to reject it all together. It still stands as a model that may serve as a kind of baseline.

The chapter has then focused on two critiques and further developments of Byram's thoughts: the transnational and the decolonial developments, which point to new conceptualisations of culture and identity in a transnational and global perspective. Taken together, they view the world not as a mosaic of different countries but as an interconnected entity characterised by inequities, hierarchies, conflicts and problems – a world that needs action, not least by globally oriented intercultural speakers and readers/writers.

References

Billig, M. (1995) *Banal Nationalism*. London: SAGE Publications.

Boesen, J. and M. Rosendal (2011) *A Piece of Cake 7–9*. Copenhagen: Alinea.

Bourdieu, P. (1990) *In Other Words: Essays Towards a Reflexive Sociology*. New York: Polity Press.

Brandelius, M. and Sundell, I. (2011) *Français Formidable*. Copenhagen: Alinea.

Buttjes, D. and Byram, M. (eds) (1991) *Mediating Languages and Cultures: Towards an Intercultural Theory of Foreign Language Education*. Clevedon: Multilingual Matters.

Byram, M. (1989) *Cultural Studies in Foreign Language Education*. Clevedon: Multilingual Matters.

Byram, M. (1997) *Teaching and Assessing Intercultural Communicative Competence*. Clevedon: Multilingual Matters.

Byram, M. (2008) *From Foreign Language Education to Education for Intercultural Citizenship: Essays and Reflections*. Clevedon: Multilingual Matters.

Byram, M. (2009) Intercultural competence in foreign languages. The intercultural speaker and the pedagogy of foreign language education. In D.K. Deardorff (ed.) *The SAGE Handbook of Intercultural Competence* (pp. 321–332). Thousand Oaks, CA: SAGE Publications.

Byram, M. (2018) An essay on internationalism in foreign language education. *Intercultural Communication Education* 1 (2), 64–82.

Byram, M. (2021) *Teaching and Assessing Intercultural Communicative Competence Revisited*. Bristol: Multilingual Matters.

Byram, M., Golubeva, I., Han, H. and Wagner, M. (eds) (2017) *From Principles to Practice in Education for Intercultural Citizenship*. Bristol: Multilingual Matters.

Byram, M. and Risager, K. (1999) *Language Teachers, Politics and Cultures*. Clevedon: Multilingual Matters.

Chapelle, C.A. (2016) *Teaching Culture in Introductory Foreign Language Textbooks*. London: Palgrave Macmillan.

Conlon Perugini, D. (2018) Discovering modes of transportation. In M. Wagner, D. Conlon Perugini and M. Byram (eds) *Teaching Intercultural Competence Across the Age Range: From Theory to Practice* (pp. 42–59). Bristol: Multilingual Matters.

Council of Europe (2018) *Reference Framework of Competences for Democratic Culture.* Strasbourg: Council of Europe Publishing.

Deardorff, D.K. (2009) *The SAGE Handbook of Intercultural Competence.* Los Angeles: SAGE Publishing.

Doyé, P. (1991) *Grossbritannien: seine Darstellung in deutschen Schulbüchern für den Englischunterricht.* Frankfurt/Main: Diesterweg.

Gagel, W. (1983) *Einführung in die Didaktik des politischen Unterrichts.* Opladen: Leske und Budrich.

García, O. and Li, W. (2014) *Translanguaging: Language, Bilingualism and Education.* Basingstoke: Palgrave Macmillan.

Geertz, C. (1975) *The Interpretation of Cultures.* London: Hutchinson.

Golubeva, I., Wagner, M. and Yakimowski, M.E. (2017) Comparing students' perceptions of global citizenship in Hungary and the USA. In M. Byram, I. Golubeva, H. Han and M. Wagner (eds) *From Principles to Practice in Education for Intercultural Citizenship* (pp. 3–24). Bristol: Multilingual Matters.

Gray, J. (2010) *The Construction of English: Culture, Consumerism and Promotion in the ELT Global Coursebook.* Basingstoke: Palgrave Macmillan.

Gudykunst, W.B. (1994) *Bridging Differences: Effective Intergroup Communication* (2nd edn). London: Sage Publications.

Guilherme, M. (2002) *Critical Citizens for an Intercultural World: Foreign Language Education as Cultural Politics.* Clevedon: Multilingual Matters.

Guilherme, M. (2015) Intercultural competence. In M. Byram and A. Hu (eds) *Routledge Encyclopedia of Language Teaching and Learning. 2nd Edition* (pp. 346–349). London and New York: Routledge.

Hannerz, U. (1992) *Cultural Complexity: Studies in the Social Organization of Meaning.* New York: Columbia University Press.

Hoff, H.E. (2020) The evolution of intercultural communicative competence: Conceptualisations, critiques and consequences for the 21st century classroom practice. *Intercultural Communication Education* 3 (2), 55–74.

Holliday, A. (2011) *Intercultural Communication and Ideology.* London: Sage.

Kramsch, C. and Vinall, K. (2015) The cultural politics of language textbooks in the era of globalization. In X.L. Curdt-Christiansen and C. Weninger (eds) *Language, Ideology and Education: The Politics of Textbooks in Language Education* (pp. 11–28). London: Routledge.

Kramsch, C. and Whiteside, A. (2008) Language ecology in multilingual settings: Towards a theory of symbolic competence. *Applied Linguistics* 29 (4), 645–671.

Liddicoat, A.J. and Scarino, A. (2013) *Intercultural Language Teaching and Learning.* Chichester: Wiley-Blackwell.

Matos, A.G. (2012) *Literary Texts and Intercultural Learning. Exploring New Directions.* Oxford: Peter Lang.

McConachy, T. (2018) *Developing Intercultural Perspectives on Language Use: Exploring Pragmatics and Culture in Foreign Language Learning.* Bristol: Multilingual Matters.

Mignolo, W. (2011) *The Darker Side of Western Modernity: Global Futures, Decolonial Options.* Durham, NC: Duke University Press.

Porto, M., Daryai-Hansen, P., Arcuri, M.E. and Schifler, K. (2017) Green Kidz: Young learners engage in intercultural environmental citizenship in an English language classroom in Argentina and Denmark. In M. Byram, I. Golubeva, H. Han and M. Wagner (eds) *From Principles to Practice in Education for Intercultural Citizenship* (pp. 131–158). Bristol: Multilingual Matters.

Porto, M. and Yulita, L. (2017) Language and intercultural citizenship education for a culture of peace: The Malvinas/Falklands Project. In M. Byram, I. Golubeva, H. Han and M. Wagner (eds) *From Principles to Practice in Education for Intercultural Citizenship* (pp. 199–224). Bristol: Multilingual Matters.

Risager, K. (1989) World studies and foreign language teaching: A perspective from Denmark. *World Studies Journal* 7 (2), 28–31.

Risager, K. (2006) *Language and Culture: Global Flows and Local Complexity*. Clevedon: Multilingual Matters.

Risager, K. (2007) *Language and Culture Pedagogy: From a National to a Transnational Paradigm*. Clevedon: Multilingual Matters.

Risager, K. (2009) Intercultural competence in the cultural flow. In A. Hu and M. Byram (Hrsg.) *Interkulturelle Kompetenz und fremdsprachliches Lernen. Modelle, Empirie, Evaluation* (pp. 15–30). Tubingen: Gunter Narr.

Risager, K. (2018) *Representations of the World in Language Textbooks*. Bristol: Multilingual Matters.

Risager, K. (2021) Language textbooks: Windows to the world. *Language, Culture and Curriculum* 34 (1), Special issue: The language textbook: Representation, interaction & learning.

Risager, K. (forthcoming) Language textbooks and popular geopolitics. Representations of the world and (post)colonial history in English and French. *Journal of Postcolonial Linguistics* 4. Special issue: Language and Popular Geopolitics, ed. by C. Levisen and S. Fernández.

Risager, K. and Svarstad, L.K. (2020) *Verdensborgeren og den interkulturelle læring* [The Global Citizen and Intercultural Learning]. Frederiksberg, Denmark: Samfundslitteratur].

Said, E.W. (1978) *Orientalism*. New York: Pantheon Books.

de Sousa Santos, B. (2014) *Epistemologies of the South: Justice against Epistemicide*. Boulder, CO: Paradigm.

Silvey, P. and Gräfnitz, S. (2018) Houses around the world. In M. Wagner, D. Conlon Perugini and M. Byram (eds) *Teaching Intercultural Competence Across the Age Range: From Theory to Practice* (pp. 22–41). Bristol: Multilingual Matters.

Tajfel, H. (1981) *Human Groups and Social Categories*. Cambridge: Cambridge University Press.

van Ek, J.A. (1986) *Objectives for Foreign Language Learning. Vol. 1: Scope*. Strasbourg: Council of Europe.

Wagner, M., Conlon Perugini, D. and Byram, M. (eds) (2018) *Teaching Intercultural Competence Across the Age Range: From Theory to Practice*. Bristol: Multilingual Matters.

2 Language Awareness and Intercultural Communicative Competence: Revisiting the Relationship

Troy McConachy

Introduction

The phenomenon of language awareness has attracted the attention of teachers and researchers working in language and intercultural education for several decades now, albeit with variation in terminology and differences in theoretical perspectives. Within Second Language Acquisition (SLA) theory, framings of language awareness typically emphasize learners' explicit knowledge of linguistic forms and functions, but only rarely take into account the relationship between language and culture or the need for the learner to reflect on this relationship in the process of learning. Meanwhile, early proponents of the language awareness movement in foreign language education saw their mission as much more than developing knowledge of the structural rules of language (see Wright & Bolitho, 1993). Rather, language awareness was framed within a broadly humanistic perspective on learning where the aim was to inspire curiosity about human languages and the ability to explore languages through analysis, reflection and discovery (e.g. Hawkins, 1994). Within intercultural language learning, language awareness is closely associated with the language learner's emerging understanding of the interrelationships between language and culture and the potential for this awareness to promote intercultural learning. In this sense, it sustains the emphasis on the humanistic development of the individual but generates new perspectives on the potential for the individual to use language awareness as a resource for mediating across cultural differences.

Although language awareness is not explicitly incorporated within Byram's (1997) model of ICC, it is attributed much importance in his pedagogical thinking (see Boye & Byram, 2017; Byram, 1991, 2012) and can be seen as interfacing with key elements of the model in important ways. This chapter takes Byram's work on language awareness as a starting point for revisiting the relationship between language awareness and ICC by critically engaging with relevant theoretical and empirical work within the field of intercultural language learning. It first considers theorizing on the interrelationship between language and culture that underpins rationales for developing language awareness and then discusses the nature of language awareness through the lens of analytical and reflective engagement. The chapter discusses work that has drawn on insights from different areas of linguistics such as pragmatics and semantics and considers what recent perspectives suggest for conceptualization of the relationship between language awareness and ICC.

Language Awareness and Conceptualizations of the Language-Culture Nexus

Work on language awareness within intercultural language learning places distinctive emphasis on learners' exploration of the interconnections between language and culture as a necessary part of becoming able to learn and use an additional language in intercultural communication. This emphasis is underpinned by the assumption of a close relationship between language and culture and the perception that learners need to develop awareness of how language functions to create cultural meanings within and across languages. The assumption that language and culture are interconnected derives from a long tradition of relativistic thinking in fields such as philosophy and linguistic anthropology, as well as more recent work in cross-cultural pragmatics, intercultural pragmatics, and cultural linguistics. Although full discussion of the complexities of the interrelationship is not possible here, it is necessary to engage with some of the key thinking that has informed approaches to language awareness within intercultural language learning.

Within Byram's early work, the rationale for developing learners' language awareness is underpinned by a view of language as a co-constitutive element of a larger cultural reality. Byram (1991: 18) explains as follows:

> Language is not simply a reflector of an objective cultural reality. It is an integral part of that reality through which other parts are shaped and interpreted. It is both a symbol of the whole and a part of the whole which shapes and is in turn shaped by sociocultural actions, beliefs and values.

This means that language not only represents culture in an abstract sense; it is also one of the primary semiotic tools by which social groups and individuals create social reality by defining and delineating the core constituents of communal life. In the context of foreign language learning,

Byram (1991) recognizes the potential for the learner to assume that a foreign language is simply a different set of linguistic tools for referring to the same cultural reality and thus emphasizes the importance of helping the learner acquire a relativistic understanding of languages and cultures through a gradual process of decentering. Language awareness plays an important role as 'the study of the nature of language as a social and cultural phenomenon' (1991: 19) and is perceived as complementary to the study of language for the purpose of skill acquisition.

Byram (1991) sees language awareness as being largely oriented toward sociolinguistic knowledge and designed to help learners reflect on their own language learning and make constructive cross-linguistic comparisons that shed light on the interconnections between language and culture. In his subsequent monograph, Byram (1997, 2021) again emphasizes that what goes on in communication is much more than an exchange of information, and that the sociolinguistic expression of meaning through phenomena such as politeness is highly consequential for building and maintaining relations across cultures. He comments that '[p]oliteness is only the visible symptom of a more complex phenomenon: the differences in beliefs, values, behaviours and meanings through which people interact with each other, differences which may be incompatible and contain the seeds of conflict' (Byram, 2021: 3–4). Thus, he points to the culture-specific nature of linguistic practices and the need for the learner to understand how linguistic choices link with underlying cultural elements.

As pointed out by Risager (2006), and acknowledged by Byram (2021) himself, this early work did not necessarily prioritize elaboration of the interrelationship between language and culture. In fact, such elaboration has proved to be a challenging task, as both of these notions are interpreted in different ways and have come to be problematized with the ascent of post-structuralist thinking within much contemporary scholarship (see Borghetti, 2019; Risager, 2020).

In early work, scholars such as Fantini (1995) draw heavily on the Whorfian tradition in arguing that language represents the worldview of cultural groups, suggesting that different constituents of language – from phonology to pragmatic patterns – come together to shape perception within a cohesive worldview. He argues for greater recognition of the role of language in intercultural encounters and the need for individuals to transcend the linguistic structuring of their own worldview.

Meanwhile, Kramsch (1993, 2009) takes a more dynamic perspective on the interrelationship between language and culture. She places particular emphasis on the notion of 'discourse' and the idea that it is in meaning-making practices that language and culture become most intertwined. She emphasizes that the construction and interpretation of linguistic meanings is dependent on the cultural knowledge and assumptions of participants, including their understandings of the interpersonal, sociocultural and historical context relevant to a spoken or written text. Kramsch

(1993), thus, criticizes approaches to awareness-raising that treat culture as 'mere information conveyed by the language, not as a feature of language itself' (1993: 8) and argues for the need to conceptualize language as an articulation of cultural meaning. In this vein, Kramsch (2006, 2011) has emphasized the importance of 'symbolic competence', which includes the ability to recognize the various connotations evoked by language use – e.g. historical, cultural, political, affective – and the ability to actively exploit and re-shape the meaning potential of (multilingual) symbolic forms and practices. In short, it involves understanding the dynamic and multifaceted nature of meaning-making and the ability to experience and express meanings that enact and renew one's positioning as a social actor.

In line with this focus on the symbolic realm, much work on language awareness within the field of intercultural language learning has adopted a view of culture as 'meaning' and aimed to identify variability in meaning-making practices, with a particularly linguistic focus. Crozet *et al.* (1999) articulate the centrality of the notion of 'linguaculture' (as used by Friedrich [1989] and parallel with 'languaculture' used by Agar [1994]) to their perspective on intercultural language learning, which emphasizes the learner's exploration of cultural differences that manifest in patterns of language structure and use and the 'linguistic experience of difference' (1999: 4). Crozet (2003) presents a way of modelling the relationship between language and culture in terms of five dimensions: level of verbosity, approaches to interpersonal relationships, approaches to politeness, level of ritualization and level of expressivity.

In a more linguistically focused formulation, Liddicoat (2009, building on Crozet & Liddicoat, 1999) models the relationship between language and culture in terms of 'articulation points' where culture influences the meaning of different units of language, including genre, pragmatic norms, norms of interaction, syntax, lexicon and paralinguistic structures. It is argued that these linguistic elements reflect a cultural group's conventions for creating meaning and representing dominant views of the social structure. Meanwhile, Risager (2007) highlights three dimensions of 'languaculture': the semantic and pragmatic dimension, the poetic dimension and the identity dimension. The first dimension parallels the work above, the second dimension relates to meaning and impressions created through phonological and prosodic features, while the third relates to the indexical relationship between language and identity positions.

Recent developments and tensions

Understanding of the influence of culture on pragmatic and semantic dimensions of meaning has progressed significantly in the past 10–15 years, and this has supported the language awareness work of a growing range of scholars. In particular, research in fields such as intercultural pragmatics and cultural linguistics is offering new ways of understanding the links between linguistic patterns and culture by identifying culture-specific schema and values that shape how words, utterances and speech act trajectories are interpreted (see McConachy & Spencer-Oatey, 2021 for a recent overview). For example, metapragmatic data, which involves language users' commentary on linguistic episodes, offers insights into perceptions of in/appropriate language use and how these are under-pinned by assumptions about different interpersonal rights and obliga-tions (Spencer-Oatey & Kádár, 2016, 2021). This contributes toward an understanding of the different cultural bases that inform evaluations of behavior, as well as the language used to frame transgressions of norma-tive behavior, especially in connection to moralized notions such as politeness, respect, dignity and so on (Haugh & Chang, 2019; Kádár, 2020). Similarly, work in cross-cultural pragmatics and cultural linguis-tics is also helping to elaborate the relationship between linguistic pat-terns and culture-specific conceptualizations of the social world and internal aspects of experience such as emotions (Sharifian, 2017; Wierzbicka, 2010). Insights from these fields are now beginning to be incorporated into theoretical, empirical and pedagogical work (e.g. Haugh & Chang, 2015; Koutlaki & Eslami, 2018; Liddicoat, 2017; Liddicoat & McConachy, 2019; McConachy, 2018; McConachy & Liddicoat, 2022; McConachy & Spencer-Oatey, 2020; Woodin, 2018). Some of this work will be explored later.

One tension that exists in all theorizing on the interrelationship between language and culture and which is highly consequential for devel-oping language awareness is how to take account of diversity within groups. For some, notions such as 'linguaculture' may be problematic because they seem to imply an inexorable relationship between linguistic patterns and cognitive patterns among speakers of a particular language and a consensus regarding preferred ways of being in the world and relat-ing as social beings. If 'language' and 'culture' are both treated as singular entities that become meshed together through the notion of 'linguacul-ture', the resultant notion has the potential to become an essentialist one. That is, it gives the impression that there is little variation among indi-viduals within the group. As critical intercultural scholars have argued, linguistic patterns and cultural ideas most visible within social groupings tend to reflect power relationships within these groupings and the work-ings of dominant ideologies (e.g. Piller, 2011). Thus, seemingly solidified patterns or ostensible consensus may obscure the fact that behaviors and ideas are always in flux and under contestation, particularly within a given nation (Kramsch, 2011; McConachy & Liddicoat, 2022).

Approached uncritically, the notion of 'linguaculture' has the poten-tial to solidify perceptions of the boundaries of nation, culture, and lan-guage and lead people to overlook the dynamic flow of cultural ideas and semiotic practices across virtual and material spaces (Risager, 2020).

Risager's work approaches the language-culture nexus in a way that transcends the boundaries of the nation and allows for separation between language and culture by emphasizing that both linguistic practices and cultural discourses flow across social networks that are essentially transnational in reach. She draws on the continental notion of 'discourse' as ways of formulating knowledge from a given perspective and therefore does not regard discourse as bound to a particular language, as ideas about particular topics flow across different languages. When discourse is understood this way, Risager (2007) argues that that language and culture can be separated given that 'any language (more or less easily) can link up with any discourse, i.e. with any subject, at this macro level language and culture are separable' (2007: 181).

There have been further challenges to the idea of the inseparability of language and culture from within scholarship on English as a lingua franca (ELF). Baker (2012) argues that the relationship between language and culture is fluid and emergent in interaction rather than pre-existing within linguistic forms themselves. That is, speakers draw on their own cultural frames of reference to impose meanings on language and negotiate these with others *in situ* (see also Kecskes, 2019). The argument is not that language is culturally neutral *per se*, but that it becomes cultural within the dynamics of interactive exchange as individuals draw on their own stock of sociocultural resources. Baker (2012) has thus advocated a notion of 'intercultural awareness' which is built upon this understanding of language and culture. He defines intercultural awareness as 'a conscious understanding of the role culturally based forms, practices, and frames of understanding can have in intercultural communication, and an ability to put these conceptions into practice in a flexible and context specific manner in real time communication' (2012: 66). This conception of awareness is useful as it foregrounds a dynamic relationship between language and culture that is congruent with the idea of the intercultural speaker who mediates between languages and cultures (Byram, 1997, 2021; Liddicoat, this volume).

A further issue of consideration is that many discussions of the interrelationships between language and culture take the viewpoint of the monolingual language learner in the process of learning a second language. While such a viewpoint is necessary, it may lead to a simplification of the interrelationship between language and culture as experienced by individuals who are already multilingual. It is, thus, important for scholars to critically reflect on the relationship between this monolingual bias and the dominance of Anglocentric assumptions in scholarship. In accordance with the multilingual turn in the field of language education and the increasing attention given to phenomena such as translanguaging (e.g. Li, 2018), any work on language awareness predicated on the assumption of a close relationship between language and culture needs to interrogate the nature of language and consider how culture is actually at play when multilingual individuals draw on particular linguistic resources from their communicative repertoire to make meaning.

Attempts to develop language awareness within the context of language learning inevitably need to be informed by ongoing research into the interrelationship between language and culture, particularly theoretical perspectives that emphasize the context-sensitive nature of this relationship and the increasingly multilingual and multimodal nature of interactions. Equally important is the nature of learners' engagement with this interrelationship and how this generates affordances for intercultural learning and the development of intercultural communicative competence.

Language Awareness as Analytical and Reflective Engagement with Language and Culture

Given that the relationship between language and culture is complex, contextual and frequently mediated by multilingual resources, many scholars and teachers seem to agree that language awareness should go beyond a rule-based understanding of language and a static understanding of the relationship between language and culture. That is not to say that there is no place for awareness of linguistic rules, norms and conventions. In fact, awareness of linguistic patterns may be essential for beginning to consider the significance of these patterns from a contextual and intercultural perspective (Liddicoat, 2005).

In line with Byram's (1997) notion of the intercultural speaker, language awareness is best theorized and cultivated within the context of analytical and reflective engagement with language. Analytical and reflective engagement refers, for example, to practices such as comparing and contrasting linguistic patterns within and across languages, reflecting on the norms for 'appropriate' language use in different contexts, exploring how language triggers judgments about speakers' backgrounds, and critically considering the significance of one's own and other's linguistic choices (Byram, 2012; Chen & McConachy, 2021; McConachy & Liddicoat, 2016). Such engagement provides opportunities for the learner to become aware of the context sensitivity of linguistic meaning and more mindful of the potential impact of cultural differences on the interpretation and production of meaning (Liddicoat & Scarino, 2013). Such a view has parallels with Svarlberg's notion of 'engagement with language' (e.g. Svarlberg, 2018), though culture is addressed more explicitly in the work above. Moreover, from an intercultural perspective, language awareness is not simply about becoming aware of cross-linguistic differences that might lead to misunderstandings but is rather linked to broader appreciation for diversity within and across languages and the goal of fostering positive intercultural relationships (McConachy & Liddicoat, 2022).

One key idea when looking at language awareness as analytical and reflective engagement is that learners' growing awareness of patterns in language structure and use should make it possible for them to construct increasingly nuanced comparisons between similar phenomena not only across different languages but also across different contexts within the same language. Although these comparisons may tend toward the superficial and stereotypical in early stages, careful reflection on what has been compared (especially when scaffolded by a teacher) allows for more nuanced and context-specific comparisons to be made over time (Kearney, 2016; McConachy & Liddicoat, 2016). For example, learners may initially be prone to making comparisons between 'greetings' in two distinct languages (e.g. greetings in English and greetings in Japanese), but later move to a more nuanced position in which regional and contextual diversity is recognized within languages as well. As comparisons come to be articulated at various scales, learners are then able to think in more varied ways about how contextual expectations shape linguistic behavior and to articulate their own understanding.

Crozet and Liddicoat (1999) emphasize that it is important for learners to develop a discourse for describing language in relation to meaning, context and cultural expectations and to reflexively engage with their own assumptions. Although this can be challenging, becoming aware of and able to articulate the nature of one's own normative assumptions about language use and how it relates to perceptions of politeness, conceptions of social roles, etc. is crucial to intercultural learning. Byram (1991) calls for learners to be encouraged to 'reflect on and explain their own key cultural concepts, however disconcerting this may be, thereby making them see themselves as others do and modifying their existing schemata and cultural competence' (1991: 26). Díaz (2013) also argues for the importance of the experience of 'dissonance' in learning and intercultural communication and the need for learners to become aware of their own 'languaculture schemas' (2013: 37). She points to the potential for dissonance to lead to transformative learning when learners are encouraged to critically reflect on their own assumptions. Whether reflection on language necessarily leads to a strong sense of dissonance or not, what is important here is that there is a willingness to examine one's own starting point perceptions about what is 'normal' and begin to decenter (crucial to Byram's *savoir être*).

Liddicoat and Scarino (2013) highlight the interconnectedness of the learner's dual roles as 'participant' and 'analyzer' in meaning-making processes, arguing that awareness is not a passive 'knowing' about the interrelationships between language and culture – it involves elaboration of this awareness in the context of action.

The intercultural is manifested through language in use, through interpreting and expressing meaning across cultural boundaries in dialogue with self and others, drawing on awareness and knowledge gained through previous experience, and recognizing the possibility of multiple interpretations of messages and the culturally embedded nature of meaning. (Liddicoat & Scarino, 2013: 50)

Such a notion that emphasizes processes of interpreting and drawing together different understandings of meaning in an intercultural context has close links with Byram's idea of *savoir comprendre* (see Liddicoat, this volume). In line with Risager's conception of linguaculture, Byram (2012) suggests that language awareness should encompass social and psychological dimensions of the language-culture nexus and that an analytical and reflective approach would allow for links to be made between the different competences within ICC (2012: 7). Engagement with the social dimension involves the learner in analysis and reflection on how language functions within social groups, whereas the latter dimension involves a more introspective analysis.

With regard to the relationship between language and social groups, there is increasing impetus for taking a critical perspective that interrogates assumed relationships between culture and named languages of the nation state (see Kramsch, 2019; Risager, this volume). While not referring specifically to the relationship between language and culture, Byram (2021) has recently argued for the importance of engaging with dominant patterns within a nation so that learners can 'challenge it, critique its values and take their own position in the exchange with those who benefit from it. It then becomes possible for them to turn this critique back on their own society and become aware of power issues around them, as seen from the vantage point of analysing another society' (2021: 26). In this sense, Byram's central notion of critical cultural awareness (*savoir s'engager*) could extend to macro sociolinguistic issues such as language hierarchies and issues of inequality within and beyond the nation that have implications for the symbolic value of learners' linguistic resources and their positioning within intercultural encounters (Kramsch, 2021).

The learner's awareness of the relationship between language and social groups is also resource for reflecting on their own relationship to these groups and how this relationship is enacted symbolically (Byram, 2012). Given the language learner's status as a developing multilingual and intercultural speaker, the learner needs to consider the significance and value that is attributed to particular languages or language varieties within the linguistic marketplace, including concrete accents, word choice, speech act strategies and more. This would provide a point of connection with Kramsch's (2009) thinking around the notion of symbolic competence, which also links critical awareness of language use in the social world and the learner's own cognitive and affective experience of language. Kramsch (2009) refers particularly to 'awareness of the symbolic value of words, ability to find the most appropriate subject position, ability to grasp the larger social and historical significance of events and to understand the cultural memories evoked by symbolic systems, ability to perform and create alternative realities by reframing the issues' (Kramsch, 2009: 113).

Making connections between the notion of symbolic competence and hermeneutic views of learning, Liddicoat and McConachy (2019) argue that learners need to become able to reflect on how they associate particular linguistic practices with particular cultural identities and how they wish to position themselves in relation to these identities (see also Kearney, 2016). Awareness of the symbolic link between linguistic practices and identities is a resource for considering one's own positioning as a multilingual speaker within particular interactions and across time and space. As Kramsch (2021) points out, however, the symbolic enactment of identity through linguistic choices is constrained by power relations and whether those who interpret them attribute credibility or authority to the speaker. Discussions of language awareness therefore need to take into account issues of symbolic power and the critical awareness the learner needs of society, social relations and self.

Examples of language awareness within analytical and reflective engagement

Increased recognition of the potential for language awareness to contribute to intercultural learning goals within foreign language education has led to empirical studies that have helped operationalize language awareness within an intercultural lens and illuminate the nature of analytical and reflective engagement in learning. These studies tend to focus on forms of language awareness associated with semantic, pragmatic and interactional features of language.

In order to emphasize that awareness emerges out of analysis and reflection, recent language awareness work drawing on pragmatics has tended to focus on the development of 'metapragmatic awareness', which represents a learner's understanding of language 'as a contextually contingent social tool in which individuals orient to pragmatic phenomena based on culturally situated frames of reference' (McConachy, 2013: 3). This definition is built on an understanding that the relationship between language and culture ultimately manifests in the ways that interactants mobilize cultural frames of reference for the production and interpretation of linguistic action in particular contexts (cf. Baker, 2012). That is, language and culture are brought into relationship when individuals draw on their world knowledge, assumptions about social relationships, intuitive and explicit understandings of appropriate behavior and language awareness in order to make meaning. This conception of metapragmatic awareness places particular emphasis on learners' awareness of their taken for granted assumptions about in/appropriate language use and the nature of their own multilingual communicative repertoire (Liddicoat, 2017; McConachy, 2019).

This line of thinking is developed in McConachy's (2018) notion of 'intercultural perspective on language use', which emerged out of a study on the intercultural learning of EFL learners in Japan. He defines this notion as 'a learner's emerging capacity for paying close attention to how language is used in context, reflecting on the construction of meaning from multiple (and conflicting) perspectives, and developing insight into the impact of cultural assumptions and frames of understanding on communication' (2018: 7). The relationship between metapragmatic awareness and an intercultural perspective on language use is that the former contributes to the development of the latter over time. That is, as learners increase their awareness of the different ways that languages embody and shape cultural meanings, they come able to make more nuanced comparisons, reflect on the impact of underlying assumptions and understand the different ways that interpretations of language feed into evaluations of people. In this sense, an intercultural perspective is a higher order construct that shapes and is shaped by language awareness.

McConachy's (2018) study placed particular importance on learners' reflexive understanding of the foundations of their own judgments of in/appropriate behavior and how these lead to judgments about individuals and groups. This means encouraging learners to experience their cognitive and affective reactions to different linguistic meanings and practices in more conscious ways and monitoring the potential for ethnocentric judgments. In terms of classroom practices, the study identified a particularly important role for 'experience talk', defined as 'descriptive, evaluative, and explanatory accounts of interactional experiences that are collaboratively constructed amongst classroom participants on the basis of reflection' (2018: 92). This is illustrated below.

Extract 1

In this extract, two Japanese students of English are discussing their experiences and perceptions of customer service in the US and Japan with their Australian teacher. Misato is a female post-graduate student in Japan who has studied English for many years but has only visited English-speaking countries for short periods of time as a tourist. Tai is an undergraduate student majoring in tourism at a Japanese university. His father lives in the US, and he has thus visited there many times for short periods of time.

1.	Teacher:	Okay, so let me ask you: how have you felt when you've been travelling overseas and the shop staff have spoken to you in a different way than in Japan?
2.	Misato:	So, when I went to San Francisco the staff asked me, 'Where did you come from, Tokyo or Osaka?' I said, 'I from Osaka', and last he asked me to shake hands.
3.	Tai:	Weird

4.	Misato:	Yeah, at last I feel a little strange. So because he asked me many things.
5.	Tai:	Yeah, I think maybe he was too friendly.
6.	Misato:	And it because I foreigner and tourist so maybe he was too friendly, I think.
7.	Tai:	Ah, but I think the relationship between customer and staff is equal in ….
8.	Misato:	Abroad?
9.	Tai:	Abroad? Yeah, I don't know about that, but maybe Western.
10.	Teacher:	Yeah, that's an interesting point. I actually feel like sometimes the shop staff are up here and the customer is down here. Sometimes in Australia you are friendly to them but they are not so friendly to you. It's kind of reversed.
11.	Misato:	I think it's because in Japan, there is the concept of 'okyakusama wa kamisama' (The customer is a God). So many customers are arrogant, I think.
12.	Tai:	Ah, but this idea 'Customer is God' was not natural in Japan because I learned that in tourism class. One hotel manager thought up have this idea and ordered his staff, 'Don't be rude to customer'. Until then, the staff say something impolite to customer like, 'This is not my job'. But now, even some job is not staff's job, they do it.

(McConachy, 2018: 108)

Whereas Misato's experience is initially evaluated in negative terms ('weird'), collaborative reflection allows for this experience to be considered from different perspectives. Specifically, as the interaction unfolds, the learners come to consider different aspects of context, including relevant role relations (customer and salesclerk), social categorization ('foreigner' and tourist) and ideologically shaped attitudes toward customer service. In terms of metapragmatic awareness, the focus here is not on internalizing an L2 norm but rather bringing into awareness through conscious articulation the different assumptions about customer service interaction and role relations that inform interpretation of this experience. This is driven by descriptive, evaluative, interpretive/explanatory accounts that are collaboratively constructed through reflective talk.

In the above, language awareness is not framed as something that helps a learner achieve 'success' in terms of behavioral objectives (i.e. making more effective performance decisions in intercultural interaction). Rather, the focus is first and foremost on re-evaluating initial impressions of behavior by considering some of the relevant elements of the context that may have had a bearing on what behavior occurred and how it was interpreted. In this sense, awareness generated through such analytical/ interpretative and reflective processes co-constructed through classroom interaction has the potential to contribute toward decentering. Although learners may make use of national-level (or even broader) comparisons at certain points, the aim is to bring learners' attention to the importance of context in the construction and interpretation of meaning. This allows for cultural stereotypes to be challenged, as a focus on the contextual provides a way of considering to what extent and under what circumstances cultural norms and values become relevant.

Another recent example of language awareness work is Woodin's (2018) study that looked at the potential for interactions around semantic meaning to provide opportunities for intercultural learning. Her study on tandem learning between L1 speakers of English and L1 speakers of Spanish shows that collaborative reflection on word meanings within and across languages can help language learners develop insights into differences in semantic meaning, including culture-specific connotations of word meanings. Learners in this study focused on words that relate closely to the social domain and social relationships, including private/*privado*, friendship/*amistad*, cooperate/*cooperar*, student/*estudiante*, education/*educación* and society/*sociedad*. Following discussion with her Spanish partner (Inés) about the meaning of student/*estudiante*, Louise comments as below.

Extract 2

Student for me doesn't mean the same as student for Inés in terms of for me it's um uh one word that brings to mind is like student debt and that, it isn't something that applies to her (.) cos the government pays a lot more um apart from that I that I think that basically we have the same ideas. (2018: 66)

Here, the impact of the different economic context surrounding education in Spain and the UK is noted as shaping the connotations of the word. Meanwhile, Inés had commented that she had come to associate the word with *borracheras* (binge drinking) based on her observations while spending time at Sheffield University, whereas it had previously been more associated with books and exams. These are not generalizations that all individuals from these nations would necessarily see things the same way, but they are instances of personal meaning-making where learners have collaboratively explored points of divergence in their own perceptions. Woodin's data also show that collaborative reflection on word meanings engages learners in multiple processes conducive to intercultural learning, such as establishing, articulating and justifying one's own perspective on meaning, taking up another person's perspective, and identifying commonality and difference. Woodin links such processes to instances of decentering, which occurs as learners move away from the assumption that L2 words must carve up semantic territory in the same way as L1 words. Awareness that the basic meaning, connotations and semantic field associated with individual words differ across languages brings cultural frames of references into focus and creates the possibility for broader appreciation of the relativity of meaning.

Semantic and pragmatic aspects of language both provide valuable entry points for individuals to begin to reflect on the nature of meaning, both in terms of meanings that are likely to be widely shared within different contexts (e.g. institutional, discourse community, regional, national, transnational) and those that are constructed from the vantage point of the individual language learner. The studies above, in addition to other work cited earlier, highlight the critical importance of analytical and reflective engagement with language, particularly when this occurs within the context of collaborative talk, whether that be with individuals from a similar or different background. They also show that language awareness has important links with intercultural abilities encompassed within Byram's model of ICC, including knowledge of self and other, knowledge of processes of interaction, skills of interpreting and relating, skills of discovery and interaction, decentering and critical awareness of the impact of cultural frames of reference on the perception of language and the consequences this has for evaluation of people marked as different from oneself.

Language Awareness as Component of ICC: Toward Integration?

Having looked at the role of language awareness within analytical and reflective engagement for intercultural learning, it is now important to consider the potential role of language awareness within a model of ICC. As Byram (2012) points out, many models of ICC (including his own) do not articulate the specific relationship between linguistic and intercultural aspects or how people experience the language-culture nexus, though he has specifically called for an integrated model.

Boye and Byram (2017) have suggested that the notion of 'languacultural awareness', which they define as 'explicit knowledge about the language-culture nexus and conscious perception and sensitivity in language learning, language teaching and language use' (2017: 442), could potentially be incorporated into Byram's model of ICC. They suggest that this would complement the knowledge of values, beliefs, behaviors and modes of social interaction already included within the model and would also encapsulate a critical stance. That is, the comparative and critical perspective already represented in the notion of critical cultural awareness within the model could be applied by learners to the phenomenon of languaculture, developed through reflective and analytical engagement with language.

As discussed earlier, the notions of 'languaculture'/'linguaculture' are useful in the sense that they highlight that language is not culturally neutral. However, these notions can also be interpreted in essentialist ways, and it would thus be imperative to unpack the 'language-culture nexus' in a way that recognizes the dynamicity and fluidity of this relationship.

Moreover, the learners' explicit knowledge about the language-culture nexus would need to be framed within a multilingual perspective that is congruent with the reality that many intercultural interactions in the current world are frequently mediated by multilingual and multimodal resources and that many language learners are already multilingual. In elaborating the role of language awareness in ICC, it will be important to consider how elements such as norms, values and assumptions interface with languages at different cultural scales (e.g. (trans)national, regional, institutional) and clarify the appropriate contexts of language use that learners should pay attention to and reflect upon. At a fundamental level, the language-culture nexus would need to be seen not as a fixed system but as something that is continually renewed or challenged, as speakers negotiate different understandings of the social world and the role of linguistic meaning in shaping such understandings (Kramsch, 2011).

A further issue that should be considered is the role of language awareness for 'native speakers'. Although the division between IC and ICC in Byram's model is largely designed to highlight the different needs and experience of communication between language learners speaking an additional language and native speakers using their only language, there are some issues to consider here. For example, Boye and Byram (2017) suggest that:

> The intercultural speaker has intercultural communicative competence, i.e. both intercultural competence and linguistic/communicative competence in a foreign language, to help them in intercultural interaction and this is something different from, and not comparable with, the competence of the monolingual native speaker. (2017: 441)

This kind of framing implies a rather strict division between those who are 'native speakers' and those who are not, which has become widely critiqued in the field and probably requires no further elaboration here. A further issue, however, is that this kind of division has the potential to create the impression that monolinguals live an existence devoid of linguistic and cultural diversity, and thus their experience of communication would not afford the opportunity to develop ICC. For example, Boye and Byram go on to state that: '... a monolingual speaker has not necessarily had the opportunity to develop the attitudes of curiosity and openness or the skills of interpreting/relating and discovery which are crucial for success' (2017: 441).

Although the experience of communicating and managing relationships through the medium of a foreign language certainly has its own distinctiveness, many individuals who speak only one dominant language are also exposed to multicultural influences and (routinely) interact with those from different linguistic and cultural backgrounds. Such communication also involves a linguistic experience of difference as meaning is negotiated amidst potential differences in accent, lexical choices, syntactic structures and speech act trajectories. Indeed, for the 'monolingual' speaker, successful communication would necessitate a willingness to adjust one's linguistic and cultural frames of reference and potentially also to incorporate features of the interlocutor's languages into the communication (Sweeney & Zhu, 2010). While there may be a difference in degree, it is also worth noting that communication among monolinguals speaking the same first language also involves a linguistic experience of difference, as individuals are inevitably positioned in different ways within the social structure and bring with them different linguistic markers of belonging that influence the meaning-making process (Gramling, 2016). Therefore, in terms of thinking about a model of ICC and the role of language awareness in particular, it will be important to understand how the negotiation of meaning unfolds and is experienced in everyday communication in diverse contexts and languages, whether individuals might technically be categorized as 'monolinguals', 'multilinguals' or other designation. It may be necessary to take on board insights from work on translanguaging and other perspectives which critique the idea of named languages and the practice of treating monolingualism as the default human condition (Gramling, 2016).

A related point here is that it is of fundamental importance that monolingual speakers are seen as equally responsible for the success of interactions. This is not simply a matter of being more 'tolerant' of different accents and communicative practices that mark the 'other' as different from 'us'. It necessitates the ability to be able to recognize the potential for cultural influences on communication and a willingness to accommodate toward an interlocutor. The notion of the 'intercultural speaker' was very useful in that it foregrounded the fact (as perceived at the time) that a language learner needs to engage in processes of reflection and mediation between languages and cultures that is not normally required of monolingual native speakers. It is now worth asking whether all individuals, including monolinguals, need to be seen as potential intercultural speakers, and for the capacities of such individuals, including their language awareness, to be seen in a new light. As the experience of linguistic difference and mediation of cultural meaning is inherent to all communication to differing degrees, it may turn out that the conceptualization of language awareness within a model of ICC needs to be framed in a way that it is not too dependent on divisions such as native/non-native, monolingual/multilingual, IC/ICC.

Conclusion

This exploratory chapter has aimed to revisit the relationship between language awareness and ICC by reviewing and reflecting on conceptions of the language-culture nexus, the nature of analytical and reflective engagement in language learning and the implications for modelling ICC.

For the language learner, the development of language awareness is an important part of coming to understand the different ways that linguistic resources are put to use to create cultural meanings within and across languages and the consequences that diversity in language use has for intercultural relations. While further work is necessary to determine how language awareness might best be incorporated within a model of ICC, it is clear that the individual's awareness of language needs to be framed within a critical and multilingual perspective that recognizes the fluidity of linguistic practices in many intercultural interactions and the dynamic ways that individuals draw on cultural assumptions as a resource for interpreting others and indexing self.

References

Agar, M. (1994) *Language Shock: Understanding the Culture of Conversation*. New York: Perennial.

Baker, W. (2012) From cultural awareness to intercultural awareness: Culture in ELT. *ELT Journal* 66 (1), 62–70.

Borghetti, C. (2019) Interculturality as collaborative identity management in language education. *Intercultural Communication Education* 2 (1), 20–38.

Boye, S. and Byram, M. (2017) Language awareness and the acquisition of intercultural communicative competence. In J.M. Cots and P. Garrett (eds) *The Routledge Handbook of Language Awareness* (pp. 435–449). New York and London: Routledge.

Byram, M. (1991) Teaching culture and language: Towards an integrated model. In D. Buttjes and M. Byram (eds) *Mediating Languages and Cultures: Towards an Intercultural Theory of Foreign Language Education* (pp. 17–30). Clevedon: Multilingual Matters.

Byram, M. (1997) *Teaching and Assessing Intercultural Communicative Competence*. Clevedon: Multilingual Matters.

Byram, M. (2012) Language awareness and (critical) cultural awareness – Relationships, comparisons, and contrasts. *Language Awareness* 21 (1–2), 5–13.

Byram, M. (2021) *Teaching and Assessing Intercultural Communicative Competence: Revisited*. Bristol: Multilingual Matters.

Chen, Y. and McConachy, T. (Online first, 2021) Translating intercultural experiences into pedagogic insights: Shifts in language teachers' perceptions of English as a language for intercultural communication. *Language Awareness*.

Crozet, C. (2003) A conceptual framework to help teachers identify where culture is located in language use. In J. Lo Bianco and C. Crozet (eds) *Teaching Invisible Culture* (pp. 39–49). Melbourne: Language Australia.

Crozet, C. and Liddicoat, A.J. (1999) The challenge of intercultural language teaching: Engaging with culture in the classroom. In J. Lo Bianco, A.J. Liddicoat and C. Crozet (eds) *Striving for the Third Place: Intercultural Competence through Language Education* (pp. 113–125). Melbourne: Language Australia.

Crozet, C., Liddicoat, A.J. and Lo Bianco, J. (1999) Intercultural competence: From language policy to language education. In J. Lo Bianco, A.J. Liddicoat and C. Crozet (eds) *Striving for the Third Place: Intercultural Competence through Language Education* (pp. 1–20). Melbourne: Language Australia.

Díaz, A.R. (2013) *Developing Critical Languaculture Pedagogies in Higher Education: Theory and Practice*. Bristol: Multilingual Matters.

Fantini, A. (1995) Introduction: Language, culture and worldview – Exploring the nexus. *International Journal of Intercultural Relations* 19 (2), 143–153.

Friedrich, P. (1989) Language, ideology, and political economy. *American Anthropologist* 91, 295–312.

Gramling, D. (2016) *The Invention of Monolingualism*. New York: Bloomsbury Academic.

Haugh, M. and Chang, W.-L.M. (2015) Understanding im/politeness across cultures: An interactional approach to raising sociopragmatic awareness. *International Review of Applied Linguistics in Language Teaching* 53 (4), 389–414.

Haugh, M. and Chang, W.-L.M. (2019) 'The apology seemed (in)sincere': Variability in perceptions of (im)politeness. *Journal of Pragmatics* 142, 207–222.

Hawkins, E. (1994) Language awareness. In R. Asher (ed.) *The Encylopedia of Language and Linguistics* (Vol. 4, pp. 1933–1938). Oxford and New York: Pergamon.

Kádár, D.Z. (2020) Capturing injunctive norm in pragmatics: Meta-reflective evaluations and the moral order. *Lingua* 237, 102814.

Kearney, E. (2016) *Intercultural Learning in Modern Language Education: Expanding Meaning-Making Potentials*. Bristol: Multilingual Matters.

Kecskes, I. (2019) *English as a Lingua Franca: The Pragmatic Perspective*. Cambridge: Cambridge University Press.

Koutlaki, S.A. and Eslami, Z.R. (2018) Critical intercultural communication education: Cultural analysis and pedagogical applications. *Intercultural Communication Education* 1 (3), 100–109.

Kramsch, C. (1993) *Context and Culture in Language Teaching*. Oxford: Oxford University Press.

Kramsch, C. (2006) From communicative competence to symbolic competence. *Modern Language Journal* 90 (2), 249–252.

Kramsch, C. (2009) *The Multilingual Subject: What Foreign Language Learners Say About Their Experience and Why It Matters*. Oxford: Oxford University Press.

Kramsch, C. (2011) The symbolic dimensions of the intercultural. *Language Teaching* 44 (3), 354–367.

Kramsch, C. (2019) Between globalization and decolonization: Foreign languages in the cross-fire. In D. Macedo (ed.) *Decolonizing Foreign Language Education: The Misteaching of English and other Colonial Languages* (pp. 50–72). New York and London: Routledge.

Kramsch, C. (2021) *Language as Symbolic Power*. Cambridge: Cambridge University Press.

Li, W. (2018) Translanguaging as a practical theory of language. *Applied Linguistics* 39 (1), 9–30.

Liddicoat, A.J. (2005) Teaching languages for intercultural communication. In D. Cunningham and A. Hatoss (eds) *An International Perspective on Language Policies, Practices and Proficiencies* (pp. 201–214). Belgrave: Fédération Internationale des Professeurs de Langues Vivantes (FIPLV).

Liddicoat, A.J. (2009) Communication as culturally contexted practice: A view from intercultural communication. *Australian Journal of Linguistics* 29 (1), 115–133.

Liddicoat, A.J. (2017) Interpretation and critical reflection in intercultural language learning: Consequences of a critical perspective for the teaching and learning of pragmatics. In M. Dasli and A.R. Díaz (eds) *The Critical Turn in Language and Intercultural Communication Pedagogy* (pp. 22–39). New York and London: Routledge.

Liddicoat, A.J. and Scarino, A. (2013) *Intercultural Language Teaching and Learning*. New York: Wiley-Blackwell.

Liddicoat, A.J. and McConachy, T. (2019) Meta-pragmatic awareness and agency in language learners' constructions of politeness. In T. Szende and G. Alao (eds) *Pragmatic Competence in L2: Focus on Politeness* (pp. 11–25). Brussels: Peter Lang.

McConachy, T. (2013) Exploring the meta-pragmatic realm in English language teaching. *Language Awareness* 22 (2), 100–110.

McConachy, T. (2018) *Developing Intercultural Perspectives on Language Use: Exploring Pragmatics and Culture in Foreign Language Learning*. Bristol: Multilingual Matters.

McConachy, T. (2019) L2 pragmatics as 'intercultural pragmatics': Probing sociopragmatic aspects of pragmatic awareness. *Journal of Pragmatics* 151, 167–176.

McConachy, T. and Liddicoat, A.J. (2016) Metapragmatic awareness and intercultural competence: The role of reflection and interpretation in intercultural mediation. In F. Dervin and Z. Gross (eds) *Intercultural Competence in Education: Alternative Approaches for Different Times* (pp. 13–25). London: Palgrave Macmillan.

McConachy, T. and Liddicoat, A.J. (eds) (2022) *Teaching and Learning Second Language Pragmatics for Intercultural Understanding*. New York and Abingdon: Routledge.

McConachy, T. and Spencer-Oatey, H. (2020) Developing pragmatic awareness. In K.P. Schneider and E. Ifantidou (eds) *Developmental and Clinical Pragmatics* (HOPS, 13) (pp. 393–427). Berlin: De Gruyter Mouton.

McConachy, T. and Spencer-Oatey, H. (2021) Cross-cultural and intercultural pragmatics. In M. Haugh, D. Kádár and M. Terkourafi (eds) *The Cambridge Handbook of Sociopragmatics* (pp. 733–757). Cambridge: Cambridge University Press.

Piller, I. (2011) *Intercultural Communication: A Critical Introduction*. Edinburgh: Edinburgh University Press.

Risager, K. (2006) *Language and Culture: Global Flows and Local Complexity*. Clevedon: Multilingual Matters.

Risager, K. (2007) *Language and Culture Pedagogy: From a National to a Transnational Paradigm*. Clevedon: Multilingual Matters.

Risager, K. (2020) Linguaculture and transnationality: The cultural dimensions of language. In J. Jackson (ed.) *The Routledge Handbook of Language and Intercultural Communication* (2nd edn) (pp. 101–115). Abingdon and New York: Routledge.

Sharifian, F. (2017) *Cultural Linguistics*. Amsterdam: John Benjamins.

Spencer-Oatey, H. and Kádár, D.Z. (2016) The basis of (im)politeness evaluations: Culture, the moral order and the East-West divide. *East-Asian Pragmatics* 1 (1), 73–106.

Spencer-Oatey, H. and Kádár, D.Z. (2021) *Intercultural Politeness: Managing Relations across Cultures*. Cambridge: Cambridge University Press.

Svarlberg, A.M-L. (2018) Researching language engagement: Current trends and future directions. *Language Awareness* 27 (1–2), 21–39.

Sweeney, E. and Zhu, H. (2010) Accommodating toward your audience: Do native speakers of English know how to accommodate their communication strategies toward nonnative speakers of English? *Journal of Business Communication* 47 (4), 477–504.

Wierzbicka, A. (2010) Cultural scripts and intercultural communication. In A. Trosborg (ed.) *Pragmatics Across Languages and* Cultures (pp. 43–78). Berlin: Walter de Gruyter.

Woodin, J. (2018) *Interculturality, Interaction and Language Learning: Insights from Tandem Partnerships*. New York and London: Routledge.

Wright, T. and Bolitho, R. (1993) Language awareness: A missing link in language teacher education? *ELT Journal* 47 (4), 292–304.

3 Intercultural Mediation in Language Teaching and Learning

Anthony J. Liddicoat

Introduction

Mediation as a concept has found increasing space in research on language teaching and learning and is an emerging part of the theoretical apparatus of researchers in the field. It has become particularly significant in interculturally-oriented thinking about teaching and learning a language. However, it is a complex concept and thinking about it, and its relevance for language learning has developed in different and at times in seemingly contradictory ways (Corbett, 2021). This chapter will examine the ways that Byram's work has introduced the concept of mediation into thinking about language teaching and learning and explore some of the issues that emerge from this work. In particular, it will consider the ways in which mediation is understood and the multiple uses that the term has in the language education literature and seek to identify the common elements that underlie these multiple uses. It will begin by examining the concept in Byram's work and then examine the ways that this idea has been elaborated in other contexts before proposing a synthesis of thinking about the concept.

Mediation in Byram's Work

Byram's work has been a significant point of departure for thinking about the idea of mediation, and the concept has evolved over time in Byram's work. The term 'mediation' is introduced in Byram (1989) as a relatively marginal idea drawn from Bochner (1982). Bochner identified four possible outcomes of intercultural contact, one of which he called 'mediating' persons, which he describes as:

> People who have the ability to act as links between different cultural systems, bridging the gap by introducing, translating, representing and reconciling cultures to each other. (Bochner, 1982: 29)

The mediator is thus someone who connects cultures, and this idea has remained central to Byram's thinking about mediation. Byram (1989) argues that developing such mediating persons should be the normal goal for language education, and while he explores what the development of such persons may entail, he does not do so in terms of developing an understanding of mediation itself.

The idea of mediation is taken up in Buttjes and Byram (1991). The main contribution about mediation in this work comes from Buttjes (1991), and Byram (1991) himself does not use the term mediation in his chapter. Buttjes discusses mediation through the lens of language acquisition comparing the acquisition processes for first and foreign languages and arguing that in first language acquisition, language is used to mediate culture, but this is substantially lacking in second language acquisition. Although he does not actually define mediation, he does associate it with the relativisation of learners' cultures, critical comparisons between cultures and negotiation of meaning. Thus, he views mediation as a process through which learners are brought into cultures. The chapters in the book, including Byram's, connect with this underlying idea, but overall, there is little discussion of what actually constitutes mediation.

In this early work, mediation is present but not developed in a substantive way. The main development of the idea in Byram's work begins with his collaboration with Zarate (Byram & Zarate, 1994, 1996) and their conceptualisation of the intercultural speaker. They argued that acting interculturally involved bringing two cultures into relationship and that one of the things that language education should develop is the ability to see how different cultures relate to each other and to act as mediators between them. They see mediation as something that learners need to do to facilitate communication between linguistically and culturally diverse interlocutors, but they also emphasise that one of the areas of mediation that learners need to accomplish is mediation between oneself and the diverse others one encounters. To be able to mediate, they argue, learners need to take an external perspective on themselves (i.e. decentre) in their interactions to analyse what happens in interaction and make adjustments where desirable. Decentring is central to their understanding of mediation, and this continues into Byram's work on intercultural citizenship (e.g. Byram, 2012; Byram et al., 2017). For example, Porto et al. (2018: 5) characterise the intercultural mediator as 'translingual, cosmopolitan, consensus-oriented, supportive and open to negotiation, i.e. they negotiate meanings with others on equal terms departing from their own positionalities'. In this case, they present the mediator as a person with qualities that allow for mediation, rather than expressing what the activity of mediation involves.

The most developed account of mediation in Byram's work is found in Byram (1997) and its later reworking (Byram, 2021),[1] which attempts to operationalise mediation as a part of intercultural communicative competence. In his discussion of the intercultural speaker, Byram indicates three things that distinguish intercultural speakers from native speakers: 'establishing relationships, managing dysfunctions and mediating' (2021: 49–50). This list seems to suggest that these three things are separate and distinguishable. However, this appears to be misleading as they are very closely related in the elaboration of mediation. Meditation is presented as one of the objectives in 'skills of interpreting and relating':

(a) Mediate between conflicting interpretations of phenomena
The intercultural speaker can use their explanations of sources of misunderstanding and dysfunction to help interlocutors overcome conflicting perspectives; can explain the perspective of each and the origins of these perspectives in terms accessible to the other; can help interlocutors identify common ground and unresolved difference. (Byram, 2021: 88)

This quote links mediation with the process of managing dysfunctions, which the intercultural speaker does through processes of explanation that bring interlocutors to understand each other. To produce such explanations, the mediator needs to have extensive knowledge of a communication problem that includes not only the perspectives of the participants but also the origins of these perspectives. Mediation is also closely linked to the idea of establishing relationships; the end result of mediation it to re-establish a relationship between interlocutors. Mediation is also included as an objective in 'skills of discovery and interaction':

(b) (ability to) use in real-time knowledge, skills and attitudes for mediation between interlocutors of one's own and a another's culture
  • can identify and estimate the significance of misunderstandings and dysfunctions in a particular situation and is able to decide on and carry out an appropriate intervention, without disrupting interaction and to the mutual satisfaction of the interlocutors. (Byram, 2021: 90)

In this case too, mediation seems to relate centrally to managing dysfunction in that it involves intervention in communication to remedy situations that have become dysfunctional.

Both of these objectives seem to imply that the mediator is separated from the communication; that is, the idea that mediators may be mediating their own meanings appears to be backgrounded, if not absent in these formulations (cf. Byram & Zarate, 1994, 1996). The language learner as mediator thus seems to be someone who is outside the problematic communication and responsible for resolving the problems of others. Also, in this formulation, the emphasis is placed on the mediator's responsibility for the success of the mediation. This would seem to be a consequence of the metaphor of competence that Byram draws on. Competence is essentially individual and internalised and thus creates a dissonance when applied to something that is essentially distributed and interpersonal, such as mediation. It cannot be assumed in mediation that interlocutors who experience problems in interaction are simply neutral participants in a mediation process who want the dysfunction to be remedied. These interlocutors have emotional and identity investments in their own meanings, and these may be challenged in moments of dysfunction in ways that preclude resolution with 'mutual satisfaction'. Interlocutors have agency in the mediation and this agency is important in understanding the outcome of mediation, as success requires interlocutors to accept and ratify different understandings not simply receive them. This means that interlocutors can exercise agency to reject mediation and the possibility of shared understanding despite the work of the mediator.

The idea of mediation is Byram's work is a fluid and evolving concept, and there appear to be three dimensions that are emphasised in different works:

- Mediation as a form of socialisation into cultures.
- Mediation as an intervention to resolve communication problems of others.
- Mediation as a reworking of one's own meanings to achieve understanding.

While I would argue that all of these are present, at least implicitly, in Byram's work, in his 1997 book, the strongest emphasis is placed on mediation as a form of problem-solving for others. This view is modified somewhat in Byram (2021), which acknowledges that mediation is more complex. What seems to be most missing in the formulations is his earlier thinking about mediation as socialisation into cultures, which is not specifically an activity of students but also involves the work of teachers.

Although mediation is important in Byram's work on intercultural communicative competence and intercultural citizenship, the fluidity and changing emphases mean that 'mediation' is something of an under-defined concept. This under-definition means that there is scope for developing a broad perspective on it that would not be the case if mediation had been narrowly defined and allows for continued elaboration and development. At the same time, under-definition can lead to a lack of clarify about the meaning of the term as an under-defined concept that is widely used risks becoming semantically empty (Piccardo, 2012) and thus less useful in both research and practice. The following discussion will examine how this term has been taken up from Byram's work and used in work on language education and the ways that this is consequential for understanding its nature and scope. This is not, however, done with the aim of providing a narrower definition of mediation but rather to understand the scope of the term to promote continued thinking and theorisation.

Elaborating Mediation as a Concept

In understanding mediation, especially as it is used in English-language research, a useful place to start is with the meaning of mediation more generally. The verb *'to mediate'* is polysemous, especially in its use in educational settings. One common meaning of the word found in general use is that of intervening in a dispute to help to resolve it. Mediation in this sense is found in many non-educational contexts. Mediation can also mean providing a link between things or people, a way of conveying something from one person to another in the sense of acting as an intermediary for others. These common meanings are used in education, but there are also more specifically educational uses. In particular, in education, mediation means to support learning through the use of symbolic tools, such as language, so that learners move from a position in which they do not know to one in which they do know, initially with support and eventually independently. This last idea, which comes from the work of Vygotsky (1934/2005, 1986), is often known as 'cultural mediation' in English. The English word *mediation* as it used in educational discourses and therefore covers three key ideas: (1) resolving problems, (2) taking an intermediary position to create a link and (3) supporting learning in socially collaborative ways. All three ideas can be seen in Byram's work and his work, but the relationships between them have not been fully articulated.

Mediation as problem-solving

The idea that mediation involves dealing with problems, including interpersonal conflicts, that result from intercultural contact is based on a premise that intercultural contact is largely shaped by miscommunication resulting from cultural differences (for a critique, see Piller, 2011). This view that the intercultural mediator works to resolve conflicts between linguistically and culturally different others is also found in the language education literature (Rubenfeld & Clément, 2012), which typically views the classroom as a site of intercultural conflict, usually between students from different cultures that needs to be resolved by teachers. Cultural differences are thus seen as a source of conflict that requires specialist intervention to bring about resolution.

If intercultural communication is understood in terms of culture-related communication breakdown, the role of the mediator is to restore communication and re-establish understanding (Gohard-Radenkovic et al., 2004a, 2004b), and a language learner thus needs to develop abilities to resolve such problems. This view of mediation has been taken up in the CEFR (Piccardo, 2020; Piccardo & North, 2020; Piccardo et al., 2019), but it does not adopt the full articulation of Byram and Zarate's intercultural speaker. The term 'cultural intermediary' is used in the discussion of intercultural skills in Chapter 5, and this links the idea of mediation specifically to conflict resolution as a cultural intermediary should be able to 'deal effectively with intercultural misunderstanding and conflict situations' (CEFR, 2001: 105). Mediation is also included in the discussion of 'Language use and the language user/learner': 'In mediating activities, the language user is not concerned to express his/her own meanings, but simply acts as an intermediary between interlocutors who are unable to understand each other directly – normally (but not exclusively) speakers of different languages' (CEFR, 2001: 87). This seems also to orient to the idea that mediation involves solving others' problems and does not involve one's own communication. The CEFR constructs mediation a language act, locating it within communicative language activities and communicative strategies, and has equated mediation with either cross-language communication (i.e. translation and interpreting), or reformulating meaning in the same language, such as by summarising or reformulating texts; that is, intercultural mediation is an interlinguistic or an intralinguistic process (Corbett, 2021; Dendrinos, 2006, 2014; Iglesias Casal & Ramos Méndez, 2020). Thus, mediation is seen in the CEFR as a linguistic reworking of meaning, although the Companion volume does acknowledge a much wider range of mediational activities in language education (Piccardo, 2020; Piccardo & North, 2020; Piccardo et al., 2019). In the CEFR, there is an expectation that the problems of others are ultimately tractable if the mediator has the relevant linguistic resources to re-language problematic messages.

When intercultural mediation is understood in terms of re-languaging, it is possible that the act of mediation becomes reduced to an act of language use, which can obscure non-linguistic dimensions of communication and the role they play in constructing and interpreting meanings (Liddicoat, 2016). In addition, it can obscure the need for mediation to go beyond the re-languaging of a text and that more and or different information may be needed to enable understanding of a message created in one linguistic and cultural context for a recipient in another, or that the message itself may need to be re-negotiated by the original speaker (Liddicoat, 2016; Stathopoulou, 2015). A second consequence is that mediators are positioned as third parties; that is, the idea of problem-solving is closely linked with the idea of the mediator as external to the communication that has caused the problem. This view of mediation coalesces two different aspects of mediation: the idea that a mediator is a problem-solver and the idea that the mediator is an intermediary and obscures other significant dimensions of mediation.

Mediation as an intermediary position

The idea that a mediator is an intermediary standing between two linguistic and cultural contexts has already been introduced in the preceding discussion of the third-person problem-solver. This idea of the mediator as an intermediary using language abilities to mediate meanings between languages and cultures has been a key feature of some definitions in the field of language education (Buttjes, 1991; Byram & Grundy, 2003; Byram & Zarate, 1994). However, in intercultural language teaching and learning, there are further ways for this to be considered beyond problem-solving. In particular, in the context of language teaching and learning, there is a mediational role associated with bringing the learner into contact with the linguistic and cultural worlds of others (Buttjes & Byram, 1991; Kohler, 2015). This mediational role is essentially that of a teacher (Iglesias Casal & Ramos Méndez, 2020), who needs to create a link between language learners and a linguistic and cultural other. This is not the same as solving problems of communication, but rather involves bringing into relationship of different possible worlds so that learners can begin to engage with the unknown. The teacher can do this in many ways: for example, by designing lessons and presenting materials, by using examples from personal experience and by engaging with what the learners already know. In the extract below, the teacher is creating such links between her (Australian) students of Indonesian that have been triggered by a student's request for a translation equivalent (see Extract 1).

Extract 1

Jodie	Miss, what's the word for 'singlet'?
Teacher	I think it's just a *baju kaus*. The reason I don't ... that I've got to really think about that is because a singlet in Indonesia is not something you'd walk around in. It would be a bit ... Jodie But what would you say for it then?
Teacher	Guys, that's another really good question. See this picture here OK some things when you translate ... when you ask me something I have to think long and hard about it. It was like the woollen jumper ... *baju wol* ... you can say ... but you really don't very often walk around Indonesia in a big woolly jumper because it's too hot. This is another classic example ... you would not walk around Indonesia like this because you wouldn't want to send ... If you were in Bali in Kuta Beach and there's hundreds of tourists sitting around you may choose to be dressed a bit more what I would call ultra informal in Indonesia OK. And if you're in the privacy of your own home and there was no-one else around then possibly but you wouldn't want to send this message to an Indonesian by walking around like this and why wouldn't you?
Charlotte	Like in Hong Kong I walked around in shorts and then everyone looked at me funny.
Teacher	And what ... then what message do you think you were sending?
Charlotte	Um, I'm a prostitute?

Teacher	Well, possibly that you're fairly carefree with your values. And why?
Charlotte	Um, because they don't wear shorts.
Teacher	When you go to Indonesia you've got to think about that and think about if you're getting a certain reaction because of your appearance and you're not happy with that reaction then what do you need to do?
Charlotte	Don't go outside in shorts.

(Source: Liddicoat & Kohler, 2012: 89–90)

This teacher takes something that is at one level unproblematic, a simple translation, and uses it as an opportunity to develop a connection between the students and the Indonesian context as she knows it. She opens a discussion of Indonesian understandings and expectations, which at this point are unknown and brings the students own worlds and possible Indonesian worlds into connection in ways that show the complexities associated with the movement between them. The intermediary is thus someone who creates the possibilities for creating links between different cultural realities.

The idea that mediation involves taking an intermediary third position raises an issue in intercultural contexts about what exactly it is that the mediator stands an intermediary for. Liddicoat (2014, 2017) argues that mediation involves not just a question of who does the mediation but also who the beneficiary of the mediation is. When the mediator is conceived as a third person outside the main communication, then the recipient of the mediation is always understood as those others engaged in the communication in which mediation is required. The view of mediators as those who need to mediate their own meanings is also a view that sees mediation as directed to the other. Liddicoat argues that mediation can be for the self as well as the other. Mediation for self involves making meaning from instances of communication with others in which meaning was not initially apparent through a process of critical reflection on processes of meaning-making considering one's own perspectives and those of others. Mediation is thus closely connected with perspective taking, which Galinsky et al. (2005: 110) define as 'the process of imagining the world from another's vantage point or imagining oneself in another's shoes'. Perspective taking involves seeing oneself from the standpoint of others and sharing feelings and perceptions. It thus involves not simply adopting an intermediary position but focuses on moving towards the other to adopt an empathic understanding of their position.

The possible constellations of participants in mediation thus appear to be complex. Mediators may be positioned outside the communication mediating for those who are inside it. Alternatively, they may be inside the communication mediating for others, or they may be inside the communication mediating for themselves. What is important in understanding mediation is not to think of the role of mediator as a position within the communication but rather to focus on the processes involved. As mediation involves processes of interpretation, reflection, reflexivity, etc., that work on meaning, then it is fruitful to consider that anyone who engages in such processes is engaged in acts of mediation and is thus a mediator.

The third person mediator, who may be the classic type of mediator in dispute resolution, is thus only one type of mediator, and perhaps not the most significant, in contexts of intercultural communication and language learning.

Mediation as teaching and learning

The third way of understanding mediation introduced above is as a way of enacting teaching and learning. This understanding draws strongly on the sociocultural educational theory (Vygotsky, 1934/2005, 1986), which argues for a dialectical relationship between thought and language in which language plays the role of a tool that shapes thought, interpretation and learning. In Vygotsky's view, learning is enacted in a societal and cultural context and involves the production of knowledge as an internalisation of social activity. It is understood a process of development from what is known to what is unknown that takes place at the point of rupture between what a learner can currently do and what they cannot yet do (Zone of Proximal Development). Between the known and the unknown lies a point at which the learner can do things with the support of a more knowledgeable other, and learning is demonstrated when the learner develops independence and autonomy. Such learning is first done at the interpersonal level and only later at the intrapersonal level. In these processes of communication, individuals use symbolic tools, such as language, to engage with, comprehend and modify their environment. Vygotsky calls these symbolic tools 'intermediaries' (посредники) because they mediate between experience and thought, construct interpretations of experience and provide affordances for learning from it. Through interactions conducted in a societal and cultural context, a person comes to learn the habits of mind of a culture, including spoken and written language, and other forms of symbolic knowledge through which people derive meaning and construct knowledge. It is through this interaction that learners develop higher mental functions and become able to engage with new aspects of their environment.

Drawing on Vygotsky's work, intercultural mediation can be conceptualised as a process through which learners learn to make and interpret meanings in languages and cultural contexts that are new for them and which occur in a context where an additional language and culture are the focus of learning. The intercultural mediator is thus a person who fulfils the role of the more knowledgeable other and, through processes of interaction, brings the learner to new understandings and new knowledge. In their work of mediation, teachers and learners are constantly building connections between the familiar and the new (Kohler, 2015), and it is in building such connections that important work of mediation takes place. The enact of such a process of mediation can be seen in Extract 2.

Extract 2

Maria: What would we put alongside here? Freedom of press, media. What about in Indonesia? Or here? (She points to the centre of a Venn diagram)

Jaxson: Indonesia tends to be stricter.

Maria: Stricter laws, policies on *apa* (what)?

Jaxson: It's too broad to narrow it down.

Maria: *Ya,* OK. On media? What issues … ? How did you come up with this? What impressions … what led you to believe … to come up with a statement like this?

Jaxson: The article on Inul Daratista.

Maria: What can you tell me about Inul?

Jaxson: She's a *dangdut* (pop music with Arab and Indian influence) dancer.

Maria: She's a *penari dangdut* … she's a *dangdut* dancer, So, what's the problem?

Jaxson: The way she dances. It's very controversial for some Islamic leaders.

Maria: So, controversial … *kontroversi* exists in Indonesian.

Jaxson: They're trying to ban her from doing it.

Maria: Right. So, *melarang dia* (forbade her) … *pemerintah* (government)? Or *tokoh* (prominent figures) …

Jaxson: *Tokoh Islam.* (Islamic leaders)

Maria: *Tokoh Islam ingin melarang show Inul Daratista karena dia sangat … tariannya sangat erotis menurut pendapat mereka … menurut pengalamannya …* [Islamic leaders wanted to ban Inul Daratista's show because she's very … her dancing is very erotic in their view … (according to their experience) from their perspective]. Do we have anything like that here? Have we heard of anything like that here?

Jaxson: No.

Maria: So, we're *bebas* (free)?

Jaxson: No. I can't say not to that degree. We're less strict on stuff like that.

Maria: Is there anything that had come up in the news like that … that you know that could be put on a par or that could say something about how we feel about that sort of thing?

Jaxson: I don't know but on a par like that you'd see stuff like on Video Hits on Saturday mornings.

Maria: *Ya,* mm. Good point. *Bagus* (Good). *Bagus sekali* (Very good). What do you see on those Video Hits?

Jaxson: Women dancing half naked.

Maria: Right, OK. So, do you think it's caused any controversy? If there were controversy where would it come from? *Dari mana?* Do you think it would come from the government?

All:	No.
Maria:	Or from political groups?
Jaxson:	*Mungkin.* (Maybe)
Maria:	But what sort of political groups?
Mark:	Maybe like local government.
Jaxson:	I don't think they'd be too upset with it. It's not an issue I think they'd deal with. I reckon it would cause more outrage with the public than it would at a higher level.
Mark:	That's like when … was it Madonna who brought out that film clip when someone got shot in a car park and they completely banned it? They made her remove the film clip. They were like a parents' committee on like a local level who took it higher and it got banned.
Maria:	But isn't that interesting. That video is to do with violence … not really sex or eroticism. So, perhaps controversy can be caused by … maybe we can conclude by saying violence is more of an issue on television than it is … not an issue but not a concern on Indonesian television as much as it is on our television. But you're right then to say that a lot of the controversy from that may come out of these Video Hits comes not from a political party but from … *orang tua* (parents) … or maybe from a political party such as Family First … maybe … *partai Kristen* (a Christian party) that have foundations that have some religious connection. *Apakah kamu setuju?* (Do you agree?)

(Source: Kohler, 2015: 173–174)

In this extract, the teacher, Maria, is working with her students to use a Venn diagram to draw connections and to identify differences between the students' home context (Australia) and Indonesia. In this extract, she uses both instructional and interactional language (see Kohler, 2020) to scaffold the process of interpretation for her learners. In constructing this activity, she challenges students to reflect on their own cultural values by scaffolding a reflective process through questions such as '*How did you come up with this? What impressions … what led you to believe … to come up with a statement like this?*' by which she engages students in articulating the ways that their own cultural assumptions influence their interpretations. She also problematises interpretations and their underlying assumptions using question such as '*So, we're bebas?*' and by getting students to consider parallels between their own context and that of others. In constructing her teaching as an intercultural mediation, Maria is engaged in a bidirectional process; she is not simply mediating the unknown other to her learners but also mediating from what is known by her learners to the unknown other, and her mediation takes the form of movement between the languages and cultures that are at play in the interaction (see also Dasli, 2011). She also paraphrases and adds to students' interpretations ('*maybe we can conclude by saying …*') to develop a more nuanced understanding of issues and indicates that her own perspective is also open to contestation ('*Apakah kamu setuju?*'). As Kohler (2015) argues, the teacher here mediates intercultural learning by creating an understanding of intercultural learning as engaging with dynamism, complexity and multiple interpretations both of learners' cultural positions and those of others and by engaging students in self-reflection through which they clarify and explain their own understandings and experiences.

While the most usual mediator in a language classroom is the teacher, the more knowledgeable participant in an interaction can take on this role. In the extract below, one of the students acts a mediator for his partner in a group task.

Extract 3

Sarah: I don't get this. She's talking about *otoosan* ((father)), but why is she talking about her father?

Jack: I think it's what she's calling her husband.

Sarah: Is that the word for husband?

Jack: No it's just that's what she calls him. Like, when I was in Japan the mother did that a lot she would say *otoosan* to him all the time. Not his name. She'd go '*otoosan otoosan*' and she meant him.

Sarah: And what did he call her?

Jack: *Okaasan.* ((mother))

Sarah: That's so weird.

Jack: It's just what they say. It's like it's their position in the family and that's how they talk about each other. He's the father and she's the mother. We use 'dad' and 'mum' just for our parents but they use them differently. Mariko used to call her brother *oniisan* ((older brother)) too. It's like using title's instead of names. And when they talked about them too they'd do the same. Like mum would say to Mariko, go get *oniisan* or something. So you say what they are in the family.

Sarah: Oh I get it, she calls him father because he's a father for the family.

(Source: Liddicoat, 2014: 270)

Kohler (2020) notes that texts and resources can act as mediating tools by presenting learners with opportunities to engage critically with linguistic and cultural constructions of diverse realities. In this case, a text in which *otoosan* is used provides the context and opportunity for mediation to occur by bringing into relationship the reality of the text and the realities of its readers through a process of reflection. Here, Sarah is unable to interpret something in the text as the naming conventions of Japanese are not familiar for her. Jack addresses the initial question but does not help Sarah to develop her understanding of the practice she has encountered.

He then follows this with a more developed account based on his experience as an exchange student in Japan that helps Sarah to build on her existing knowledge of the terms and to construct a new understanding, which she states in the final line of the extract. Here, Jack has helped Sarah to construct a new understanding of an initially unknown cultural practice by explaining the cultural context and describing his observations in Japan. When Sarah responds that this behaviour is *weird*, based on her intracultural perspective, he begins to develop a more interpretative account of the practice that helps her to shift her understanding from an intracultural one to an intercultural one. In doing this, he uses the idea of family relationships, which is already known by Sarah, and locates the use of *otoosan* within this understanding of family membership developing a cultural rationale for the observed pattern of language use. In developing his interpretation, he frames language use within its own cultural context and attempts to make explicit the cultural fame in which the behaviour is reproduced.

Synthesising mediation

Each of the ways of thinking about mediation discussed above can be considered as a lens through which to view mediation as a practice in intercultural language teaching and learning. In considering intercultural mediation, it is important to take all of these possible ways of thinking into account, and to be aware of the ways each can limit understandings of the nature of mediation, and consequently educational practice. The various ways of approaching mediation discussed above may look to be disparate, but in reality, there is much overlap and communality between them. In developing an elaborated view of mediation, it is therefore important to consider what lies at the heart of mediation as described above and to consider the affordances and constraints that each lens brings with it.

Mediational work is often considered as being explanatory, and this idea is present in Byram's (1997, 2021) formulation of the objectives discussed above. It is evident in the discussion above that explaining is involved in the contexts discussed above. However, the ability to explain has pre-requisites; one can only explain what one has come to know. This raises the question of how a multilingual individual comes to know in order to be able to explain some meaning that is understood differently in different linguistic and cultural contexts. This question itself raises further issues about the ways that learning is understood. Sfard (1998) conceptualises learning in terms of two dominant metaphors: *acquisition* and *participation*. She argues that acquisition constructs knowledge as a commodity, and learning is seen as the process of receiving, accumulating or gaining possession of that commodity through its transfer from the teacher to the learner. Participation constructs knowledge as an aspect of practice, and learning involves a process of active construction of knowledge integrated into the process of becoming a participant in communities of shared practice. Sfard argues that neither of the metaphors should be understood as a complete theory of learning but rather sees that theories of learning need to find complementarity between the metaphors. Paavola *et al.* (2004) have added a third metaphor to Sfard's description, which they call the knowledge-creation metaphor in which learning is a creative process that involves drawing upon tacit knowledge and transforming it into explicit knowledge, by experimenting with new conceptual modelling and theory-building. Liddicoat and Scarino (2013) argue that there is a further facet of learning and argue for a hermeneutic view in which learning is understood as a process of interpretation and coming to understand (Ashworth, 2004; Gallagher, 1992).

The interpretation of multiple meanings is fundamental for all of the understandings of mediation discussed above. In problem-solving, coming to understand interpretations is central to identifying and addressing problems. When a mediator acts as an intermediary between people, it is to work with them to expose and communicate meanings. In teaching and learning, it is interpretation that lies at the heart of coming to know.

For a language learner or teacher acting as an intercultural mediator, the ability to interpret multiple and divergent meanings as they occur in communication and to connect these meanings for participants in communication is a central part of mediational work. In engaging with meaning, a mediator is involved in acts of interpretation, especially in contexts where meaning is not shared between participants and thus where understanding is in some ways problematic (Kohler, 2020). Interpreting in the context of mediation is not simply a search for the correct meaning of some element in the communication (cf. Schleiermacher, 1977) as in any communication, and particularly in intercultural communication, multiple meanings are potentially present and potentially valid (Gadamer, 2011; Ricoeur, 1965). Gadamer and Ricoeur argue that interpretations are personal and meaning results from the perspectives and resources that an interpreter brings to the act of interpreting, which is made possible only by the context of the individual's experiences and life world. Gadamer argues that interpretation is the result of fore-understanding (*Vorverstehen*), anticipations of meanings based on a previous history of interpreting others' messages. Fore-understandings are the necessary pre-conditions for interpretation to happen. As personal experiences of meaning-making must inevitably differ between individuals, interpretations inevitably differ. Gadamer argues that reaching a shared interpretation involves a fusion of horizons – the horizons reflected in the interpreter's initial presuppositions and the horizon of the other person or text with which the interpreter engages – through dialogue between different interpretations. This involves each participant coming to know the presuppositions of the other so that shared understanding and shared interpretation can be achieved. This process of dialogic negotiation of meaning is fundamentally a linguistic act in which the languages(s) of the participants provide a resource though which meanings can be shared. In contrast to Schleiermacher (1977), Gadamer (2011) argues that a shared meaning is not the identification of a correct meaning, but rather the connecting of personal meanings, with an acknowledgement of differences. This is centrally important for understanding intercultural mediation as it recognises that the meanings of all participants have validity, and the act of mediation is not to privilege one meaning over another but rather to bring meanings into relationship. As Ricoeur (1970) argues, the focus of interpretation needs to be placed on exposing multiple possible meanings in order to highlight the motivations behind and the implications of each.

Intercultural mediation is a process that involves the ability to understand through a process of reflection on multiple possible interpretations, and using this understanding to facilitate communication across languages and cultural contexts. Mediation itself is therefore not simply an interpretative process, as it involves more than just coming to know multiple interpretations and requires the mediator to work to bring diverse interpretations into relationship for participants in communication. This requires the mediator not just to understand meanings but to be aware of and to reflect on the process of meaning-making itself. It is thus closely linked to Kramsch's (2006, 2011) conceptualisation of symbolic competence. Reflection on the process of meaning-making means attending to how the meanings that are potentially present in a moment of communication are realised for the participants in the interaction (both for self and others) and understanding what prompts these realisations of meaning potential. The ability to decentre is important for reflection and reflexivity, and this is something that has been present in thinking about mediation since the work of Byram and Zarate (1994, 1996) and is a core part of their conceptualisation of *savoir être*. Mediation is not simply a form of engagement with interaction but the ability to step outside the interaction and to take multiple perspectives of it (Byram *et al.*, 2002).

Regardless of the entry point into thinking about intercultural mediation (problem-solving, acting as an intermediary or supporting learning), the processes of coming to know the previously unknown, interpreting and reflecting on interpretations, and applying the results of these processes to communication appear to be central. Focusing on such central processes allows seemingly disparate entry points to be brought into relationship in ways that clarify the communalities of thinking rather than the diversities of application.

Conclusion

This chapter began by arguing that mediation has been under-defined in the field of language teaching and learning. It then examined how this under-defined idea has been operationalised in research in the field to identify some of the different ways that definition has been given to the term. Under-defined concepts have the advantage that they do not overly constrain thinking about the concept, and this can be important in the exploration of a concept that has newly entered into an intellectual field. Definitions can impose boundaries on thinking that can limit possibilities. However, under-definition can also lead to fragmentation where there is little sense of what holds the concept together. I would argue that what is needed to advance thinking about mediation in language teaching and learning is an open definition, akin to Wittgenstein's (1974) idea of a concept-word, defined by its core not by its boundaries. This chapter has attempted to identify what might be found in this core.

In language learning for intercultural communication, mediation is both a process through which learning happens and a goal to which learning leads. The aim of language learning is for learners to become able to understand and reflect on meaning-making and interpretation, to enter into the multiplicity of meanings present in acts of communication and then respond to these in their communication with others. The process through which mediation is learnt is a process of mediation in which leaners come to understand meaning-making and interpretation through the actions of more capable others. This duality brings complexities to understandings of the nature of mediation in language learning that need to be acknowledged and engaged with in research and teaching, and require an elaborated understanding of mediation. Discussing different ways of understanding mediation and mediators necessarily involves creating distinctions between views. However, the creation of such distinctions is not the aim of this chapter. These distinctions help to illuminate the possibilities for understanding mediation, but ultimately an elaborated view that responds to the complexities of language learning and use needs to bring these into relation. Bringing these into relation is not always harmonious, but the conflicts and tensions between ways of perceiving mediation are often productive for developing new and more cogent understandings.

Note

(1) The quotes below are taken from Byram (2021), although they differ little from the versions found in Byram (1997).

References

Ashworth, P. (2004) Understanding as the transformation of what is already known. *Teaching in Higher Education* 9 (2), 147–158.

Bochner, S. (1982) The social psychology of cross-cultural relations. In S. Bochner (ed.) *Cultures in Contact: Studies in Cross-Cultural Interaction* (pp. 5–44). Oxford: Pergamon.

Buttjes, D. (1991) Mediating languages and cultures: The social dimension restored. In D. Buttjes and M. Byram (eds) *Mediating Languages and Cultures: Towards an Intercultural Theory of Foreign Language Education* (pp. 3–16). Clevedon: Multilingual Matters.

Buttjes, D. and Byram, M. (eds) (1991) *Mediating Languages and Cultures: Towards an Intercultural Theory of Foreign Language Education.* Clevedon: Multingual Matters.

Byram, M. (1989) *Cultural Studies in Foreign Language Education.* Clevedon: Multilingual Matters.

Byram, M. (1991) Teaching culture and language: An integrated model. In D. Buttjes and M. Byram (eds) *Mediating Languages and Cultures: Towards an Intercultural Theory of Foreign Language Education* (pp. 17–30). Clevedon: Multilingual Matters.

Byram, M. (1997) *Teaching and Assessing Intercultural Communicative Competence.* Clevedon: Multilingual Matters.

Byram, M. (2012) Conceptualizing intercultural (communicative) competence and intercultural citizenship. In J. Jackson (ed.) *Routledge Handbook of Language and Intercultural Communication* (pp. 85–97). Abingdon: Routledge.

Byram, M. (2021) *Teaching and Assessing Intercultural Communicative Competence: Revisited.* Bristol: Multilingual Matters.

Byram, M. and Grundy, P. (2003) *Context and Culture in Language Teaching and Learning.* Clevedon: Multilingual Matters.

Byram, M. and Zarate, G. (1994) *Définitions, objectifs et évaluation de la compétence socio-culturelle* [Definitions, Objectives and Evaluation of Socio-cultural Competence]. Strasbourg: Report for the Council of Europe.

Byram, M. and Zarate, G. (1996) Defining and assessing intercultural competence: Some principles and proposals for the European context. *Language Teaching* 29, 239–243.

Byram, M., Gribkova, B. and Starkey, H. (2002) *Developing the Intercultural Dimension in Language Teaching: A Practical Introduction for Teachers.* Strasbourg: Council of Europe.

Byram, M., Golubeva, I., Han, H. and Wagner, M. (2017) Introduction. In M. Byram, I. Golubeva, H. Han and M. Wagner (eds) *From Principles to Practice in Education for Intercultural Citizenship* (pp. xvii–xxxiv). Bristol: Multilingual Matters.

Corbett, J. (2021) Revisiting mediation: Implications for intercultural language education. *Language and Intercultural Communication* 21 (1), 8–23.

Council of Europe (2001) *Common European Framework of Reference for Languages: Learning, Teaching, Assessment.* Cambridge: Press Syndicate of the University of Cambridge.

Dasli, M. (2011) Reviving the 'moments': From cultural awareness and cross-cultural mediation to critical intercultural language pedagogy. *Pedagogy, Culture & Society* 19 (1), 21–39.

Dendrinos, B. (2006) Mediation in communication, language teaching and testing. *Journal of Applied Linguistics* 22, 9–35.

Dendrinos, B. (2014) Testing and teaching mediation. *Directions in Language Teaching and Testing.* https://rcel2.enl.uoa.gr/directions/issue1_1f.htm

Gadamer, H.-G. (2011) *Wahrheit und Methode. Grundzüge einer philosophischen Hermeneutik* [Truth and Method. Fundamentals of a Philosophical Hermeneutics]. Berlin: Akademie Verlag.

Galinsky, A.D., Ku, G. and Wang, C.S. (2005) Perspective-taking and self-other overlap: Fostering social bonds and facilitating social coordination. *Group Processes & Intergroup Relations* 8 (2), 109–124. doi: 10.1177/1368430205051060

Gallagher, S. (1992) *Hermeneutics and Education.* Albany, NY: SUNY Press.

Gohard-Radenkovic, A., Lussier, D., Penz, H. and Zarate, G. (2004a) Cultural mediation in language learning and teaching as a process. In G. Zarate, A. Gohard-Radenkovic, D. Lussier and H. Penz (eds) *Cultural Mediation in Language Learning and Teaching* (pp. 215–226). Strasbourg: Council of Europe Publishing.

Gohard-Radenkovic, A., Lussier, D., Penz, H. and Zarate, G. (2004b) La Médiation culturelle en didactique des langues comme processus. In G. Zarate, A. Gohard-Radenkovic, D. Lussier and H. Penz (eds) *La Médiation culturelle et didactique des langues* (pp. 225–238). Strasbourg: Council of Europe Publishing.

Iglesias Casal, I. and Ramos Méndez, C. (2020) Mediación y competencia comunicativa intercultural en la enseñanza del español LE/L2 [Mediation and intercultrual communicative competence in the teaching of Spanish FL/L2]. *Journal of Spanish Language Teaching* 7 (2), 89–98. doi: 10.1080/23247797.2020.1853368

Kohler, M. (2015) *Teachers as Mediators in the Foreign Language Classroom*. Bristol: Multilingual Matters.

Kohler, M. (2020) *Developing Intercultural Language Learning*. Cham: Palgrave Macmillan.

Kramsch, C. (2006) From communicative competence to symbolic competence. *Modern Language Journal* 90 (2), 249–252.

Kramsch, C. (2011) The symbolic dimensions of the intercultural. *Language Teaching* 44 (3), 354–367.

Liddicoat, A.J. (2014) Pragmatics and intercultural mediation in intercultural language learning. *Intercultural Pragmatics* 11 (2), 259–277.

Liddicoat, A.J. (2016) Intercultural mediation, intercultural communication and translation. *Perspectives: Studies in Translatology* 24 (3), 347–353.

Liddicoat, A.J. (2017) Interpretation and critical reflection in intercultural language learning: Consequences of a critical perspective for the teaching and learning of pragmatics. In M. Dasli and A. Díaz (eds) *The Critical Turn in Language and Intercultural Communication Pedagogy: Theory, Research and Practice* (pp. 22–39). London and New York: Routledge.

Liddicoat, A.J. and Kohler, M. (2012) Teaching Asian languages from an intercultural perspective: Building bridges for and with students of Indonesian. In X. Song and K. Cadman (eds) *Bridging Transcultural Divides: Teaching Asian languages and Cultures in a Globalising Academy*. Adelaide, SA: University of Adelaide Press.

Liddicoat, A.J. and Scarino, A. (2013) *Intercultural Language Teaching and Learning*. Chichester: Wiley-Blackwell.

Paavola, S., Lipponen, L. and Hakkarainen, K. (2004) Models of innovative knowledge and three metaphors of learning. *Review of Educational Research* 74 (4), 557–576.

Piccardo, E. (2012) Médiation et apprentissage des langues: Pourquoi est-il temps de réfléchir à cette notion. [Mediation and Language Learning: Why is it Time to Reflect on This Notion]. *Ela. Études de linguistique appliquée* 167, 285–297.

Piccardo, E. (2020) La mediazione al cuore dell'apprendimento linguistico per una didattica 3.0. *Italiano LinguaDue* 12 (1), 561–585.

Piccardo, E. and North, B. (2020) The dynamic nature of plurilingualism: Creating and validating CEFR descriptors for mediation, plurilingualism and pluricultural competence. In S.M.C. Lau and S. Van Viegen (eds) *Plurilingual Pedagogies: Critical and Creative Endeavors for Equitable Language in Education* (pp. 279–301). Cham: Springer International Publishing.

Piccardo, E., North, B. and Goodier, T. (2019) Broadening the scope of language education: Mediation, plurilingualism, and collaborative learning: The CEFR Companion Volume. *Journal of E-Learning and Knowledge Society* 15 (1), 17–36. doi: 10.20368/1971-8829/1612

Piller, I. (2011) *Intercultural Communication: A Critical Introduction*. Edinburgh: Edinburgh University Press.

Porto, M., Houghton, S.A. and Byram, M. (2018) Intercultural citizenship in the (foreign) language classroom. *Language Teaching Research* 22 (5), 484–498. doi: 10.1177/1362168817718580

Ricoeur, P. (1965) *De l'interprétation: Essai sur Freud* [On Interpretation: Essay on Freud]. Paris: Seuil.

Ricoeur, P. (1970) *Freud and Philosophy: An Essay on Interpretation* (D. Savage, Trans.). New Haven, NY: Yale University Press.

Rubenfeld, S. and Clément, R. (2012) Intercultural conflict and mediation: An intergroup perspective. *Language Learning* 62 (4), 1205–1230.

Schleiermacher, F. (1977) *Hermeneutik und Kritik: Mit einem Anhang sprachphiloso-phischer Texte Schleiermachers* (M. Frank, ed.) [Hermenuetics and Criticism: With an Appendix of Schleiermacher's Philosophical Texts]. Frankfurt am Main: Suhrkamp.

Sfard, A. (1998) On two metaphors for learning and the dangers of choosing just one. *Educational Researcher* 27, 4–13.

Stathopoulou, M. (2015) *Cross-Language Mediation in Foreign Language Teaching and Testing*. Bristol: Multilingual Matters.

Vygotsky, L.S. (1934/2005) Мышление и речь [Thought and Language]. Moskow: Smysl.

Vygotsky, L.S. (1986) *Thought and Language* (A. Kozulin ed). Massachusetts: The MIT Press.

Wittgenstein, L. (1974) *Philosophical Grammar* (A. Kenny, trans., R. Rhees, ed). Oxford: Blackwell.

4 From Intercultural Communicative Competence to Intercultural Citizenship: Preparing Young People for Citizenship in a Culturally Diverse Democratic World

Martyn Barrett and Irina Golubeva

Introduction

Over the past 25 years, the intercultural communicative competence model developed by Michael Byram (1997) has proved to be one of the most influential models, especially in the field of foreign language education. This model describes the elements of intercultural communicative competence that Byram judges to be teachable and assessable in the language classroom, and it stands out among other well-known models by emphasizing the role of critical cultural awareness and political education. It is therefore not surprising that this model has been adapted and developed to formulate the theory and practice of intercultural citizenship education (Byram, 2008; Byram *et al.*, 2017; Byram & Golubeva, 2020; Porto *et al.*, 2018), not only within foreign language education but also in a broader context, across the entire curriculum (Byram *et al.*, 2009a, in press a; Wagner *et al.*, 2019). In this chapter, we provide an overview of this trajectory that has been taken by Byram from intercultural communicative competence to intercultural citizenship, to show the development of his ideas. Our purpose is also to reveal how some of the international initiatives and projects in which Byram has participated have created new intellectual challenges, in response to which new formulations relating to both intercultural communication and citizenship have been developed – formulations which in turn have had a substantial impact on citizenship education in particular.

Byram's (1997) Model of Intercultural Communicative Competence

We start by providing an overview of Byram's 1997 model, and with an important distinction that he draws between intercultural competence and intercultural communicative competence. This distinction is most simply expressed through two diagrams – see Figures 4.1 and 4.2.

Figure 4.1 summarises the key factors that Byram proposes are required for intercultural communication but omitting those that are primarily linguistic. He uses the term 'intercultural competence' to denote these five factors (1997: 49 and 73). Byram notes that the success of intercultural interactions can be judged not only in terms of the effective exchange of information but also in terms of the establishing and maintenance of human relationships (Byram, 1997: 32–33). The latter, in particular, requires the individuals concerned to apply sets of attitudes, knowledge and skills within the interaction.

As Figure 4.1 shows, Byram suggests that intercultural competence consists of five factors, which he calls *savoirs*: (1) attitudes of relativising self and valuing others (*savoir être*), (2) knowledge of self and other, and of individual and societal interaction (*savoirs*), (3) skills of interpreting and relating (*savoir comprendre*), (4) skills of discovering and/or interacting (*savoir apprendre/faire*) and (5) critical cultural awareness (*savoir s'engager*). Byram explicitly associates critical cultural awareness with

	Skills interpret and relate *(savoir comprendre)*	
Knowledge of self and other; of interaction; individual and societal *(savoirs)*	**Education** political education critical cultural awareness *(savoir s'engager)*	**Attitudes** relativising self valuing other *(savoir être)*
	Skills discover and/or interact *(savoir apprendre/faire)*	

Figure 4.1 Factors in intercultural communication (from Byram, 1997: 34, reproduced with permission)

political education, and he chooses the label of *savoir s'engager* to draw attention to its relevance for citizenship education. Critical cultural awareness involves a reflective, analytical and critical approach to the cultural perspectives, practices and products that are present within both the learner's own culture and other people's cultures. It takes intercultural learning to a more abstract level, to the level of metacognition. The positioning of critical cultural awareness at the center of the diagram is intended to convey the core role that education plays in the development of this component of learners' intercultural competence (Byram, 1997: 46). Otherwise, the model is neutral concerning the inter-relationships between the five factors.

This model is not intended to be an exhaustive specification of every possible personal, social or interactive factor that might be applied in the context of intercultural interaction, but only the most important factors which Byram judges should be taught and assessed in the classroom. In order to spell out what this means in practice, he reformulates each of the five factors in terms of specific objectives (see Table 4.1). While the descriptions of the factors are frequently cited by other authors, the refinement of the descriptions into objectives for the purposes of teaching and assessment is less frequently referred to. However, this refinement is actually what makes Byram's model so useful for educational purposes, far beyond foreign language education. Indeed, through the objectives, the model has implications for curriculum design, teaching and learning, assessment and teacher education.

In addition to this model of intercultural competence (Figure 4.1), Byram (1997) proposes a more comprehensive model of intercultural communicative competence (see Figure 4.2). The latter includes the entirety of intercultural competence, but also includes linguistic, sociolinguistic and discourse competences as further components. This model is intended to provide a description of the components of the intercultural communicative competence that is required by a foreign language learner who communicates and interacts with people from another cultural group through the use of a foreign language. It is therefore possible to distinguish between intercultural competence and intercultural communicative competence. In the former, individuals have the ability to interact in their own language with people who have other cultural affiliations, drawing on their knowledge, attitudes and skills in order to do so; in the latter, individuals have the ability to interact with people who have other cultural affiliations *in a foreign language* and are able to negotiate a way of communicating and interacting which is satisfactory to both themselves and their interlocutor (Byram, 1997: 70–71). Like the model of intercultural competence (Byram, 1997: 34), the model of intercultural communicative competence (Byram, 1997: 73) is an educational model; although the latter includes educational objectives linked to linguistic, sociolinguistic and discourse competences, the relation between these competences is not spelled out in detail by

Table 4.1 Intercultural competence defined in terms of objectives (Based on Byram, 1997: 50–53)

Factor in the IC model	Description of the factor	Objectives (refinement of the description for the purposes of teaching and assessment)
Attitudes	curiosity and openness, readiness to suspend disbelief about other cultures and belief about one's own	• willingness to seek out or take up opportunities to engage with otherness in a relationship of equality; this should be distinguished from attitudes of seeking out the exotic or of seeking to profit from others; • interest in discovering other perspectives on interpretation of familiar and unfamiliar phenomena both in one's own and in other cultures and cultural practices; • willingness to question the values and presuppositions in cultural practices and products in one's own environment; • readiness to experience the different stages of adaptation to and interaction with another culture during a period of residence; • readiness to engage with the conventions and rites of verbal and non-verbal communication and interaction
Knowledge (of/about)	of social groups and their products and practices in one's own and in one's interlocutor's country, and of the general processes of societal and individual interaction	• historical and contemporary relationships between one's own and one's interlocutor's countries; • the means of achieving contact with interlocutors from another country (at a distance or in proximity), of travel to and from and the institutions which facilitate contact or help resolve problems; • the types of cause and process of misunderstanding between interlocutors of different cultural origins; • the national memory of one's own country and how its events are related to and seen from the perspective of one's interlocutor's country; • the national memory of one's interlocutor's country and the perspective on it from one's own; • the national definitions of geographical space in one's own country and how these are perceived from the perspective of other countries; • the national definitions of geographical space in one's interlocutor's country and the perspective on them from one's own; • the processes and institutions of socialisation in one's own and one's interlocutor's country; • social distinctions and their principal markers, in one's own country and one's interlocutor's; • institutions, and perceptions of them, which impinge on daily life within one's own and one's interlocutor's country and which conduct and influence relationships between them; • the processes of social interaction in one's interlocutor's country
Skills of interpreting and relating	ability to interpret a document or event from another culture, to explain it and relate it to documents from one's own	• identify ethnocentric perspectives in a document or event and explain their origins; • identify areas of misunderstanding and dysfunction in an interaction and explain them in terms of each of the cultural systems present; • mediate between conflicting interpretations of phenomena

(Continued)

Table 4.1 (Continued)

Factor in the IC model	Description of the factor	Objectives (refinement of the description for the purposes of teaching and assessment)
Skills of discovery and interaction	ability to acquire new knowledge of a culture and cultural practices and the ability to operate knowledge, attitudes and skills under the constraints of real-time communication and interaction	• elicit from an interlocutor the concepts and values of documents or events and to develop an explanatory system susceptible of application to other phenomena; • identify significant references within and across cultures and elicit their significance and connotations; • identify similar and dissimilar processes of interaction, verbal and non-verbal, and negotiate an appropriate use of them in specific circumstances; • use in real-time an appropriate combination of knowledge, skills and attitudes to interact with interlocutors from a different country and culture, taking into consideration the degree of one's existing familiarity with the country and culture and the extent of difference between one's own and the other; • identify contemporary and past relationships between one's own and the other culture and country; • identify and make use of public and private institutions which facilitate contact with other countries and cultures; • use in real-time knowledge, skills and attitudes for mediation between interlocutors of one's own and a foreign culture
Critical cultural awareness/political education	an ability to evaluate critically and on the basis of explicit criteria perspectives, practices and products in one's own and other cultures and countries	• identify and interpret explicit or implicit values in documents and events in one's own and other cultures; • make an evaluative analysis of the documents and events which refers to an explicit perspective and criteria; • interact and mediate in intercultural exchanges in accordance with explicit criteria, negotiating where necessary a degree of acceptance of them by drawing upon one's knowledge, skills and attitudes

Byram. In addition, the objectives for these three competences are not specified in the same level of detail as those for intercultural competence. However, the model of intercultural communicative competence does include specifications of the locations in which learning may occur and of the roles of the teacher and the learner in those locations. The locations include the classroom, fieldwork and independent learning, in each of which teachers and learners have differing roles and relationships. The teacher's role is, of course, most prominent in the context of the class-room; however, the teacher may also provide guidance and structure for fieldwork but play a minimal role or no role at all in independent learning. Byram suggests that these three locations for learning link differently to the various objectives of the model (as listed in Table 4.1). In order to sup-port and stimulate the process of learning in all three locations, learners can use a portfolio for collecting evidence which documents their

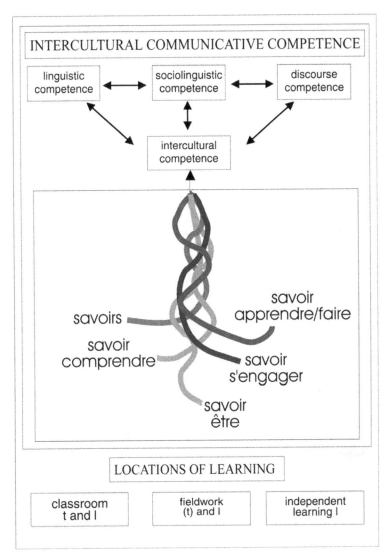

Figure 4.2 Model of intercultural communicative competence (from Byram, 1997: 73, reproduced with permission)

learning, and for reflecting on their progress and on how they may develop their competences further in the future (for an example of such a portfolio, see Byram *et al.*, 2021).

Byram's model has been challenged on several fronts since it was published 25 years ago. One criticism is that the frequent references to 'country' in the book indicate that Byram equates culture with country and that his model focuses excessively on the components of intercultural competence that contribute to the ability to communicate and interact with people from other countries (Hoff, 2020; Matsuo, 2012; Risager, 2007). However, Byram (1997: 54–55, footnote 1) does explicitly state that, although he refers to 'countries' throughout the book for the sake of clarity, his discussion of intercultural competence also applies to interactions with members of other types of cultural groups such as ethnic minorities, and indeed one of the extended examples discussed in the book concerns the teaching of French in Canada, which is viewed by some Canadian teachers as facilitating better understanding of and interaction with francophone Canadians (Byram, 1997: 24–25).

A second criticism is that his model is tied to an oversimplified notion of culture, with the people from a national culture being treated as homogeneous and adhering to the same national perspective and cultural practices, and with people from different countries being treated as inherently different from one another – in short, Byram has been criticised for holding an essentialised view of culture (Belz, 2007; Dervin, 2016). However, Byram himself states that members of cultural groups are constantly negotiating their understandings of aspects of their culture and that as a result, over time, major changes in beliefs, behaviours or meanings can occur (1997: 17). He further states that it is important to be 'aware of the dangers of presenting "a culture" as if it were unchanging over time or as if there were only one set of beliefs, meanings and behaviours in any given country' (Byram, 1997: 39). These statements clearly offer a non-essentialised view of culture. That said, it is arguable that the implications of these statements are not pursued with sufficient rigour in the formulation of some of the details of the model (e.g. in the references to 'national memory' and 'national definitions' in the objectives listed under the heading of 'Knowledge' – see Table 4.1).

A third criticism that has been expressed is that Byram's model is a componential model, which only describes the components of intercultural competence and intercultural communicative competence without specifying the interrelationships between these components; it therefore fails to clarify the connections between attitudes, skills and knowledge (apart from the central positioning of learners' political and critical cultural awareness) and fails to illuminate learning processes and sequences of development (Kearney, 2019). However, it may actually be a strength of the model that it is componential. This is because we know that the development of intercultural attitudes – including the relationships between cultural self-ascriptions on one hand and attitudes to other cultural groups on the other hand – vary profoundly, not only across cultural settings but also across learners within individual settings (for reviews, see Barrett, 2007; Barrett & Davis, 2008). By not attempting to specify these relationships on a priori grounds, Byram's model displays a suitable level of humility in its claims, leaving it to future research to identify empirically the nature of these relationships in different settings and in different individuals. In addition, while it might be tempting to claim *a priori* that attitudes provide the initial entry point into, or the foundations for, the development of the other components of intercultural competence (cf. Deardorff, 2006), there is evidence which shows that the opposite pattern of influence can occur in practice, with changes to cultural knowledge and beliefs sometimes impacting directly on intercultural attitudes rather than vice versa (see, e.g. Halperin *et al.*, 2012; Saguy & Halperin, 2014). Once again, by avoiding the premature *a priori* specification of sequences in development, Byram's model leaves it to future research to identify the sequences that occur in practice within particular cultural settings and individuals.

Other critiques are that Byram pays too little attention to the nexus of language and culture (Risager, 2006) and to symbolic competence (Kramsch, 2009, 2011). These critiques deserve consideration given that a close relationship between language, communication and culture is an important premise underlying Byram's model (see Chapters 2 and 3, this volume).

Finally, it should be re-emphasised here that Byram's intention in the book is not to present an exhaustive or definitive description of all the possible components of either intercultural competence or intercultural communicative competence. Instead, the intention is to describe those particular components that can be formulated as pedagogical objectives in a way which makes them usable for teaching and assessment, so that they can then be utilised by teachers, especially teachers of foreign languages, for planning their teaching and assessment (Byram, 1997: 49, 56 and 88).

The Autobiography of Intercultural Encounters

Byram's 1997 book arose out of work that he had been conducting for the Language Policy Division of the Council of Europe (CoE) during the 1990s, and he continued working as an advisor to the Division for many years thereafter. In 2006, he initiated a new CoE project to develop an educational tool which would help learners to reflect critically on their encounters with people from other ethnic, national, religious and linguistic backgrounds. If interaction within such encounters is to be appropriate, effective and respectful, learners need to be able to apply the components of their intercultural competence within the context of these encounters in real time. It was envisaged that by supporting learners' reflections on their own intercultural encounters, and by encouraging their analysis of their reactions and behaviour during these encounters, this tool would, first, help to promote the development of the competences that learners require to engage in respectful intercultural dialogue, and second, encourage learners to engage in subsequent actions which would promote a deeper understanding of different cultural practices and world views and contribute to the common good. The tool that emerged from this project was the *Autobiography of Intercultural Encounters* (AIE) (Byram *et al.*, 2009a), and in the course of its development, Byram and colleagues articulated a new expanded model of intercultural competence.

The components reflected in the AIE tool were not intended to be used as a basis for developing teaching objectives as such, and this is one reason why the 2009 conceptualisation of ICC differs from the 1997 model. The components were instead conceptualised as a larger set of competences that learners require if they are to engage effectively and appropriately in intercultural encounters and are to take action in pursuit of the common good (Byram *et al.*, 2009b). Ten such competences were identified (see Table 4.2).

The AIE itself was then constructed to aid the development of these competences through the process of reflection. The AIE consists of a structured sequence of questions designed to support learners in thinking about a specific intercultural encounter which they themselves have experienced, and these questions are designed to stimulate the development of the 10 competences. The order in which the questions are asked progressively scaffolds the learner's reflections. The AIE begins with relatively simple descriptive questions about the encounter and the learner's own behaviours within the encounter, before more challenging questions are

Table 4.2 The model of intercultural competence underlying the design of the Autobiography of Intercultural Encounters (AIE) (Adapted from Byram *et al.* (2009b), © Council of Europe, reproduced with permission.)

- *Respect for otherness:* curiosity and openness, readiness to suspend belief about the 'naturalness' of one's own culture and to believe in the 'naturalness' of other cultures.
- *Acknowledging the identities of others:* taking full notice of other people's identities and recognising them for what they are.
- *Tolerance for ambiguity:* the ability to accept ambiguity and lack of clarity and to be able to deal with this constructively.
- *Empathy:* the ability to project oneself into another person's perspective and their opinions, motives, ways of thinking and feelings.
- *Skills of interpreting and relating:* the ability to interpret a document or event from another culture, to explain it and relate it to documents or events from one's own.
- *Skills of discovery and interaction:* the ability to acquire new knowledge of a culture and cultural practices and the ability to operate knowledge, attitudes and skills under the constraints of real-time communication and interaction.
- *Communicative awareness:* the ability to recognise different linguistic conventions, different verbal and non-verbal communication conventions – especially in a foreign language – and their effects on discourse processes, and to negotiate rules appropriate for intercultural communication.
- *Knowledge:* knowledge of social processes, and knowledge of illustrations of those processes and products; the latter includes knowledge about how other people see oneself as well as some knowledge about other people.
- *Critical cultural awareness:* the ability to evaluate, critically and on the basis of explicit criteria, perspectives, practices and products in one's own and other cultures and countries.
- *Action orientation:* the willingness to undertake some activity alone or with others as a consequence of reflection with the aim of making a contribution to the common good.

asked about the other person's behaviours and their thoughts, feelings and reactions. The questions progress on to issues concerning the communicative behaviours that took place and how the learner could find out more about the other person's culture. The AIE then culminates in the most challenging questions, which ask the learner to analyse similarities and differences between their own culture and that of the other person, and to evaluate the encounter critically. The final questions in the AIE ask the learner to reflect on the actions which they either have undertaken already or could undertake in the future as a consequence of the encounter.

Two versions of the AIE were developed, a standard version for use by older learners and adults, and a version for younger learners who need help from an adult in reading and writing and in thinking back over their encounter. In two follow-up projects, the AIE team went on to develop the *Autobiography of Intercultural Encounters through Visual Media* (AIEVM) (Barrett *et al.*, 2013), which was designed to promote the development of the competences required for deconstructing images of cultural others encountered in visual media such as television, cinema, magazines, newspapers, etc., and the *Autobiography of Intercultural Encounters through the Internet* (AIETI) (Byram *et al.*, in press a, b), which was designed to support the development of the competences required for engaging in respectful intercultural exchanges through social media and social networking sites. Again, both a standard version and a younger learners' version of the AIEVM and the AIETI were developed.

It is noteworthy that the AIE competence model shown in Table 4.2 incorporates all of the attitudes, skills, knowledge and awareness that had appeared in Byram's 1997 model, but additionally includes several further competences, including tolerance for ambiguity and empathy, some of which had been discussed in his 1997 book (see, e.g. p. 16) but had not been incorporated into his earlier model. The inclusion of action orientation, where the emphasis is placed on making a contribution to the common good, should be noted. Byram had also discussed the concept of action orientation in his 1997 book, using it to forge a link between foreign language teaching and political education, but again he did not explicitly embed it within his own model at the time. Embedding the concept explicitly in the AIE model marks an important shift in Byram's thinking towards the concept of intercultural citizenship. As will be discussed later in this chapter, intercultural citizenship has become a much more prominent theme in Byram's more recent work.

Developing Intercultural Competence through Education

Further development work on the nature of intercultural competence subsequently took place through the CoE, most notably on a project entitled *Developing Intercultural Competence through Education* (DICE) (Barrett *et al.*, 2013/2014, initially published as an internal CoE paper in

2013 and subsequently published in book format, 2014). This project was aimed at developing a rationale and conceptual framework for the full integration of the teaching and learning of intercultural competence into school systems – a much broader ambition than that of either the 1997 book or the AIE. The project examined the nature and significance of intercultural competence, the components of intercultural competence, how these components can be developed through education and the various educational methods, approaches and activities that can be used for this purpose. However, DICE did not attempt to formulate the specific objectives or learning outcomes that might be achieved through the use of these methods, approaches and activities.

The account of intercultural competence presented in DICE represents a further step in an evolving conception of intercultural competence. There are five significant new features of the DICE conception that should be noted.

First, there is a clear and explicit adoption of a non-essentialist view of culture. DICE argues that there is variability within all cultural groups. This is because the cultural resources (e.g. values, norms, beliefs, practices, customs, etc.) that are perceived to be associated with membership of cultural groups are always contested by the members of the groups, and because different group members appropriate and use different subsets of the total pool of resources that are provided by the culture.

Second, DICE argues that all individuals belong to multiple cultural groups (e.g. to family, generational, gender, social class, educational, occupational, lifestyle, ethnic, national and language groups). This means that all individuals have multiple cultural affiliations and identities, and their cultural affiliations intersect in such a way that each individual occupies a unique cultural positioning. These intersections further contribute to the internal variability that exists within cultural groups.

Third, it is noted by DICE that all cultural groups constantly develop over time. This is due to a number of factors: interactions with and influences from other cultural groups; political, economic and historical events and developments; and the internal contestation of the cultural resources of the group.

Fourth, DICE argues that individuals' cultural affiliations are fluid and dynamic, with the subjective salience of these affiliations and their associated identities fluctuating as individuals move from one situation to another. For this reason, different affiliations – or different subsets of intersecting affiliations – are highlighted depending on the particular social and cultural contexts that are encountered.

Fifth, because the subjective salience of cultural affiliations fluctuates according to context, intercultural encounters can arise in any situation where the context makes a specific cultural difference perceptually salient to an individual. In such a situation, the individual does not respond to the other person (or people) on the basis of their personal characteristics alone. Instead, the response is based, at least in part, on their perceptions of the cultural affiliations of the other person, which are perceived to differ from their own affiliations.

A further way in which the conception of intercultural competence that is presented in DICE differs from the earlier conceptions is that intercultural competence is construed as being broader than the set of attitudes, skills, knowledge and behaviour involved in face-to-face communication with others. DICE proposes that intercultural competence may also be deployed when reading texts about, thinking about, viewing images of or making judgements about people who are perceived to have different cultural affiliations from oneself. In other words, intercultural competence is required for understanding, appreciating and respecting people who are perceived to have different cultural affiliations from oneself even when no interaction or communication takes place with those people. Hence, in this respect, intercultural competence is construed by DICE as being broader than intercultural communicative competence.

As might be expected, given this broader conception, DICE provides a more expansive list of the components of intercultural competence. The components that are specified in the report are listed in Table 4.3.

Table 4.3 The components of intercultural competence specified in the DICE report (Adapted from Barrett *et al.* (2013/2014), © Council of Europe, reproduced with permission.)

Attitudes
- Valuing cultural diversity and pluralism of views and practices
- Respecting people who have different cultural affiliations from one's own
- Being open to, curious about and willing to learn from and about people who have different cultural orientations and perspectives from one's own
- Being willing to empathise with people who have different cultural affiliations from one's own
- Being willing to question what is usually taken for granted as 'normal' according to one's previously acquired knowledge and experience
- Being willing to tolerate ambiguity and uncertainty
- Being willing to seek out opportunities to engage and cooperate with individuals who have different cultural orientations and perspectives from one's own

Skills
- Multiperspectivity – the ability to decentre from one's own perspective and to take other people's perspectives into consideration in addition to one's own
- Skills in discovering information about other cultural affiliations and perspectives
- Skills in interpreting other cultural practices, beliefs and values and relating them to one's own
- Empathy – the ability to understand and respond to other people's thoughts, beliefs, values and feelings
- Cognitive flexibility – the ability to change and adapt one's way of thinking according to the situation or context
- Skills in critically evaluating and making judgements about cultural beliefs, values, practices, discourses and products, including those associated with one's own cultural affiliations, and being able to explain one's views

(Continued)

Table 4.3 (Continued)

- Skills of adapting one's behaviour to new cultural environments – for example, avoiding verbal and non-verbal behaviours which may be viewed as impolite by people who have different cultural affiliations from one's own
- Linguistic, sociolinguistic and discourse skills, including skills in managing breakdowns in communication
- Plurilingual skills to meet the communicative demands of an intercultural encounter, such as use of more than one language or language variety, or drawing on a known language to understand another ('intercomprehension')
- The ability to act as a 'mediator' in intercultural exchanges, including skills in translating, interpreting and explaining

Knowledge and understanding
- Understanding the internal diversity and heterogeneity of all cultural groups
- Awareness and understanding of one's own and other people's assumptions, preconceptions, stereotypes, prejudices, and overt and covert discrimination
- Understanding the influence of one's own language and cultural affiliations on one's experience of the world and of other people
- Communicative awareness, including awareness of the fact that other peoples' languages may express shared ideas in a unique way or express unique ideas difficult to access through one's own language(s), and awareness of the fact that people of other cultural affiliations may follow different verbal and non-verbal communicative conventions which are meaningful from their perspective
- Knowledge of the beliefs, values, practices, discourses and products that may be used by people who have particular cultural orientations
- Understanding of processes of cultural, societal and individual interaction, and of the socially constructed nature of knowledge

Actions
- Seeking opportunities to engage with people who have different cultural orientations and perspectives from one's own
- Interacting and communicating appropriately, effectively and respectfully with people who have different cultural affiliations from one's own
- Cooperating with individuals who have different cultural orientations on shared activities and ventures, discussing differences in views and perspectives, and constructing common views and perspectives
- Challenging attitudes and behaviours (including speech and writing) which contravene human rights, and taking action to defend and protect the dignity and human rights of people regardless of their cultural affiliations, for example, by:
  - Intervening and expressing opposition when there are expressions of prejudice or acts of discrimination against individuals or groups
  - Challenging cultural stereotypes and prejudices
  - Encouraging positive attitudes towards the contributions to society made by individuals irrespective of their cultural affiliations
  - Mediating in situations of cultural conflict

The list of actions included at the end of this list represents a much more detailed and explicit account of what is entailed in 'action orientation' than had been specified in the AIE. DICE further argues that intercultural competence provides an essential foundation for being a global citizen. It proposes that intercultural competence entails developing one's capacity to build common projects, to assume shared responsibilities and to create common ground to live together in peace. In short, equipping learners with intercultural competence empowers them to take action in the world as intercultural citizens.

A second characteristic of the components of intercultural competence as described in DICE is the explicit identification of a value – valuing cultural diversity and pluralism of views and practices – under the heading of 'Attitudes'. There is also an implicit value embedded in the fourth bullet under 'Actions' – valuing the dignity and human rights of people regardless of their cultural affiliations. Values became a more distinctive feature in the next iteration of intercultural competence that took place at the CoE, in the *Reference Framework of Competences for Democratic Culture*.

The Council of Europe's Reference Framework of Competences for Democratic Culture (RFCDC)

The direction of travel from Byram's 1997 model, through the AIE and DICE, is clear: a progressively greater articulation of the components of intercultural competence, and also of the links between intercultural competence and citizenship. That said, the proliferation of components in the DICE model, without linking them to specific objectives, makes it somewhat unwieldy for practical applications, especially for teaching purposes. Furthermore, the fact that values were not explicitly identified and separated out in the description of the components represents a lack of conceptual clarity in the report.

These two issues were directly addressed in the development of the RFCDC (Council of Europe, 2018), to which Byram made significant contributions as a member of the authoring group. Work on the RFCDC began in 2013, as a result of a political initiative by the member state of Andorra, which held the Chairmanship of the CoE in 2012–2013. Andorra was particularly concerned to ensure that formal education in European countries promotes the competences that young people need to be able to engage in intercultural dialogue and to act as responsible democratic citizens. Importantly, one of the documents that fed into the formulation of the Andorran initiative was DICE, which was presented at a Chairmanship conference in Andorra La Vella in February 2013.

In accordance with the Andorran proposal, the RFCDC was designed to provide guidance to the member states on how the intercultural and democratic competences of learners can be promoted through formal education. It was published in 2018, in three volumes (Council of Europe, 2018). The first volume describes a conceptual model of the competences that young people need to acquire in order to engage effectively in intercultural dialogue and active democratic citizenship; the second volume provides lists of scaled descriptors for all of the competences contained in the conceptual model and the third volume provides guidance for ministries of education and for education practitioners on how the model and the descriptors can be used to inform education policy and practice in six areas – curriculum, pedagogy, assessment, the use of a whole school approach, teacher education and the use of education for combatting radi-calisation. Of most relevance to the current chapter is the conceptual model, which is presented in the first volume.

This RFCDC model incorporates in its entirety the conceptualisation of culture that had previously been articulated in DICE. The model proposes that 20 specific competences are required for what may be termed 'intercultural and democratic competence' (i.e. the ability to meet the demands and challenges of intercultural and democratic situations). These 20 competences fall into four broad categories: values, attitudes, skills and knowledge and critical understanding (see Figure 4.3). The RFCDC argues that these competences are psychological resources that learners need to acquire if they are to engage effectively and appropriately in inter-cultural dialogue and act as responsible and effective democratic citizens. Each of these 20 competences is described in detail by the RFCDC. Some of the competences, such as openness and empathy, may be targeted from a relatively early age at pre-school and primary school. However, others, such as knowledge and critical understanding of politics, law and econo-mies, are more suitable for targeting in upper secondary school and higher education. This is not to say that criticality (e.g. the ability to make criti-cal judgements about equality, equity and fairness) is not present in young

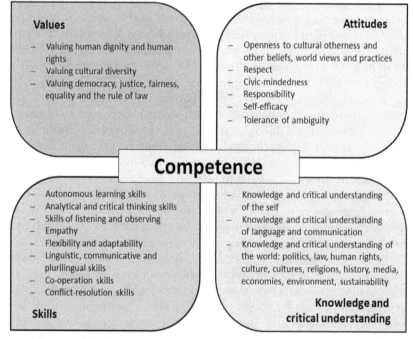

Figure 4.3 The 20 competences required for participating effectively and appropri-ately in democratic culture within culturally diverse societies, according to the RFCDC (From Council of Europe (2018), © Council of Europe, reproduced with permission.)

children – it clearly is (see, e.g. Killen *et al.*, 2018) – nor that openness and empathy are not important during adulthood – they clearly are (e.g. Butrus & Witenberg, 2013); instead, the suggestion is that different competences may be more suitable for promotion through education at different levels of education. For this reason, the RFCDC proposes that promoting the development of these competences is a task that applies across all levels of formal education, from preschool through primary and secondary education to higher education.

Three characteristics of the RFCDC competence model should be noted. First, despite the wider scope of the model (which covers not only intercultural competence but also democratic competence), there is a reduction in the total number of components vis-à-vis the DICE model. This was achieved by reconceptualising the components and grouping them at a more general level, rather than at the specific level that had been used in DICE – thus, aspects that had been differentiated in the DICE model were combined in the RFCDC model under superordinate headings. Through this means, the RFCDC model is more comprehensive while simultaneously containing fewer component competences than the DICE model.

Second, unlike the competences in the DICE model, all 20 competences contained in the RFCDC model are broken down into sets of specific objectives through the descriptors. These descriptors are formulated using the language of learning outcomes, and they provide detailed specifications of the objectives for each individual competence at three levels of proficiency: basic, intermediate and advanced.

Third, three sets of values are present in the model, these being the values that are essential for engaging in respectful intercultural dialogue and democratic behaviour. The appearance of values in this model as a separate category of competences, rather than subsuming them under the heading of attitudes, is a novel and distinctive feature of the RFCDC. There are several characteristics that differentiate values from attitudes: their generality, trans-situational applicability, focus on desirable goals and prescriptiveness (Schwartz, 2006). These differences motivated the separation of values from attitudes in the RFCDC model. The RFCDC proposes that, in real-life situations, the 20 competences are rarely mobilised and used individually. Instead, they are much more likely to be applied in clusters. Depending on the situation and the specific demands, challenges and opportunities of that situation, as well as the specific needs of the individual within that situation, different subsets of competences will be activated and deployed. Furthermore, any given situation also changes over time. For this reason, an effective and adaptive response requires the constant monitoring of the situation and the appropriate ongoing adjustment of the competences being deployed. In other words, a competent individual mobilises and deploys clusters of competences in a fluid, dynamic and adaptive manner in order to meet the constantly shifting demands, challenges and opportunities that arise in intercultural and democratic situations.

Five concrete illustrations of how this process occurs are provided in the RFCDC: interacting during an intercultural encounter; taking a stand against hate speech; participating in political debate; encountering propaganda advocating a violent extremist cause; and post-conflict reconciliation. These illustrations reveal the close relationship between intercultural and democratic competence when acting in real-world situations in which cultural diversity is salient. In short, they provide vivid illustrations of one of Byram's key concerns: intercultural citizenship.

Another key concern of Byram's, namely the role of language in education, is addressed in the RFCDC in a separate guidance document on this topic, which Byram co-authored with Mike Fleming (Council of Europe, 2020a). This document discusses the central importance of language to success in all subjects of study at school, the need for education systems to ensure that learners have a sufficient command of the language of learning/schooling and the need for teachers to understand the role that language plays in fostering intercultural and democratic values, attitudes, skills, knowledge and understanding. The document argues that education for values, attitudes and critical understanding, in particular, requires a high level of language competence, and it is therefore crucial for teachers to be aware of the language competence of their learners and the extent to which this might be impacting on their intercultural and democratic competence.

The RFCDC has already made a major contribution to education within Europe. While the RFCDC was still under development, it was the main focus of the *25th Session of the Council of Europe Standing Conference of Ministers of Education* in April 2016, at which the Education Ministers from 50 European states issued a *Final Declaration* strongly endorsing the RFCDC and calling on the CoE to assist member states in examining and implementing it in their national education systems. A CoE survey, conducted in April 2019, revealed that the RFCDC was already being implemented either in whole or in part in Andorra, Azerbaijan, Belarus, Belgium (French-speaking community), Cyprus, Finland, Greece, Italy, Latvia, Moldova, Montenegro, North Macedonia, Portugal, Romania, San Marino, Serbia and Ukraine.

In order to support uptake of the RFCDC in the member states, a number of new tools have been developed. These include a tool to support teachers' critical reflections on intercultural and democratic competence and on their own professional practices (Council of Europe, 2020b) and a portfolio that can be used by learners for collecting materials documenting their developing proficiency in the use of the 20 competences – the portfolio is designed to stimulate learners' critical reflections on their competences, and to support them in identifying how to further develop their competences (Byram *et al.*, 2021). In addition, revised editions of the

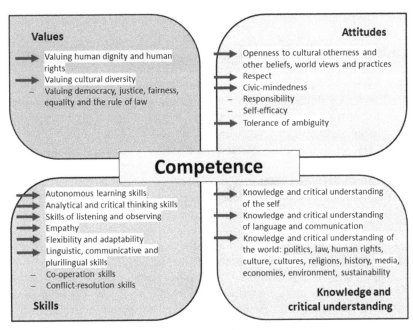

Figure 4.4 The specific RFCDC competences (marked with arrows) that are promoted through the use of the AIE, AIEVM and AIETI (From Byram *et al.* (in press b), © Council of Europe, reproduced with permission.)

AIE, AIEVM and AIETI were produced (Byram *et al.*, in press b). In these revisions, the components contained in the original model of intercultural competence used to design the AIE (Table 4.2) were mapped onto one or more of the competences contained in the RFCDC model (Figure 4.3). The results of this mapping are shown in Figure 4.4, which indicates the subset of RFCDC competences required for participating in face-to-face intercultural encounters as well as intercultural encounters that are experienced through visual or digital media.

Byram's Concept of Intercultural Citizenship

A parallel stream of work that Byram led, while working on these various CoE projects, was dedicated to conceptualising intercultural citizenship and intercultural citizenship education (Byram, 2008, 2012; Byram & Golubeva, 2020; Byram *et al.*, 2017; Porto & Byram, 2015; Porto *et al.*, 2018; Porto *et al.*, 2021; Wagner *et al.*, 2019).

The concept of intercultural citizenship has expanded over the years. Initially, the term was devised to emphasise those additional dimensions, such as linguistic and intercultural competences, that need to complement citizenship competences because most contemporary communities are multilingual and multicultural. While the term 'citizenship' has traditionally denoted one's legal status in relationship to a country, individuals may actually have a subjective sense of belonging to communities at a variety of levels – the local, regional, national, transnational or global level – and they might engage in civic activities at any or all of these levels. This complexity cannot be ignored. Furthermore, in order to function effectively as a citizen in these communities today, the learner needs to become an 'intercultural citizen', that is, a person who has the attitudes, knowledge and skills of intercultural competence which enable them to participate in multilingual and multicultural communities. In this sense, the notion of intercultural citizenship accommodates multiple forms of belonging and active citizenship at all of these various levels.

Byram (2008) went on to develop the concept of education for intercultural citizenship in considerable detail. He notes that traditional citizenship education aims to equip learners with the competences that are required for action in their local and national communities, but usually fails to direct learners' attention to the transnational and global levels as additional sites for civic action. Conversely, foreign language education directs learners' attention to the transnational level, especially to those countries in which the language that is being learned is spoken. But while foreign language education equips learners with the competences that are required to act as intercultural speakers, it does not equip them with the active citizenship competences that are required to take action at the transnational level. Byram recognised that his concept of critical cultural awareness, which was originally intended to act as the link between intercultural competence and citizenship competence in his 1997 model, was insufficient to perform this role insofar as it only involves the reflective and critical evaluation of the cultural perspectives, practices and products in the learner's own culture and other people's cultures – in itself, it does not involve taking action for the common good (indeed, this was the motivation for including not only critical cultural awareness but also action orientation in the model of intercultural competence underpinning the AIE – with action orientation itself then becoming an important facet of civic-mindedness in the RFCDC).

As a consequence, Byram (2008) synthesised citizenship education and national and foreign language education into a new curriculum area which he calls 'education for intercultural citizenship', in order to enable the synergies between these two complementary approaches to be achieved. He identifies five domains that need to be addressed by this area: the evaluative orientation (in which the objectives are defined in terms of values and attitudes), the cognitive orientation (focused on both propositional and procedural knowledge), the comparative orientation (which focuses on the comparison with otherness), the communicative orientation (covering linguistic, sociolinguistic and discourse competence) and the action orientation (the capacity to live and cooperate with others, resolve conflicts and disputes, and take part in public debates and make choices in real-life situations). Three of these orientations (the evaluative, cognitive and action orientations) are addressed by both citizenship education and national and foreign language education, but the remaining two (the comparative and communicative orientations) are only addressed by language education. In a series of detailed tables, Byram (2008: 180–184) unpacks the specific objectives which are associated with each of these five orientations. The overall aim of this new curriculum area is:

> to ensure that those who leave an education system ... have a sense of belonging to an international community, a capacity to interact on socio-political matters with people of other languages and cultures, with a critical awareness of the particular nature of socio-political action and interaction in international and intercultural contexts. (Byram, 2008: 185)

While his 2008 book focuses on the theoretical principles of education for intercultural citizenship, a subsequent book edited by Byram and colleagues reports a series of studies in which these principles were implemented in practice at a variety of educational levels from primary through to higher education (Byram *et al.*, 2017). A crucial feature of all of the studies in this book was *criticality*, which is the central element in both intercultural competence (in the form of critical cultural awareness) and intercultural citizenship. The difference is that:

> models of intercultural competence and the concept of the intercultural speaker limit the activity of the individual to mediation. Intercultural citizenship goes beyond this, involving both activity with other people in the world, and the competences required for dialogue with people of other linguacultures. (Byram & Golubeva, 2020: 77)

Thanks to criticality, for example, intercultural citizens would not fall under the influence of populism – instead, they would engage in *critical action* (Byram *et al.*, 2017). This is how intercultural citizenship and active citizenship are related. Active citizenship implies participation in civil society, but it cannot be taken for granted that active citizenship is always associated with positive intentions (for detailed discussion, see Golubeva, 2018):

> In today's societies, both positive and negative examples of social and political activation can be observed ... [A]n active citizen may also share the views and values of radicals, populists, or ... even commit acts of terrorism, vandalism or participation in riots and violent protests. (Golubeva, 2018: 9)

Hence, there are compelling reasons to intensify intercultural citizenship education to empower individuals to act in socially responsible, non-violent ways. Active citizenship makes sense if it is combined with principles of intercultural and democratic citizenship.

Table 4.4 Characteristics of education for intercultural citizenship (Adapted from Byram *et al.*, 2017: xxv)

- a critical questioning of assumptions through the process of juxtaposition and comparison;
- emphasis on becoming conscious of working with Others (of a different group and culture) through (a) processes of comparison/juxtaposition and (b) communication in a language (L1 or L2/3/...) which influences perceptions and which emphasises the importance of learners becoming conscious of multiple identities;
- creating a supranational community of action and communication which is composed of people of different beliefs, values and behaviours which are potentially in conflict – without expecting conformity and easy, harmonious solutions;
- having a focus and range of action which is different from that which is available when not working with Others, where 'Others' refers to all those of whatever social group who are initially perceived as different, members of an out-group;
- emphasizing becoming aware of one's existing identities and opening options for social identities additional to the national and regional, etc.;
- paying equal attention to cognition/knowledge, affect/attitude, behaviours/skill;
- all of the above with a conscious commitment to values (i.e. rejecting relativism), being aware that values sometimes conflict and are differently interpreted, but being committed, as citizens in a community, to cooperation.

Education for intercultural citizenship can therefore be viewed as encompassing the characteristics listed in Table 4.4.

Revisiting Byram's (1997) Model of Intercultural Competence

While the present chapter was being written, the second revised edition of Byram's 1997 book was published. In the Preface to the revised edition, Byram (2021) reports that, essentially, he remains satisfied with what he wrote in 1997 which remains useful for the future, albeit while recognising its weaknesses. We concur with this judgement. Most other models of intercultural competence and intercultural communicative competence that have appeared since 1997 (and there have been many) fail to articulate the components of these competences with sufficient clarity and detail to enable these components to be linked explicitly to teaching and educational assessment through the specification of practical objectives that may be used by teachers in the classroom. Consequently, while there is now a more comprehensive model of the intercultural and democratic competences that are required for active democratic citizenship available through the RFCDC, Byram's 1997 models of intercultural competence and intercultural communicative competence still have considerable educational importance and relevance, particularly for foreign language education.

That said, the new edition of the book contains many useful additions (e.g. concerning value pluralism, mediation, and political education), as well as some more subtle changes in details of the model (e.g. to the definition of critical cultural awareness). These additions and minor revisions mean that the new edition will inevitably become a further landmark publication in this field.

Conclusion

In this chapter, we have provided an overview of how Michael Byram has contributed to the understanding of intercultural competence and intercultural communicative competence and to the theory and practice of education for intercultural citizenship, over the past 25 years. As we have seen, his contributions have been highly productive in terms of both theory and practice. Furthermore, we believe that his work is now more important than ever. We are living in times of global crisis and conflicts and are desperately searching for solutions to these problems. It is important to understand that whatever solutions we find or invent, it will be impossible to implement them without educating intercultural citizens who are ready and willing to take responsible action in the interests of the global and local communities. Recent events, such as the COVID-19 pandemic, have confirmed what humanity has been trying to learn from the historical events that have impacted the world both in the past and the present: that it is crucial for our well-being to develop a sense of global interconnectedness and a sense of responsibility for other members of our communities. The task and the ultimate goal of both foreign language education and education for intercultural citizenship is to help young people to develop this sense of interconnectedness and responsibility, and a desire to take action for improving collective well-being and the common good.

Acknowledgements

We would like to express our grateful thanks to Paloma Castro, Ulla Lundgren and Jane Woodin and to an anonymous reviewer, for their insightful comments on earlier drafts of this chapter.

References

Barrett, M. (2007) *Children's Knowledge, Beliefs and Feelings about Nations and National Groups*. Hove: Psychology Press.

Barrett, M., Byram, M., Ipgrave, J. and Seurrat, A. (2013) *Images of Others: An Autobiography of Intercultural Encounters through Visual Media*. Strasbourg: Council of Europe.

Barrett, M., Byram, M., Lázár, I., Mompoint-Gaillard, P. and Philippou, S. (2013/2014) *Developing Intercultural Competence through Education*. Strasbourg: Council of Europe.

Barrett M. and Davis, S.C. (2008) Applying social identity and self-categorization theories to children's racial, ethnic, national and state identifications and attitudes. In S.M. Quintana and C. McKown (eds) *Handbook of Race, Racism and the Developing Child* (pp. 72–110). Hoboken, NJ: John Wiley & Sons.

Belz, J.A. (2007) The development of intercultural communicative competence in telecollaborative partnerships. In R. O'Dowd (ed.) *Online Intercultural Exchange: An Introduction for Foreign Language Teachers* (pp. 127–166). Clevedon: Multilingual Matters.

Butrus, N. and Witenberg, R.T. (2013) Some personality predictors of tolerance to human diversity: The roles of openness, agreeableness, and empathy. *Australian Psychologist* 48, 290–298.

Byram, M. (1997) *Teaching and Assessing Intercultural Communicative Competence.* Clevedon: Multilingual Matters.

Byram, M. (2008) *From Foreign Language Education to Education for Intercultural Citizenship: Essays and Reflections.* Clevedon: Multilingual Matters.

Byram, M. (2012) Conceptualizing intercultural (communicative) competence and intercultural citizenship. In J. Jackson (ed.) *Routledge Handbook of Language and Intercultural Communication* (pp. 85–97). London: Routledge.

Byram, M. (2021) *Teaching and Assessing Intercultural Communicative Competence: Revisited.* Bristol: Multilingual Matters.

Byram, M., Barrett, M., Aroni, A., Golubeva, I., Jouhanneau, C., Kumpulainen, K., Losito, B., Natsvlishvili, N., Rus, C., Styslavska, O. and Tranekjær, L. (2021) *A Portfolio of Competences for Democratic Culture: Standard Version.* Strasbourg: Council of Europe Publishing. https://www.coe.int/en/web/reference-framework-of-competences-for-democratic-culture/portfolios (date accessed 29 September 2021).

Byram, M., Barrett, M., Davcheva, L., Gomez Mejia, G., Ipgrave, J., Lindner, R. and Seurrat, A. (in press a) *Autobiography of Intercultural Encounters through the Internet.* Strasbourg: Council of Europe.

Byram, M., Barrett, M., Ipgrave, J., Jackson, R. and Méndez García, M.C. (2009a) *Autobiography of Intercultural Encounters.* Strasbourg: Council of Europe.

Byram, M., Barrett, M., Ipgrave, J., Jackson, R. and Méndez García, M.C. (2009b) *Autobiography of Intercultural Encounters: Context, Concepts and Theories.* Strasbourg: Council of Europe.

Byram, M., Barrett, M., Ipgrave, J., Jackson, R. and Méndez García, M.C. (in press b) *Autobiography of Intercultural Encounters: Context, Concepts and Theories* (2nd revised edn). Strasbourg: Council of Europe.

Byram, M. and Golubeva, I. (2020) Conceptualizing intercultural (communicative) competence and intercultural citizenship. In J. Jackson (ed.) *Routledge Handbook of Language and Intercultural Communication* (2nd edn) (pp. 70–85). London: Routledge.

Byram, M., Golubeva, I., Han, H. and Wagner, M. (eds) (2017) *From Principles to Practice in Education for Intercultural Citizenship.* Bristol: Multilingual Matters.

Council of Europe (2018) *Reference Framework of Competences for Democratic Culture* [3 volumes]. Strasbourg: Council of Europe.

Council of Europe (2020a) *Reference Framework of Competences for Democratic Culture: Competences for Democratic Culture and the Importance of Language.* Strasbourg: Council of Europe.

Council of Europe (2020b) *RFCDC Teacher Self-Reflection Tool.* Strasbourg: Council of Europe. https://www.coe.int/en/web/reference-framework-of-competences-for-democratic-culture/-reflection-tool-for-teachers (date accessed 29 January 2021).

Deardorff, D.K. (2006) Identification and assessment of intercultural competence as a student outcome of internationalization. *Journal of Studies in International Education* 10 (3), 241–266.

Dervin, F. (2016) *Interculturality in Education: A Theoretical and Methodological Toolbox.* London: Palgrave Macmillan.

Golubeva, I. (2018) *The Links between Education and Active Citizenship/Civic Engagement. NESET II Report.* Luxembourg: Publications Office of the European Union. https://nesetweb.eu/wp-content/uploads/2019/06/NESET2_AHQ1.pdf (date accessed 29 January 2021).

Halperin, E., Crisp, R.J., Husnu, S., Trzesniewski, K.H., Dweck, C.S. and Gross, J.J. (2012) Promoting intergroup contact by changing beliefs: Group malleability, intergroup anxiety, and contact motivation. *Emotion* 12 (6), 1192–1195.

Hoff, H.E. (2020) The evolution of intercultural communicative competence: Conceptualisations, critiques and consequences for 21st century classroom practice. *Intercultural Communication Education* 3 (2), 55–74.

Kearney, E. (2019) Professional (re)visions of language teaching for interculturality. In B. Dupuy and K. Michelson (eds) *Pathways to Paradigm Change: Critical Examinations of Prevailing Discourses and Ideologies in Second Language Education, AAUSC 2019 Volume – Issues in Language Program Direction* (pp. 248–275). https://scholarspace.manoa.hawaii.edu/bitstream/10125/69800/2019_11.pdf (date accessed 28 September 2021).

Killen, M., Elenbaas, L. and Rizzo, M.T. (2018) Young children's ability to recognize and challenge unfair treatment of others in group contexts. *Human Development* 61 (4–5), 281–296.

Kramsch, C. (2009) Discourse, the symbolic dimension of intercultural competence. In A. Hu and M. Byram (eds) *Interkulturelle Kompetenz und Fremdsprachliches Lernen. / Intercultural Competence and Foreign Language Learning* (pp. 107–121). Tubingen: Gunter Narr Verlag.

Kramsch, C. (2011) The symbolic dimensions of the intercultural. *Language Teaching* 44 (3), 354–367.

Matsuo, C. (2012) A critique of Michael Byram's intercultural communicative competence model from the perspective of model type and conceptualization of culture. *Fukuoka University Review of Literature & Humanities* 44, 347–380.

Porto, M. and Byram, M. (2015) A curriculum for action in the community and intercultural citizenship in higher education. *Language, Culture and Curriculum* 28 (3), 226–242.

Porto, M., Golubeva, I. and Byram, M. (2021) Channelling discomfort through the arts: A Covid-19 case study through an intercultural telecollaboration project. *Language Teaching Research*. Advance Online Publication.

Porto, M., Houghton, S.A. and Byram, M. (2018) Intercultural citizenship in the (foreign) language classroom. Editorial. *Language Teaching Research* 22 (5), 484–498.

Risager, K. (2006) *Language and Culture: Global Flows and Local Complexity.* Clevedon: Multilingual Matters.

Risager, K. (2007) *Language and Culture Pedagogy: From a National to a Transnational Paradigm.* Clevedon: Multilingual Matters.

Saguy, T. and Halperin, E. (2014) Exposure to outgroup members criticizing their own group facilitates intergroup openness. *Personality and Social Psychology Bulletin* 40, 791–802.

Schwartz, S.H. (2006) Les valeurs de base de la personne: Théorie, mesures et applications [Basic Human Values: Theory, Measurement, and Applications]. *Revue française de sociologie* 42, 249–288.

Wagner, M., Cardetti, F. and Byram, M. (2019) *Teaching Intercultural Citizenship across the Curriculum: The Role of Language Education.* Alexandria, VA: American Conference on the Teaching of Foreign Languages.

5 Intercultural Dialogue and Values in Education

Paloma Castro, Ulla Lundgren and Jane Woodin

Introduction

The term *intercultural dialogue* reached prominence in Europe particularly through the 2008 Year of Intercultural Dialogue and the concurrent Council of Europe (CoE) White Paper, as a policy response for managing cultural diversity. It is defined by the Council of Europe as 'a process that comprises an open and respectful exchange of views between individuals and groups with different ethnic, cultural, religious and linguistic backgrounds and heritage, on the basis of mutual understanding and respect' (CoE, 2008: 17). Over the past few years, the authors of this chapter – all educationalists working in European universities – have been considering the relevance of this notion for higher education policy and practice; to do so was one of the recommendations of the White Paper, which recognizes the potential for developing 'intercultural intellectuals' (CoE, 2008: 31).

During the process of developing a framework for implementing an intercultural dialogue (ICD) approach[1] in the internationalization of higher education (Lundgren *et al.*, 2020; Woodin *et al.*, 2011), we have increasingly realized the importance of changing the focus from *products* of internationalization (as can be found in many international barometers and rankings), towards less outwardly measurable *processes* of internationalizing higher education. This shift from product to process, through taking an ICD approach, has led us to understand the importance of values in higher education. The more we, together with colleagues in our recent edited volume (Lundgren *et al.*, 2020), have moved deeper into an ICD approach, the more crucial value orientations and actions have become to our own educational philosophy, embracing an educationalist approach in the spirit of intercultural dialogue.

When using the term *values*, we adhere to the definition of the term as described in the Reference Framework for Competences for Democratic Cultures (RFCDC): 'A value is a belief about a desirable goal that motivates action and serves as a guiding principle in life across many situations' (CoE, 2018: 78).[2]

For us, educational values in an ICD approach can be linked to a modern humanistic concept of *Bildung*, as will be explained later. Our work is also influenced by the work of colleagues in Cultnet – most notably, its founder Mike Byram – to whom this volume is dedicated, and whose contribution is noted throughout this chapter.

Being European scholars in higher education with an interest not only in language education but in intercultural education in general, the horizon from which we are looking at values is limited by having lived predominantly in Western Europe and working largely through the medium of a European language. We recognize that this chapter is limited through a largely European perspective and that this may not be without objections from other levels of education and parts of the world.

The chapter will start with an overview of the context of the Council of Europe's initiatives on Intercultural Dialogue. We then consider its relevance for education and, in particular, in the context of internationalization of higher education. We argue that the use of an intercultural dialogue (ICD) approach, the development of which has been influenced by the work of Mike Byram, can maintain a focus on educational values and purposes in the *Bildung* sense.

Intercultural Dialogue in Context

The concept of intercultural dialogue discussed in this chapter relates largely – but not entirely – to that which is used in the Council of Europe's White Paper (CoE, 2008) on the subject. The White Paper was developed to encourage European citizens to engage in intercultural interactions; this came at a point in time when 13 countries had recently joined the European Union.[3] There was some concern over the seeming failure of a policy of multiculturalism within national borders, and the tendency for groups within Europe to function largely within similar cultural, ethnic and linguistic circles, with little interaction with other groups living nearby. The White Paper openly acknowledges intercultural dialogue as a way of respecting individuals' rights to 'choose' their culture (whether inherited or adopted) while recognizing our common future and our need to participate responsibly in diverse societies. Creating physical spaces to facilitate doing things together across cultural groups are central aspects of fostering intercultural dialogue for the CoE, with a focus on all of us as responsible for making this happen. The White Paper makes it clear that this cannot be left to governments alone, but needs to involve us all at a citizen level, through our various communities as well as through institutional support and focus. It is the *process* of mutual exchange, which characterizes intercultural dialogue, rather than a focus on *solutions* to issues or problems:

> Intercultural dialogue is understood as an open and respectful exchange of views between individuals, groups with different ethnic, cultural, religious and linguistic backgrounds and heritage on the basis of mutual understanding and respect. It operates at all levels – within societies, between the societies of Europe and between Europe and the wider world (CoE, 2008: 10–11).

Recognizing that 'equal' is not something which can be assumed or ignored, the CoE White Paper takes the position that **'the challenge of living together in a diverse society could only be met if we can live together as equals in dignity'** (2008: 10) (emphasis in original). This means less attention on 'getting things done together' (which focuses on product-orientation), and more on 'doing things together' (which focuses on the process of the joint activity). For the CoE, this is always within the framework of what are called the core and fundamental values of Europe: 'The cornerstones of a political culture valuing diversity are the common values of democracy, human rights and fundamental freedoms, the rule of law, pluralism, tolerance, non-discrimination and mutual respect' (CoE, 2008: 25).

It is interesting to note that much of what is understood by the CoE as intercultural dialogue is also evident in academic discussions of the term *dialogue*. Dialogue is used in a wide variety of contexts and meanings, for example, in politics and international relations as a means to resolve political conflicts and bring about peace. Dialogue also has a strong presence in faith circles.[4] Linguists have classified dialogue in a range of ways, considering sociolinguistic features (e.g. linking to power relationships in dialogue) or communicative/pragmatic compositional features (e.g. informative, or artistic dialogue), which often have multi-purposes (Radkevych, 2015). It is generally seen as a process which involves more than one person (although according to some, e.g. Vygotsky (1970), it can also be an internal process). Tannen (1995) reminds us that dialogue is something which is jointly constructed and that utterances of one interlocutor are highly dependent on those of the other interlocutor(s). Moreover, any dialogue is not a stand-alone event, but also needs to be understood in the context of other dialogues and communications of which this dialogue is a part. For Bakhtin (1986), it references meanings from outside of the dialogue itself: 'Each utterance is filled with the echoes and reverberations of other utterances to which it is related by the communality of the sphere of speech communication' (1986: 91). Hierarchical relationships are evident in utterances, as Bakhtin states: 'The basic stylistic tone of an utterance is therefore determined above all by who is talked about and what his relation is to the speaker – whether he is higher or lower than or equal to him on the scale of the social hierarchy' (cited in Morris, 2003: 170).

Dialogue itself as a term can hold different meanings. In earlier work (Lundgren *et al.*, 2020), we referred to the fact that the meaning of dialogue may change across languages/cultures (e.g. Wierzbicka, 2006).

Dialogue, then, is jointly constructed, allows for mutual understanding, has an element of reciprocity and can lead to change, joint creativity and new ways of thinking. Bohm (1996) talks about dialogue as a 'stream of meaning', flowing in, among and between us. He makes a useful distinction between *discussion* (people arguing from fixed positions and attempting to persuade others over to their perspective) and *dialogue* which is not about superiority, right or wrong, or indeed defending positions. All of these, he argues, obstruct creativity, whereas dialogue is about mutual participation and the development of something together, through listening to each other and jointly building and developing understanding.[5]

> Ordinarily people pay very little attention to each other, each one has his(sic) own opinion which is based on his own conditioning (…) if 10 or 20 or 30 people could really think together with one mind, I think they could liberate a tremendous energy. (Bohm, 1979 – recorded interview)

The question of paying attention to each other (or indeed not) is characterized by Buber (1971) in his work on dialogue as relationship with others. His distinction between the I-It and I-You (or thou) mode of dialogue with others illustrates how we may orient to others as 'things' (I-It), as opposed to orienting to the whole person, seeing others as whole (I-You).

Developing joint understanding does not mean that difference should be minimized. According to Ganesh and Holmes (2011), understanding dialogic encounters as intercultural 'is particularly evident in studies that position *difference* as key points or moments of negotiation in dialogic processes' (2011: 82). Dialogue allows individuals to acknowledge the complexity and diversity of relationships and work towards solutions in situations of conflict (Holmes, 2014). Leeds-Hurwitz (2013), in a recorded plenary speech, reminds us however that the goal of intercultural dialogue is not to reach consensus but that it is 'a specific form of communication, where participants, having their own perspective, still recognize the existence of other different perspectives, and remain open to them'. Differentiating it from monologue or debate (see Bohm, 1979, recorded interview), it requires 'listening to the other and seriously attempting to understand what is said' – this may result in participants changing some of their assumptions; but Leeds-Hurwitz argues, this is not the goal of dialogue. She also notes that difference is assumed: 'people who already share all of their assumptions have no need for dialogue'.[6]

We understand intercultural dialogue as a process of working together as equals, assuming difference or the possibility of difference (religious, cultural, ethnic, linguistic as described in the White Paper, 2008). The *intercultural* in intercultural dialogue, therefore, does not refer to cross-national dialogue alone (if at all), but to the process of engaging in listening and understanding people from diverse backgrounds and in diverse contexts; people who we understand (or who understand us) as culturally different, whose perspective is not the same as ours and whose perspective we wish to understand for the sake of understanding it, as 'equals in dignity' (CoE, 2008: 10).

Equals in dignity, however, is not a situation that is easy to create, simply through creating spaces for intercultural dialogue to take place. As Bourdieu (1991) notes (albeit in relation to linguistic power and an interactionist perspective in particular), interactions cannot be assumed to be a 'closed world', but the 'whole social structure is present in each interaction' (1991: 67). Dialogue between an Arabic-speaker and a French speaker of a formerly colonized nation (to use one of Bourdieu's examples) will be affected not only by the interaction between the individuals but also by the relations between the groups who speak those languages.

Relationships of power are not limited to individuals or groups; social institutions (such as governmental, religious, or educational institutions) can also reinforce individual or group power, thereby reducing the opportunity for equality and dialogue. The question then is whether spaces for dialogue can be effective in building the kind of dialogic space which is advocated in the White Paper, when so many influences around the dialogue are power-laden (Woodin et al., 2020).

This issue is recognized to some extent in the CoE White Paper, which notes that while all citizens need to be involved in this endeavor, it is also important to build structures within our organizations and institutions that address the process of living together as equals in diverse communities (CoE, 2008: 39). The White Paper offers universities in particular as examples where intercultural dialogue should – and could – be fostered. This important work was documented in relation to universities in a seminar (Wächter, 2009), where the need to recognize and articulate values in higher education policies was emphasized, and has since been developed, as follows in the next section.

Intercultural Dialogue in Policies and Practices

One way in which institutions can build structures addressing the processes of living together as equals in dignity is through developing policies and practices which encourage open and respectful exchange of views. Citing universities as an example, the White Paper states:

.... [T]he university is ideally defined precisely by its universality – its commitment to open-mindedness and openness to the world, founded on enlightenment values. The university thus has great potential to engender "intercultural intellectuals" who can play an active role in the public sphere. (CoE, 2008: 31)

The need for universities to embrace an intercultural dialogue perspective within – and beyond – the boundaries of their institutions is also recognized in the CoE White Paper (2008), and through subsequent seminars (e.g. Wächter, 2009). In the following section, we present two examples of how an intercultural dialogue approach has been adopted in internationalization policies and practices: one within the context of higher education, and the other within the broader context of education in general.

A framework for an intercultural dialogue (ICD) approach in higher education

With the purpose of tracking the traces of intercultural dialogue in internationalization policies within higher education, we have previously argued that such policies offer an opportunity to openly recognize core values of democracy, human rights and the rule of law and a commitment to mutual respect and understanding (Woodin *et al.*, 2011). In our analysis of national and local policy documents from three European universities, we found sporadic and implicit evidence for a commitment to intercultural dialogue, mainly through evidence of educationalist approaches in policy at local rather than national level (often at the very local level of the classroom). We concluded that the concept of intercultural dialogue 'offers an opportunity to re-orient, clarify and justify in human (individual and social) development terms internationalization policies, strategies and activities, thus moving from the discourse of instrumentalism to that of educationalism' (Woodin *et al.*, 2011: 129). We understood that to address the issue of internationalization from an ICD perspective, higher education institutions need to become aware of their underlying discourses of internationalization though making their own position explicit and adopt social and educational values and practices. We proposed a framework for implementing an ICD approach in higher education that is intended to help readers to consider the rationales underlying the national and local policy of their university as a two-way process, offering examples of what would need to happen in universities.

In a recent edited volume (Lundgren *et al.*, 2020), contributors offered reflections on theory and practice that address internationalization of higher education in ways which encompass an ICD approach as a vehicle for possible development and transformation of individuals in a process of active engagement. It aligns with an educational approach to internationalization, 'which recognizes the personal and societal value of learning itself, contributes to a person's self-understanding and stimulates meta-reflection' (Lundgren *et al.*, 2020: xxii).

Building on this work and learning from the suggestions and challenges from colleagues in the edited volume (Lundgren *et al.*, 2020), we proposed a revised[7] framework for implementing an ICD approach in universities. It was built through a process of dialogue with the contributors to the edited volume that brought a range of perspectives. It focused – among other aspects – on the role of multiple languages and perspectives, including the term 'intercultural' itself (Ortiz *et al.*, 2020), staff development (Golubeva, 2020; Savvides, 2020), multiple perspectives in planning internationalization (Schuessler, 2020), engagement of those outside universities (Porto, 2020), the need for an integrated approach (Wang & Holmes, 2020) which does not simply focus on 'foreign' international students but learning from home diversity (Deardorff & Woodin, 2020), the question of intercultural learning in the context of internationalization at home (Borghetti & Zanoni, 2020), financial constraints on policies (Clarke & Yang, 2020), the contribution of student perspectives on internationalization (Saurwein *et al.*, 2020), the integration of internationalization in a dialogic and educationalist perspective (Risager & Tranekjær, 2020), the need to make explicit the value-base in internationalization strategy (Lundgren, 2020) and the importance of identifying and addressing historic inequalities (Parmenter *et al.*, 2020).

A framework for a democratic culture approach in education

A second example of intercultural dialogue within policies and practices is the Reference Framework of Competences for Democratic Culture (RFCDC) published by the Council of Europe (2018). This document aims to offer a systematic approach for the 'empowerment' of social actors 'within any social group, for example in an education institution, a workplace, a political system (local, national, international), a leisure organisation, or an NGO' (CoE, 2018: 20). It provides a framework for teaching, learning and assessment of competences for democratic culture. It is intended for use by educationalists in all sectors of education systems, founded on the values promoted by the CoE of human rights, democracy, and the rule of law:

> The Framework will help to create education which ensures that humanity flourishes, that the individual's human rights are protected and that democratic values are expressed through public bodies and other institutions that affect citizens. The competences specified by the Framework define a capacity to create or restructure institutions or processes in a peaceful manner, in order to generate and reinforce democratic societies. This includes citizens complying with existing practices and also actively engaging in practices judged to be in need of change. (CoE, 2018: 15)

What is important to note is the key role given not only to education institutions but also to practitioners ('educationalists' as referred in the RFCDC, p. 65) to foster a culture of democracy and intercultural dialogue to empower the individuals/learners to become autonomous and respectful democratic citizens. From this educational perspective, the learners are at the core of their own learning process which requires active engagement within and outside the institutions as a whole person, activating their intellect, emotions and experiences.

The RFCDC Framework proposes 20 competencies required for democratic citizenship (see Chapter 4, this volume). Embedded within what has become commonly known as the 'butterfly model' because of its four-winged shape (see CoE, 2018), these competences are likely to be applied in clusters, depending on the situation. The four wings of this model represent the overarching categories of attitudes, skills, knowledge and critical understanding, and values. It offers an opportunity for operationalizing an intercultural dialogue approach within institutional policies and practices; it adopts an educational pedagogy, counteracting instrumentality, based on humanistic ideas and reflected in the concept of *Bildung* (discussed below).

Once the concept of intercultural dialogue is brought into an institution, it becomes an educational approach to policy and practice that requires greater emphasis on educational *processes*. If shared aims in encounters (in the broadest sense of the word) relate to understanding and respecting each other, this necessarily means that we will need to know more about what we believe in, what are our values, whether as individuals or groups (or indeed institutions).

Values in Educational Policies and Practices

So far, the focus of this chapter has been on intercultural dialogue (CoE, 2008) as a processual concept underlying the two presented examples of frameworks for policy and practice in education: an ICD approach, based on the White Paper, and specifically composed for internationalization in higher education (Lundgren *et al.*, 2020; Woodin *et al.*, 2011) and the RFCDC developed to promote and enhance education at all levels for democratic citizenship, human rights education and intercultural education (CoE, 2018). Here, we shift the focus to the values of these frameworks and their foundation and consider their ideological base. Our intention is now to analyze how they resonate with the overriding concept of *Bildung* and with Mike Byram's works.

Values can be individual and societal; they are prescriptive, lead to action and constitute a desirable goal (CoE, 2018: 78):

> A value is a belief about a desirable goal that motivates action and serves as a guiding principle in life across many situations. Values have a normative prescriptive quality about what should be done or thought. (…) At the individual psychological level, values are internalised social representations or moral beliefs that people appeal to as the ultimate rationale for their actions. However, values are not simply individual traits but social agreements about what is right, good, or to be cherished. They are codes or general principles guiding action (…).

Teachers at all levels continuously take actions by asking themselves the important questions about the contents, methods and purpose of their own teaching: *What? How?* and *Why?* Every educator constantly makes personal choices, consciously or unconsciously, based on epistemology, ideology and conceptions of the world. How an educator constructs the meaning of relevant concepts is of vital importance for the impact of her students' learning. Underlying the *Why?* question is the value base, which in its turn leads up to the purpose of the activity and practice. This educational discussion was vivid during the last decades of the previous millennium. The old concept of *Didaktik* had its revival in a number of European countries, a word that may have different connotations to an English-speaking audience. This concept refers to critical questions about contents, methods and purpose and has created a new educational field, having in common a critical stance to the process of teaching and learning, recognizing that education is based on values.

We return now to the two examples of educational frameworks discussed above and consider how values are articulated in each of them. The ICD approach requires open and respectful exchanges of perspectives with the aim of understanding diverse views and practices and valuing others, as an end in itself. These values are clearly aligned with those of the CoE (given that the ICD approach developed from the 2008 White Paper). The values articulated in the RFCDC framework are explicitly named as part of the 'butterfly' model, as: valuing human dignity and human rights; valuing cultural diversity; and valuing democracy, justice, fairness, equality, and the rule of law. In both these cases, the underpinning values resonate with the broader educational philosophy of *Bildung* and its values. This concept cannot be ignored in this chapter as there are clear influences from *Bildung* in RFCDC (see above), in an ICD approach and a strong presence in Byram's works.

Bildung as a value base

This term is German, and the concept is used in Germany and Scandinavia (*bildning* in Swedish and *dannelse* in Norway and Denmark). The English translation 'education' does not cover it completely. *Bildung* is a complex concept which we are unable to give exhaustive attention to in this chapter. Yet *Bildung,* as a humanistic educational concept, may be useful when trying to link values and purposes of learning and practice in intercultural approaches to education.

With its roots in Ancient Greece, the concept of *Bildung* was coined by Wilhelm von Humboldt in the 18th century, and it has returned in modern times in differently interpreted shapes. H.G. Gadamer has developed it in *Wahrheit und Methode* (1960) and argues that understanding is always created within a 'horizon of understanding' (Gadamer cited in Bohlin, 2013: 396). We interpret everything we encounter, from the horizon of understanding that we internalize from primary (home) and secondary (school) socialization during our upbringing.[8]

An example of *Bildung* in our time is exemplified in degree programs such as Liberal Arts as they appear in US universities, whose philosophical background is discussed in Martha Nussbaum's book *Cultivating Humanity: A Classical Defence of Liberal Education* (1997).[9] As authors of this chapter, we recognize the connection to a humanistic view on education as pleaded by Gustavsson (2014: 109): 'The very aim and meaning of *Bildung* is to humanize what is often considered to be an instrumental education and society, governed by goal-rationality or goal-means efficiency'. This rhymes with Coghlan and Brydon-Miller (2014) who understand that contemporary *Bildung* provides 'a counter to commodification of education and professional development' (2014: 79).

Taylor (2017: 419) argues that 'the notion of *Bildung* may offer conceptual sustenance to those who wish to develop educative practices to supplement or contest the prevalence and privileging of market and economic imperatives in higher education'.

Bohlin (2013) reminds us of the connection between intercultural dialogue, *Bildung* and higher education:

> I propose, civic *Bildung* is best understood as a disposition and competence to engage in dialogical encounters with people of different identities and background. This is not only a civic and democratic capacity, but also a capacity to develop as an individual by learning from others. The challenge for universities, then, is to find ways to promote the development of this capacity (...) [U]niversities should not only prepare students for future careers and provide them with a broad knowledge base, but also prepare them for life as active citizens in a democratic society and enable their personal development. (2013: 398)

Bohlin's understanding of *Bildung* echoes the value base of the CoE and shows us how the concept is related to intercultural dialogue. As noted earlier in this chapter, the CoE White Paper (2008) has a vital mission recognizing intercultural dialogue in higher education.

> Higher-education institutions play an important role in fostering intercultural dialogue, through their education programmes, as actors in broader society and as sites where intercultural dialogue is put into practice. (CoE, 2008: 32)

If we consider intercultural dialogue from a value-based perspective, the dilemma for universities arises as to how – and on what basis – their role is to tell students what values to accept (such direction is usually limited to secondary school activity). Referring to the moral and value-led aspects of *Bildung,* Bohlin (2013) recognizes this dilemma and proposes that the solution is to refer to transformative learning theory (Gadamer, 1989).[10]

As educators in higher education, we can lead and encourage students to self-cultivation (Bohlin, 2013). Democratic and humanistic values are, then absolute conditions of *Bildung*, and go hand in hand with an educational aim of developing a disposition and competence to engage in dialogical encounters with people of different identities and background.

Understanding intercultural dialogue as a developmental process (CoE, 2008; Lundgren *et al.*, 2020; Woodin *et al.*, 2011) echoes with this broader educational philosophy, *Bildung* and its values, in the sense of 'a rich process of bringing out (*educere* in Latin) the potentials of students in the *Bildung* meaning which implies transformation' (Byram, 2020: 16).[11] In the next section, we explore the work of Mike Byram, who brings our attention to the 'complementarity of Bildung and action' (2010: 320). Byram's work is a valuable contribution to understand the transformative dimension of intercultural dialogue in the field of Education. Below, we will be drawing on his work, in particular on Intercultural Communicative Competence (ICC) (1997, 2021), Intercultural Citizenship (2008) and internationalism (2020).

Values in Mike Byram's work

Bildung – 'that interplay between the individual and the world that is the "formation", perhaps "transformation", of the individual – continues to be central to debate about all education' (Byram, 2010: 319). *Bildung* is a central motivation for Byram in his development of the concepts of Intercultural Communicative Competence (ICC) and Intercultural Citizenship. ICC[12] (Byram, 1997) is an educational model which Byram has revisited more than two decades later (Byram, 2021). His major aim for returning to this widely known model is to make his first version more transparent as it sometimes has been misinterpreted. He also wants to make reference to the vast area of research which has followed since 1997. He has further developed and clarified the fifth component of his model, *critical cultural awareness (savoir s'engager)* (Byram, 2021: Preface). It is defined in his work as

> an ability to evaluate, critically and on the basis of an explicit systematic process of reasoning, values present in one's own and other cultures and countries (...) This educational component (...) adds for purposes of clarifying one's own ideological perspective and engaging with others consciously on the basis of this perspective. (Byram, 1997: 101; Byram 2021: 140)

The 1997 book is particularly focused on language learning with a 'critical as well as open approach' (1997: 113) to Self and Other and arguing that 'a critical stance is based on clearly articulated set of beliefs' (1997: 113). Critical cultural awareness forms the key value base for his later work on Education for Intercultural Citizenship (2008) where criticality as value becomes even more focused. Criticality in the 2008 book is more clearly connected to intercultural citizenship education, which has been applied not only to language learning but all education. The aim is to develop as a democratic and politically engaged citizen of the world, extending but not excluding national citizenship. Byram's work with the RFCDC model (CoE, 2018) has resulted in a greater and a more developed focus on critical cultural awareness as Risager points out (in the foreword to Byram, 2021: ix). Underlying ICC is the idea of the learner as 'an engaged and responsible citizen' (Byram, 2021). In the middle of his model of ICC is the concept of education, which he relates to *Bildung*. The mission of the teacher is to create opportunities for the student to develop as an individual, not mainly for private good but for public good.

Action in the world[13] is vital when Byram (2020) discusses internationalism as the preferred ideology behind internationalization in higher education, a recent field where he puts values in the foreground. He defines the concept of internationalism as 'a particular set of values and ideas forming a basis for action in the world' (2020: 16), arguing that,

> internationalism has a moral dimension which rejects ethnocentricity and puts in its place a set of liberal values. Change in an internationalist view will come through groups of people who act together (...) as an international entity to overcome the limits of what they could do within their nation and state (...). Internationalism can be the basis of change for good in the world (...). (Byram, 2020: 23–24)

According to Byram (2020), internationalization without the moral dimension of internationalism is just a set of organizational activities.

Byram acknowledges that his work for decades with the CoE has influenced his academic writing (Byram, 2021: 153–154). The influence of his ICC model can be discerned in *The Common European Framework of Reference for Languages* (CEFR) (CoE, 2001), although critical cultural awareness was not included in this framework. Byram's work with CoE teams on the Autobiography of Intercultural Encounters (CoE, 2009) focuses more strongly on the core values of critical cultural awareness in the portfolio connected to RFCDC (CoE, 2018), a further 'attempt to deal systematically with interculturality in ways that the CEFR had not managed to do' (Byram, 2021: Conclusion).

Concluding Remarks

We have considered *Bildung* and the contribution of Mike Byram's work as essential to recognize an intercultural dialogue (ICD) approach in Education. Within *Bildung* we find elements that highlight further the values of intercultural dialogue as presented in the CoE documents and that imply an engagement in dialogic encounters with people of different identities and backgrounds; these we also find in Byram's work (and in the ICD and RFCDC frameworks discussed above).

Once the concept of intercultural dialogue is introduced in an institutional context, the focus of work becomes more process-oriented than product-oriented, and the role of values becomes all the more essential in developing meaningful educational purposes: 'At the heart of theory and practice (...) in education in general is the need to clarify purposes' (Byram, 2010: 317). Underpinning the democratic and humanistic values of *Bildung* are the educational purposes of self-cultivation, personal development and a process of transforming one's perspective in encounters with others: developing the individual for life as an active intercultural citizen for public good.

The CoE White Paper, an ICD approach, RFCDC, Byram's work and a contemporary *Bildung* concept all have in common a process-oriented educational purpose based on a similar set of values. They all focus on the development of the individual learner (or citizen) in and outside educational institutions in order to become an active responsible intercultural citizen encompassing democratic and humanistic values.

The focus on values in intercultural dialogue brings with it an uncomfortable feeling too. It can be easy for moral relativism to creep in while our relatively 'rich nations' of the world congratulate ourselves on succeeding in being inclusive and responding to others in an equal and respectful manner (Woodin *et al.*, 2020). As recognized earlier in this chapter, we wonder: how possible is it to have equal encounters in such an unequal world? We have not done justice to this pressing perspective in this chapter, but hope that the discussion here can offer some contributions in this direction, if only through recognizing the limitations of our work.

Finally, we would like to make a personal reflection about the importance of dialogue in our own development as researchers. As explained at the beginning of this chapter, we, the three authors, recognize that our work would not have arrived at the place it has if we had undertaken it independently. Our (intercultural) research dialogue brings us to new spaces – not necessarily third spaces – but where we are more than the sum of our parts. It is thanks to our meeting at Cultnet – the initiative started by Mike Byram in 1997 – that we have had this opportunity to work together and share thoughts and experiences in a rich intercultural dialogue with colleagues from across the world.

We cannot ignore the unequal power relationships involved between a professor in a top UK university and PhD students grappling with finding a voice and/or understanding the meaning of their research. In the early days of Cultnet, this was the typical scenario in the cold room of the School of Education in Durham.[14] Typically, we would be 10–15 PhD students from European[15] higher education institutions, between 1 and 3 members of Durham academic staff, spending two days listening to each other's thoughts, research reports, questions, challenges, etc. The magic of those events was – and still is – in the open spaces facilitated by Mike, where each member had the same length of time to use in whatever way they wished – to explain their issues, blocks, pressing questions, research approaches, with a sense of mutual respect, and joint endeavor in understanding our challenge to grasp and promote intercultural competence. It is thanks to Mike's powerful ability to relinquish power at the points needed to develop the I-You spaces of Buber's relationship-building where we could share our common humanity (CoE). This affirmation of who we were at whatever stage we were at in our research journey has had a longer-lasting effect on our motivation than any quick or clever intellectual response to an academic challenge. It is our destiny now to continue this and adopt intercultural dialogue processes in all aspects of our lives.

Notes

(1) We have opted to keep the acronym when intercultural dialogue approach (ICD) is referred to and leave intercultural dialogue with no acronym when referring to the concept.

(2) For a more extensive CoE definition, see section 'Values in Educational Policies and Practices'.

(3) https://ec.europa.eu/neighbourhood-enlargement/policy/from-6-to-27-members_en

(4) See, for example, the work of the dialogue society (http://www.dialoguesociety.org/), or Bohm, Factor & Garrett http://www.david-bohm.net/dialogue/dialogue_proposal.html (accessed 17.08.20).

(5) The term understanding can also be understood differently; see, for example, Bredella (2003).

(6) A Bakhtinian perspective would also argue that the multiplicity of perspectives is evident in dialogue.

(7) For a first version, see Woodin et al. (2011).

(8) Byram (1997: 34) talks about a process of tertiary socialization when an individual is 'relativizing self and valuing others'.

(9) The relationship to the concept of Bildung is clearly evidenced in Nussbaum's book, although she does not specifically use the term Bildung.

(10) For transformative learning theory, see also, for example, Taylor and Cranton (2012).

(11) For an extensive discussion on Education, see Fleming (2009).

(12) See Chapter 1 of this volume.

(13) See Barnett (1997).

(14) Early Cultnet meetings always took place in December; we regularly found ourselves searching the local charity shops for an additional warm jumper or scarf to counteract the day-long concentration on research discussions.

(15) Soon, PhD students from other parts of the world joined our Cultnet meetings.

References

Bakhtin, M. (1986) *Speech Genres and Other Late Essays* (C. Emerson and M. Holquist, eds; V. McGee, trans.). Austin: University of Texas Press.

Barnett, R. (1997) *Higher Education: A Critical Business*. Buckingham: Society for Research into Higher Education and the Open University Press.

Bohlin, H. (2013) Bildung and intercultural understanding. *Intercultural Education* 24 (5), 391–400. https://doi.org/10.1080/14675986.2013.826019

Bohm, D. (1979) Interview with David Suzuki, 26 May 1979, for CBC Canada TV 'The nature of things [Video]. https://www.youtube.com/watch?v=r-jI0zzYgIE

Bohm, D. (1996) *On Dialogue*. Oxon: Routledge.

Borghetti, C. and Zanoni, G. (2020) Student and staff perspectives on Internationalisation at Home: A local investigation. In U. Lundgren, P. Castro and J. Woodin (eds) *Educational Approaches to Internationalization through Intercultural Dialogue. Reflections on Theory and Practice* (pp. 169–182). Oxon and New York: Routledge.

Bourdieu, P. (1991) *Language and Symbolic Power* (Gino Raymond and Matthew Adamson, transl.). Cambridge, MA: Harvard University Press.

Bredella, L. (2003) For a flexible model of intercultural understanding. In G. Alred, M. Byram and M. Fleming (eds) *Intercultural Experience and Education* (pp. 31–49). Clevedon: Multilingual Matters.

Buber, M. (1971) *I and Thou* (Walter Kaufmann, transl.). New York. Touchstone.

Byram, M. (1997) *Teaching and Assessing Intercultural Communicative Competence.* Clevedon: Multilingual Matters.

Byram, M. (2008) *From Foreign Language Education to Education for Intercultural Citizenship: Essays and Reflections.* Clevedon: Multilingual Matters.

Byram, M. (2010) Linguistic and cultural education for Bildung and citizenship *Modern Language Journal* 94 (2), 317–321.

Byram, M., Golubeva, I., Han, H. and Wagner, M. (eds) (2017) *From Principles to Practice* in *Education for Intercultural Citizenship.* Bristol: Multilingual Matters.

Byram, M. (2020) An internationalist perspective on internationalisation. In U. Lundgren, P. Castro and J. Woodin (eds) *Educational Approaches to Internationalization through Intercultural Dialogue. Reflections on Theory and Practice* (pp. 15–26). London: Routledge.

Byram, M. (2021) *Teaching and Assessing Intercultural Communicative Competence: Revisited.* Bristol: Multilingual Matters.

Carbaugh, D., Khatsevich, E., Saito, M. and Shin, D. (2011) 'Dialogue' in Japanese, Korean, and Russian: A cultural discourse analysis of communication codes. *Journal of International and Intercultural Communication* 4 (2), 87–108.

Castro, P., Lundgren, U. and Woodin, J. (2020) Intercultural dialogue: An educational approach. In U. Lundgren, P. Castro and J. Woodin (eds) *Educational Approaches to Internationalization through Intercultural Dialogue: Reflections on Theory and Practice* (pp. 3–14). Oxon and New York: Routledge.

Clarke, M. and Hui Yang, L. (2020) Strategic approaches to internationalisation and intercultural dialogue: Policy and practices in the Republic of Ireland. In U. Lundgren, P. Castro and J. Woodin (eds) *Educational Approaches to Internationalization through Intercultural Dialogue. Reflections on Theory and Practice* (pp. 57–70). Oxon and New York: Routledge.

Coghlan, D. and Brydon-Miller, M. (2014) *The SAGE Encyclopedia of Action Research* (Vols. 1–2). Los Angeles: SAGE Publications Ltd. https://dx.doi.org/10.4135/9781446294406

Council of Europe (2001) *Common European Framework of Reference for Languages: Learning, Teaching, Assessment.* Cambridge: Cambridge University Press.

Council of Europe (2008) *White Paper on Intercultural Dialogue: "Living Together as Equals in Dignity".* Council of Europe. www.coe.int/t/dg4/intercultural/WhitePaper_InterculturalDialogue_2_en.asp#

Council of Europe (2009) *Autobiography of Intercultural Encounters.* Strasbourg: Council of Europe.

Council of Europe (2018) *Reference Framework of Competences for Democratic Culture. Volume 1. Context, Concepts and Model.* Strasbourg: Council of Europe.

Deardorff, D. and Woodin, J. (2020) Higher education internationalization process in the USA: Successes and lessons learned in relation to intercultural dialogue. In U. Lundgren, P. Castro and J. Woodin (eds) *Educational Approaches to Internationalization through Intercultural Dialogue: Reflections on Theory and Practice* (pp. 126–136). Oxon and New York: Routledge.

Fleming, M. (2009) Introduction. Education and training: Becoming interculturally competent. In A. Feng, M. Byram and M. Fleming (eds) *Becoming Interculturally Competent through Education and Training* (pp. 1–12). Bristol: Multilingual Matters.

Gadamer, H.G. (1989) *Truth and Method*. (2nd rev. edn). Sheed and Ward (German original *Wahrheit und Methode,* first published 1960).

Ganesh, S. and Holmes, P. (2011) Positioning intercultural dialogue – Theories, pragmatics, and an agenda. *Journal of International and Intercultural Communication* 4 (2), 81–86. https://doi.org/10.1080/17513057.2011.557482

Golubeva, I. (2020) Enhancing faculty and staff engagement in internationalisation: A Hungarian example of training through intercultural dialogue. In U. Lundgren, P. Castro and J. Woodin (eds) *Educational Approaches to Internationalization through Intercultural Dialogue. Reflections on Theory and Practice* (pp. 183–194). Oxon and New York: Routledge.

Gustavsson, B. (2014) Bildung and the road from a classical into a global and postcolonial concept. *Confero* 2 (1), 109–131.

Holmes, P. (2014) Intercultural dialogue: Challenges to theory, practice and research. *Language and Intercultural Communication* 14 (1), 1–6.

Lähdesmäki, T., Koistinen, A-K. and Ylönen, S.C. (2020) *Intercultural Dialogue in the European Education Policies. A Conceptual Approach*. Cham: Palgrave Macmillan.

Leeds-Hurwitz, W. (2013) What is intercultural dialogue? Harron Lecture at Villanova University on November 11, 2013, available at https://www.youtube.com/watch?v=9YSQPcEFp48 (accessed 10 October 2018).

Lundgren, U., Castro, P. and Woodin, J. (eds) (2020) *Educational Approaches to Internationalization through Intercultural Dialogue: Reflections on Theory and Practice*. Oxon and New York: Routledge.

Lundgren, U. (2020) Internationalization as individual development: A national strategy through an intercultural dialogue lens. In U. Lundgren, P. Castro and J. Woodin (eds) *Educational Approaches to Internationalization through Intercultural Dialogue: Reflections on Theory and Practice* (pp. 43–56). Oxon and New York: Routledge.

Morris, P. (ed.) (2003) *The Bakhtin Reader: Selected Writings of Bakhtin, Medvedev, Voloshinov*. London: Arnold Publishers.

Nussbaum, M.C. (1997) *Cultivating Humanity: A Classical Defense of Reform in Liberal Education*. Cambridge, MA: Harvard University Press.

Ortiz, J.M., Usma, J.A. and Gutierrez, C.P. (2020) Critical intercultural dialogue opening new paths to internationalization in HE: Repositioning local languages and cultures in foreign language policies. In U. Lundgren, P. Castro and J. Woodin (eds) *Educational Approaches to Internationalization through Intercultural Dialogue: Reflections on Theory and Practice* (pp. 71–85). Oxon and New York: Routledge.

Porto, M. (2020) Intercultural citizenship as an opportunity for bottom-up intercultural dialogue internationalization in South America. In U. Lundgren, P. Castro and J. Woodin (eds) *Educational Approaches to Internationalization through Intercultural Dialogue: Reflections on Theory and Practice* (pp. 150–168). Oxon and New York: Routledge.

Parmenter, L., Bowell, T., Calvert, S., Longhurst, R. and Tiakiwai, S.-J. (2020) Intercultural dialogue in an Aotearoa New Zealand university: Strategy and curriculum. In U. Lundgren, P. Castro and J. Woodin (eds) *Educational Approaches to Internationalization through Intercultural Dialogue: Reflections on Theory and Practice* (pp. 86–97). Oxon and New York: Routledge.

Radkevych, V. (2015) Studying dialogue in linguistics: Main aspects. *The Advanced Science Journal* 3, 68–71.

Risager, K. and Tranekjær, L. (2020) Intercultural dialogue in a critical and multilingual perspective. In U. Lundgren, P. Castro and J. Woodin (eds) *Educational Approaches to Internationalization through Intercultural Dialogue: Reflections on Theory and Practice* (pp. 139–149). Oxon and New York: Routledge.

Risager, K. (2021) Foreword. In M. Byram *Teaching and Assessing Intercultural Communicative Competence: Revisited* (pp. ix–xi). Bristol: Multilingual Matters.

Saurwein, L., Pauzenberger, C. and Hang Xu, F. (2020) Are internationalization strategies and intercultural competence a fitted glove? A case study of part-time management students' learning experience through intercultural dialogue. In U. Lundgren, P. Castro and J. Woodin (eds) *Educational Approaches to Internationalization through Intercultural Dialogue. Reflections on Theory and Practice* (pp. 195–208). Oxon and New York: Routledge.

Savvides, N. (2020) Internationalising the curriculum: Education lecturers' understandings and experiences at a UK university. In U. Lundgren, P. Castro and J. Woodin (eds) *Educational Approaches to Internationalization through Intercultural Dialogue: Reflections on Theory and Practice* (pp. 98–110). Oxon and New York: Routledge.

Schuessler, M. (2020) The intersection of internationalisation: Constructing a knowledge framework grounded in intercultural dialogue. In U. Lundgren, P. Castro and J. Woodin (eds) *Educational Approaches to Internationalization through Intercultural Dialogue: Reflections on Theory and Practice* (pp. 27–40). Oxon and New York: Routledge.

Tannen, D. (1995) Waiting for the mouse: Constructed dialogues in conversation. In D. Tedlock and B. Mannheim (eds) *The Dialogic Emergence of Culture* (pp. 198–217). Champaign: University of Illinois Press.

Taylor, C. (2017) Is a posthumanist Bildung possible? Reclaiming the promise of Bildung for contemporary higher education. *Higher Education* 74 (3), 419–435.

Taylor, E.W. and Cranton, P. (2012) *The Handbook of Transformative Learning: Theory, Research, and Practice*. San Francisco: Jossey-Bass.

Vygotsky, L.S. (1970) *Thought and Language*. Cambridge, MA: The MIT Press.

Wang, C. and Holmes, P. (2020) The role of informal curricula in furthering intercultural dialogue: internationalization in a Chinese university. In U. Lundgren, P. Castro and J. Woodin (eds) *Educational Approaches to Internationalization through Intercultural Dialogue: Reflections on Theory and Practice* (pp. 111–125). Oxon and New York: Routledge.

Wierzbicka, A. (2006) The concept of 'dialogue' in cross-linguistic and cross-cultural perspective. *Discourse Studies* 8 (5), 675–703.

Woodin, J., Lundgren, U. and Castro, P. (2011) Tracking the traces of intercultural dialogue in internationalization policies of three EU universities: Towards a framework. *European Journal of Higher Education* 1 (2–3), 119–134.

Woodin, J., Castro, P. and Lundgren, U. (2020) Internationalization and higher education: questions from an educationalist/intercultural dialogue perspective. In U. Lundgren, P. Castro and J. Woodin (eds) *Educational approaches to Internationalization through Intercultural Dialogue: Reflections on Theory and Practice* (pp. 211–226). Oxon and New York: Routledge.

Wächter, B. (2009) Intercultural dialogue on the university campus. In S. Bergan and J.-P. Restoueix (eds) *Intercultural Dialogue on Campus* (pp. 133–140). Strasbourg: Council of Europe.

6 From Critical Cultural Awareness to Intercultural Responsibility: Language, Culture and Citizenship

Manuela Guilherme

An Autobiographical Introduction

It is impossible to start this chapter that celebrates Michael Byram's work without bringing an autobiographical note. Mike was my PhD supervisor and, in this role, he guided this section of my life through the last four years of the past century. I entered the 21st century waving a PhD certificate in Education from Durham University in December 2000, in a tremendous ceremony in an imposing building next to the Cathedral and, moreover, entitled to wear a ravishing gown for life …! That was the end of a marathon in my life and the beginning of a new one. However, Mike has remained my mentor and confidant, to whom I turn when I need wise advice with regard to my research activities. I spent three enriching years in Durham, besides the valuable experience of teaching Portuguese at the University of Newcastle. It was precisely then when Mike generously started to organise the annual Cultnet meetings, which was then a network of doctoral students who were digging the same new field, all inspired by Mike's work. Mike and Marie-Thérèse were incredible hosts both for the occasional Cultnet participants as well as for the regular doctoral students. These events at their cosy home provided the background for more informal conversations about our common research projects, our countries of origin and our life experiences in Durham which would naturally establish a special 'intercultural' complicity and affection for life between all of us. There is a sense of belonging to a 'family'.

Byram's work fell into my hands for the first time at the main library at Stanford University, in 1991, while doing research for my Master's thesis on North-American Bilingual/Bicultural educational programmes. I remember reading then through his 1989 book, *Cultural Studies in Foreign Language Education* (Byram, 1989), which impressed me most because it responded precisely to my research interest at that moment. I was already a mid-career tenured secondary school teacher of English and German who had become a certified teacher educator in 1987, first under a national programme with the Ministry of Education for teacher trainers which aimed to design new curricula and introduce culture in language classes, followed by a job at the Nova University in Lisbon which required mainly the coordination of pre-service training centres for English teachers, including supporting seminars on teaching theories and methodologies. In the late 80s and through the 90s, I was regularly awarded study grants which enabled me to carry out research on this topic in various universities in the United States. It was thrilling to find out about a scholar in Europe who was developing a strong school, with a combination of theory and practice, in the same line of thought and experience. Besides, I was already cherishing the idea of progressing into a doctoral programme, if possible, abroad. Portugal had just joined the 'European Community', and it was the right moment to take an adventure in family and also provide my sons with the opportunity to live and study abroad. I had not long ago travelled with my eldest son to Scotland, and I could remember how fascinated we were as we looked at Durham Cathedral from inside the train; we could not then imagine the powerful symbolism that building would bring to our lives. But, in Palo Alto, in 1991, such possibility appeared as no more than a dream, and it still took another five years to make it happen.

I had only been contemplating a distant possibility to move to Durham when I received Byram, Morgan and colleagues' 1994 book, *Teaching-and-Learning Language-and-Culture* and read the magic key statement in its very last page: 'The resulting attitude might best be defined as **"critical cultural awareness"**, not only a critical stance but also an action-orientation' (1994: 187, my emphasis). If I still had any hesitation, it vanished at that moment. This keyword and its definition resonated with Paulo Freire's critical pedagogy on which I had been working and applying to our field of language teaching. Despite the personal and funding obstacles I would have in the way, I felt I had received the keyword for my new adventure; it was not any more a matter of considering other options. Moving to Durham and study what this 'critical cultural awareness' might mean, under Professor Michael Byram's supervision, started to seem like the Freire's utopian 'inédito viável', which I have translated elsewhere as 'the viable unknown' (2017a).

In the national teacher trainers' training programme, led by the Ministry of Education, designed and coordinated by Maria Emília Galvão, in which I had formally participated for two years, the main goal was to implement a daring curriculum development based on authentic materials and geared to introduce culture in language education with a critical approach. This valuable programme had abruptly ended due to changes in the government and in the Ministry of Education and Maria

Emília's move to Brussels. I then moved myself to the *Universidade Nova* in Lisbon to coordinate the pre-service English teacher training programme and start a Master's degree on Cultural Studies with a focus on American studies. In the summer of 1995, I was awarded a one-month grant to go to the School of Education, Durham University, in order to do some research under the supervision of Professor Mike Byram. When I first met him in person, I had their 1994 book in my hand and told him, pointing my finger to its last page and said: I would like to do my PhD thesis on this concept 'critical cultural awareness'! On my way back to Lisbon, I had to overcome each one of all sorts of obstacles, personal and professional, but one year later, I was already living in Durham, had registered as a PhD student at the School of Education and started as a Portuguese lecturer at Newcastle University, supported by the Instituto Camões. My eldest son was starting an MSci in the Department of Chemistry, and my youngest had become an A-level student at Durham Johnstone School. It had not been easy nor was it going to be, but it was certainly worth it. It definitely changed our lives, for the three of us. None of us would be doing what we have been doing, in the way we have been doing, without our Durham adventure. In their simple way, Mike Byram and Marie-Thérèse touched the lives of many of us who are now scattered around the world and part of a larger and larger network.

Well, finally arrived here and now, I am going to revisit the introduction of the 'critical cultural awareness' concept by Mike Byram in the early 90s (Byram, 1994), to describe how I developed it during the following decade (Guilherme, 2002) and finally reflect on how and why this argument has lost steam and given way to other terminologies and ideas which have responded to other trends in Europe. I will then argue for an adapted terminology, that of 'critical intercultural awareness' which I have adopted (Guilherme & Souza, 2019), since I find it more appropriate for current times, and finally discuss the conceptual framework within which I have developed the idea of 'intercultural responsibility' (Guilherme, 2020a, 2020b). The development of critical cultural awareness meant a tremendous challenge to language teachers, not only those who were still adopting grammar and functional approaches to language education but also for those already exploring communicative approaches, and considering that then nations mainly defined personal identities and linguistic entities. It opened the door for an interdisciplinary approach to language education, greatly supported by sociolinguistics and sociology of education. Critical intercultural awareness then pushed language education into a much more dynamic process by contextualising it in complex conceptual frameworks, namely that of the 'intercultural', and placing it within the political and social challenges in current times of transnationalisation. Finally, my proposal for the development of intercultural responsibility, both in the contexts of education and research, aims to move beyond European borders by adopting a decolonial, critical and inter-epistemic stand towards knowledge and cognitive and social justice. It provides a challenge for language and citizenship education as well as for interdisciplinary and transnational research.

Mike Byram's Proposal of 'Critical Cultural Awareness'

In the late 80s and early 90s, Byram was involved in national and international projects in Europe on language teaching with a focus on 'cultural awareness', the role of language and culture teaching in the curriculum, its relationship with mother tongue education and its impact on social life through intercultural citizenship education. These interrelated topics reflect how Byram presented a broader understanding of language education with a strong influence on language teachers' development programmes at university level and on language education curricula, at all levels, in Europe and worldwide. It is evident in Byram's work the strong link between practice and theory which I believe also relies in his early experience as a secondary school teacher. In every dimension, Byram is a 'teacher', not in the sense that he aims to transmit knowledge but that he attempts to elicit knowledge creation from his audience, based on practice. Hence, his view of education is broader, contextual and developmental. Byram explained: 'It is evident from this perspective that to speak a language is to speak a culture, to exchange language which embodies a particular way of thinking and living, some parts of which are highly specific to the social group in question' (1992: 169). His publications brought researchers on language teaching to Durham University School of Education and, from there, many international and intercontinental networks were established. At the turn of the century, Byram managed to turn the School of Education at Durham University into an international and intercontinental hub in research on language teaching.

By that time, he also became very active at the Council of Europe and participated in the elaboration of important documents, at the European level to start with, but which were also adopted worldwide. This has lately been an argument against his work, that of being Eurocentric, which is rather hollow and biased because one thing is that Europe is indeed, and legitimately, Byram's 'locus of enunciation', that is, his theoretical and practical background is mainly rooted in international Europe, broadly speaking. However, this does not mean that we may assume that his stand is closed in itself, ethnocentric, nationalistic, not dialoguing with the world, which is absolutely not the case. Such, self-called non-Eurocentric, arguments are themselves as biased, oblivious and blind as the genuinely Eurocentric ones.

Byram first addresses the term 'cultural awareness' in reference to the report of the Working Party on Modern Foreign Languages, issued in the late 1980s, in the context of the elaboration of a new version of the National Curriculum in England, which proposed that 'cultural awareness should be given explicit and systematic attention in the Programme of Study', although 'the Working group does not define either culture or cultural awareness' according to Byram *et al.* (1995: 5). At least not sufficiently which leads Byram to undertake that task while coordinating national and international projects where teachers are elicited about those concepts. Byram was therefore setting the stage for the development of cultural awareness which would lead to his concept of 'critical cultural awareness'. In this regard, Byram touched specific issues such as, for example, culture and language learning in higher education which should provide students with interdisciplinary knowledge, for example, about institutions of target societies (1993) and cultural awareness as vocabulary learning, in relation to which Byram appropriately reminds us that 'the essence of understanding the cultural content of words is in their connotations' (1997a: 52). Both elements, that of an interdisciplinary approach to cultural content and that of the encounter of different conceptual frameworks which determine clashes between word connotations, have revealed to be decisive for a critical perception of cultural awareness. It cannot be forgotten that Byram's approach to language and culture teaching is very much inspired by both the British School of Cultural Studies, namely Raymond Williams et al. (Byram, 1997a, 1997b), as well as by the communicative approach to language which had been developing by sociolinguistis, such as Hymes, Stern and van Ek, for example (Byram, 1997c).

In the meantime, in a joint authorship (Byram *et al.*, 1994), Byram continued to develop the background for his idea of critical cultural awareness and claimed for a 'critical perspicacity and a neutral empathetic construction of cultural norms [which] is necessary to appreciate the relevant cultural context' in cultural awareness (1994: 29). However, combining a '**critical** perspicacity' and a '**neutral** empathetic construction' (my emphasis) in order to define (critical) cultural awareness may seem contradictory, not only in between these elements but also, and foremost, when associated with the notion of *savoir s'engager* to which it is linked in later publications (Byram, 1997c). *Savoir s'engager* – critical cultural awareness was the fifth dimension of Intercultural Communicative Competence, a matrix developed in collaboration with Geneviève Zarate under the umbrella of Sociocultural Competence put forward by the Council of Europe in preparation of the Common European Framework of Reference for Languages, a document with a strong impact in language education in Europe and worldwide at the turn of the century. To the four *savoirs*, namely *savoir être, savoir faire, savoir apprendre* and *savoirs*, Byram added *savoir s'engager*, by which he meant critical cultural awareness/ political education, and defined as 'an ability to evaluate critically and on the basis of explicit criteria perspectives, practices and products in one's own and other cultures and countries' (Byram, 1997c: 63). On the whole, Byram aims to make cultural awareness explicitly reflexive, comparative and evaluative and hence considers it the 'educational' component of

Intercultural Communicative Competence *par excellence* and, therefore, a 'crucial' aim for foreign language teaching (Byram, 1997c: 101–103). Therefore, the 'political' element, which inspired his contributions to the formulation of Intercultural Citizenship Education, also drawn on Doyé's concept of 'political education' (Byram, 1996, 2002), had the purpose 'of clarifying one's own ideological perspective and engaging with others consciously on the basis of that perspective' which 'may include conflict in perspectives, not only harmonious communication' (Byram, 1997c: 101). Byram's proposal of critical cultural awareness included some ingredients, namely that of being explicit, ideological and conflictual, when unavoidable, in a perspective which might seem to call for radical and transformative action. However, his critical and political approach to critical cultural awareness remained very much tied with communication, while action and transformation are left within the constraints of social and political systems in place, more clearly, without envisaging structural changes in power relations. I am not talking about undemocratic revolution, but about thick interrogation and adopting deep cultural and epistemological decolonisation. It is perhaps not a matter of character but one of degree. In this line, Byram's work pays tribute to sociolinguistic theories of communication and dialogue and coincides, in several aspects, with Habermas' Theory of Communicative Action while he calls 'for socialisation into a common political culture as a minimum basis for an integrated Europe' (Byram & Risager, 1999: 47). Ultimately, Byram remains a pragmatist, very much according to the British tradition and also in Dewey's style, as I argued elsewhere (Guilherme & Menezes de Souza, 2019c, see below).

Byram (2002) explains what he means by 'politics in education' which he considers 'is the role education, including language education, plays in changing societies for the better' and leaves what he means by 'better' for further debate while referring to Dewey's statement that democracy is the best means to achieve a better society (2002: 45). Yet, Byram leaves us with the doubt about what makes this role political, what must/can be changed and how. Later, Byram is more specific about critical cultural awareness/political education which, according to him, implies 'introducing a perspective of mediation and communication that does not presuppose democracy as the only source of values and governance' since it only 'offers apparent common ground' as 'it is understood differently in different societies' (2008: 165). Although this perception of democracy is not developed along this line in the book, except for the 'importance of individuals being aware of their own ideology – political or religious ...' (2008: 165), we may infer that it nevertheless implies an intercultural understanding of critical cultural awareness, to be discussed later below.

More recently, in an interview (Porto, 2013), Byram provides us with his mature understanding of this term 'critical cultural awareness', which he had offered to the world two decades earlier, to which many horizons had been added and to which he eventually sets some limits. Critical cultural awareness/political education, the term *savoir s'engager* is here only briefly mentioned, calls for action, but not political action, since the teacher cannot have a political agenda and must remain essentially neutral. In sum, the teacher's role demands, on the whole, that they urge students to have a questioning attitude to what they have taken for granted. Here, as before (Byram, 2002), Byram endorses his proposal as moral education too, and it is in this confluence that citizenship education is settled.

Manuela Guilherme's Development of the 'Critical Cultural Awareness'

I brought my theoretical background on language education, cultural studies, bilingual/bicultural educational programmes and Freire's critical pedagogy together with my practical experience as an international researcher, curriculum developer and teacher educator along to my doctoral thesis to be focused on Byram's term 'critical cultural awareness'. I departed from a discussion of Freire's dialogical theory on critical pedagogy from a perspective of cultural politics, citizenship education and teacher development (Guilherme, 2002). I addressed critical pedagogy in language and cultural education as a language of critique and possibility along with the analysis of the Freirean concepts of reflection, dissent, difference, dialogue, empowerment, action and hope. While analysing these leading concepts in Freirean critical pedagogy, I also drew on various other authors, among them Henry Giroux, Catherine Walsh, Antonia Darder, Michel Foucault, Chantal Mouffe and John Dewey. The latter was an important source for complementing the idea of citizenship education in relation to Freire's critical pedagogy, despite the differences between both approaches. In sum, to enclose my contribution to critical (inter)cultural awareness or to intercultural competence into one single perspective, that is, by putting it into an already existing box, as it has often been attempted, misses its essential character of a border, frontier, intercultural, inter-epistemic, intercontinental, South-North-South approach.

Freire was introduced to Dewey's work by another important Brazilian scholar in the beginning of the 20th century, Anisio Teixeira, who had met Dewey at the University of Columbia while taking a Master's in education there. To my knowledge, Freire only mentioned Dewey once, in a remarkable introductory text to Giroux's 1988 book, both entitled 'Teachers as Intellectuals', and he did it in the following terms:

> I believe that central to a realizable critical pedagogy is the need to view schools as democratic public spheres. This means regarding schools as democratic sites dedicated to forms of self and social empowerment. ...

> This position owes a great deal to John Dewey's views on democracy, but it goes beyond his position in a number of ways, and these are worth mentioning. … it points to the role that teachers and administrators might play as transformative intellectuals who develop counterhegemonic pedagogies that not only empower students … but also educate them for transformative action. … This is very different from Dewey's view, because I see democracy as involving not only a pedagogical struggle but also a political and social struggle. (1988: xxxii–xxxiii)

I have more recently undertaken a comparative analysis between Freire and Dewey's theoretical proposals and respective practical implementation, in the form of two articles published in Brazil. There, an intercultural dialogue is established between Freire's and Dewey's works through a comparative analysis between the (post)colonial matrices of the Americas, as if putting the North and the South between mirrors. Differences between both (post)colonial matrices are examined as well as their impact into the respective political and social frameworks which contextualise each of their bodies of work (Guilherme, 2018). Both colonisation matrices and decolonisation processes are compared to each other, which allows for an analysis of how these built the conceptual frameworks of democratic life in each territory and how Freire and Dewey's ideas of language, cultural diversity and education emerge from such historical backgrounds. In Guilherme (2017b), Freire's and Dewey's visions of the future are dealt with by taking into account their positions in time and space, their philosophical and epistemological standings with regard to reflexive thinking, pedagogy, knowledge and action. Both influential scholars aim to build the future of their societies through education, either by 'problem posing' (Freire) or by 'problem solving' (Dewey) and the difference between these two proposals determine their educational goals.

It seems appropriate, at this stage, to recall a comparative appreciation of Byram and Guilherme's interpretations of 'critical cultural awareness' which, by coincidence, refers to Dewey and Freire:

> Their approaches differ, from the beginning, in that, in our understanding, Byram's approach to critical awareness in language and culture education may be characterised as one of a pragmatist Deweyan kind while Guilherme's is more inspired by the utopian Freirean proposal, in the sense that Paulo Freire refers as the accomplishment of the "inédito viável" that Guilherme translates as the "[viable unknown] the 'not yet' that is still deemed feasible". (Guilherme & Menezes de Souza, 2019c: 8)

However, I expanded the philosophical foundations of 'critical cultural awareness' to the Frankfurt School's 'Critical Theory', by analysing the theoretical underpinnings developed by its different generations from Horkheimer to Habermas and 'post-modernism' in general, together with a focus on individual authors such as Lyotard, Derrida, Baudrillard, Foucault and Rorty, etc. (2002). The approach to such philosophical foundations has been misunderstood (by e.g. Ferri, 2018; Holliday, 2011), for its relevance in Freire's background for critical pedagogy has been ignored. The perspective taken at the referred philosophical foundations aimed to demonstrate that they brought support to one possible vision of 'critical cultural awareness' which explored Freire's development of criticality, culture, education and pedagogy providing a new epistemological and ontological proposal from the Global South (deeply contextualised in Latin America and Africa), not only geographically situated but also metaphorically illustrated. Yet, Freire's approach was very knowledgeable of the above-mentioned insider European critique of modernism – the latter constituting the bulk of epistemological colonialism – whose critique transpires throughout Freire's work. The authors mentioned above, who undertook a critique of modernism from inside, were also taken into account by Freire, as it has been recognised by his closest colleagues and carers of his legacy (e.g. Morrow & Torres, 2002; Torres, 2014; Walsh, 2015).

I then formulated the following definition of critical cultural awareness (2002), which does not contradict Byram's definition above:

> From the theoretical discussions and the empirical findings, we may conclude that critical cultural awareness entails *a philosophical, pedagogical, and political attitude towards culture.* It may be defined as *a reflective, exploratory, dialogical and active stance towards cultural knowledge and life that allows for dissonance, contradiction, and conflict as well as for consensus, concurrence, and transformation. It is a cognitive and emotional endeavour that aims at individual and collective emancipation, social justice, and political commitment.* (Guilherme, 2002: 219)

The understanding of critical cultural awareness here goes one step further in the direction of emancipation, social justice and political commitment; that is, it moves beyond a language of critique, and therefore questioning, into the language of possibility, that of Freire's 'inédito viável' (the viable unknown), the language of resistance and structural transformation.

Although the theory underlying the concept of 'critical cultural awareness' *per se*, put forward by Byram more than two decades ago, has not been much developed, theoretically speaking, it has been widely but marginally addressed under the umbrella theme of Intercultural Competence as can be confirmed, for example, across the issues of the *Language and Intercultural Communication* journal, which coincides chronologically with the time span under attention here. In this case and also in other journals, such as the *Language Learning Journal* (for example, Vences & Fay, 2015, about Mexican universities; Moncada Linares, 2016, from

Colombia; Afshar & Yousefi, 2019, from Iran), the term has often been referred to with regard to language teaching practices in different parts of the globe. It has also been inspirational to many articles where its three compounding words have been partially re-created in different combinations, although still under the umbrella theme of Intercultural Communicative Competence. A theoretical and practical study about this concept is also reported in a recent chapter (Guilherme & Sawyer, 2021), about a smaller replication in 2013 by Mark Sawyer of Guilherme's 2000 study, both with Portuguese and Japanese secondary school teachers of English, carried out both in Portugal and Japan. Critical cultural awareness was also the contents of Chapter 2 in Holliday (2011) and, more recently, has earned a renewed focus by Elinor Parks (2018, 2020a, 2020b), who has revived the implications of critical cultural awareness in higher education. In sum, the term and the concept of 'critical (inter)cultural awareness' remains promising as a legacy for the next decades when times force us out of the most recent 'quick fixes' (Phipps, 2010) which have rested at the surface of intercultural communication.

Critical Intercultural Awareness

Since it was introduced, the concept of critical cultural awareness was always embedded in an intercultural environment, once it was considered, by its author, as a key capacity within the Intercultural Communicative Competence framework and as a strong component of the 'intercultural speaker' (Byram, 1997c). It did not happen immediately, but it was only natural that, with an increasing inter-culturalisation of life, the term 'critical **inter**cultural awareness' had been smoothly introduced by other authors.

Byram provides us with his interpretation of the idea of the 'intercultural' mainly through his description of the 'intercultural speaker' whom he describes 'as a social actor whose interaction with others is coloured by the social identities he/she brings to communication situations and how those identities are perceived by other speakers of the language, both natives and non-natives' (1997b: 56). In this description, the power relations imbalance between social identities is not openly taken into account, although Byram (1996) refers to 'the horizontal dimension of European citizenship – [which] draws upon people's multiple identities' and argues that education must help young people 'to reflect upon their affective response, outside the classroom, to the vertical and horizontal relationships of citizenship' (1996: 66). Yet, we are left to wonder to what extent such 'affective' responses meet the demands of *savoir s'engager*. As far as the 'intercultural speaker' is concerned, Byram (1997c) adds to this character in such a way that the speaker 'is aware of potential conflict between their own and other ideologies and is able to establish common criteria ... and ... is able to negotiate agreement on places of conflict and acceptance of difference' (1997c: 63). Again, asymmetrical power which underlies dialogical consensus and corresponding pressure which manipulates final acceptance are again not problematised. Ultimately, Byram seems to advocate a standing of 'problem posing', by questioning what is taken for granted; however, his ultimate goal is one of pragmatic 'problem solving' based on dialogue, consensus and final acceptance.

Later, Byram shared his thoughts about what he meant by 'being intercultural' or 'acting interculturally' as opposed to 'being bilingual/bicultural'. Byram (2003) explains that, although being bilingual/bicultural may involve having 'a greater meta-awareness of language and an ability to decentre', 'acting interculturally involves a level of analytical awareness which does not necessarily follow from being bicultural' (2003: 64). And beyond, 'being intercultural and the state of "interculturality" may follow from acting interculturally' (Byram, 2012: 86). We may therefore conclude that, according to him, an intercultural mindfulness can be learned and practiced so that one eventually feels intercultural. To this definition of the state of 'interculturality', Byram (2012) still adds 'the notion of 'interculturalism', i.e. a belief in the value of being and acting as an intercultural person ... Like other '-isms', interculturalism is an ideology or belief system' (2012: 86). We are then led to understand that being and acting interculturally entails an ideological position. More than an ideology, according to Byram (2009), interculturality/ism also implies a moral standing, in that 'the intercultural speaker has a morality that is consciously brought to bear on the perspectives, practices, and products and that the morality is founded in the Kantian tradition' (2009: 324). Byram does not expand much on the philosophical, or even political, debates about the notion of 'the intercultural'; instead, he provides us with an analysis, amply illustrated, on the purposes of Intercultural Communicative Competence and the intercultural speaker.

I have devoted much of my attention searching for different meanings of 'the intercultural' and their correlates, both semantically, that is, by examining its variability depending on prefixes and suffixes, and interculturally, that is, the intercultural understanding of the very concept (2019a). I have often attempted to define the term, *per se* or in different combinations, such as intercultural competence, intercultural citizenship and intercultural responsibility. For example, I was invited to contribute with a definition of the term *per se* for the online ALICE Dictionary, in Portuguese:

> The 'Intercultural' concept spreads over a broad semantic area that goes from the idea of a 'melting pot' – half assimilationist, half segregationist – up to a critical discussion about the practice of an emancipatory and intercultural citizenship, at the local, national and global levels. However, the nature of the intercultural discourse is, at its core, ideological, epistemological and political. ... The 'intercultural' can simply be defined by the

capacity to cope with the unknown. However, identifying a difference of 'perspective' is much more complex than it may appear. ... In its contemporary theorisation, this concept offers room and potential for recognition, in equity, as well as peer and reciprocal dialogue between cultures and languages and, finally, for the critical construction of plural and radically democratic societies. (Guilherme, 2019b, my translation)

ALICE – *Strange Mirrors, Unsuspected Lessons: Leading Europe to a new way of sharing the world experiences* (2011–2016) was a large project whose research activities were held in various countries in Europe, Latin America, Africa and Asia, funded by the European Research Council and coordinated by Boaventura de Sousa Santos. Almost coinciding in time, I was carrying out the Glocademics project (2014–2017) in Brazil and Coimbra, also funded by the European Commission. In one of the books emerging from this project (Routledge, 2019), I formally adopted/adapted the term 'critical intercultural awareness' in its title – *Glocal Languages and Critical Intercultural Awareness: The South answers back*:

We adopt here the term "critical intercultural awareness", instead of "critical cultural awareness" precisely because this book intends to provide the readers with illustrations of a decolonial "intercultural translation" across and within language(s) and culture(s) rather than simply on the (post)colonial meeting of languages and cultures. Accordingly, we intend to respond to a particular cultural fabric of miscegenation that is evident in the Brazilian society and that responds to its specific colonial history. Our emphasis on a critical view of interculturality (a word that, in our work, only attempts to translate into English the term *interculturalidad(e)*, both in Spanish and Portuguese) is also heavily grounded on the vast work by Walsh (2007, for example) throughout her long experience in Ecuador, about her concept "interculturalidad crítica" which is endorsed by the editors of this book. (Guilherme & Menezes de Souza, 2019c: 8)

I had been adopting/adapting this term 'critical interculturality' from before and is mainly based on, besides my own research work, the combination of four sources: (a) the work of Michael Byram on 'critical cultural awareness' (2008); (b) Paulo Freire's 'critical pedagogy' (1974); (c) Catherine Walsh's 'interculturalidad crítica' (2018) and (d) Boaventura de Sousa Santos' 'intercultural translation' (2018). The notion of 'critical intercultural awareness' has therefore become foundational for my theoretical and empirical development from 'Intercultural Competence' to 'Intercultural Responsibility' to be discussed below.

Intercultural Responsibility

In the first edition of the Routledge *Encyclopaedia of Language Teaching and Learning* (2000), I was caught by surprise by Byram's invitation to contribute with a definition of Intercultural Competence (IC), and I was brief therefore and cautious '... the ability to interact effectively with people from cultures that we recognise as different from our own' (Guilherme, 2000: 297). I then focused my argument on the theory of 'critical cultural awareness' and 'the intercultural speaker'. Ten years later, for the second edition, I revisited my previous definition and radically changed it into a 'general capacity ... [that] combines notions of communication and interaction across languages and cultures by focusing on the readiness to establish fluid relationships at the interstices of different and multiply-determined identities whilst having a purpose or task in mind' (2013: 346). I then expand my argument into 'the limits and possibilities of IC', 'a global notion of IC' and 'From Intercultural Competence to Intercultural Responsibility', a term I had introduced before at the ICOPROMO project (2013–2016). At the same time, the term intercultural responsibility (IR) was earning some international recognition, namely from the UNESCO's 'Intercultural Competences', a document that singled out IR as one of the terms that 'highlight aspects of intercultural competences that otherwise might be ignored' and can 'provide important vocabulary permitting examination of specific aspects of intercultural competences worthy of more attention than received to date' (2013: 17).

Theoretically speaking, my idea of Intercultural Responsibility has emerged from desk research on, among many others, mainly Byram's, Freire's, Walsh's and Santos' works. At the practical level, it has been developed out of my research carried out within the context and teamwork across different international/transnational projects, namely on Intercultural Competence for Professional Mobility (Guilherme *et al.*, 2010), on the Intercultural Dimension of Citizenship Education, on Equity and Social Cohesion Policies in Higher Education and on power relations between languages/cultures within and between research groups.

Walsh has developed a theory on decolonial critical intercultural pedagogies, inspired by Freire to start with and by discussing, in depth, criticality from different rationalities and *interculturalidad* from the perspective of indigenous communities in Latin America, namely from her experience with her Ecuadorian students and her intellectual activism. She affirms that 'interculturality, from this perspective, is not an existing condition or a done deal. It is a process and project in continuous insurgence, movement, and construction, a conscious action, radical activity, and praxis-based tool of affirmation, correlation, and transformation', to which she adds that 'interculturality extends its project of an *otherwise*, a transformation conceived and impelled from the margins, from the ground up, and for society at large' (Walsh, 2018: 59). Walsh's struggle in Latin America for radical social and political transformation, following the steps of Paulo Freire, has included her participation in the fabric of new pluri-national constitutions where intercultural/indigenous legacies have been introduced (e.g. in Bolivia and Ecuador) and where interculturality has earned its legitimate role and renewed meanings. Santos (2018) has also introduced a regenerated terminology regarding 'intercultural translation' under the umbrella theme of the 'Epistemologies of the South'. In this context and concerning 'the postabyssal pedagogies called for by the epistemologies of the South', he defines the objective of 'intercultural translation' as one which aims 'to articulate and entertain a conversation among different knowledges that, in some instances, are anchored in different cultures' (2018: 16). Furthermore, it is 'specifically aimed at enhancing reciprocal intelligibility without dissolving identity, thus helping to identify complementarities and contradictions, common grounds and alternative visions' (2018: 32). Both concepts 'critical decolonial interculturality' and 'intercultural translation', the latter within a theory built around the idea of the 'Epistemologies of the South', and both aiming at cognitive and epistemological justice, are main foundational pillars for the idea of 'intercultural responsibility'.

Theoretically, I have been developing the idea of intercultural responsibility by analysing the post-Second World War proposals of a pluralistic interpretation of responsibility, mainly by Jewish writers, namely Arendt, Jonas, Levinas, Derrida, etc. (2020a). In addition, I have been trying to complement it further with the Philosophy of Liberation (Enrique Dussel and Orlando Fals Borda) and the 'decolonial turn' (put forward by Castro-Gomez, Walter Mignolo, Ramon Grosfoguel, Enrique Dussel, Anibal Quijano and Catherine Walsh) as well as postcolonial theories such as that of Gayatri Spivak. Therefore, responsibility that is assumed to be intercultural is here understood as to be grounded on a far-reaching, intricate and challenging perception of interculturality. Intercultural responsibility is meant to amplify glocally, both in breadth and in depth, interdisciplinary fields such as critical plurilingual and intercultural citizenship education as well as transnational research group work. I have also addressed, in response to the challenge to Intercultural Responsibility contained in the UNESCO document on Intercultural Competences (2013), the 17th UNESCO Sustainable Development Goal, which aims 'to revitalize the partnerships for the goals' (https://www.un.org/sustainabledevelopment/globalpartnerships/) (Guilherme, 2020b). Given the pandemic and the environmental sustainability crises, intercultural responsibility aimed at 'glocal' solidarity and cooperation (entangled global and local partnerships) can be paramount in contributing for the survival, well-being and growth of the planetary components. The concepts of critical intercultural awareness and intercultural responsibility may also bring valuable ideas to be developed in relation to the 4th UNESCO-SDG on Quality Education (e.g. forthcoming *Language and Intercultural Communication* special issue on 'Critical Pedagogy and Quality Education (UNSDG-4): The Legacy of Paulo Freire for Language and Intercultural Communication' ed. by J. Corbett and M. Guilherme).

With regard to transnational research, I have also discussed the relationship between Intercultural Responsibility and the concept of Responsible Research and Innovation put forward in the context of the EU-Horizon 2020 research framework and made a comparative analysis with university outreach programmes in the surrounding communities (*programas de extensão universitária*) in Latin American universities (Guilherme, 2022).

Conclusion

Times to come will be demanding. It will not be enough to touch the surface of reality, to surf the globalisation wave, pretending that you are grabbing the clouds. Knowledge homogenisation, that is framed in one language and one set of cultural criteria, will not be up to the challenges we are going to face, and we will not have the sufficient resources to go without heterogeneous capacities and multiple approaches to one problem. This chapter has intended to describe the author's walk from learning about critical cultural awareness, as proposed by Mike Byram, to proposing intercultural responsibility which also aims to respond to contemporary challenges in language education, intercultural citizenship and plurilingual and intercultural transnational research. I intended to highlight the important contribution of 'critical cultural awareness' – *savoir s'engager*, introduced by Mike Byram which I believe that it has not yet been given as much attention as it deserves and, therefore, not yet fulfilled all its promises. This chapter has also aimed to call attention to the potential that the adopted and adapted concept of 'critical **inter**cultural awareness' can offer to be developed in different directions, both across disciplines and in the entanglement of the global and the local dimensions. Intercultural responsibility represents one in many paths where it can be explored.

References

Afshar, H.S. and Yousefi, M. (2019) Do EFL teachers 'critically' engage in cultural awareness? A mixed-method investigation. *Journal of Intercultural Communication Research* 48 (4), 315–340.

Byram, M. (1989) *Cultural Studies in Foreign Language Education*. Clevedon: Multilingual Matters.

Byram, M. (1992) Language and culture learning for European citizenship. *Language and Education* 6 (2–4), 165–176.

Byram, M. (1993) Introduction. *Language, Culture and Curriculum* 6 (1), 1–3.

Byram, M. (1995) Defining and describing 'cultural awareness'. *Language Learning Journal* 12, 5–8.

Byram, M. (1996) Introduction: Education for European citizenship. *Evaluation and Research in Education* 10 (2–3), 61–67.

Byram, M. (1997a) 'Cultural awareness' as vocabulary learning. *Language Learning Journal* 16, 51–57.

Byram, M. (1997b) Cultural studies and foreign language teaching. In S. Bassnett (ed.) *Studying British Cultures: An Introduction* (pp. 53–64). London: Routledge.

Byram, M. (1997c) *Teaching and Assessing Intercultural Communicative Competence* (2nd edn: 2021). Clevedon: Multilingual Matters.

Byram, M. (2002) Foreign language education as political and moral education – An essay. *Language Learning Journal* 26, 43–47.

Byram, M. (2003) On being 'bicultural' and 'intercultural'. In G. Alred, M. Byram and M. Fleming (eds) *Intercultural Experience and Education* (pp. 50–66). Clevedon: Multilingual Matters.

Byram, M. (2008) *From Foreign Language Education to Education for Intercultural Citizenship: Essays and Reflections*. Clevedon: Multilingual Matters.

Byram, M. (2009) Intercultural competence in foreign languages: The intercultural speaker and the pedagogy of foreign language education. In D.K. Deardorff (ed.) *The SAGE Handbook of Intercultural Competence* (pp. 321–332). Los Angeles: Sage.

Byram, M. (2012) Conceptualizing intercultural (communicative) competence and intercultural citizenship. In J. Jackson (ed.) *The Routledge Handbook of Language and Intercultural Communication* (pp. 85–97). New York and London: Routledge.

Byram, M. and Risager, K. (1999) *Language Teachers, Politics and Cultures*. Clevedon: Multilingual Matters.

Byram, M., Morgan, C. and colleagues (1994) *Teaching-and-Learning Language and Culture*. Clevedon: Multilingual Matters.

Ferri, G. (2018) *Intercultural Communication: Critical Approaches and Future Challenges*. Cham, Switzerland: Palgrave Macmillan.

Freire, P. (1974) *Education for Critical Consciousness*. London: Sheed and Ward.

Freire, P. (1988) Introduction. In H.A. Giroux (ed.) *Teachers as Intellectuals* (pp. xxix–xxxvi). New York: Bergin & Garvey.

Guilherme, M. (2000) Intercultural competence. In M. Byram (ed.) *Encyclopaedia of Language Teaching and Learning* (pp. 297–300). London: Routledge.

Guilherme, M. (2002) *Critical Citizens for an Intercultural World: Foreign Language Education as Cultural Politics*. Clevedon: Multilingual Matters.

Guilherme, M. (2013) Intercultural competence. In M. Byram and A. Hu (eds) *Encyclopaedia of Language Teaching and Learning* (pp. 346–349). London: Routledge.

Guilherme, M. (2017a) Freire's philosophical contribution for a theory of intercultural ethics: A deductive analysis of his work. *Journal of Moral Education* 46 (4), 422–434.

Guilherme, M. (2017b) Visões de futuro em Freire e Dewey: Perspectivas interculturais das matrizes (pós)coloniais das Américas. *ECCOS* 44, 205–223.

Guilherme, M. (2018) O diálogo intercultural entre Freire & Dewey: O Sul e o Norte nas matrizes (pós)coloniais das Américas. *Educação e Sociedade* 142, 89–105.

Guilherme, M. (2019a) Introduction: The critical and decolonial quest for intercultural epistemologies and discourses. *Journal of Multicultural Discourses* 14 (1), 1–13.

Guilherme, M. (2019b) "Intercultural", *Dicionário Alice*. https://alice.ces.uc.pt/dictiona ry/?id=23838&pag=23918&id_lingua=1&entry=24306

Guilherme, M. (2020a) Intercultural responsibility: Transnational research and glocal critical citizenship. In J. Jackson (ed.) *The Routledge Handbook of Language and Intercultural Communication* (2nd edn, Ch. 21). New York and London: Routledge.

Guilherme, M. (2020b) Intercultural responsibility: Critical inter-epistemic dialogue and equity for sustainable development. In W. Leal Filho, A.M. Azul, L. Brandli, A. Lange Salvia and T. Wall (eds) *Partnership for the Goals: Encyclopedia of the UN Sustainable Development Goals*, vol. 17. Cham: Springer. https://doi. org/10.1007/978-3-319-71067-9_75-1

Guilherme, M. (forthcoming in 2022) 1. Glocademia: Intercultural responsibility across North/South epistemologies. In M. Guilherme (ed.) *A Framework for Critical*

Transnational Research: Advancing Plurilingual, Intercultural, and Inter-epistemic Collaboration in the Academy. London and New York: Routledge.

Guilherme, M., Keating, C. and Hoppe, D. (2010) Intercultural responsibility: Power and ethics in intercultural dialogue and interaction. In M. Guilherme, E. Glaser and M.C. Méndez García (eds) *The Intercultural Dynamics of Multicultural Working* (pp. 77–94). Bristol: Multilingual Matters.

Guilherme, M. and Menezes de Souza, L.M.T. (2019) Introduction: Glocal languages, the South answering back. In M. Guilherme and L.M.T. Menezes de Souza (eds) *Glocal Languages and Critical Intercultural Awareness: The South Answers Back* (pp. 1–13). London and New York: Routledge

Guilherme, M. and Sawyer, M. (2021) How critical has intercultural learning and teaching become? A diachronic and synchronic view of "critical cultural awareness" in language education. In M.D. López-Jiménez and J. Sánchez-Torres (eds) *Intercultural Competence Past, Present and Future: Respecting the Past, Problems in the Present and Forging the Future* (pp. 185–208). Singapore: Springer.

Holliday, A. (2011) *Intercultural Communication and Ideology.* London: SAGE.

Moncada Linares, S. (2016) Othering: Towards a critical cultural awareness in the language classroom. *HOW Journal* 23 (1), 129–146.

Morrow, R.A. and Torres, C.A. (2002) *Reading Freire and Habermas: Critical Pedagogy and Transformative Social Change.* New York: Teacher's College Press, Columbia University.

Parks, E. (2018) *Communicative criticality* and *savoir se reconnaître*: Emerging new competencies of criticality and intercultural communicative competence. *Language and Intercultural Communication* 18 (1), 107–124.

Parks, E. (2020a) The separation between language and content in Modern Language degrees: Implications for students' development of critical cultural awareness and criticality. *Language and Intercultural Communication* 20 (1), 22–36.

Parks, E. (2020b) *Developing Critical Cultural Awareness in Modern Languages: A Comparative Study of Higher Education in North America and the United Kingdom.* New York and London: Routledge.

Phipps, A. (2010) Training and intercultural education: The danger in 'good citizenship'. In M. Guilherme, E. Glaser and M.C. Méndez García (eds) *The Intercultural Dynamics of Multicultural Working* (pp. 59–73). Bristol: Multilingual Matters.

Porto, M. (2013) Language and intercultural education: An interview with Michael Byram. *Pedagogies: An International Journal* 8 (12), 143–162.

Santos, B. (2018) *The End of the Cognitive Empire: The Coming of Age of Epistemologies of the South.* Durham: Duke University Press.

Torres, C. (2014) *First Freire: Early Writings in Social Justice Education.* New York: Teacher's College Press, Columbia University.

UNESCO (2013) *Intercultural Competences: Conceptual and Operational Framework.* Paris: UNESCO.

Vences, P.T. and Fay, R. (2015) Developing general cultural awareness in a monocultural English as a foreign language context in a Mexican university: A wiki-based critical incident approach. *The Language Learning Journal* 43, 222–233.

Walsh, C. (2007) Shifting the geopolitics of critical knowledge. *Cultural Studies* 21 (2–3), 224–239.

Walsh, C. (2015) Decolonial pedagogies walking and asking. Notes to Paulo Freire from Abya Yala. *International Journal of Lifelong Education* 34 (1), 9–21.

Walsh, C. (2018) On decolonial dangers, decolonial cracks, and decolonial pedagogies rising. In W.D. Mignolo and C. Walsh (eds) *On Decoloniality: Concepts, Analytics, Praxis* (pp. 81–98). Durham and London: Duke University Press.

7 Conflict and the Cognitive Empire: Byram's Critical Cultural Awareness

Alison Phipps

Introduction

The year 1997 saw the European Union in its ascendency. Eight years after the Fall of the Berlin wall, seven years after German Reunification, the post-Soviet era was well under way, and it was clear that the new era of globalisation and movement of people, goods and capital were sweeping all before them. 9/11 had not yet destabilised the anticipation of the beginning of the new millennium (Yurchak, 2006), and the greatest active fears lay with the Balkan wars, Rwandan genocide and Y2K computer compliance. Peace time Europe was fully alive with its potential and consolidating approaches to its European project. Into this context *Teaching and Assessing Intercultural Communicative Competence* (Byram, 1997) brought a particular focus on the role of critical cultural awareness. It was necessary. The intercultural project was in its infancy – the term 'intercultural' largely one developed in North America and with roots in NATO – and the work of peace needed some gentle probing through democratic educational initiatives, and ones which would play well with Lyotard's Postmodern Condition (Lyotard, 1984).

Any fair critique of Byram's undeniable contribution to intercultural education worldwide must begin with this philosophical and material context.

In this chapter, I will review some of the ways in which critical engagement of Byram's work has proceeded (Gramling, 2016; Guilherme, 2002; Hoff, 2014; MacDonald & O'Regan, 2013; Phipps, 2014) and the paradigms from which they have emerged. I shall consider the dangers of presentism in critiques of work which was part of the architecture of an era already very different to our own, and the importance of the foundation Byram's work lays for precisely the kinds of critical cultural awareness he advocates.

Importantly, however, I shall engage with the present decolonial context and the ways in which Byram's work might be interpreted and stands in comparison to, for instance, present critiques and the postcolonial projects of the 1990s (Gregory, 2014; Nyamnjoh, 2019). To this end, I will utilise the work of Santos and his critique of cognition and awareness in models designed for peace time (Santos, 2018) and suggest ways of acknowledging and also hoping for an age when we might return to the utility of models which are designed for kinder conditions of life and learning.

Decolonising Intercultural Communicative Competence

It would be easy to begin a chapter on Byram's extensive work, in 2021, after the rise and rise of the #BlackLivesMatter movement, and the rise and rise of calls for 'decolonising' every aspect of the Western curriculum in schools and universities, with a simplistic critique. 'Presentism' is the term used in critical assessments of work which fails to take the context of writing, the material possibilities of an age and the nuance of which avenues are available for exploration, into account. Presentism is what we find in any assessment of Byram's work which argued that his contribution was problematic because it offers Anglo-normative, Eurocentric curricular models which reflect the position of a white, male, professor at an elite university. This would also be a grossly unfair assessment of the work. Twenty-five years on from the writing of *Teaching and Assessing Intercultural Communicative Competence* and from the publication of quite frankly more books than many have had hot dinners, Byram's contribution to intercultural language education, to the development of diverse and nuanced models of assessment of learning in schools, universities and teacher education worldwide, is unparalleled. It is empirically grounded, theoretically modelled and has stood the test of time in policy and curricular terms. It has enabled mainstream education to embed intercultural models in its practice and training.

This present age, however, has concerns of its own, which are not those of the 1990s and 2000s, when Byram was capacitating a large, global, and yes – largely European cohort of postgraduate and postdoctoral early career scholars through Cultnet, through many, varied publishing initiatives and collaborations. That Byram's work – and the work of the majority of scholars working in the nascent European context of intercultural studies in the 1990s – was predominantly white, Anglophone or Francophone, with some strong German publications – reflects the material base supporting the publication of work in this area. This, in and of itself, reflects the processes within education and research which produced the context of the 1990s, into which work which was seeking to produce a European skillset, an integration and a citizenry, was pitched. Raymond Williams contended that, 'Form always has an active material base'

(Williams, 1977: 190) as he sought to work culturally, through the limitations of traditional Marxist thought with its determinisms of base and superstructure. In short, Williams was allowing for dynamism, agency, fluidity, the ways in which escape could be made from simple economic determinism.

The presentisms of a simplistic critique in 2021 would analyse Byram's references in his 1997 text for the presence of scholars from the Global South. It would see if the now canonical decolonial, and postcolonial scholars, were present – the Fanons and N'gũgis. It would read only his work in English, ignoring the body of work undertaken with Genevieve Zarate, for instance, and the pioneering equality of writing with women which is a hallmark of Byram's scholarship. It would look for contributions from Black scholars in the Americas, and Africa. It would, with the first filters of search terms, draw more or less a blank, and draw conclusions which are limited, presentist and structurally naïve. But the damage would be done.

With this opening, it will be clear, that I wish to read against the grain of the present moment of decolonial scholarly anger, while at the same time contributing myself to the development of a decolonising scholarship of multilingual, decolonial action, and being greatly in sympathy, critically and aesthetically with the anger and its effect. In recent work, I have argued that there is no pure place to stand in the work to change the economic and material base, the cultural structures which allow equal access to elite education, higher education, worldwide, and within our own state in the UK (Fassetta, 2020; Phipps, 2018, 2019; Phipps et al., 2020). I am clear that an intercultural scholarship will need to weigh questions of structural equity carefully and build on the work undertaken in the struggles for post and decolonial freedoms across the former British Empires, and other European Empires – as described by Santos (2002). It builds substantially out of critiques and elaborations of Byram's work, notably by scholars setting a context for Eurocentricity and pointing to wider global frameworks, postcoloniality, languages beyond the monolingualisms of Europe and the tendency of the scholarship in intercultural studies towards the transcendent, rather than the immanent in its prescriptions (Gramling, 2016; Guilherme, 2002; Hoff, 2014; MacDonald & O'Regan, 2013; Phipps, 2014).

Language and Culture

The 'quick' of Byram's scholarship – what binds his project of intercultural communicative competence and intercultural citizenship together over time – is found in the debates of the 1970s and 1980s on language and culture. Language as an articulation of the superstructure, culture as a noun, a verb, a way of life, a distinctive patterning of societies were all examined meticulously via a variety of critical and deconstructive lens.

There was much in the project of linguistic and cultural deconstruction that was yet to find a practical and pragmatic articulation and some of the tropes and approaches to Byram's scholarship can be found in his firm footing within empirical education sciences and his work on qualitative methodological innovations for the study of culture and construction of intercultural competence. Particular works such as *Language Learners as Ethnographers* (Roberts *et al.*, 2001) and *Developing Intercultural Competence in Practice* (Byram *et al.*, 2001) point to this methodological and pedagogical concern. In an expanding Europe, with ERASMUS and SOCRATES projects in development, the practicality was an urgent task and responded to reports, for instance, of failings in student programmes and placements abroad in modern and foreign language education in particular (Coleman, 2001).

Beyond Europe, in what was then referred to as the 'third world', and is now referred to as 'the Global South', the scholarship was largely postcolonial in nature, and equally marked by the pragmatism and theoretical polarisations that were broadly present in European scholarship at this time. Responses to the Ethiopian famine, development of the millennium development goals and Make Poverty History/Jubilee 2000 campaigns, together with the rise in islamophobia, responses to the 'War on Terror' post-2001 all made the ecosystems of scholarship both practical and highly theoretical. The postcolonial work which was able to tread water through Said's Orientalism (Said, 1995); Mbembe's De La Postcolonie (Mbembé, 2000), Pratt's Imperial Eyes (Pratt, 2008) and the work of translation studies (Bassnett-McGuire, 1980; Bassnett & Trivedi, 1999; Cronin, 2000) up until the urgency of the second decolonial wave, developed largely apart from education and pedagogy, and within the arts and humanities. Attempts to bridge these fields came from within the *International Association for Languages and Intercultural Communication* (IALIC) but were uneasy, marked by suspicions, and more pragmatically, different journals and book series and doctoral training programmes which funnelled work into separate disciplines, despite the interdisciplinary claims and aspirations of the fields. The merging of work in the field of social sciences with arts and humanities is a long and difficult, enduring interdisciplinary tasks. As Bourdieu (1988) has noted, academic scholarly work is set in fields with their own norms, rituals and markers of distinction, and the overcoming of these for interdisciplinarity takes time. It also requires risk and the ability to work within new fields which have not yet attained the same markers of distinction such as journals with history and standing or academic associations with several decades of meetings and sufficient capital to sustain their work, and to institutionalise their new fields. The first personal chairs in the field of intercultural studies were only established around 10 years ago in the UK, and it's only in 2015 that funding to develop work undertaken in education on intercultural communicative competence began to have real structural influence in the field of modern languages through the work of the Translating Cultures thematic funding from the Arts and Humanities Research Council project Transnationalising Modern Languages (Spadaro *et al.*, 2019).

Despite all these strong material, political and structurally disciplining dimensions, Byram's work bears consideration for the role it plays in creating conditions for and sustaining work from and with the Global South. This may not be the mainstay of his work, but it is present.

In 2000, Manuela Guilherme successfully defended her PhD thesis, under Byram's supervision, in which she pursued a critical pedagogy approach to the concept of intercultural communicative competence, and the '*Savoirs*' in the Common European Framework of Reference. The subsequent book of her thesis was published in the Multilingual Matters book series, Languages for Intercultural Communication and Education, which Byram established with myself, in 1999 (see Guilherme, 2002). It was the third book to be published in this series and it took, in part what, in today's academic terminology, would be called a 'southern epistemological' theoretical position. It rests on scholars from the Global South, notably the work of Paolo Freire, and melds these with the critical political scholarship of North American scholars, Giroux and McClaren, but also situates the work within the criticality of post war European philosophy and the work of Habermas, and of poststructuralisms of Derrida, Foucault, Baudrillard and Lyotard (Freire, 1998, 2003, 2006; Giroux, 1988; Guilherme, 2000, 2002; McLaren, 1995). Byram's supervision of this thesis and openness to a critical pedagogical development of his own frameworks is in many ways typical of the collaborative and capacitating approach to scholarship.

A second book in the early list of the LICE book series also requires consideration. As series editors, many proposals passed over our desks. Our practice was always to appraise independently and then share our views, and we are not always on the same page by a long way. This would usually lead to better work as we debated and proposed avenues for authors to explore. Gradually, a shape and direction emerged to the series which was global in scope and which prioritised empirical work and much school-based curriculum policy and development largely across the global north and South East Asia. Again, this reflected trends in higher education at the time when neoliberal expansion of higher education into China was in its ascendency, in particular. In the early days, as the series was still finding its feet, a proposal was received which was energisingly different and un-European in feel and philosophy.

Vernacular Palaver: Imaginations of the Local and Non-native Languages in West Africa stands out as different from the variations on the themes of intercultural competence, languages and education which dominated our series. Moradewun Adejunmobi, now Professor of African American and African Studies at the University of California, Davis, offered the series a stunning work of intercultural scholarship from the perspective of West African speech and popular culture (see Adejunmobi, 2004). That this has not become a default cited text in intercultural studies and education shows that even when the material conditions are put in place for publication by Black scholars from the South, and knowledge from and of the intercultural contexts of West Africa offered for further development in a largely European context, scholars and students do not necessary follow those threads at the time. Rather, they may come back to them in later years only to find the apparent 'new' concerns of their age already well reflected in previous publications. Racism and the consumption of knowledge are intimately linked and take more than a publication in a series to overcome, or even changed citation practices. Structural and systemic problems require structural and systemic change of which series editing is a small part.

Entente Cordiale: Peace Not War

The forms of hegemonic zeal which consume a knowledge-hungry student body and inform decolonial student politics is one which Byram, I believe, was also keen to facilitate with his model of critical cultural awareness and his '*savoir être*' – the knowing how to be, which has ethical valence for individual intercultural citizens in formation. If anything, in the wake of the fall of the Berlin Wall and the aftermath of the Balkans war and genocide on the borders of the new European enlargements, a street politics of education seemed remote within the conditions of knowledge and theoretical developments of intercultural language education. There was a practical, steady, pragmatic peace-building task to hand – that of enabling multilingual and intercultural language education for Europe and beyond, into contexts with strong neoliberalising curricular development.

Byram's work and models, with their stated ontological and critical dimensions, fitted perfectly into these contexts, and importantly into those of the post-Enlightenment European philosophical tradition, alongside that of American pragmatism and British empiricism. Having shared panel discussions and chaired debates with Mike Byram over two decades, it's clear that one of his favourite, and often most exasperated answers to questions or to any critical impasses in a theoretical debates, would be, 'that would be an empirical question'. The ability to test a hypothesis, develop an empirical knowledge base for theoretical pursuits is a vital part of his scholarship and for understanding how it developed. And as part of the material conditions enabling this empiricism and these debates comes European freedom of movement and European funding. Of course his work is that of a European scholar. He was working in the heyday of European Union scholarship, working with the Council of Europe to shape this to be fit for purpose within the context of ascendant neoliberal ideologies and the recourse to critique and to ontology as counterweights.

In November 1991, the General Conference of UNESCO invited the Director General 'to convene an international commission to reflect on education and learning for the 21st Century'. Similar to the commissioning of Lyotard's earlier 1984 *The Postmodern Condition: A Report on Knowledge*, but less performative in its assessment of the directions for education (Lyotard, 1984), Jacques Delors submitted *Learning: The Treasure within* (Delors *et al.*, 1996). In it, an outline was presented which was rooted in lifelong learning and a holistic and integrated vision of education. It included the four dimensions, each found in Byram's Intercultural Communicative Competence framework, of learning to be, to know, to do, and to live together. In the introduction, education is presented as 'a necessary utopia'.

> In confronting the many challenges that the future holds in store, humankind sees in education an indispensable asset in its attempt to attain the ideals of peace, freedom and social justice. As it concludes its work, the Commission affirms its belief that education has a fundamental role to play in personal and social development. (Delors *et al.*, 1996: 11)

In many ways, this was the pragmatic and empirical outworking of the revolutions in consciousness that had occurred through engagement with the work of Cultural Studies, the foregrounding of questions of cultural identity, race gender and class, the Birmingham School, and the consequences for mainstream education under neoliberal paradigms. Both the Delors report and the models Byram elaborated towards his 1997 publication were exceptional attempts to draw often incompatible political streams into a workable, education model that was fit for purpose for a system that had undergone a revolution across the global north.

In many ways, the Delors report and the work Byram and his contemporaries and colleagues undertook through the 1990s onwards in their engagement with this work is the equivalent of engagement today with the normative frameworks of the Sustainable Development Goals. Fundamentally, the questions were questions for peace time, and for a point in human history that pre-dated the attacks on the World Trade Center and the Pentagon in the United States in 2001, and the ushering in of the war on terror and its consequences for any form of education for mutual flourishing and mutual respect, under new and diffuse conditions of warfare, and now cultural warfare. In 1997, cultural and intercultural education and dialogue were instrumental in the pursuance of a politics of education for peace, with Byram's work very much at the forefront of this particular moment.

Byram's work also fits firmly into models of educational practice, and ways of doing scholarship which pre-date the SDGs in other ways too. In 1997, Erasmus and Tempus schemes were beginning to really show what enhanced mobility on a number of levels, across the dimensions of lifelong learning, might achieve. The decade following the 1997 publication saw scholars meeting, conferencing, researching and publishing together across the European Union and forging bonds many of which are still in evidence in work continuing today, and despite Brexit. Entente Cordiale Scholarships between Britain and France began in 1995, focusing on continuing the cordial relations between the two states, forged off the back of centuries of colonial territory disputes in 1904, but again revealing the political importance of French and of Europe in the 1990s.

The lens is European, not global, despite the later iterations and fits of models to global contexts. The scholarship is rooted in Enlightenment and European scholarship, critically. The work on decolonising of the 1980s and as part of postcolonial scholarship was largely unreflected in debates on education but confined to the work in literature and modern language departments (Bassnett & Trivedi, 1999; Forsdick, 2005; Pratt, 1991, 2008). It takes time for theories to move through and into new disciplines, from deconstruction and decolonisation and its no surprise that its only now, in 2021, that the advocacy and activism of #BlackLivesMatter and decolonising higher education has begun to fuse with a seam of scholarship that has largely been located in history and literature and thought, not strongly within mainstream education outwith Europe.

Conflict, Conviviality, Conclusions

Intercultural Communicative Competence, in the pursuance of personal and social development under the peace time conditions of Europe is a convivial goal. It locates politics in the personal and civic space but is nonetheless transformational in intent and also pragmatic in its non-revolutionary aims. Steady building up of education as formation with multicultural, multilingual experiences and societies can serve to create a citizenship with intercultural communicative competence over time. These people can meet, greet, work, play, love and also disagree in ways which will not produce the devastations of the past on European soil, and these may also then be lessons for others which the Common European Framework of Reference has now enabled, in part.

Questions of conviviality look very different when the world's conflicts are made proximate by both social media and mass displacements of people, when in the UK numbers seeking asylum since the 1997 publication have fundamentally altered and added to questions of intercultural communicative competence and brought questions of conflict centre stage. In her Nobel lecture, Judith Butler (Butler, 2012) poses the new dilemma of care for lives which are more or less grievable in conflicts worldwide, but also the question of how it can be that citizens come to care about the fate of another who is not proximate, not an immediate neighbour or citizen but in a far off conflict, suffering and in need of both advocacy and attention. The politics of the second and third decades of the 21st century, facilitated by technologies, are producing new questions of the place of education as a necessary utopia, of the limits to personal competence as a survival stratagem, and of the global and climate scope required of intercultural imagination and communication which takes leave of the immediately social and also brings the more than human world in as an addressee.

But at root, and what remains constant, from Byram's scholarship, as the world changes, is the clear focus on the empirical, the steady in the service of education that might lead to convivial ways of being similar and different, equal and also radically unequal but capable of dialogue.

The South African scholar Francis Nyamnjoh refers to education and higher education in particular as requiring conviviality, a state which is less bound and fraught with the distresses of the political and even environmental sphere:

> [...] a convivial scholarship that dwells less on zero-sum games of absolute winners and losers, encourages a disposition of incompleteness and humility through the reality of the ubiquity of debt and indebtedness, and finds strength in themes of interconnections, interdependences, compositeness, and incompleteness [...]. (Nyamnjoh, 2019)

This would also be a fitting description of the methods of scholarship and nurturing of intercultural education scholars which many of us have experienced from Mike Byram's own work in the academy. It also allows us to begin again at a point in time where the terms 'intercultural' and 'competence' are beginning to sound dated and rather blunt from excessive use. Intercultural programmes are stagnating, and the world is talking of climate change, conflict, displacement and the COVID pandemic. People cannot travel and sitting together is now a technological pursuit on Zoom and Teams and in the hands of Big Tech. Political power is dangerously dominated by politicians who have made an art out of not displaying any intercultural communicative competence at all, and fear grips and does its corrosive work.

What succeeds this moment in global human history is as yet unknown, but the seeds are sown in Byram's decentring scholarship and even more importantly in the holistic, ontological methods that persist. Santos has elaborated some critical trajectories for social and legal frameworks for this age, which he calls 'the coming of age of epistemologies of the south' (Phipps, 2007; Santos, 2014, 2018). He argues powerfully, and against the grain of the European traditions, for human scale thought, and also from within an engaged scholarship of social movements, for which the critical cognitive frameworks of 300 years of European scholarship are inadequate. It's not an easy thing, looking at one's own scholarship on, for instance, the year abroad for language study in Europe, and to see it seemingly, from within UK higher education at least, discontinued and the scholarship rendered defunct, as has occurred for those of us who worked within the European project. Nor is Santos wrong to see certain approaches to knowledge as having run their course and needing to pause, take stock, philosophically, of new, material conditions. This is not a *tabula rasa* for intercultural scholarship, however, but rather the critical work of offering revised concepts and shaping a field anew. For Santos, there was a focus on concepts such as 'intercultural translation' and a move from thinking of Universities to 'pluriversities or subversities' as organising entities.

In Byram's 2008 monograph, he focused on 'Intercultural Citizenship' and concluded with a pragmatic agenda for education for citizenship sitting alongside that of language education. He is unapologetic about using 'Education' twice in the title of this book, and sees the steps for the decade following the 1997 publication as forging bonds between intercultural communicative competence and intercultural citizenship: 'a focus of citizenship education on the understanding and action involved when one is a member of an international society, especially an international civil society' (2008: 229).

What the decade following the publication of this agenda for engagement in action has brought has been a heightened awareness globally of what it means not to belong, not to be documented, not to have franchise, not to be included, or to be tolerated and included in such a way as to overburden and fetishise. Intercultural citizenship remains a Delorsian goal, a necessary education utopia, a vision for what seems to be an ever-receding future faced with the monumental challenges encapsulated by the Sustainable Development Goals, and COP26 meeting in Glasgow in November 2021.

But, and this 'but' is part of holding fast to Byram's vision and agenda for engagement for intercultural citizenship, yesterday (6 May 2021) the Scottish Parliament elections were held, following a long engagement and multilingual campaign, and voting rights were extended to refugees in Scotland. 'It means we are considered part of the community' said refugees, who had learned English, and who have lived in Scotland for 14 years (https://youtu.be/C2IbfGUmgUk). Social media was full of reports and happy selfies from some of the 20,000 refugees able to vote for the first time, reporting feeling not just of being included but trusted, part of things, about to be exactly what Byram envisages – Intercultural Citizens.

It sometimes seems like an ever-receding future and a long way off, the vision and outworking of Byram's intercultural agenda, globally, but on 6 May 2021, it was also right here in Scotland, where I live, work, learn, act and educate, and it was made real.

References

Adejunmobi, M. (2004) *Vernacular Palaver: Imaginations of the Local and Non-Native Languages in West Africa*. Clevedon: Multilingual Matters.

Bassnett, S. and Trivedi, H. (1999) *Postcolonial Translation: Theory and Practice*. London: Routledge.

Bassnett-McGuire, S. (1980) *Translation Studies*. London & New York: Methuen.

Bourdieu, P. (1988) *Homo Academicus*. Cambridge: Polity.

Butler, J. (2012) Precarious life, vulnerability, and the ethics of cohabitation. *The Journal of Speculative Philosophy* 26 (2), 134–151.

Byram, M. (1997) *Teaching and Assessing Intercultural Communicative Competence*. Clevedon: Multilingual Matters.

Byram, M. (2008) *From Foreign Language Education to Education for Intercultural Citizenship: Essays and Reflections*. Clevedon: Multilingual Matters.

Byram, M., Nichols, A. and Stevens, D. (eds) (2001) *Developing Intercultural Competence in Practice*. Clevedon: Multilingual Matters.

Coleman, J. (2001) What is residence abroad for?: Intercultural competence and the linguisitic, cultural academic, personal and professional objectives of student residence abroad. In R. Di Napoli, L. Polezzi and A. King (eds) *Fuzzy Boundaries? Reflections on Modern Languages and the Humanities* (pp. 121–140). London: CILT.

Cronin, M. (2000) *Across the Lines: Travel, Language and Translation*. Cork: Cork University Press.

Delors, J. *et al.* (1996) *Learning: The Treasure Within*. Report to UNESCO of the International Commission on Education for the Twenty-first Century. Paris: UNESCO.

Fassetta, G., Al-Masri, N. and Phipps, A. (eds) (2020) *Multilingual Online Academic Collaborations as Resistance: Crossing Impassable Borders*. Bristol: Multilingual Matters.

Forsdick, C. (2005) *Travel in Twentieth Century French and Francophone Cultures: The Persistence of Diversity*. Oxford: Oxford University Press.

Freire, P. (1998) *Teachers as Cultural Workers*. Boulder, CO: Westview Press.

Freire, P. (2003) *Pedagogia Da Esperança: Um reencontro com a Pedagogia do oprimido*. São Paulo: Pax e Terra.

Freire, P. (2006) *Pedagogia do Oprimido* (Vol. 43). São Paulo: Paz e Terra.

Giroux, H. (1988) *Teachers as Intellectuals: Toward a Critical Pedagogy of Leaning*. New York: Bergin & Garvey.

Gramling, D. (2016) *The Invention of Monolingualism*. New York and London: Bloomsbury.

Gregory, D. (2014) *The Colonial Present*. Oxford: Blackwell.

Guilherme, M. (2002) *Critical Citizens for an Intercultural World: Foreign Language Education as Cultural Politics*. Clevedon: Multilingual Matters.

Guilherme, M.M. (2000) Critical Cultural Awareness: The Critical Dimension in Foreign Culture Education. PhD dissertation submitted to University of Durham.

Hoff, H.E. (2014) A critical discussion of Byram's model of intercultural communicative competence in the light of bildung theories. *Intercultural Education* 25 (6), 508–517.

Lyotard, J.-F. (1984) *The Postmodern Condition: A Report on Knowledge*. Manchester: Manchester University Press.

MacDonald, M.N. and O'Regan, J.P. (2013) The ethics of intercultural communication. *Educational Philosophy and Theory* 45 (10), 1005–1017.

Mbembé, J.-A. (2000) *De la postcolonie: Essai Sur L'imagination Politique Dans L'Afrique Contemporaine*: Paris: Karthala.

McLaren, P. (1995) *Critical Pedagogy and Predatory Culture*. London: Routledge.

Nyamnjoh, F.B. (2019) Decolonising the university in Africa. In *Oxford Research Encyclopedia*. Oxford: Oxford University Press.

Phipps, A. (2007) Other worlds are possible: An interview with Boaventura de Sousa Santos. *Language and Intercultural Communication* 7 (1), 91–101.

Phipps, A. (2014) 'They are bombing now': 'Intercultural Dialogue' in times of conflict. *Language and Intercultural Communication* 14 (1), 108–124.

Phipps, A. (2018) Language plenty, refugees and the post-Brexit world: New practices from Scotland. In M. Kelly (ed.) *Languages after Brexit: How the UK Speaks to the World* (pp. 95–107). London: Plagrave Macmillan.

Phipps, A. (2019) *Decolonising Multilingualism: Struggles to Decreate*. Bristol: Multilingual Matters.

Phipps, A., Sitholé, T., Tordzro, N.D. and Tordzro, G. (2020) English last: Displaced publics and communicating multilingually as social act and art. In E. Scandrett (ed.) *Public Sociology as Educational Practice: Challenges, Dialogues and Counter-Publics* (pp. 183–198). Bristol: Bristol University Press.

Pratt, M.L. (2008) *Imperial Eyes: Travel Writing and Transculturation*. London: Routledge.

Said, E. (1995) *Orientalism* (Vol. 2). London: Penguin.

Santos, B.D.S. (2002) Between Prospero and Caliban: Colonialism, postcolonialism, and inter-identity. *Luso-Brazilian Review* 39 (2), 9–44.

Santos, B.D.S. (2014) *Epistemologies of the South: Justice against Epistemicide*. London: Routledge.

Santos, B.D.S. (2018) *The End of the Cognitive Empire: The Coming Age of Epistemologies of the South*. Durham and London: Duke University Press.

Spadaro, B., Burdett, C., Creese, A., Forsdick, C. and Phipps, A. (2019) In conversation: Translating cultures. *The Translator* 25 (4), 1–14.

Williams, R. (1977) *Marxism and Literature*. Oxford: Oxford University Press.

Yurchak, A. (2006) *Everything Was Forever, Until It Was No More*. Princeton: Princeton University Press.

Part 2

Intercultural Development in Diverse Contexts: Perspectives and Practices

8 Intercultural Development in the Context of Mobility

Jane Jackson, Sin Yu Cherry Chan and Tongle Sun

Introduction

It is often assumed that individuals who participate in an academic mobility scheme will become more interculturally competent, global-minded and proficient in a second language (L2). Participants themselves may expect to easily make friends with locals and become fluent speakers of local languages simply by being present in the host environment. Despite these expectations of immersion and personal transformation, contemporary study abroad (SA) researchers have discovered that a complex interplay of internal elements (e.g. agency, motivation, intercultural attitudes) and external factors (e.g. host receptivity, access to local communities of practice) can result in starkly divergent learning trajectories and outcomes (Iwasaki, 2019; Jackson, 2018a, 2018b). While some participants do indeed transform through SA, without a pedagogical intervention, others experience little or no gains in language proficiency or intercultural competence (Jackson & Oguro, 2018; Paige & Vande Berg, 2012; Vande Berg, 2015). Some may even return home with reinforced stereotypes and a reduced desire to use their L2 to initiate intercultural interactions (Iwasaki, 2019; Jackson & Schwieter, 2019).

To promote interculturality and help L2 participants make the most of their time abroad, more and more SA scholars advocate research-driven pedagogical interventions that draw on relevant models of intercultural competence development (e.g. Byram & Dervin, 2008; Howard, 2019; Jackson, 2018a, 2018b, 2018c) and recent advances in critical pedagogy and online education (e.g. social constructionism, eLearning platforms) (Jackson, 2019b, 2020; Jackson & Oguro, 2018; Plews & Misfeldt, 2018). Building on the seminal work of Byram (1997) and colleagues (e.g. Alred & Byram, 2002; Byram & Dervin, 2008; Byram & Feng, 2006), this chapter offers concrete examples of ways to scaffold, deepen and extend the language and intercultural development of participants before, during and after academic mobility.

Intercultural Competence Development

Within the context of academic mobility, several models of intercultural competence development have impacted the design, implementation and evaluation of intercultural interventions, including Byram's (1997) model of intercultural communicative competence, Deardorff's (2008) process model of intercultural competence and Bennett's (1998, 2012) developmental model of intercultural sensitivity. Although each has unique features, all of them emphasize the developmental nature of intercultural competence. Among them, Byram's work has been especially influential in the intercultural education of L2 participants as his conception of interculturality underscores the importance of the language dimension (Byram & Golubeva, 2020; Jackson, 2018a).

Drawing on the earlier work of linguists (e.g. Canale & Swain, 1980; Hymes, 1966, 1972) and the construct of 'communicative competence' in L2 teaching and learning, Byram (1997) coined the term 'intercultural communicative competence' to refer to 'the ability [of second language speakers] to see and manage the relationships between themselves and their own cultural beliefs, behaviours and meanings, as expressed in a foreign language, and those of their interlocutors, expressed in the same language – or even a combination of languages – which may be the interlocutors' native language, or not' (1997: 12). In this capacity, Byram maintained that second language speakers serve as a bridge between interlocutors who have a different linguistic and cultural background. It is this notion of mediation that underpins his conception of intercultural competence development.

In the first part of his model, Byram (1997) cites the following *linguistic* elements as characteristic of an interculturally competent L2 speaker: linguistic competence (the ability to apply knowledge of the rules of a standard version of the language to produce and interpret spoken and written language), sociolinguistic competence (the ability to give to the language produced by an interlocutor – whether native speaker or not – meanings which are taken for granted by the interlocutor or which are negotiated and made explicit with the interlocutor) and discourse competence (the ability to use, discover and negotiate strategies for the production and interpretation of monologue or dialogue texts which follow the conventions of the culture of an interlocutor or are negotiated as intercultural texts for particular purposes) (1997: 48).

The second part of his framework centers on five *savoirs* or components that are linked to the *cultural* dimension. The first two are considered essential for successful intercultural/interlingual communication: intercultural attitudes or *savoir être* (curiosity and openness, readiness to suspend disbelief about others' cultures and belief about one's own intercultural attitudes) and knowledge or *saviors* (of social groups and their products and practices in one's own and interlocutor's country). The remaining components include skills of interpreting and relating or *savoir comprendre* (the ability to interpret a document or event from another culture, to explain it and relate it to documents or events from one's own), skills of discovery and interaction or *savoir apprendre/faire* (the ability to acquire new knowledge of a culture and to operate this knowledge in real-time communication) and critical cultural awareness or *savoir s'engager* (the ability to evaluate critically and on the basis of explicit criteria, perspectives, practices and products in one's own and other cultures and countries) (Byram, 1997, 2009; Byram *et al.*, 2002).

Byram's model is not without critics, however. Risager (2007) and Liddicoat and Scarino (2010), for example, maintain that the relationship between intercultural and linguistic communication is not sufficiently clear. Sercu (2004) further argues that Byram's framework lacks a meta-cognitive dimension that can help to explain how L2 learners plan and monitor their intercultural communication. Liddicoat and Scarino (2010, 2020) concur and suggest that more attention should 'focus specifically on the interplay of language and culture in both communication and learning as they occur in variable contexts in diversity' (Liddicoat & Scarino, 2020: 398).

Despite these limitations, the *saviors* model (Byram & Zarate, 1994, 1996) remains influential and has been adopted by the Council of Europe's (2001, 2018) *Common European Framework of Reference for Languages* (CEFR), which, in turn, has impacted the design and delivery of intercultural programming for both mobile and non-mobile L2 students throughout Europe and beyond.

The Intercultural Speaker or Mediator

A discussion of the *saviors* would be incomplete without reference to the construct of the 'intercultural speaker'. Linked to the intercultural competence development model, this term was put forward by Byram (see Byram & Zarate, 1996) to describe foreign language/culture learners who successfully establish intercultural relationships through the use of their L2. Intercultural speakers 'operate their linguistic competence and their sociolinguistic awareness ... in order to manage interaction across cultural boundaries, to anticipate misunderstandings caused by difference in values, meanings and beliefs, and ... to cope with the affective as well as cognitive demands of engagement with otherness' (Byram, 1995: 25). Depicted as competent, flexible L2 communicators (Byram, 2012; Byram & Zarate, 1994, 1996), intercultural speakers 'engage with complexity and multiple identities' and 'avoid stereotyping which accompanies perceiving someone through a single identity' (Byram *et al.*, 2002: 5). Expanding on this notion, Guilherme (2004: 298) defines *critical* intercultural speakers as individuals who are able to 'negotiate between their own cultural, social and political identifications and representations with those of the other' and, in the process, become aware of 'the multiple, ambiva-lent, resourceful, and elastic nature of cultural identities in an intercul-tural encounter'.

Byram's (1997) model of intercultural communicative competence encourages SA educators to view their L2 students as intercultural speak-ers who co-construct meaning through the use of language in intercultural interactions by drawing on various linguistic and cultural resources, and their complex self-identities. Byram (2008) later employed the term 'inter-cultural mediator' to draw attention to the ability of L2 speakers to use both speaking and listening skills to mediate or negotiate cultural bound-aries and differences through a shared language. This notion resonates with the idea of 'thirdness', that is, 'the ability to be both "inside" an interaction and to remain sufficiently "outside" that one can observe, reflect, and develop a critical perspective, different to that of L1 [first lan-guage] speakers' (Wilkinson, 2020). This follows the increasing emphasis on criticality and reflexivity in intercultural practice (Byrd Clark, 2020).

While the constructs of intercultural speaker and intercultural media-tor remain influential, critical theorists argue that it is important to be mindful of the power dimension in intercultural interactions such as in host-sojourner communication that takes place in the host language in SA contexts (Phipps & Gonzalez, 2014; Wilkinson, 2020). As Noels *et al.* (2020: 59) suggest, 'This inequity in power relations is inherent in the learning context as the hosts do not necessarily need to hear the voices of the newcomers, but the newcomers do need to be heard and accepted to be members of the society'. Building on the work of Holliday (2011, 2012), Wilkinson (2020: 294) cautions that the concept of intercultural commu-nication 'connotes connection and crossing and reifies difference and sep-arateness, suggesting, as it does, exchange *between* (*inter*) at least two cultures that exist as definable and more or less bounded entities'. She concludes that despite the recent criticisms, '... used with care within the context of language education and with caution elsewhere ... the intercul-tural speaker still has a place in our research and practice' (2020: 294).

Intercultural Interventions Within the Context of Academic Mobility

In the past two decades, we have seen growth in the diversity of schemes that strive to deepen and extend the language and intercultural learning of participants in academic mobility schemes (Jackson & Oguro, 2018; Plews & Misfeldt, 2018), including some that have drawn on the work of Byram (1997) and his colleagues (e.g. Alred & Byram, 2002; Byram & Dervin, 2008; Byram & Feng, 2006) as well as other scholars such as Bennett (2012). In particular, there is increasing emphasis on reflexivity and criticality in study abroad programming (Byrd Clark, 2020; Jackson, 2018a). While many initiatives are limited to the pre-departure phase, others focus on supporting students while they are in the host speech community. A much smaller number target the intercultural learning and meaning-making of returnees (e.g. Jackson, 2015; Lee, 2018). In some contexts, Byram's vision has helped to inspire the development of comprehensive intercultural education programs that span all phases of the academic mobility cycle from pre-departure to re-entry (e.g. Cuenat, 2018). Advances in theory-building, research, pedagogy, assessment and communications technology are enabling the creation of innovative intercultural interventions in academic mobility contexts throughout the world, and increasingly many place more emphasis on both self-reflection and critical engagement (e.g. Byrd Clark, 2020; Jackson, 2018a, 2019b; Lee, 2018).

Pre-departure preparation

Intercultural L2 educators have identified and explored the challenges that newcomers may face in an unfamiliar speech community, drawing attention to the strategies that may ease the adjustment process and facilitate language and intercultural learning (e.g. Furnham, 2015; Kim, 2012). Inspired by this material and models of intercultural competence development (e.g. Byram, 1997; Deardorff, 2008), intercultural educators have been devising a range of pre-departure interventions (e.g. Bennett, 2009; Hepple, 2018; Holmes *et al.*, 2015).

If participants are to take full advantage of their time in the host community, Byram *et al.* (2001) argue that they need to be 'well prepared pedagogically' (2001: 4) for the experience. Pre-academic mobility interventions (e.g. workshops, intercultural communication courses) can raise awareness of the benefits of setting realistic sojourn goals, encourage reflection on potential adjustment/L2/intercultural communication issues and explore language and culture learning strategies that could be used to maximize stays abroad (Bathurst & La Brack, 2012; Jackson, 2018b; Jackson & Oguro, 2018). Intervening at this stage can provide students with a frame of reference to help them process their L2/intercultural experience and ease their adjustment in the new environment.

Programmers may incorporate specific characteristics of the academic mobility scheme (e.g. SA aims, duration, housing, language component) into the design of the pre-departure intervention. Detailed profiles of the participants, including an assessment of their L2 proficiency and intercultural sensitivity, can help to shape the intervention (Almarza *et al.*, 2015; Harsch & Poehner, 2016). An understanding of the cohort's language and intercultural attitudes, motivation, readiness for intercultural learning and SA aims can help to guide the selection and sequencing of materials and activities (Byram, 1997; Jackson, 2018b; Paige, 2013, 2015). In accord with the principles of experiential learning and the basic tenets of learner-centered teaching, intercultural educators may then build on the participants' (inter)cultural knowledge (*savoirs*) (Byram, 1997), L2 expertise, and previous international/intercultural experience (Jackson, 2018b; Passarelli & Kolb, 2012). This phase should help students to develop a more critical, reflective mindset, which can then aid the processing of intercultural/L2 experience in a metacognitive way (by 'thinking about thinking') (Byrd Clark, 2020; Penman & Ratz, 2015).

If the pre-departure orientation is for a group of students who will study in the same host country, intercultural educators may encourage the participants to gather culture-specific information (e.g. sociopragmatic norms of politeness, local vocabulary). Byram (1997) refers to this as the enhancement of cultural knowledge or *savoirs*. For example, participants may be prodded to develop some understanding of the history, geography, and religion(s) of the host country, as well as the linguistic and sociopolitical landscape. Contemporary critical theorists also underscore the need for facilitators to raise awareness of diversity *within* cultures and draw attention to the potentially harmful effects of Otherisation and essentialism (Holliday, 2011, 2012, 2020; Jackson, 2018a, 2019a; Ladegaard, 2020).

Prior to the arrival in the host country, intercultural educators may draw attention to the subtle ways in which primary socialization can influence one's behavior, values, identities and outlook. This reflective process can also raise awareness of negative orientations of the hosts or sojourners (Anya, 2017) and help to cultivate what Byram (1997) refers to as intercultural attitudes (*savoir être*). With enhanced self-awareness and a more positive outlook, participants are better positioned to push past stereotypes and consider the impact of their own attitudes, preconceptions and behaviors (e.g. conflict communication style) on intercultural interactions (Alred & Byram, 2002; Ladegaard, 2020).

Prior to SA, intercultural educators may familiarize students with language and culture-learning strategies that could help them to deal more effectively with the natural ups and downs of intercultural transitions (e.g. see Bennett, 2015; Deardorff & Arasaratnam-Smith, 2017; Jackson & Oguro, 2018). Experiential learning activities (e.g. ethnographic interviews with international students on their home campus) can encourage students to gain valuable intercultural/L2 experience and reflect on the challenges of intercultural adjustment before studying abroad (Jackson, 2016; Passarelli & Kolb, 2012; Roberts *et al.*, 2001). Students may also be presented with sojourner accounts (e.g. blog posts, diary entries, interview excerpts), critical incidents (e.g. brief scenarios that illustrate intercultural miscommunication) or SA cases (e.g. problem-based narratives that illustrate intercultural situations) to analyze and discuss. Activities like this have the potential to lessen anxiety while nurturing a more positive mindset, thereby increasing the willingness of the students to use their L2 to initiate intercultural interactions. In essence, when skilfully managed, interventions of this nature can promote the knowledge and skills that feature in Byram's (1997) model (e.g. knowledge or *savoirs*; skills of interpreting and relating or *savoir comprendre*; skills of discovery and interaction or *savoir apprendre/faire*).

Intercultural educators also recognize that SA returnees can be a valuable resource in pre-departure orientations, especially if these individuals have taken an active role in the host environment, displayed positive intercultural attitudes and enhanced their intercultural communicative competence. Returnees can provide encouragement for reticent students who are about to embark on overseas studies. Drawing on their own international experience, returnees could share the strategies and intercultural attitudes (*savoir être*) that helped them to cope with acculturative stress and construct meaningful intercultural, L2 relationships. The returnees could encourage the setting of realistic goals and also inspire newcomers to diversify their social networks early on to optimize their experience in the host environment.

The stay in the host environment

While in the host country, newcomers receive varying degrees of support, depending on the nature, length and format of their program, as well as available funding and staff expertise. In many academic mobility programs, there are no intercultural interventions, and students are expected to quickly adjust and immerse themselves in their new surroundings. With more awareness of the research that points to the benefits of intercultural interventions in SA programs, we are witnessing growth in the number and diversity of pedagogical initiatives that seek to enhance intercultural learning and engagement (e.g. Jackson & Oguro, 2018; Jackson & Schwieter, 2019; Plews & Misfeldt, 2018).

Some faculty-led academic mobility schemes for L2 students now incorporate intercultural education into the curriculum, drawing on Byram's model and recent advances in our understanding of the importance of criticality and reflexivity (Byrd Clark, 2020; Jackson, 2014, 2018b, 2020). Instructors from both home and host institutions may collaborate on the design and implementation of activities to promote intercultural learning and engagement in the host country. Credit-bearing intercultural education courses or optional workshops may be offered to newcomers, which may include contact with locals. International exchange participants may enroll in intercultural communication courses in the host institution or, when available, join an online intercultural transitions course hosted by their home institution to help them make sense of their experience in the host environment (e.g. Jackson 2017, 2018b, 2018c). Newcomers may also benefit from the support offered by counsellors who have received special training to work with international students (e.g. ease intercultural transitions) (Arthur, 2004). A growing number of host institutions offer orientations, intercultural social activities and/or 'buddy' programs that match international students with local partners to help the newcomers more quickly adjust to their new surroundings and advance their intercultural communicative competence. It is also possible that the host environment may offer little or no support for newcomers or the new arrivals may choose not to participate in events organized by their hosts.

Intercultural educators have been creating a range of tasks to prompt what Byram (1997) defines as critical cultural awareness or *savoir s'engager*. The writing of a diary, journal, wiki log or blog can stimulate critical reflection, dialogue and self-analysis (Anya, 2017; Jackson & Oguro, 2018; Passarelli & Kolb, 2012) and foster a more in-depth understanding of the host environment (Péron, 2019). Reflecting on and writing about intercultural experiences can provide an emotional release (Ochs & Capps, 2001) and help newcomers deal with the ups and downs that are a natural part of the adjustment process (Brewer & Moore, 2015; Savicki, 2015). Critical engagement and reflection can bring about a deeper awareness of the complex ways in which hosts and newcomers collaboratively construct, negotiate or contest gender, race, ethnicity, sexuality and social class identities (Anya, 2017; Péron, 2019).

Thinking and writing about intercultural experience can help students to become more attuned to their own intercultural attitudes and positioning in the host environment. With the guidance and support of a skilled intercultural educator, SA students can become more cognizant of their reactions to linguistic and cultural difference, and the ways in which they approach intercultural interactions. A reflective mindset can help to reduce negative emotions and create the space and distance needed to learn from unsatisfactory intercultural interactions as well as ones that are deemed successful. By revisiting intercultural experiences through writing and discussion, students can deepen their metacognitive awareness and learn to assume more responsibility for their own intercultural attitudes, actions and outcomes.

To bolster language and (inter)cultural awareness in the host environment, intercultural educators may require participants to keep a blog, diary, e-journal or visual account of their international, intercultural learning (e.g. audio or video recordings, hypermedia web logs or vlogs). This process, including periodic reviews of entries, can bring about new insights (e.g. awareness of a negative, self-defeating attitude, the benefits of an open mindset) and help to raise awareness of gaps or growth in intercultural competence. This, in turn, can facilitate the revision of language and intercultural learning goals.

As the participants deepen their intercultural knowledge and gain relevant 'real-world' experience in the host environment, intercultural educators can prompt the systematic 'unpacking' of intercultural interactions and conflict situations (e.g. using a direct style of communication in a context where indirectness is the norm) and consider what they might do differently in similar situations in the future. Thus, more and more inter-culturalists (e.g. Byram, 1997; Dasli & Díaz, 2017; Jackson & Oguro, 2018) recommend that intercultural education include critical reflection as a core element. While in the host environment, students may be routinely encouraged to critically reflect on their past, current and future intercul-tural interactions.

Intercultural educators need to create a safe environment to host debriefing sessions that encourage newcomers to discuss sensitive intercul-tural issues that are impacting their stay abroad (e.g. discriminatory prac-tices, positioning, unfamiliar 'cultures of learning' or other ways of being). For these sessions to work well, it is vital that the facilitator be empathetic, practice active listening and genuinely encourage the free expression of ideas and experiences in a respectful manner. Participants may be prompted to revisit their SA goals and consider what they can realistically accomplish in the remainder of their stay in the host environment.

Students in faculty-led programs who have received ample pre-sojourn preparation may conduct small-scale ethnographic projects in the host environment. Through sustained contact in a particular setting, they may investigate local cultural practices and gain exposure to different world-views in addition to authentic communication styles and speech genres (Jackson, 2016; Roberts *et al.*, 2001). As they carry out their research, they can systematically observe, listen, interpret and analyze the behavior and discourse of their 'informants'. Additionally, projects of this nature can provide students with a purpose for intercultural interactions and inspire more in-depth, meaningful dialogue; this can be especially helpful for students who are less confident of their L2/social/intercultural com-munication skills (Jackson, 2008, 2017a; Roberts *et al.*, 2001). As Wilkinson (2020) explains, '[t]he idea behind these programs is not only to equip students with the ethnographic tools to facilitate general observa-tion of aspects of daily life in the foreign country, but to encourage a deeper engagement with a particular aspect of that culture through researching and writing up a specific ethnographic project' (2020: 290–291). Proponents of the use of ethnography in academic mobility schemes contend that it can deepen students' awareness of social and cultural ele-ments in the host environment and facilitate the development of intercul-tural communicative competence.

Besides ethnography, intercultural educators have devised other cre-ative modes of experiential learning (e.g. weekly tasks that require inter-cultural interactions, informal interviews with hosts) to encourage students to become more engaged in the host environment (Jackson & Oguro, 2018; Passarelli & Kolb, 2012) and further develop their intercul-tural communicative competence (Byram, 1997; Byram & Golubeva, 2020). Without these interventions, one cannot assume that language and intercultural learning will occur in the host environment. Participants may not take advantage of affordances in the host community and end up spending all of their free time conversing in their L1 with co-nationals, contrary to their pre-departure expectations and aspirations.

Intercultural educators may also encourage SA students to take some time to prepare for their return to their home country (Kartoshkina, 2015; La Brack, 2015). Learner-centered debriefing sessions (face-to-face or online) can motivate students to revisit their pre-SA goals and take stock of their language and (inter)cultural learning and personal growth. With prompting, students may also consider how to sustain their multicultural ties and extend their language and intercultural learning once they are back home (e.g. keep their 'global self' alive in their home environment).

Re-entry

Within the context of academic mobility, most intercultural interventions are implemented before and during the stay abroad; however, recent research has revealed that returnees may experience readjustment issues and find it difficult to continue their language and intercultural development in meaningful ways once they return home (Bathurst & La Brack, 2012; La Brack, 2015; Szkudlarek, 2010). Accordingly, more face-to-face, blended or fully online re-entry schemes are being devised to deepen and extend the intercultural communicative competence development of returnees (Byram, 1997) through the offering of intercultural transition courses, re-entry workshops, study abroad alumni conferences and other interventions (Jackson, 2015, 2017, 2018b, 2018c; Jackson & Oguro, 2018).

Even if the period abroad has been brief, returnees may experience readjustment issues, especially if they have developed a broader worldview, diversified their social network, become more at ease with informal discourse in their L2, developed positive intercultural attitudes, and honed a more inclusive mindset (Byram, 1997; Furnham, 2015; Jackson, 2015; Savicki, 2015). Much to their surprise, some find themselves ill-prepared to deal with the malaise and identity confusion that can fester once they are back home. Intercultural educators can help them to make sense of their emotions and experiences, and set positive, realistic goals for their future language and intercultural learning.

More sensitive to the need for re-entry interventions, intercultural educators are providing more opportunities for returnees to share their experiences and critically reflect on their international, intercultural learning and re-entry. Discussions and activities (e.g. reflective writing tasks, small group discussions) that center on identity-related issues may be designed to encourage returnees to consider how to apply their enhanced L2 and intercultural communication skills in their current life and future career. The participants may also be prompted to recognize and seize affordances in their home environment to engage in intercultural interactions, develop a multicultural social network and nurture their 'global self'. This continued emphasis on the intercultural skills and attitudes identified by Byram (1997) draws further attention to the life-long nature of intercultural communicative competence development.

Comprehensive Interventions That Target All Phases of the Study Abroad Cycle

A number of schemes encompass all phases of the academic mobility cycle from pre-departure to re-entry. In Europe, drawing on the work of Byram, Holliday and other applied linguists, collaborative schemes have brought about the creation of materials and guidebooks that aim to enrich the intercultural learning of mobile students. The European Centre for Modern Languages, for example, created *PluriMobil*, a pedagogical tool that provides materials and ideas for activities that aim to deepen the plurilingual and intercultural development of students before, during and after academic mobility (Cuenat, 2018; European Centre for Modern Languages, 2015).

The *Intercultural Educational Resources for Erasmus Students and their Teachers* (IEREST) project, a multilateral, intercultural education scheme, seeks to promote mobility and enhance the intercultural learning of participants during all phases of the academic mobility cycle (IEREST, 2015). Drawing on critical notions of interculturality and intercultural competence development (e.g. Byram, 1997; Byram & Zarate, 1994, 1996), IEREST developed a European network of higher education institutions which brought about the development and testing of intercultural teaching modules that strive to enhance the intercultural awareness and personal growth of SA participants (Beaven & Borghetti, 2016; Borghetti, 2016; Borghetti & Beaven, 2018; Holmes *et al.*, 2016) (also see http://www.ierest-project.eu/).

Summary and Future Directions

Within the context of academic mobility, this chapter reviewed some of the exciting developments that have taken place in intercultural pedagogy in the past few decades, paying particular attention to the ways in which the work of Byram and his colleagues has provided valuable inspiration. While there have been impressive gains in the intercultural education of SA participants, much more work needs to be done to optimize the potential of academic mobility. Unintentionally, some programs still foster Otherisation and essentialism (Holliday, 2020; Jackson, 2018b). Instead of scaffolding and encouraging higher levels of intercultural awareness and sensitivity, and the attributes and actions associated with critical intercultural mediators (Byram & Golubeva, 2020; Wilkinson, 2020), some interventions focus so much on cultural difference that pre-existing stereotypes and ethnocentrism are reinforced (Ladegaard,

2020). To counter this, contemporary critical interculturalists increasingly recommend that pedagogical interventions transcend traditional conceptions of culture that are bounded by the nation-state (Holliday, 2011, 2020), enhance critical self-awareness and recognition of one's positionality and identities in new environs and raise more awareness of diversity *within* cultures and the notion of multiple, complex identities (e.g. Jackson & Oguro, 2018; Komisarof & Zhu, 2016).

By adopting some of the pedagogical approaches that were described in this chapter, intercultural educators can prompt SA participants to push past 'them vs us' discourse and display a more critical awareness of themselves and their positioning in the world. For this to happen, educators must have a solid understanding of interculturality and intercultural (communicative) competence (e.g. Byram & Golubeva, 2020; Holliday, 2011, 2020; Liddicoat & Scarino, 2020; Wilkinson, 2020), intercultural development theories (e.g. Byram, 1997; Byram & Zarate, 1994, 1996; Deardorff, 2008; Jackson, 2018a) and advances in research-inspired pedagogy (e.g. Jackson & Oguro, 2018; Plews & Misfeldt, 2018).

The promotion of intercultural awareness, empathy and global-mindedness is challenging but vital to optimize international educational experience and prepare students for the globalized world in which we live. Finally, just as research and theories should inform practice, systematic reviews of pedagogical interventions must be carried out and shared publically to provide direction for the enhancement of intercultural teaching and learning in academic mobility contexts.

References

Almarza, G.G., Martinez, R.D. and Llavador, F.B. (2015) Identifying students' intercultural communicative competence at the beginning of their placement: Towards the enhancement of study abroad programmes. *Intercultural Education* 26 (1), 73–85.

Alred, G. and Byram, M. (2002) Becoming an intercultural mediator: A longitudinal study of residence abroad. *Journal of Multilingual and Multicultural Development* 23 (5), 339–352.

Anya, U. (2017) *Racialized Identities in Second Language Learning: Speaking Blackness in Brazil*. London: Routledge.

Arthur, N. (2004) *Counseling International Students: Clients from Around the World*. Boston, MA: Springer.

Bathurst, L. and La Brack, B. (2012) Shifting the locus of intercultural learning: Intervening prior to and after student experiences abroad. In M. Vande Berg, R.M. Paige and K.H. Lou (eds) *Student Learning Abroad: What Our Students Are Learning, What They're Not, and What We Can Do About It* (pp. 261–283). Sterling, VA: Stylus.

Beaven, A. and Borghetti, C. (2016) Interculturality in study abroad. *Language and Intercultural Communication* 16 (3), 313–317.

Bennett, J.M. (2009) Cultivating intercultural competence: A process perspective. In D. Deardorff (ed.) *The Sage Handbook of Intercultural Competence* (pp. 121–140). Thousand Oaks, CA: Sage.

Bennett, J.M. (2015) Essential principles for intercultural training. In J.M. Bennett (ed.) *The Sage Handbook of Intercultural Competence* (Vol. 1, pp. 293–297). Thousand Oaks, CA: Sage.

Bennett, M.J. (1998) Intercultural communication: A current perspective. In M.J. Bennett (ed.) *Basic Concepts of Intercultural Communication: Selected Readings* (pp. 1–34). Yarmouth, ME: Intercultural Press.

Bennett, M.J. (2012) Paradigmatic assumptions and a developmental approach to intercultural learning. In M. Vande Berg, R.M. Paige and K.H. Lou (eds) *Student Learning Abroad: What Our Students Are Learning, What They're Not, and What We Can Do About It* (pp. 90–114). Sterling, VA: Stylus.

Borghetti, C. (2016) Intercultural education in practice: Two pedagogical experiences with mobile students. *Language and Intercultural Education* 16 (3), 502–513.

Borghetti, C. and Beaven, A. (2018) Monitoring class interaction to maximise intercultural learning in mobility contexts. In J. Jackson and S. Oguro (eds) *Intercultural Interventions in Study Abroad* (pp. 37–54). London: Routledge.

Brewer, E. and Moore, J. (2015) Where and how do students learn abroad? Using reflective writing for meaning-making and assessment. In V. Savicki and E. Brewer (eds) *Assessing Study Abroad: Theory, Tools, and Practice* (pp. 145–161). Sterling, VA: Stylus.

Byram, M. (1995) Acquiring intercultural competence. In L. Sercu (ed.) *Intercultural Competence: A New Challenge for Language Teachers and Trainers in Europe* (pp. 53–69). Aalborg: Aalborg University Press.

Byram, M. (1997) *Teaching and Assessing Intercultural Communicative Competence.* Clevedon: Multilingual Matters.

Byram, M. (2008) *From Foreign Language Education to Education for Intercultural Citizenship: Essays and Reflections.* Clevedon: Multilingual Matters.

Byram, M. (2009) Intercultural competence in foreign languages: The intercultural speaker and the pedagogy of foreign language education. In D.K. Deardorff (ed.) *The Handbook of Intercultural Competence* (pp. 321–332). Thousand Oaks, CA: Sage.

Byram, M. (2012) Conceptualizing intercultural (communicative) competence and intercultural citizenship. In J. Jackson (ed.) *The Routledge Handbook of Language and Intercultural Communication* (pp. 85–97). London: Routledge.

Byram, M. and Dervin, F. (eds) (2008) *Students, Staff, and Academic Mobility.* Newcastle: Cambridge Scholars Publishing.

Byram, M. and Feng, A. (eds) (2006) *Living and Studying Abroad: Research and Practice.* Clevedon: Multilingual Matters.

Byram, M. and Golubeva, I. (2020) Conceptualizing intercultural (communicative) competence and intercultural citizenship. In J. Jackson (ed.) *The Routledge Handbook of Language and Intercultural Communication* (2nd edn, pp. 70–85). London: Routledge.

Byram, M., Gribkova, B. and Starkey, H. (2002) *Developing the Intercultural Dimension in Language Teaching: A Practical Introduction for Teachers.* Strasbourg: Council of Europe.

Byram, M., Nichols, A. and Stevens, D. (2001) Introduction. In M. Byram, A. Nichols and D. Stevens (eds) *Developing Intercultural Competence in Practice* (pp. 1–8). Clevedon: Multilingual Matters.

Byram, M. and Zarate, G. (1994) *Définitions, objectifs et évaluation de la compétence socio-culturelle.* Strasbourg: Council of Europe.

Byram, M. and Zarate, G. (1996) Defining and assessing intercultural competence: Some principles and proposals for the European context. *Language Teaching* 29 (4), 239–243.

Byrd Clark, J. (2020) Reflexivity and criticality for language and intercultural communication research and practice. In J. Jackson (ed.) *The Routledge Handbook of Language and Intercultural Communication* (2nd edn, pp. 86–106). London: Routledge.

Canale, M. and Swain, M. (1980) Theoretical bases of communicative approaches to second language teaching and testing. *Applied Linguistics* 1, 1–47.

Council of Europe (2001) *Common European Framework of Reference for Languages.* Cambridge: University of Cambridge Press and Council of Europe.

Council of Europe (2018) *Common European Framework of Reference for Languages: Learning, Teaching, Assessment: Companion Volume with New Descriptors.* Strasbourg: Council of Europe.

Cuenat, M. (2018) Plurimobil: Pragmatic enhancement of intercultural learning in study abroad contexts. In J. Jackson and S. Oguro (eds) *Intercultural Interventions in Study Abroad* (pp. 175–190). London: Routledge.

Dasli, M. and Díaz, A.R. (eds) (2017) *The Critical Turn in Language and Intercultural Communication Pedagogy: Theory, Research and Practice.* London: Routledge.

Deardorff, D.K. (2008) Intercultural competence: A definition, model, and implications for education abroad. In V. Savicki (ed.) *Developing Intercultural Competence and Transformation: Theory, Research, and Application in International Education* (pp. 32–52). Sterling, VA: Stylus.

Deardorff, D.K. and Arasaratnam-Smith, L. (eds) (2017) *Intercultural Competence in International Higher Education: International Approaches, Assessment and Application.* London: Routledge.

European Centre for Modern Languages (2015) *Plurilingual and Intercultural Learning Through Mobility: Practical Resources for Teachers and Teacher Trainers.* http://plurimobil.ecml.at/

Furnham, A. (2015) Mobility in a global era. In J.M. Bennett (ed.) *The Sage Handbook of Intercultural Competence* (Vol. 2, pp. 630–634). Thousand Oaks, CA: Sage.

Guilherme, M. (2004) Intercultural competence. In M. Byram (ed.) *Routledge Encyclopedia of Language Teaching and Learning* (pp. 297–300). London: Routledge.

Harsch, C. and Poehner, M.E. (2016) Enhancing student experiences abroad: The potential of dynamic assessment to develop student interculturality. *Language and Intercultural Communication* 16 (3), 470–490.

Hepple, E. (2018) The first step in embedding intercultural learning through study abroad within an Australian university: Designing and implementing pre-departure intercultural workshops. In J. Jackson and S. Oguro (eds) *Intercultural Interventions in Study Abroad* (pp. 18–36). London: Routledge.

Holliday, A. (2011) *Intercultural Communication and Ideology.* Thousand Oaks, CA: Sage.

Holliday, A. (2012) Culture, communication, context and power. In J. Jackson (ed.) *The Routledge Handbook of Language and Intercultural Communication* (pp. 37–51). London: Routledge.

Holliday, A. (2020) Culture, communication, context and power. In J. Jackson (ed.) *The Routledge Handbook of Language and Intercultural Communication* (2nd edn, pp. 39–50). London: Routledge.

Holmes, P., Bavieri, L. and Ganassin, S. (2015) Developing intercultural understanding for study abroad: Students' and teachers' perspectives on pre-departure intercultural learning. *Intercultural Education* 26 (1), 16–30. https://doi.org/10.1080/14675986.2015.993250

Holmes, P., Bavieri, L., Ganassin, S. and Murphy, J. (2016) Interculturality and the study abroad experience: Students' learning from the IEREST materials. *Language and Intercultural Communication* 16 (3), 452–469

Howard, M. (ed.) (2019) *Study Abroad, Second Language Acquisition and Interculturality.* Bristol: Multilingual Matters.

Hymes, D.H. (1966) Two types of linguistic relativity. In W. Bright (ed.) *Sociolinguistics* (pp. 114–158). The Hague: Mouton.

Hymes, D.H. (1972) On communicative competence. In J. Pride and J. Holmes (eds) *Sociolinguistics* (pp. 269–293). Harmondsworth: Penguin.

IEREST (2015) *Intercultural Education Resources for Erasmus Students and Their Teachers*. Koper: Annales University Press.

Iwasaki, N. (2019) Individual differences in study abroad research: Sources, processes and outcomes of students' development in language, culture and personhood. In M. Howard (ed.) *Study Abroad, Second Language Acquisition and Interculturality* (pp. 237–262). Bristol: Multilingual Matters.

Jackson, J. (2008) *Language, Identity, and Study Abroad: Sociocultural Perspectives*. London: Equinox.

Jackson, J. (2014) The process of becoming reflexive and intercultural: Navigating study abroad and reentry experience. In J.S. Byrd Clark and F. Dervin (eds) *Reflexivity in Language and Intercultural Education: Rethinking Multilingualism and Interculturality* (pp. 43–63). London: Routledge.

Jackson, J. (2015) Becoming interculturally competent: Theory to practice in international education. *International Journal of Intercultural Relations* 48, 91–107. https://doi.org/10.1016/j.ijintrel.2015.03.012

Jackson, J. (2016) Ethnography. In H. Zhu (ed.) *Research Methods in Intercultural Communication: A Practical Guide* (pp. 239–254). New York, NY: Wiley and Sons.

Jackson, J. (2017) Intercultural communication and engagement abroad. In D.K. Deardorff and L.A. Arasaratnam-Smith (eds) *Intercultural Competence in Higher Education: International Approaches, Assessment and Application* (pp. 197–201). London: Routledge.

Jackson, J. (2018a) *Interculturality in International Education*. New York: Routledge.

Jackson, J. (2018b) Optimizing intercultural learning and engagement abroad through online mentoring. In J. Jackson and S. Oguro (eds) *Intercultural Interventions in Study Abroad* (pp. 119–137). London: Routledge.

Jackson, J. (2018c) Intervening in the intercultural learning of L2 study abroad students: From research to practice. *Language Teaching* 51 (3), 365–382.

Jackson, J. (2019a) Intercultural competence and L2 pragmatics. In N. Taguchi (ed.) *The Routledge Handbook of Second Language Acquisition and Pragmatics* (pp. 479–494). London: Routledge.

Jackson, J. (2019b) *Online Intercultural Education and Study Abroad: Theory into Practice*. London: Routledge.

Jackson, J. (2020) The language and intercultural dimension of education abroad. In J. Jackson (ed.) *The Routledge Handbook of Language and Intercultural Communication* (2nd edn, pp. 442–446). London: Routledge.

Jackson, J. and Oguro, S. (2018) Introduction: Enhancing and extending study abroad learning through intercultural interventions. In J. Jackson and S. Oguro (eds) *Intercultural Interventions in Study Abroad* (pp. 1–17). London: Routledge.

Jackson, J. and Schwieter, J.W. (2019) Study abroad and immersion. In J.W. Schwieter and A. Benati (eds) *Cambridge Handbook of Language Learning* (pp. 727–750). Cambridge: Cambridge University Press.

Kartoshkina, Y. (2015) Bitter-sweet re-entry after studying abroad. *International Journal of Intercultural Relations* 44, 35–45.

Kim, Y.Y. (2012) Beyond cultural categories: Communication adaptation and transformation. In J. Jackson (ed.) *Routledge Handbook of Language and Intercultural Communication* (pp. 229–243). London: Routledge.

Komisarof, A. and Zhu, H. (2016) Introduction. In A. Komisarof and H. Zhu (eds) *Crossing Boundaries and Weaving Intercultural Work, Life and Scholarship in Globalizing Universities* (pp. 1–20). London: Routledge.

La Brack, B. (2015) Reentry. In J.M. Bennett (ed.) *The Sage Handbook of Intercultural Competence* (Vol. 2, pp. 723–727). Thousand Oaks, CA: Sage.

Ladegaard, H. (2020) Constructing the cultural Other: Prejudice and stereotyping. In J. Jackson (ed.) *The Routledge Handbook of Language and Intercultural Communication* (2nd edn, pp. 191–203). London: Routledge.

Lee, L. (2018) Employing telecollaborative exchange to extend intercultural learning after study abroad. In J. Jackson and S. Oguro (eds) *Intercultural Interventions in Study Abroad* (pp. 137–154). London: Routledge.

Liddicoat, A.J. and Scarino, A. (2010) Eliciting the intercultural in foreign language education at school. In A. Paran and L. Sercu (eds) *Testing the Untestable in Language Education* (pp. 52–73). Bristol: Multilingual Matters.

Liddicoat, A.J. and Scarino, A. (2020) Assessing intercultural language learning. In J. Jackson (ed.) *The Routledge Handbook of Language and Intercultural Communication* (2nd edn, pp. 395–409). London: Routledge.

Noels, K., Yashima, T. and Zhang, R. (2020) Language, identity, and intercultural communication. In J. Jackson (ed.) *The Routledge Handbook of Language and Intercultural Communication* (2nd edn, pp. 55–69). London: Routledge.

Ochs, E. and Capps, L. (2001) *Living Narrative: Creating Lives in Everyday Storytelling.* Boston, MA: Harvard University Press.

Paige, R.M. (2013, August 16) Factors Impacting Intercultural Development in Study Abroad. Paper presented at Elon University, Elon, North Carolina, United States.

Paige, R.M. (2015) Interventionist models for study abroad. In J.M. Bennett (ed.) *The Sage Handbook of Intercultural Competence* (Vol. 2, pp. 563–568). Thousand Oaks, CA: Sage.

Paige, R.M. and Vande Berg, M. (2012) Why students are and are not learning abroad. In M. Vande Berg, R.M. Paige and K.H. Lou (eds) *Student Learning Abroad: What Our Students Are Learning, What They're Not and What We Can Do About It* (pp. 29–59). Sterling, VA: Stylus.

Passarelli, A.M. and Kolb, D.A. (2012) Using experiential learning theory to promote student learning and development in programs of education abroad. In M. Vande Berg, R.M. Paige and K.H. Lou (eds) *Student Learning Abroad: What Our Students Are Learning, What They're Not and What We Can Do About It* (pp. 137–161). Sterling, VA: Stylus.

Penman, C. and Ratz, S. (2015) A module-based approach to foster and document the intercultural process before and during the residence abroad. *Intercultural Education* 26 (1), 49–61.

Péron, M. (2019) Don't write on walls! Playing with cityscapes in a foreign language course. In A. James and C. Nerantzi (eds) *The Power of Play in Higher Education: Creativity in Tertiary Learning* (pp. 185–194). London: Palgrave Macmillan.

Phipps, A. and Gonzalez, M. (2004) *Modern Languages: Learning and Teaching in an Intercultural Field.* Thousand Oaks, CA: Sage.

Plews, J. and Misfeldt, K. (2018) *Second Language Study Abroad: Programming, Pedagogy, and Participant Engagement.* Cham: Springer.

Risager, K. (2007) *Language and Culture Pedagogy: From a National to a Transnational Paradigm.* Clevedon: Multilingual Matters.

Roberts, C., Byram, M., Barro, A., Jordan, S. and Street, B. (2001) *Language Learners as Ethnographers.* Clevedon: Multilingual Matters.

Savicki, V. (2015) Stress, coping, and adjustment. In J.M. Bennett (ed.) *The Sage Handbook of Intercultural Competence* (Vol. 2, pp. 776–780). Thousand Oaks, CA: Sage.

Sercu, L. (2004) Assessing intercultural competence: A framework for systematic test development in foreign language education and beyond. *Intercultural Education* 15 (1), 73–89.

Szkudlarek, B. (2010) Reentry: A review of the literature. *International Journal of Intercultural Relations* 34 (1), 1–21.

Vande Berg, M. (2015) Developmentally appropriate pedagogy. In J.M. Bennett (ed.) *The Sage Encyclopedia of Intercultural Competence* (Vol. 1, pp. 229–233). Thousand Oaks, CA: Sage.

Wilkinson, J. (2020) From native speaker to intercultural speaker and beyond: Intercultural (communicative) competence in foreign language education. In J. Jackson (ed.) *The Routledge Handbook of Language and Intercultural Communication* (2nd edn, pp. 283–298). London: Routledge.

9 Intercultural Education through Civic Engagement: Service Learning in the Foreign Language Classroom

Petra Rauschert and Claudia Mustroph

Introduction

Not only the 2019 Global Peace Index but also a glance at the daily news shows that many conflicts and crises that have emerged in the past decade remain unresolved. Moreover, the COVID-19 pandemic has further exacerbated the situation in many countries and clearly demonstrated that peaceful coexistence in this globalized world is a goal that can only be achieved together. Teachers and curriculum developers play a major role in this process as they set the course of development for future generations. While educators in all subjects contribute in their own unique way, foreign language teachers are particularly well positioned to equip learners with the ability to engage in dialogue with people who have different linguistic and cultural affiliations, develop appreciation for otherness and establish sustainable relations worldwide. Intercultural Service Learning is a pedagogy that combines these dimensions of curricular learning and intercultural education with civic engagement. Thus, students not only identify local or global issues but use foreign languages to contribute to their resolution. This approach is closely related to Intercultural Citizenship Education, a pedagogy developed by Byram (2008). As early as 1997, Byram declared that foreign language learning should have broader educational aims, arguing that an intercultural approach to language education should be integrated within a philosophy of political education. About 10 years later, he formalized these ideas within a Framework for Intercultural Citizenship Education (Byram, 2008: 238f.). Here, he argued that 'the objectives of Education for Citizenship go further than those for Intercultural Communicative Competence, by encouraging engagement and action' (Byram, 2008: 74). Intercultural Service Learning (ISL) and Intercultural Citizenship Education (ICE) have different origins, but they share the assumption that educational institutions should provide students with the opportunity to use what they learn in class to exercise active citizenship on a local and global level.

The purpose of this chapter is to suggest how ISL can enhance foreign language education by linking intercultural learning and civic engagement. We will first present Service Learning from a theoretical perspective and define ISL as a special subtype of this pedagogy (Bringle, 2011; YSA, 2007). Additionally, we will map related pedagogies and highlight commonalities (Byram, 2008; Rauschert & Byram, 2017; UNESCO, 2014). A practical example, the Global Peace Path project, will be presented to illustrate how ISL can be implemented in foreign language education and provide insights into the effects it can have on participating students.

Service Learning: A Theoretical Perspective

Service Learning projects combine institutionalized learning and civic engagement (Seifert & Zentner, 2010). According to Sliwka and Frank (2004), this pedagogical approach has its origin in the US-American tradition of experiential learning, which aims to enhance education by offering learning opportunities beyond the classroom that address real-world questions (Lester et al., 2005). The idea of Service Learning is often regarded as a response to the educational philosopher John Dewey (1859–1952) and his book *Democracy and Education* (1916), which advocates for learning through and for civil society responsibility (Reinders, 2016). The strong link between educational aims and philanthropic work in Service Learning also becomes evident in Minor's (2001: para. 2) definition: 'Service learning is a union of community service and formal learning. It involves students going into their communities and using what they learn in class to help people, and then bringing what they learn in their community back into the classroom to enhance their academic learning. It is service with learning objectives and learning with service objectives'.

Service Learning is a type of community-based learning that 'can interest and motivate students by providing a foundation for exploring intellectual and social issues through rigorous engagement, discussion, and reflection' (Clifford & Reisinger, 2018: 6). The terms *engagement* and *service* are mainly used synonymously in the literature. However, along with a shift 'from working *with* rather than *for* communities' (Clifford & Reisinger, 2018: 5), the term *civic engagement* has a slightly stronger political connotation, while *community service* places stronger emphasis on charitable work.

Due to the wide range of different Service Learning projects that have been carried out worldwide, the definitions of the concept are equally varied. However, the majority reference three didactical principles: (1)

reality, (2) reciprocity and (3) reflection (Godfrey *et al.*, 2005: 315). The first principle, reality, implies that Service Learning projects cannot be carried out solely in an academic setting but must take place in the real world and respond to genuine support needs in the community. Reciprocity relates to the relationship between all participants (service providers and service recipients). The final didactical principle, reflection, indicates that participants in a Service Learning project need sufficient time and guidance to reflect on the relationship between institutional learning and their experience in the community.

As more projects based on the concept of Service Learning have been carried out, related research and evaluation of these projects have increased. Internationally, the eight quality criteria for good Service Learning initiatives published by the National Youth Leadership Council in 2008 have been rather influential (Figure 9.1). The scope of this article does not allow us to discuss all the quality criteria, including their indicators, in detail; however, the main idea of each criterion shall be adumbrated.

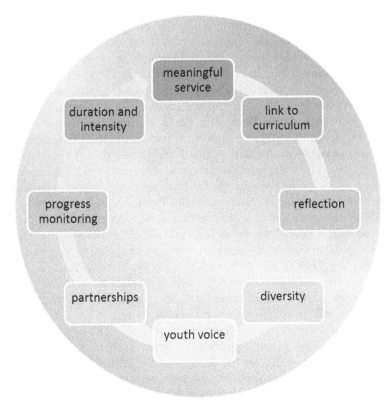

Figure 9.1 K-12 Service Learning standards for quality practice (based on: National Youth Leadership Council, 2008)

The first quality criterion, meaningful service, is designed to ensure the match between service activities and participants. This includes aspects such as age appropriateness and personal interests but also encompasses a general understanding of the social context of the service activity. In addition, it needs to be ensured that the project 'leads to attainable and visible outcomes that are valued by those being served' (National Youth Leadership Council, 2008: 1). Very much in line with the overall definition of the pedagogical concept is the second quality standard. In contrast to other activities such as volunteer work, Service Learning is characterized by its strong link to the curriculum. Consequently, it is designed with clear learning goals in mind and aligns closely with the school or academic curriculum. Due to its particular importance, reflection is not only one of the three didactical principles but also constitutes one of the standards for quality practice. It is only through extensive and instructor-led reflection that participants can actually transfer their experience into new knowledge (National Youth Leadership Council, 2008: 2). A further standard is diversity, which requires an atmosphere of mutual understanding and respect among all participants of a project. The next quality criterion is related to the participants' age. Service Learning is usually designed for young people, encourages them to make a difference in their societies, and therefore 'provides youth with a strong voice in planning, implementing and evaluating' (National Youth Leadership Council, 2008: 3). As Service Learning projects involve collaboration between teachers, students and community members, partnership is a further essential aspect. In order to ensure successful completion of projects, the quality principle of progress monitoring also plays an important role. It urges all participants to evaluate the advancement of the project and invites them to optimize the project flow. The final quality standard, duration and intensity states that Service Learning projects need to be of appropriate length to achieve the envisioned outcomes (National Youth Leadership Council, 2008: 4).

While the question of what makes a good Service Learning project received a great deal of attention during the development of the pedagogical approach, and some studies also investigated the impact on the communities (e.g. Düx et al., 2008; Melchior, 1999; Metz & Youniss, 2005), recently, more research has been conducted on the effects of the projects on the learners. With regard to the latter, meta-analyses show that Service Learning significantly affects learners in four areas: academic, civic, social and personal characteristics (Reinders, 2016: 54). The extent to which Service Learning can have a positive influence on these features depends on the didactical quality of the project (Billig, 2007: 18), among other factors. How far these positive effects can be seen in the Global Peace Path Project will be discussed later in the article. First, we would like to outline the theoretical background of the project, i.e. ISL, a particular form of Service Learning.

Intercultural Service Learning: A Special Type of Service Learning

Whereas Service Learning projects, as we explained in the previous section, do not prescribe specific curricular content, in ISL the focus is on intercultural learning (De Leon, 2014: 21). Modifying Bringle and Hatcher's (1995: 122) definition of International Service Learning, a closely related approach, De Leon (2014) also emphasizes this aspect when she describes ISL as:

> a structured academic experience in which students (a) participate in an organized service activity that addresses identified community needs; (b) learn from direct interaction and cross-cultural dialogue with others in which they can apply course content; and (c) reflect on the experience in such a way as to further understanding of course content, deepen understanding of global and intercultural issues, broaden appreciation of cultural difference, and enhance a sense of their own responsibility as local and global citizens. (2014: 21)

The intercultural dimension of ISL manifest mainly in two respects: (1) the aim of developing students' intercultural competence and (2) the expanded notion of community service that includes local and global communities. In view of the learning objectives of ISL, there is a great deal of overlap with the aims of foreign language learning, and it is therefore particularly useful in language education. For example, the goals to 'learn from direct interaction and cross-cultural dialogue with others', 'deepen understanding of global and intercultural issues' and 'appreciation of cultural difference' (2014: 21) are inherent in the descriptions of intercultural and communicative competences in many curricula and educational standards for foreign language learning (Council of Europe, 2001; KMK, 2012; National Standards Collaborative Board, 2015). In ISL projects, the foreign language serves as a means that allows learners to engage in meaningful dialogue with partners who have different cultural affiliations, discuss societal issues and collaboratively take action. While the foreign language has instrumental value here, its function needs to be further explored in regard to the intercultural dimension of ISL. With and through (foreign) languages learners encounter contrasting perspectives, engage in critical study of the world and experience how languages shape identities and relationships.

Unlike Service Learning, Intercultural Service Learning is still a comparably new approach (Morgan & Barnhart, 2015: 528). In order to concretize the intercultural competences that students are to develop when practicing ISL in the foreign language classroom, Byram's widely acclaimed model of Intercultural Communicative Competence (1997) provides the necessary categories. Byram argues in *Teaching and Assessing Intercultural Communicative Competence* (1997), that it is not only linguistic competences that determine whether an exchange between two people from different cultures is fruitful. Rather, in his view, what is equally important is the establishment and 'maintenance of human relationships' (Byram, 1997: 33). This necessitates the development of intercultural competence, defined by Byram (1997) on the basis of the following five savoirs:

- attitudes: relativizing self, valuing other (*savior être*)
- skills: interpret and relate (*savior comprendre*)
- skills: discover and/or interact (*savoir apprendre/faire*)
- knowledge of self and other, of interaction: individual and societal (*saviors*)
- education: political education, critical cultural awareness (*savoir s'engager*). (1997: 34)

The domains knowledge, skills and attitudes are grouped around the term education, which is specified as 'political education/critical cultural awareness' (Byram, 1997: 34). While intercultural competence can be acquired in formal or informal learning contexts, Byram argues that the central term of 'education' is particularly relevant in formal educational institutions, where there is a need for an evaluative orientation that, for example, allows learners to critically analyze values present in their own and their interlocutor's cultures.

While ISL aims to foster all five *saviors*, it is the central position of critical cultural awareness that makes his model a particularly valuable source for ISL. This concept was even developed further in the revised edition of Byram's 1997 volume, for example, by making explicit the notion of power differentials (Byram, 2021: Chap. 2). We already emphasized the importance of reflection in the context of Service Learning; however, this practice seems even more crucial in the context of ISL. Since the experience itself does not automatically lead to a favorable learning outcome, learners should reflect critically. For example, when students encounter beliefs or behaviors that contradict their previously accepted cultural norms, reflection can be used as a tool to question existing assumptions and modify them (De Leon, 2014: 22). If this step is omitted, participants might be overstrained by their service experience and, as a result, reach unwanted conclusions that may even perpetuate stereotypes. This danger is particularly imminent with regard to the relationship between project members. As there is usually a group of service providers and a group of service recipients, it is essential to be mindful of the hierarchical structures and power relationships present in society and to ensure that patterns of domination and inequality do not develop within the project work itself. Thus, rather than establishing clear boundaries between both groups, accomplishing a shared goal should be the focus.

A further distinction between Service Learning and ISL relates to the notion of community service. Traditional Service Learning projects often focus on a local or a national level; ISL, in contrast, can take a broader perspective. Thanks to the internet, even geographically remote people can now interact with one another. As a consequence, the notion of community is expanding more and more to groups with a joint communication channel. The increasing global interconnectedness is not only leading to global communities but more diversity within local communities that are marked by migration flows. The following three categories offer a way to systematize the different forms of ISL (Youth Service America, 2007: 3):

(1) ISL within one country: People who live in the same country but have different cultural affiliations collaborate on a project;
(2) ISL between countries: Students stay in their country and remotely collaborate with people from a different country during a project;
(3) ISL abroad: Service is provided during a stay abroad.

An example of the first type is the Global Peace Path, which will be outlined later in this chapter. Rauschert (2014) also conducted an ISL project between countries when she, her learners in Germany, and their partners in India created a magazine entitled *Happiness in India and Germany*. The magazine provided information and education while its earnings were used to build a school in India (see pp. 148–169).

Intercultural Service Learning and Intercultural Citizenship Education: Six of One, Half a Dozen of the Other?

There has not yet been extensive research on ISL's connection to foreign language education. Only with the introduction of the term intercultural citizenship, Byram's publication *From Foreign Language Education to Education for Intercultural Citizenship: Essays and Reflections* (2008) added a new perspective to language learning. De Leon interprets this concept as 'an extension of "intercultural competence"' (2014: 81), which results in foreign language education that urges learners to not only question their own viewpoints and those dominant in society but to also take active part in social activity within and beyond the nation.

One noteworthy question relates to the extent that local and global issues should be made a matter of discussion in Intercultural Citizenship Education (ICE) in the foreign language classroom. Byram (2018) advocates for a view of internationalism that is realized through

> the importance of (humanistic) values and understanding others, the critical reflection on one's own self and country, the developing link with education for (active) citizenship and participation in democratic processes which go beyond the borders of the nation and state. (2018: 71)

Byram illuminates his argument by encouraging discussions in the foreign language classroom that deal with themes seemingly far too large for a single nation to solve, such as world peace, gender equality and climate change. This selection of themes also holds true for ISL, especially based on the broad concept of community that we established earlier. A third pedagogical approach that advocates for the discussion of global issues in schools is Global Citizenship Education (GCE) as promoted by the United Nations Educational, Scientific and Cultural Organization (UNESCO): 'GCE aims to empower learners to engage and assume active roles, both locally and globally, to face and resolve global challenges and ultimately to become proactive contributors to a more just, peaceful, tolerant, inclusive, secure and sustainable world' (UNESCO, 2014: 15).

Even though both ICE and ISL involve some kind of civic engagement, be it on a local, national, or global level, so far, only in ISL is there a clear distinction between different forms of engagement. According to Rauschert and Byram (2018), a more standardized approach that facilitates categorizing civic action across different pedagogies might be helpful in this respect. Therefore, the following four categories could be applicable to both ICE and ISL: first, Seifert and Zentner (2010) distinguish between *direct* and *indirect engagement*. The former refers to projects in which the service providers have direct contact with the recipients, whereas the latter involves projects in which the providers may raise money for beneficiaries they do not know in person, for instance. A further form is *engagement through advocacy*, which means that project participants, for example, raise awareness of the suppression of an ethnic minority. The final form is *engagement through research*, a project form in which participants do research and find information to support solving an issue (p. 21ff.).

As for the learning aims, ISL and ICE both focus on similar goals, i.e. promoting intercultural competence, encouraging reflection and actively taking part in the community. However, Service Learning and ISL projects need to pay more attention to the group dynamics between all participants involved to ensure that the endeavor is realized as a joint effort. Whereas in ISL projects there is usually a clear provider and recipient of service, in ICE, teams from two different countries work together and do not differ significantly in terms of their role within the project. Furthermore, in ICE, the ideas of political engagement and criticality play a more prominent role. Barnett's approach to criticality (1997) lays the groundwork for the evaluation of ICE projects. Barnett proposes a model with three domains in which learners can or should become critical. The first domain relates to what the learners learn about the world. The second domain encompasses the learners' internal world and urges them to self-reflect critically. The last domain applies to the external world and becomes visible in what learners do as a result of their critical thinking. Barnett further distinguishes between different levels of criticality. At the least complex level, he sees the acquisition of skills that learners need to be critical. At the second level, he proposes applying this new knowledge to the learners' world and themselves. At the third level, criticality is supposed to trigger change and modify what has, until now, been perceived as common sense in all three domains. The final level goes one step further and not only requires the learner to alter what has been common sense but urges them to transform it and create something completely new (Barnett, 1997). From these contemplations on criticality, Byram *et al.* (2017) derive the following features of good ICE projects. They:

- create a sense of international identification with learners in the international project;
- challenge the 'common sense' of each national group within the international project;
- develop a new 'international' way of thinking and acting (a new way which may be either a modification of what is usually done OR a radically new way);
- apply that new way to 'knowledge', to 'self' and to *'the world'*. (2017: xxviii, emphasis in original)

These guidelines can also be adopted to plan and evaluate ISL projects. Together with Barnett's observations, they even allow the organizers of such a project to roughly assess the level of criticality that the participants reached through their activities.

All in all, the review of both ISL and ICE shows that although the two pedagogies differ in their focus on criticality and, depending on the project design, assign different roles to their participants, they nevertheless pursue very similar goals and apply similar methodology. This holds especially true when ISL is practiced in the foreign language classroom, as ICE was originally developed for this field. Rauschert and Byram (2018) therefore point to the potential for synergies. This idea could be expanded by integrating further related approaches. For future theoretical reasoning and the design of upcoming projects, both based on ISL or ICE, the concept of GCE may, for example, be of additional value since it offers useful recommendations for educating learners to be citizens of the world and to solve global issues. Only if the advocates of different approaches make use of each other's experiences and vantage points will there be a possibility to reach the joint goal, which in Ban Ki-moon's words is: 'Education must fully assume its essential role in helping people to forge more just, peaceful and tolerant societies' (UNESCO, 2014: 11).

Intercultural Service Learning in Practice: The Global Peace Path Project

After discussing the theoretical basics of ISL, this part of the chapter presents a practical example, the Global Peace Path. The project involves students creating peace poetry in multicultural teams, publicly displaying their work and, by doing so, starting a worldwide peace campaign. It is thus an example of ISL with engagement through advocacy. The project exemplifies how ISL can be implemented in foreign language classrooms to foster democratic culture and intercultural dialogue competences. This chapter will outline the process of the project and show how the eight Service Learning standards (National Youth Leadership Council, 2008) introduced in the first section of this article were applied to ensure high-quality practice. It will also provide insight into the research results, which reveal that this kind of ISL can substantially contribute to the academic and personal growth of its participants.

Participants

The Global Peace Path project was developed and started at the Department of Teaching English as a Foreign Language (TEFL) of the University of Munich (LMU) in Germany. In summer semester 2018, the authors conducted a collaborative project with 22 university students and 19 participants with refugee status. The university students were enrolled in programs leading to either a teaching qualification or a master's degree in English studies. The course they took was entitled *Recent developments in intercultural education: Setting up a Global Peace Path* and included in the English didactics module. Conducting the project over a full semester met the Service Learning standard of 'duration and intensity' that suggests a duration of several weeks or months (National Youth Leadership Council, 2008). The 10 participating master's students were an international group from Bulgaria, China, Chile, Hong Kong, Japan, Russia, Serbia and the USA. The 12 student teachers were mainly from Germany. The participants with refugee status were also a mixed group from Afghanistan, Mali, Nigeria, Senegal, Sierra Leone, Somalia, Pakistan and Syria. Contact was established through cooperation with a vocational school in Munich, which eight of the refugees attended, and a local Helpers-Circle Asylum. The 11 refugees who attended through the Helpers-Circle Asylum were, at the time of the project, attending secondary school, undergoing vocational training, working part-time or awaiting a verdict on their asylum application.

Project aims and learning objectives

In accordance with the definition of Service Learning, the project included formal learning and civic engagement. The civic engagement, which corresponds with the standard of 'meaningful service' (National Youth Leadership Council, 2008), had a local and global dimension as it aimed to contribute to the integration of refugees into German society as well as promote peace worldwide. As both the foreign master's students and the refugees were comparatively new in Germany, unlike the master's students who were already part of the university community, many of the refugees found it difficult to make contact with locals. Reducing contact anxiety and establishing friendly relations was therefore considered a first important step towards integration. This is closely related to the overarching goal of the project – promoting peace – because in addition to the poetry-based, global peace campaign the participants started, peaceful coexistence and collaboration were practiced on a local level, albeit limited to the project context.

Intercultural communicative competence was the major focus of the curricular content. As future English teachers, the students further developed this competence themselves but also became acquainted with pedagogies they could later apply in their classes to foster intercultural competence in their pupils. The project also included language-related goals. Creating multilingual poetry together, which included all 13 languages present in the project group ranging from Arabic to Chinese to Urdu, required, for example, creative writing skills and mediation of meanings. Due to the different proficiency levels of the project participants in English and German, the workshops were held bilingually. This not only facilitated mutual understanding but also allowed all project participants to practice at least one foreign language.

Concrete learning objectives were drawn from Byram's work and the *Reference Framework of Competences for Democratic Culture* (RFCDC, Council of Europe, 2018). The *RFCDC* incorporates the idea of a combination of both language and political education as it comprises 'competences that need to be acquired by learners if they are to participate effectively in a culture of democracy and live peacefully together with others in culturally diverse democratic societies' (2018: 11). However, as a cross-curricular model applicable to all sectors of education, the *RFCDC* includes and highlights further competences in the field of democratic education. This ties in well with ISL pedagogy because, in addition to intercultural competences, democratic competences related to the civic engagement can be drawn from the model. The *RFCDC* includes 20 competences subdivided into four domains: values, attitudes, skills and knowledge and critical understanding (see the model of CDC competences in Council of Europe, 2018: 38). The Global Peace Path project aimed to foster competences in all four domains of the *RFCDC*. Special emphasis was placed on valuing the human right to peace, valuing cultural diversity and developing an attitude of civic-mindedness.

Project phases

The project structure follows five interdependent phases: investigation, preparation and planning, action, demonstration and reflection (Kaye, 2010: 15, see Figure 9.2). The investigation phase includes identifying a real need or problem in the community (the term community may be used in its local or global sense). In this case, the starting point was what

Figure 9.2 Project structure (five phases of Service Learning based on Kaye, 2010: 15)

some people called 'the refugee crisis', perceived tendencies of political radicalization and xenophobia, and the existence of worldwide wars and conflicts. Thus, a need for cultural exchange and peaceful relationships was identified. Generally, Service Learning pedagogy aims at self-induced action by the students in all phases of the project. Since the project required some prearrangements (e.g. finding project partners, obtaining permission for the permanent poetry exhibition) and had to be completed within a single semester, the topic was predefined by the course instructors.

In the preparation and planning phase, the project goals and design were concretized, with students having a voice in all decisions. The Global Peace Path project is a literature-based approach of citizenship education as it requires students to create poetry or poetic statements as a means to promote peace. Since it was intended to exhibit the poetry permanently, funding for the printing had to be secured as well. The students prepared for the encounter by researching information on the home countries of their project partners.

The encounter and the actual project work, i.e. the project group taking action, took place during two full-day workshops. In the first workshop, labeled 'Meet & Write', the entire project team consisting of university students and participants with refugee status met and got to know each other. In mixed groups of two to three people, they wrote the first version of their poem. In the second workshop, 'Meet & Mediate', they translated their poems, so all poems would be available in three languages: English, German and a language of the international participants (i.e. the languages of the refugees and the international master's students). The multilingualism of the poems reflects the idea of intercultural dialogue and understanding: German functioned as the local language,

English as the international language or lingua franca and the third language as a bridge to the cultures of the international participants. In this phase of the project, the Service Learning standards of 'diversity' and 'partnerships' played a central role since the success of the project depended on the participants' ability to respectfully collaborate in diverse teams.

The final stage, demonstration, included the project participants presenting their peace poetry to the public. The poems were printed on signs and permanently displayed at a lakeside near Munich. A public opening event of this first station of the Global Peace Path was organized where the project team recited the poetry and encouraged the visitors to engage in intercultural dialogue. For example, locals and project participants discussed the different perspectives on peace expressed in the poetry and conversed about the home countries of the authors. In addition to the poetry exhibition, a website (www.lmu.de/globalpeacepath) was created that not only presents the poetry of this project but also invites other educational institutions from Germany and around the world to conduct follow-up projects, creating a Global Peace Path.

'Reflection', another Service Learning standard, was included in every phase of the project. Service Learning is a form of experiential education, hence why it is also described as 'learning through reflected experience' (Sliwka & Frank, 2004: 10, our translation from German). Special emphasis was therefore placed on reflecting on the actions performed, the interactions that took place, and the affective components involved.

Project organization and data collection

The project was accompanied by intensive research to gain further insight into the impact of ISL in foreign language education. The student-oriented approach of Service Learning was also integrated into the research design. In addition to the action research conducted by the course instructors, two empirical studies were led by students who wrote their final theses[1] on the Global Peace Path. This procedure corresponds with the standards 'youth voice' and 'progress monitoring' (National Youth Leadership Council, 2008). The project was evaluated on the basis of seven sets of data: two questionnaires in a pre-test/post-test format, two workshop evaluation sheets, the *Autobiography of Intercultural Encounters* (Council of Europe, 2009), a placemat activity and a prompted reflection activity. The research followed a mixed-method approach with particular emphasis on qualitative data. The questionnaires also provided quantitative data. Through data triangulation, results were validated and complemented. The scope of this chapter does not allow a complete presentation of results, but a choice of representative findings will provide insights into how the ISL project fostered competences for democratic culture and intercultural dialogue. One of the questionnaires and the workshop evaluation sheets were filled in by the entire project team ($N =$ 41), and evidence was found that the project had very positive effects on the participants with refugee status as well. For example, they reported that the workshops helped them overcome their fear of making contact with Germans despite their limited language skills. However, since this article examines the impact of ISL in foreign language education, the focus will be on the effects on the university students ($N = 22$).

Project outcomes

Data analysis showed that the students progressed in all four domains of democratic competence as defined in the *RFCDC* (Council of Europe, 2018). Before the project, only 5% of the students rated their knowledge about the home countries of the participating refugees on a five-level Likert scale as sufficient or better.[2] This increased to 68% after the project (Bauer, 2018: 38). Students reported not only having expanded their factual knowledge but also their critical understanding, by reflecting 'on his/her prejudices and stereotypes and what lies behind them' (Council of Europe, 2018: vol. 2, p. 22).

This aspect is interrelated with the domain attitudes because prejudice reduction is a prerequisite for becoming open-minded to cultural otherness. The data provide evidence that the ISL project had a major impact on the students' attitudes. Precisely, 72% of the students stated that, before the project, they were prejudiced against refugees (Bauer, 2018). In the post-test, these students reported attitudinal changes: 'I have learned that my "fears" of conversations with refugees were unfounded' and 'that the exchange with people from different cultural backgrounds can be very exciting and fulfilling' (Nora, our translation from German[3]). Another student explained: 'I only knew things about refugees through news reports but there is much more behind it I learnt from the refugees' (Simon). The data reveal that both university students and participants with refugee status entered the project with fears and prejudices that could be reduced through the encounter. These findings are supported by a psychologically oriented study on the Global Peace Path that investigated the effects of intergroup contact on prejudice and explored stereotype content differences between the subgroups: 'Results from the post-test phase confirm the importance of intergroup contact while showing that refugees were perceived as warmer and more competent after the encounter' (Marić, 2020: 35). The study supports Allport's (1954) contact hypothesis, which states that contact is a crucial means to reduce prejudice and promote harmonious intergroup relations if certain conditions are met (Spears & Tausch, 2014). In the Global Peace Path project's case, '[t]hese positive developments may be related to three important conditions this intercultural encounter was framed by, namely institutional support, cooperation and common superordinate goals' (Marić, 2020: 30).

As part of the category *valuing cultural diversity*, the *RFCDC* claims that 'intercultural dialogue should be used to develop respect and a culture of 'living together' (Council of Europe, 2018: vol. 2, p. 16). Ninety percent of the students declared in the post-test that the project helped to build rapport and stated, for example: 'I actually think that the refugees and the foreign master's students now feel more like part of our society here, e.g. some of us met for dinner the other day and we just like spending time as a group' (Laura[4]). Further statements, such as 'We all melted together as one union/team' (Simon) or 'In the end I felt like a member of a big family' (Ayla), corroborate the assumption that the students not only valued engaging in dialogue with others who have different cultural affiliations but also developed – and be it only for the duration of the project – what Byram calls 'international group identity' (Rauschert & Byram, 2017: 364). The fact that some students and refugees met outside of class as a result of the collaboration and began to use the pronoun 'we' inclusively (e.g. 'we just like spending time as a group') suggests that the juxtaposition of 'us' and 'them' shifted in favor of identification as an international group.

While the findings above illustrate the contribution to intercultural learning, it was also analyzed if the ISL project had an impact on the students' civic-mindedness, a democratic competence assigned to the category attitudes in the *RFCDC* (Council of Europe, 2018), which particularly relates to the service component of ISL. All but two students declared that the project increased their awareness of the necessity of social participation and their willingness to actually solve problems. The ones who stated that their awareness had not changed argued that they had already been aware of this need before the project started. It must be noted though that volition does not automatically lead to self-induced action. This became clear when some students pointed out that they would 'follow but not initiate' (Lien) civic action. Others explain the project impact as follows: 'This experience has inspired me to look for similar projects and maybe someday even organize my own' (Milo) or 'I realized that every one of us is needed to change the world and society' (Ayla). The fact that afterwards two students organized follow-up projects on their own initiative, and so continued the Global Peace Path in other places, can be taken as an indicator that the experience was sustainable and had a long-term effect.

The data provide clear evidence that the ISL project fostered intercultural and democratic competences with particularly strong effects in the domains of attitudes and values as defined in the *RFCDC*. The students used the foreign language to engage in intercultural dialogue and accomplish a shared goal. Interestingly, the data suggest that the impact on the student group was even higher than on their partners with refugee status. This reflects previous Service Learning research (e.g. Astin *et al.*, 2000; Claus & Ogden, 1999) and the conclusion that – especially in educational settings – community service linked to formal learning and regular phases of reflection is more efficient than mere community service.

Conclusion

Service Learning and, consequently, ISL are based on Dewey's ideas from the early 20th century. More than a century later, his ideas have not lost their relevance; on the contrary, they appear even more significant because of newly arising conflicts due to, for example, the effects of the COVID-19 pandemic. In spite of the challenges, we need to invest time and effort to reach our common goal: a peaceful world. Educational approaches that promote active citizenship, such as ICE and ISL, are of great importance in this process because they engage the younger generation in building a 'creative' (Dewey, 1939) or 'strong democracy' (Barber, 1984: 152).

In times of social distancing, visiting the permanent display of the first stage of the Global Peace Path near Munich may be challenging. Thanks to the project's website, it is still possible to get a first impression of the initial stage of the project and its steadily growing number of new successors, at this point about 20 follow-up projects in Germany, Fiji, India, Japan and the Netherlands. Furthermore, the ramifications of the pandemic render the organization of ISL projects more difficult and possibly even unfeasible in some contexts. Nevertheless, it is important to ensure that projects are of high didactical quality and can fully develop their potential to positively influence academic, civic and personal characteristics. Only if the projects provide enough room for guided reflection can ISL enhance students' intercultural competence. In the current situation, digital learning environments may present a good alternative setting to traditional ISL projects. People with different cultural backgrounds can, for instance, use video conferencing tools or chat programs to meet and get to know each other. Joint work can also be facilitated by using collaborative software such as Google Docs, Padlet or Dropbox. Applying these ideas to the Global Peace Path Project, the different project phases could easily be transferred to a digital meeting on Zoom. Thanks to the wide accessibility of these web-based tools, the inclusion of participants from more countries might become even easier since physical presence at the project location is no longer obligatory. Furthermore, the software allows for creation of multiple group workspaces where multicultural teams can interact and create their texts together. The empirical research accompanying the project in Munich revealed a positive effect on intercultural competence and students' civic-mindedness. So far, it is not clear whether the same effects can also be achieved in digital ISL projects. Further research would need to be conducted to investigate how transferring the project to a digital space would influence the achievement of the intended learning goals. The transfer would bring challenges: In digital communication, there is often less opportunity to focus on the interpersonal level. That is why the development of intercultural competences, which are closely linked to affective dimensions, may be harder to reach in a digital ISL context. Furthermore, project organizers must keep in mind that access to digital tools is not a given. It often depends on the participants' socioeconomic background and, consequently, can present a threat to an equal relationship between service providers and recipients. Only if these new challenges are carefully considered is there a realistic opportunity for digital ISL projects to reach their goal: educating 'learners to resolve persistent challenges related to sustainable development and peace that concern all humanity' (UNESCO, 2014: 11).

Acknowledgements

Part of the content of this article was presented in the keynote speech *Internationalism, Service Learning and Citizenship in Language Teaching: Concepts and Implementations* that Professor Michael Byram and Petra Rauschert gave at the conference Intercultural Education: Innovative Approaches and Practices in Higher Education in Le Mans, France, on 22 November 2018. We would like to thank Michael Byram for this collaboration.

Notes

(1) Bavarian teacher trainees must complete a *Zulassungsarbeit*, which is comparable to a master's thesis, at the end of their academic studies.
(2) The five-level Likert scale included the following items: *very good – good – sufficient – poor – hardly any.*
(3) The data collected by means of questionnaires took place with anonymous codes. The students were free to respond in English or German. Unless marked as translation, the original quotations were used.
(4) For data protection reasons, pseudonyms are used here instead of the participants' real names.

References

Allport, G.W. (1954) *The Nature of Prejudice.* Boston, MA: Addison-Wesley.
Astin, A.W., Vogelgesang, L.J., Ikeda, E.K. and Yee, J.A. (2000) *How Service Learning Affects Students.* Los Angeles, CA: Higher Education Research Institute.
Barber, B.R. (1984) *Strong Democracy.* Berkeley, CA: University of California Press.
Barnett, R. (1997) *Higher Education: A Critical Business.* Buckingham: Society for Research into Higher Education and the Open University Press.
Bauer, V. (2018) *Die Entwicklung interkultureller und demokratischer Kompetenzen durch Intercultural Service Learning. Eine empirische Studie zum Projekt 'Global Peace Path'* [Developing intercultural and democratic competences through Intercultural Service Learning. An empirical study on the project 'Global Peace Path'] [Zulassungsarbeit]. University of Munich (LMU). www.lmu.de/globalpeacepath
Billig, S.H. (2007) Unpacking what works in service-learning: Promising research-based practices to improve student outcomes. In J.C. Kielsmeier, M. Neal and N. Schultz (eds) *Growing to Greatness 2007: The State of Service-Learning* (pp. 18–28). Saint Paul, MN: National Youth Leadership Council.

Bringle, R.G. and Hatcher, J.A. (1995) A service-learning curriculum for faculty. *Michigan Journal of Community Service Learning* 2, 112–122.

Byram, M. (1997) *Teaching and Assessing Intercultural Communicative Competence.* Clevedon: Multilingual Matters.

Byram, M. (2021) *Teaching and Assessing Intercultural Communicative Competence: Revisited.* Bristol: Multilingual Matters.

Byram, M. (2008) *From Foreign Language Education to Education for Intercultural Citizenship: Essays and Reflections.* Clevedon: Multilingual Matters.

Byram, M. (2018) An essay on internationalism in foreign language education. *Intercultural Communication Education* 1 (2), 64–82.

Byram, M., Golubeva, I., Han, H. and Wagner, M. (2017) Introduction. In M. Byram, I. Golubeva, H. Han and M. Wagner (eds) *From Principles to Practice in Education for Intercultural Citizenship* (pp. xvii–xxxiv). Bristol: Multilingual Matters.

Claus, J. and Odgen, C. (1999) *Service Learning for Youth Empowerment and Social Change.* Pieterlen and Bern: Peter Lang Publishing.

Clifford, J. and Reisinger, D. (2018) *Community-based Language Learning: A Framework for Educators.* Washington, DC: Georgetown University Press.

Council of Europe (2001) *Common European Framework of Reference for Languages: Learning, Teaching, Assessment.* Cambridge: Press Syndicate of the University of Cambridge.

Council of Europe (2009) *Autobiography of Intercultural Encounters.* Strasbourg: Council of Europe. https://www.coe.int/en/web/autobiography-intercultural-encounters

Council of Europe (2018) *Reference Framework of Competences for Democratic Culture.* Strasbourg: Council of Europe. https://www.coe.int/en/web/education/competences-for-democratic-culture

Dewey, J. (1939) Creative democracy – The task before us. *John Dewey and the Promise of America* 14, 12–17.

De Leon, N. (2014) Developing intercultural competence by participating in intensive intercultural service-learning. *Michigan Journal of Community Service Learning* 21 (1), 17–30.

Godfrey, P.C., Illes, L.M. and Berry, G.R. (2005) Creating breadth in business education through service-learning. *Academy of Management Learning & Education* 4 (3), 309–323.

Institute for Economics & Peace (2019) *Global Peace Index 2019: Measuring Peace in a Complex World.* http://visionofhumanity.org/reports

KMK (Sekretariat der Ständigen Konferenz der Kultusminister der Länder in der Bundesrepublik Deutschland). *Bildungsstandards für die fortgeführte Fremdsprache (Englisch/Französisch) für die Allgemeine Hochschulreife. Beschluss der Kultusministerkonferenz vom 18.10.2012.* https://www.kmk.org/themen/qualitaetssicherung-in-schulen/bildungsstandards.html

Lester, S.W., Tomkovick, C., Wells, T., Flunker, L. and Kickul, J. (2005) Does service-learning add value? Examining the perspectives of multiple stakeholders. *Academy of Management Learning & Education* 4 (3), 278–294.

Marić, M. (2020) *Overcoming Prejudice in Intercultural Encounters. The 'Global Peace Path' Project as a Vehicle of Reducing Prejudice.* [Zulassungsarbeit]. University of Munich (LMU). www.lmu.de/globalpeacepath

Minor, J.M. (2001) Using service-learning as part of an ESL program. *The Internet TESL Journal* 7 (4). http://iteslj.org/Techniques/Minor-ServiceLearning.html

Morgan, T.W. and Barnhart, E. (2015) Intercultural service learning. In J.M. Bennett (ed.) *The SAGE Encyclopedia of Intercultural Competence* (pp. 526–528). Thousand Oaks, CA: Sage, Inc.

National Youth Leadership Council (2008) *K-12 Service-Learning Standards for Quality Practice.* https://cdn.ymaws.com/www.nylc.org/resource/resmgr/resources/lift/standards_document_mar2015up.pdf

The National Standards Collaborative Board (2015) *World-Readiness Standards for Learning Languages* (4th edn). Alexandria, VA: Author.

Rauschert, P. (2014) *Intercultural Service Learning im Englischunterricht. ein modell zur förderung interkultureller kompetenz auf der Basis journalistischen Schreibens.* [Intercultural service learning in English language teaching: A model to foster intercultural competence on the basis of journalistic writing]. Münster: Waxmann.

Rauschert, P. and Byram, M. (2017) Service learning and intercultural citizenship in foreign language education. *Cambridge Journal of Education* 48 (3), 353–369.

Reinders, H. (2016) *Service Learning: Theoretische überlegungen und empirische studien zu lernen durch engagement.* [Service learning: Theoretical considerations and empirical studies]. Weinheim: Beltz Juventa.

Seifert, A. and Zentner, S. (2010) *Service-Learning – Lernen durch engagement: Methode, qualität, ceispiele und ausgewählte schwerpunkte. Eine Publikation des Netzwerks Lernen durch Engagement.* [Service learning: Method, quality, examples, and selected focal points]. Weinheim: Freudenberg Stiftung.

Sliwka, A. and Frank, S. (2004) *Service Learning: Verantwortung lernen in schule und gemeinde.* [Service learning: Learning responsibility at school and in the community]. Weinheim: Beltz.

Spears, R. and Tausch, N. (2014) Vorurteile und Intergruppenbeziehungen. [Prejudices and intergroup relations]. In K. Jonas, W. Stroebe and M. Hewstone (eds) *Sozialpsychologie* (pp. 507–564). Cham: Springer.

UNESCO (2014) *Global Citizenship Education: Preparing Learners for the Challenges of the 21st Century.* UNESCO. https://unesdoc.unesco.org/ark:/48223/pf0000227729

Youth Service America (2007) *Addressing Diversity and Global Challenges Through Intercultural Service Learning.* http://tools.ysa. org/downloads/modules/InterculturalService-LearningModule.pdf

10 Revisiting Intercultural Communicative Competence in Language Teacher Education: Perspectives from Colombia

Beatriz Peña Dix

> The foreign language teacher [...] encourages and expects learners
> to challenge their own society, and this is a major responsibility.
> (Byram, 2021: 122)

Introduction

With the impact of accelerated globalisation, real and virtual mobility and proliferation of Information and Communication Technologies on the communicative landscape, language teacher education now needs to evolve to prepare learners for ethical intercultural engagement (Crozet, 2017; Porto & Byram, 2015). This means that, like all education, foreign language education and language teacher education should take a reflective and critical approach to issues such as human rights, racism, discrimination, exclusion and stereotyping and foster skills of critical analysis that privilege peace and social justice (De Leo, 2010). Human-rights education, for example, is considered an underpinning principle of education for intercultural understanding. In the words of Byram and Wagner (2018: 140), 'language teaching needs to be linked to other disciplines in order to develop an approach that integrates insights from citizenship education'.

The intercultural dimension in foreign language teaching aims to develop learners as intercultural mediators able to engage with complexity and multiple identities (Byram *et al.*, 2002) and as builders of spaces of dialogue and negotiation. This means that teachers and students participate in a different dynamic with and through the language that is being taught/learnt. They see beyond instrumental dimensions of language teaching and learning and come to see language as a whole entity embracing new knowledge, skills and strategies to oppose monocultural, anti-diverse views which may emerge in different educational spaces (Dervin, 2016). Therefore, in its broadest sense, teacher education means preparing successful and effective teachers who can help learners meet the challenges of a changing world by 'sensitising' them to their own values and culture and helping them to appreciate the values of others and see/ experience the world from the vantage point of different languages and cultures (Fonseca-Greber, 2010: 102).

This chapter addresses the role of Intercultural Communicative Competence (ICC) in language teacher education. It aims to highlight that although many acknowledge the importance of integrating an intercultural dimension into language teacher education, a number of theoretical and practical challenges remain. The first part of this chapter discusses different theoretical positionings and research on ICC in language teacher education. These perspectives – many of which are inspired by the works of Byram (1997, 2011, 2021) – represent important trajectories of scholarly inquiry in the field of intercultural language teaching and learning. At the intersection of these theoretical understandings, the second part of the chapter draws on my own research that examines teachers' ICC understandings in Colombia. I examine teachers' perspectives on the incorporation of ICC in the English language classroom given that ICC in language teacher education programmes has been seldom explored in the country. As Moya-Chaves *et al.* (2018: para. 1) explain:

> [In Colombia,] the discussion on interculturality is usually limited to the anthropological treatment of a folklore tradition and its implementation in the classroom still seems to be marginal [...] In the field of language T&L [teaching and learning] and in teacher education, this seems to be even more remote.

The chapter provides an emerging initiation ICC model to aid language teachers in exploring Intercultural English language teaching (IELT) for the first time. This model informs language teacher educators about several fundamental considerations related to ICC and offers a potential statement of philosophy to set ICC English language teaching standards in the Colombian context. It is my hope that this may also offer insights for teacher educators working in different national contexts.

Understanding the Role of ICC in Language Teacher Education

As introduced above, interculturally oriented pedagogy in foreign language teaching (FLT) positions the language teacher as an agent of change and pedagogical progress (Guilherme, 2007) and sees ICC not as something to be added to teaching and learning, but rather something central and integral to the interactions that already and inevitably take place in the classroom and beyond (Liddicoat, 2008: 282). Work on ICC points to the importance of developing critical cultural awareness (hereafter, CCA) in both teachers and learners so they can actively and responsibly participate and take action in a global society by exploring appropriate ways to interact with people from other cultures (Byram, 2021). Drawing on strong empirical research (Byram, 2011, 2021; Guilherme, 2007; Porto & Byram, 2015), ICC – the foundation for intercultural citizenship – has already become an important component of language curricula in some parts of the world, while in others, explorations are underway to find out how it can be incorporated into language teaching and learning. It has, thus, become a major concern for foreign language educators who now see ICC as a fundamental objective in the foreign language classroom. Many now advocate that, with the proper support, scaffolding and follow-up, language teachers can contribute to the realisation of an education for cosmopolitan citizenship (Byram, 2021; Guilherme, 2007).

ICC teacher education assumes that individuals cannot be reduced to their collective identities and, thus, strengthens values such as open-mindedness, tolerance of difference and respect for *Self* and *Other* (Skopinskaja, 2009). This underscores the importance of preparing individuals to engage and collaborate within a global society by discovering appropriate ways to interact with people from other cultures (Byram, 2021). One important example is Sercu's (2006) advocacy for the Foreign Language and Intercultural Competence teacher or the *FL&IC teacher*, which offers broad possibilities to promote a more international approach to teacher education in order to achieve world citizenship. She makes claims about the existence of specific characteristics that constitute a proficient profile for a good foreign language and intercultural competence (FL&IC) teacher:

> Teachers should be able to employ teaching techniques that promote the acquisition of savoirs, savoir-apprendre, savoir-comprendre, savoir-faire and savoir-être. [...] They should be able to select appropriate teaching materials and to adjust these materials [...] In addition to being skilful classroom teachers, teachers should also be able to use experiential approaches to language-and-culture teaching. (2006: 58)

Sercu's FL&IC teacher profile presupposes a language education system ready to scaffold the process of intercultural language teaching-learning and promote more enriching views of the language teaching professions. However, one real issue is that there is often a significant gap between the rather ambitious goals associated with the promotion of ICC and actual teaching practices. This chapter comes back to this idea of a theory-practice gap after first looking at dominant conceptualisations of ICC.

Dominant Conceptualisations of ICC and ICC Teaching in the Field of Language Teacher Education

A range of conceptual frameworks and models for ICC have relevance for the field of language learning and language teacher education. Among the most credited and frequently referenced include Byram's multidimensional model of ICC (1997); Guilherme's interdisciplinary model for teaching/learning foreign cultures (2002); Deardorff's pyramid model of IC (2006); Liddicoat and Scarino's five-principled intercultural learning model (2013) and Dervin's IC model (2020). First, Byram's pioneering conceptualisation of intercultural communicative competence (ICC) can be defined as a multi-layered, interdisciplinary concept.

According to Byram's influential proposal (1997; also revisited in the 2021 2nd edition), IC involves key *savoirs* for communicating and building relations with individuals from different cultures: *savoirs* (knowledge of the culture), *savoir comprendre* (skills of interpreting/relating), *savoir apprendre* (skills of discovery/interaction), *savoir être* (attitudes of curiosity/openness) and *savoir s'engager* (critical cultural awareness, CCA). Byram *et al.* (2002) also emphasise 'the ability to ensure a shared understanding by people of different social identities, and the ability to interact with people as complex human beings with multiple identities and their own individuality' (2002: 10). When an individual develops ICC, they are able to build relationships with and through language by building new symbolic representations. CCA, originally embedded in *savoir s'engager*, encourages language educators to create learning opportunities to turn individuals into critical thinkers who are aware of interconnections between classroom lessons and real-world issues (Nugent & Catalano, 2015). As a result, a foreign language teacher inspired by Byram's model is expected to create learning situations not only to learn and use the foreign language but also to engage learners in processes of developing intercultural knowledge, skills, attitudes and awareness of cultural values (Smakova & Paulsrud, 2020).

With a similar perspective, Guilherme's contribution to foreign language education includes her 'interdisciplinary model for teaching/learning foreign cultures' (2002: 209–210), which integrates a triad of interdisciplinary areas within which foreign language-culture education should operate: Critical Pedagogy, Cultural Studies and Intercultural Communication. She advocates for a general multiple-perspective framework for foreign culture education and grounds her proposal on the tenet that foreign language-culture education and teacher development programmes should consider Human Rights Education and Education for Democratic Citizenship as permanent references. Guillerme's advocacy for IC critical citizenship (2002), inspired by Byram's ICC savoir s'engager and its CCA, proposes the *critical intercultural speaker* as an individual aware of the multiplicity of cultural identities and their interfaces in an intercultural encounter. According to Guilherme, foreign language-cultural education should become a dialogue-constructed space to reflect upon the ways knowledge and culture are constructed according to historical, social and political constraints. Guilherme's ICC critical citizenship and her *critical intercultural speaker* builds on the Self, the Other and the world, with increased teacher and learner motivation to explore and cross multi-diverse borders – real or imaginary – by becoming critically aware of the multiple levels of their cultural and political identities to participate in transformative action (Guilherme, 2002: Chapter 5).

On the same topic, Deardorff (2009) advocates that IC should become a curricular baseline carried out by interculturally competent educators and a strategic learning objective in the classroom. Deardorff's (2006) pyramid model of IC proposes three elements, which, similar to Byram (1997), are attitudes, knowledge and skills. However, internal and external outcomes are also included, and these are hierarchically organised in levels – from the lowest to the highest levels to build IC. Deardorff (2009), moreover, reorganises the pyramid model into a process model of IC, which describes the synergy between internal outcomes (attitudes, knowledge and skills leading to flexibility, adaptability, an ethnorelativism and empathy) and external outcomes (appropriate behaviour and effective communication). For Deardorff, intercultural values such as curiosity, openness, respect and discovery work harmoniously as a social mechanism that helps individuals move beyond their comfort zone to motivate both teachers and learners in a continuous collaborative IC learning process with and through language. This compositional model of IC establishes the skills of observation, interpreting, evaluation and relating. Attitudes (or the affective component), knowledge and skills lead to adaptability, flexibility and empathy. At the capstone of the pyramid lies the desired external outcome, which is the manifestation of the internal components through appropriate behaviour in communication (Deardorff, 2011).

Meanwhile, for Liddicoat and Scarino (2013), a key understanding of the interculturally competent individual is that cultures are relative, and there is no one correct or established way of doing things – all behaviours are culturally malleable and variable (Liddicoat & Scarino, 2013). For teachers, this implies the need for understanding of language and culture diversity as well as how this relates to the teaching profession. This means that language teaching from an intercultural perspective is an activity in which intercultural principles and theoretical positions affect practice at every level. The authors reject static cultural knowledge and believe in active engagement with language and culture. Intercultural knowledge and awareness operate in a synergetic, mutual relationship that is far from unidirectional. Engaging with languages and cultures allows language teachers and learners to develop self- and other's awareness and analytical strategies to elaborate this awareness or a 'meta-level of awareness (or meta-awareness)' (2013: 50). Liddicoat and Scarino's (2013) idea of 'reflection' is one precondition to being able to achieve an intercultural perspective for language teaching (Liddicoat, 2008; Liddicoat *et al.*, 2003; Liddicoat & Scarino, 2013). Reflection is an important component of teachers' growth and empowerment and is closely linked to 'the capacity of decentring, of stepping outside one's existing, culturally constructed, framework of interpretation and seeing things from a new perspective' (Liddicoat & Scarino, 2013: 58).

In addition to the perspectives above, Dervin's (2020) recent works explore criticism of the concept of interculturality and what he regards as its Western-centric ideology and connotation. Dervin, overall, is suspicious of what he regards as static models of IC and their monological, self-centred nature that frequently ignore the 'other' as a real companion in the co-construction of IC, and show lack of ethical reflection, in addition to an overemphasis on difference (Dervin, 2016). The author also places critical reflexivity at the core of IC to delegitimise established discourses and remarks that researchers and educators are not spectators of reality. Instead, they have a direct impact on what is negotiated, constructed, and performed in intercultural transactions. In the same way, Dervin (2020) urges caution about the relationship between interculturality and the concept of power as the former may contribute to unbalanced power relations because of the multiplicity and intersectionalities of identities present in encounters. In other words, interculturality does not encompass neutrality in intercultural transactions but celebrates interactions between individuals whose viewpoints may oppose or clash under given circumstances.

Dervin (2020) advocates for the intrinsic intercultural dimension of education, and how in this context interculturality becomes 'the negotiation of everyone's diversities with others' (2020: 60). Dervin's Post-Modern Model grounded in Critical and Reflexive Interculturality aims at developing theoretical and methodological reflexivity that is fundamental to support pre-service teachers' actions and reflections on the different interactions they have, in addition to aiding their pedagogical and ethical choices in their teaching endeavours. Dervin himself expressed certain dissatisfaction with the model he developed, pointing that 'the model still tends to be theoretically and methodologically Eurocentric, based on ideologies developed mostly in the "West" (postmodernist ideologies)' (2020: 63). In Dervin's (2020) view, his Postmodern Model 'lacks individual and interactional ethical aspects', which made him 'look for some alternatives and complementary perspectives' (2020: 63).

Along similar lines of thought, and complementary to the Post-Modern Model, the Confucian Model refers to Dervin's efforts to approach Confucian's ethics and *Analects*, which emphasise ongoing self-improvement and social interaction. Furthermore, the Model re-situates

Dervin's own understandings of intercultural encounters from an *in situ* ethical Confucian perspective. This new Confucian Model is still a work in progress, but the principles on which it is based may make it applicable for peer- and self-assessment by teachers and student teachers to think about what is happening in the classroom and reflect on their IC. According to Dervin (2020), his two models should be able to trigger 'discussions and negotiations of things that are often silenced in education (e.g. negative representations, conflicts, modesty, etc.)' (2020: 65).

Despite merging or opposing views, these models (Byram, 1997; Deardorff, 2006; Dervin, 2020; Guilherme, 2002; Liddicoat & Scarino, 2013) represent an effort to understand the complex nature of human interactions when a foreign language is put in contexts that deserve dialogue, mediation, and mutual understanding – the realities of which are built with the language that is being taught/learned. The authors have made important efforts in an attempt to transform foreign language classrooms into spaces of solidarity – 'a mode or act of inclusion of a person or persons into a group or institution structured discursively' (Pensky, 2009: xi) – for horizontal dialogue, permanent altruistic collaboration and mutual recognition of what brings us closer to or more distant from each other. ICC gives language education a new epistemological floor to build beyond linguistic competence in such a way that both students and teachers carry out their own intercultural explorations using the language they teach/learn, in and outside the classroom, in order to participate in the world and contribute to the co-construction of new social realities.

The Problem of the Knowledge-Practice Gap

Although there has been significant evolution in understandings of the intercultural dimension in FLT, there is still an unfortunate gap between theory and practice in many contexts. Research shows that although many teachers regard culture as important, they tend to lack the knowledge and theoretical background regarding how to address intercultural goals in language teaching (Fernández-Agüero & Garrote, 2019; Guilherme, 2002; Sercu *et al.*, 2005). Guilherme (2002) also notes that attempts to integrate an intercultural focus in teaching can be characterised by reservation or lack of seriousness. Similarly, Nguyen (2013) and Smakova and Paulsrud (2020) discovered tensions between teacher willingness to teach intercultural competence and the way in which they currently shape their teaching practice. Thus, in spite of teachers having positive views (or at least not negative) to support the integration of the ICC in FLT, their limited conceptions of ICC, lack of teacher training, teacher development opportunities and expert support and guidance on the topic restrict possibilities for successfully integrating ICC at the level of classroom practice (Alonso-Belmonte & Fernández-Agüero, 2013).

It is at this point, that I address the issue in the Colombian context. My own research aimed to be a contribution to the field of IELT as a qualitative constructivist study that aimed to investigate Colombian (public sector) English language teachers' existing or prospective intercultural communicative competence (ICC). In my study, teachers' perspectives on culture and interculturality were explored based on the underpinning assumption that there is a need to transform language education in Colombia moving forward to the 'intercultural turn'. Within this vision of language teaching, teachers can become, in the near future, intercultural mediators who enlarge the objectives of contemporary language teaching to build *Third Spaces* for dialogue and negotiation through English. Another important aim was providing a comprehensive understanding of current English language teaching in Colombia, including teachers' experiences and perspectives on culture and interculturality. Key findings showed that teachers feel positively disposed to intercultural pedagogies and to IELT, but their profile does not meet yet the expectations pertaining to the knowledge, skills and attitudes that are desirable for IELT. Based on these findings, a tripartite initiation model is proposed to help English language teachers move forward towards ICC, which will be explained later in the chapter.

Reflecting on English Language Teachers' Perceptions and Approaches Towards ICC in Colombia

Colombia, the third most populous country in Latin America, possesses a rich and diverse linguistic heritage; this is far from the label of being monolingual and monocultural, which has been mistakenly applied to the country due to the predominance of Spanish. From a sociolinguistic perspective, additional language groups in Colombia generally speak Spanish as a second language and have a minority community language as their mother tongue: either a native Amerindian language, an English or Spanish-based Creole (Islander English and *Palenquero*), Colombian Sign Language, or Romani language, spoken by Colombians of Romani descent (Bonilla Carvajal & Tejada Sánchez, 2016).

English in Colombia has become mandatory in both public and private education as the National Ministry of Education has ruled it as a priority in the national agenda (Vélez-Rendón 2003). However, proficiency in English may vary considerably due to the difference in quality between public and private education. Today, English can be considered a pillar in Colombian education. Undergraduates from many universities need to demonstrate English language proficiency by taking an international examination (TOEFL, IELTS) as a requirement to graduate. Employers at almost every level are requesting a basic or intermediate command of English. As explained by de Mejía (2004: 392), 'Career advancement in Colombia is dependent to a large degree on English language proficiency'. As such, language educational policies have been designed to shape the State's goals and promote proficient English speakers as a part of the international economic strategy towards advanced globalisation (Alesina & Farrera, 2005).

There have been a series of proposals that have endeavoured to consolidate English language educational policies in Colombia. However, tensions and criticism towards these policies include claims that most foreign language policies, educational reforms and government regulations are imposed without concern of the needs and wishes of those who are either affected by them or expected to carry them out (Fandiño, 2011). Key language policies have been implemented in Colombia over the past two decades: The English Language Syllabus (1982, Programa de Inglés); the COFE Project (1991–1997, Proyecto COFE); the General Law of Education (1994, Ley General de Educación, ley 115); the Curricular Guidelines for foreign languages (1999, Lineamientos curriculares para lenguas extranjeras); Bilingual Colombia (Colombia Bilingüe) and the National English Programme, 2015–2025 (Programa Nacional de Inglés, 2015–2025). These policies are not 'finished products', and they do not appear to follow from each other. Instead, some of them were abruptly stopped and replaced by new proposals due to political changes (British Council, 2015).

Despite criticisms of ELT marketisation and the imposition of foreign language policies, English is widely taught as a foreign language of considerable prestige, ruled to be a priority in the national education agenda (Jaime Osorio & Insuasty, 2015). English is extensively seen as an agent of development, progress, wealth and prosperity. Today, English can be considered a pillar in Colombian education, and its teaching in public and private sectors has become a contested arena for debates about learner and teacher proficiency, quality language education, access or exclusion to opportunities (Bonilla Carvajal & Tejada Sánchez, 2016). Undergraduates from many universities need to demonstrate English language proficiency by taking an international examination (TOEFL, IELTS) as a requirement to graduate. Employers at almost every level are requesting a basic or intermediate command of English. As explained by de Mejía (2004: 392), 'career advancement in Colombia is dependent to a large degree on English language proficiency'. As such, language educational policies have been designed to shape the State's goals and promote proficient English speakers as a part of the international economic strategy towards advanced globalisation (Alesina & Farrera, 2005; Fairclough, 2006).

In contrast, 'interculturality' in ELT is a relative recent field of study in the country and has earlier been equated with ethnoeducation, as well as to examine how indigenous cultural traditions differ from those of the national standardised culture (López, 2009). Interculturality in the context of group diversity or other additional cultures or collectives (e.g. regional, national diversity; youngsters' urban cultures, LGTBI collectives, among others) and languages within the same country (e.g. Palenquero, Creole, Romani) have rarely been explored empirically. However, in Colombia, interest in ICC in the field of language teaching has increased gradually over the past decade. This has resulted in empirical research into how foreign language education goals and teaching pedagogies can be reformulated in terms of ICC. A considerable number of qualitative studies – interview-based, case studies, pedagogical innovations, skill-based strategies to foster IELT, conceptual explorations, course and workshop design, instructional materials analysis, examination of related publications, virtual teams and study groups, etc. – and few quantitative or mixed-method approaches (survey-based enquiry) have taken place analysing how intercultural sensitiveness, awareness and/or ICC are developed after the implementation of specific procedure, pedagogical strategies or academic contents (e.g. Benavides-Jimenez & Mora-Acosta, 2019; Cuartas Álvarez, 2020; Henao *et al.*, 2019).

An Exploratory Study with English Teachers

To further contribute to explorations of language and culture teaching and IELT in Colombia, I collected data for 15 months as part of a qualitative exploratory research study in Bogotá, Colombia with 25 teachers of English from the public sector. The study explored teachers' existing or prospective intercultural communicative competence (ICC) based on the underpinning assumption that there is a need to transform language education in Colombia and move forward from the 'cultural turn' to the 'intercultural turn' (Dasli & Díaz, 2017). The main research question focused on teachers' perceptions of what is needed to advance towards more intercultural approaches, and how IELT could be fostered in their current praxis. Different kinds of data were collected: a set of 25 semi-structured interviews, classroom observation data, information emerging from two focus groups, short narrative accounts from a blog and the researcher's journal entries.

Thematic analysis was used as an appropriate strategy to make sense of the data in detail and develop interpretations (Braun & Clarke, 2006). ATLAS-Ti computer-assisted qualitative data analysis was selected to store, organise, group and retrieve data. Last, but not least, ethical considerations were taken into account which included: ethical approvals; abundant, transparent information before, during and after the research process; informed consents, copies of transcripts to participants, which included translation of some interview data originally in Spanish and copies of the research report to those who were interested.

Some key findings showed that Colombian English teachers recognise the importance of culture teaching in the ELT classroom, and their perspectives and practices are oriented towards the inclusion of essentialist views of culture, factual culture, trivia and culture-as-content teaching.

Teachers also expressed their receptiveness to ICC and have a positive attitude towards IELT. However, some declared that their knowledge on the topic is limited, and, as a result, they end up emphasising static cultural knowledge and cross-cultural comparisons. In this sense, they return to the culture teaching momentum of CLT rather than adopting a more critical, multifaceted approach. Teachers seem to arrive at a conceptual bottleneck that hinders them from advancing towards IELT and therefore request more scaffolding, guidance and support to develop their practice. Some of the following answers represent participants' reactions about this situation: 'Es claro que no sabemos como integrar el componente intercultural en nuestras aulas de inglés; la mayoría de mis acciones son intuitivas' ['It is clear that we do not know how to integrate the intercultural component in our English classrooms; most of my actions are intuitive', our translation from Spanish.] Another participant claimed that:

> Quiero decir que sin apoyo de expertos, sin una guía o algo sirva como orientación, no se puede avanzar [hacia IELT], puesto que por mucho que uno lea sobre los temas, no se pueden llevar a la práctica tan fácilmente ['I want to say that without the support of experts, without a guide or something that serves as an orientation, you cannot advance [towards IELT], since no matter how much one reads about the topics, they cannot be put into practice so easily', our translation from Spanish].

Findings also revealed teachers' strong connection with some components of Byram's ICC model, and their perceptions of interculturality partially addressed savoir (knowledge as primarily knowledge) and savoir comprendre (skills to interpret). Participant teachers spoke about a desired ICC English language teacher profile: 'un profesor de mente abierta, capaz de comprender al Otro Cultural' [An open-minded teacher able understand the cultural Other]; 'Valorar otras culturas' [Value other cultures] and 'capacidad de apreciar otras culturas' [Capacity to appreciate other cultures]. These appeared to include Byram's ideas of attitudes and dispositions (savoir-être). This data referring to culture-as-knowledge, to cross-cultural recurrent classroom strategies, and to valuing the native culture and the target cultures suggest that the savoirs and savoir comprendre components of Byram's model are the most recognised parts. Findings also suggested that participants see in Byram's postulates a plausible, accessible guideline they can adhere to as a starting point. Because communicative language teaching (CLT) is taken as a major reference for teachers here, explorations of Byram's (1997) ideas can be perceived as an advancement if ICC is seen as a continuation in the continuum of communicative approaches.

In addition to advocacy for Byram's savoirs and savoir comprendre, critical thinking and reflective teaching practice were also underscored by teachers as part of an advancement towards ICC-based language teaching. Reflexivity and criticality are thus integral parts of Byram's ICC tenets.

However, even more importance should be attributed to them to sensitise English language teachers' incipient ICC. Also, in addition to some well-acknowledged ICC attitudes (e.g. tolerance, open mindedness, respect), there were two values – *fraternity* and *solidarity* – mentioned by participant teachers as being important qualities in intercultural attitudes or *savoir-être*. These values are particularly significant for the Colombian collectivist society in which the group, and not the individual, is at the core of social relationships. Even though solidarity has not frequently been mentioned in other models of ICC (e.g. Byram, 1997; Deardorff, 2009; King & Baxter Magolda, 2005; Spitzberg & Changnon, 2009), it is well acknowledged by international organisations including UNESCO, one of its principles advocates, that '[i]ntercultural education provides all learners with cultural knowledge, attitudes and skills that enable them to contribute to respect, understanding and *solidarity among individuals*, ethnic, social, cultural and religious groups and nations' (UNESCO, 2013: 27).

Concomitantly, fraternity, or bonds of brotherhood, friendship and solidarity were also identified as an important characteristic for the intercultural teacher. These values together underscore the importance of ICC as part of a collective, collaborative learning task because they are values that, because of their very nature, emphasise the relationships between groups of individuals in need of strategies for their mutual understanding, appreciation and permanent dialogue. Seen from this perspective, fraternity and solidarity could represent a Colombian, or a Latin American contribution to the intercultural attitudes or *savoir-être* English language teachers should develop.

Grounded in my own research on teaching English developing ICC in the language classroom, emerging themes from interviews, elicited beliefs and knowledge on the topic of interculturalising ELT, a guideline or proposal for teachers approaching ICC in the English language classroom – an ICC initiation model – should necessarily adhere to the following characteristics (Peña Dix, 2018: 224–225):

(1) A data-driven emerging model that comes from participant teachers' elicited opinions on interculturality and ICC.
(2) A plain model that aids teachers who are for the first time approaching the issue of interculturalising ELT.
(3) A model that recognises a departing stance from culture teaching at any level and should be located on the wide spectrum of culture and language instruction.
(4) A model that promotes reflection as to how teaching practices should evolve from structural to more constructivist, anti-essentialist standpoints.
(5) A model that leads to a process of increasing intercultural sensitivity. This should not be something that works as an inventory to determine presence-absence relationships but as breakthrough-in-progression.

(6) A model that capitalises upon English language teachers' previous knowledge and experiences.
(7) A model the core of which includes CCA due to its consolidation of some of Byram's postulations combined with reflective teaching practices and higher order thinking skills.
(8) A non-prescriptive model, although this may sound paradoxical, that acknowledges its transitory validity and continuous construction of concepts. It can be seen as a guideline or a thinking-and-reflecting tool for English language teachers to find their own ways to access intercultural English language teaching.

Based on these tenets, aspects from developmental models become relevant as competence evolves over time, and these models provide stages of progression or maturity that entail relationships that can become more competent through on-going interaction (Spitzberg & Changnon, 2009). It is also understood that due to its processual nature, 'ICC is not to be acquired in a short space of time or in one module. It is not a naturally occurring phenomenon but **a lifelong process** which needs to be addressed explicitly in learning and teaching' [Emphasis added] (McKinnon, 2012: para. 4). It is not inaccurate to say that Colombian English language teachers are in their infancy of ICC language teaching (Álvarez Valencia, 2014), and evolving towards an ICC 'maturity' appears to be a feasible route to taking ICC from an initial to more mature stages (King & Baxter Magolda, 2005). Thus, achieving ICC involves time, and the processes of becoming intercultural not only depend upon external factors, but also on teachers' internal intrinsic aspects relating to their autonomy, disposition and personality. Achieving ICC does not have to do with an age or language proficiency level, but rather it involves professional maturation and reflective critical praxis that capitalises on experience and 'self-authorship' (Kegan, 1994: 185).

The next section presents an emerging initiation model (Figure 10.1) that suggests how teachers can advance towards ICC in ELT. The proposal is inspired by the triadic dimension of Byram's ICC critical thinking reflective teaching and translates into the development of a continuous process of knowledge, attitudes and beliefs as cyclical operations within the language teaching-learning spiral process that can be revisited in order to reflect on intercultural experiences inside and outside the classroom. Convergence with Byram's multidimensional model, critical thinking and reflective teaching practice are embedded in the concept of CCA. Through CCA, teachers build an open environment of inquiry to discover by themselves the origins of judgements or stereotypes (Byram & Guilherme, 2000). As teachers learn to deconstruct stereotypes and prejudice, they become mature intercultural learners and mediators ready to share this knowledge in the classroom together with the tasks required for learning the language.

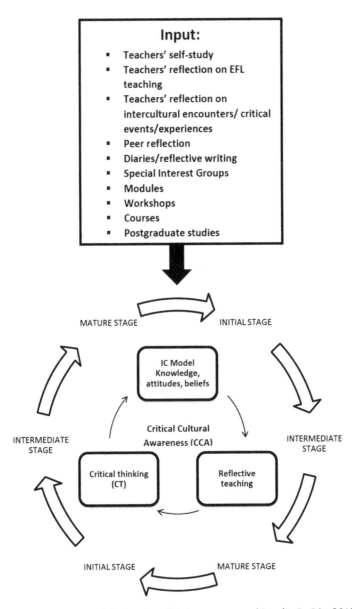

Figure 10.1 Initiation model of ICC English language teaching (Peña Dix, 2018)

The initiation model

This initiation model is a dynamic continuum in which multidirectional processes are cyclical, and in which teachers are hopefully motivated to learn, change, evolve and transform over time (Nugent & Catalano, 2014). The circularity of the diagram and the arrows can indicate the freedom and flexibility to transit between categories to achieve a certain action orientation that can be understood as the crucial link between interculturality and intercultural citizenship (Barrett, 2008; Guilherme, 2002). The model also suggests that 'maturity' is achieved within a process of multiple revisions of the triad of concepts that, at some point, interrelate and merge. The initial or intermediate stages in some aspects of the *savoirs* do not exclude being mature in some other aspects; growth in a competence does not mean that all processes grow evenly due to teachers' experiences, backgrounds and self-motivations. For this reason, establishment and maturation of ICC happens because time and praxis aid teachers to revisit attitudes, knowledge and skills, and they assume the roles of reflective, critical thinkers and English teaching practitioners.

Deardorff (2009) relates ICC to critical thinking by explaining how ICC 'promotes effective and appropriate decision making' (2009: 479). ICC allows an individual to become an effective interlocutor in intercultural communication (Soboleva & Lomakina, 2018). To develop ICC, a conscious attitude to intercultural communication as a way of understanding the world, its goals and objectives is required. Successful intercultural communication helps minimise misunderstandings and conflicts on an intercultural basis. Thus, a competent critical thinker will be able to cope with prejudices because:

> Critical thinking skills help learners develop ICC and contribute to more appropriate and effective communication across cultures. Thus, developing knowledge of other cultures and communicative practices in a FL classroom has to parallel fostering the ability to critically reflect on and adapt knowledge by means of reasoning. (Sobkowiak, 2016: 712)

With regard to reflective teaching, language teachers can examine their attitudes, assumptions and beliefs about language learning and teaching, to make critically reflective decisions about their teaching (Richard & Lockhart, 1994). This implies a continuous IC exercise applied to the teaching practice and to the pedagogical principles ruling the teaching of languages.

Concomitantly, based on my research and on my initiation model, if the next step is to create a comprehensive ELT national curriculum, I propose an empirically based *Statement of philosophy* as a necessity to set prospective ICC English language teaching guidelines. It would read as follows:

> The relationship between language and culture, and how foreign language teaching objectives will be insufficient without reflection on building Intercultural Communicative Competence (ICC) in language teaching must be a major concern in a globally interconnected world. Language teacher education in Colombia should embrace a multidimensional

approach in which, in addition to linguistic and pedagogical knowledge, the development of intercultural competence and critical cultural awareness, gradually leading up to intercultural citizenship, are at the core. In an envisaged near future, ICC forms an integral part of the language curriculum. Language teachers embrace interculturalism to mediate and develop a new vision of the language in their learners which can help them access cultures, experience intercultural encounters, and participate in national and international intercultural dialogue as they become citizens of the world.

This statement of philosophy assumes that ICC in language teaching is a gradual process of critical awareness in which language educators overtake an informed, intercultural turn to ELT. English language teachers also become learners – 'teachers by profession, but [...] students of [their] profession' (Senese, 2017: 104) – since they learn and grow in ICC together with their language students and with other colleagues. In this way, the language classroom develops its own intercultural ecology as an open space for language and culture teaching, self and collective learning, and intercultural dialogue and mediation with and through English, which helps build multiple, coexisting voices and realities.

Conclusions

This chapter has discussed the importance of ICC in the context of contemporary language teacher education. Despite complexities, coincidences and discrepancies when exploring ICC and ICC models, as well as their scope and reach, scholars get to common ground when they express that language education seems a natural context for the development of interculturality. For this reason, we are now witnessing a gradual transformation in the role of language teachers as agents of change and pedagogical progress that originates from the necessity to widen teacher knowledge, skills and attitudes to integrate intercultural critical stances into teacher education and praxis. To ameliorate the knowledge-practice gap, intercultural language teacher education should create inclusive, human-rights based curricula to educate and support teachers to become interculturalists themselves so as they can scaffold ICC language learning aims and contribute to more harmonious societies (Hoff, 2016). Humans rights-based curricula fosters ICC and intercultural communication through the promotion of 'freedoms, rights, equality, equal access and opportunities for all, [...] ensuring that every person has equal opportunity regardless of their race, culture, language, religion, gender or disability. Education should therefore enable learners to participate effectively at local, national and global levels' (De Leo, 2010: 14).

In the concrete case of Colombia, data reported here were congruent with international research regarding how the ICC dimension is still challenging in the foreign language classroom despite teachers often having positive dispositions towards incorporating ICC in ELT. Participant teachers expressed an interest in some components of Byram's ICC model as a starting point to become knowledgeable about and trained in ICC in their ELT praxis – they partially addressed *savoir* (knowledge as primarily knowledge) and *savoir comprendre* (skills to interpret). Findings were conclusive that Byram's proposal is of particular value to my research – 'Byram's writings have, to a great extent, been responsible for the growing significance attributed to the cultural component within foreign language education [...] and for making teachers more interested in adding a critical dimension to it' (Guilherme, 2002: 143) – because *critical cultural awareness* as a goal represents an inclusive aim encompassing reflection, criticality, and maturity in ICC in the foreign language classroom. This triad has emerged from teachers' views and assumptions. Based on what teachers expressed, a statement philosophy for ICC and a situated initiation tripartite model which integrates Byram's thoughts, reflective teaching practices and critical thinking skills were formulated to gradually and conscientiously develop mature ICC awareness and competence (Byram, 2012).

Altogether, intercultural language education and teacher training now require collective efforts and readiness of all education stakeholders to build into the future critically and optimistically. Achieving ICC in the foreign language classroom will require significant changes concerning emphasis on how language teachers and learners create and re-create multilayered realities with and through language to build more democratic, open spaces for dialogue and understanding. Unanswered questions may address the issue of teachers' level of preparation to promote students' understanding of the world and empower them to engage in action and participate in society. Language teacher education curricula will learn from each other about how to promote innovative ICC language instruction and adjust language teacher education and training so as to facilitate the development of interculturality and intercultural citizenship in the field of foreign language teaching and learning (Byram & Wagner, 2018).

References

Álvarez Valencia, J.A. (2014) Developing the intercultural perspective in foreign language teaching in Colombia: A review of six journals. *Language and Intercultural Communication* 14 (2), 226–244.

Alesina, A. and Ferrara, E.L. (2005) Ethnic diversity and economic performance. *Journal of Economic Literature* 43 (3), 762–800. https://www.aeaweb.org/articles ?id=10.1257/002205105774431243

Benavides-Jimenez, F. and Mora-Acosta, Y.L. (2019) Beliefs of two culturally diverse groups of teachers about intercultural bilingual education. *Profile: Issues in Teachers' Professional Development* 21 (2), 63–77.

Bonilla Carvajal, C.A. and Tejada-Sanchez, I. (2016) Unanswered questions in Colombia's foreign language education policy. *Profile: Issues Teacher Professional Development* 18 (1), 185–201.

Braun, V. and Clarke, V. (2006) Using thematic analysis in psychology. *Qualitative Research in Psychology* 3 (2), 77–101.

British Council (2015) *English in Colombia: An Examination of Policies, Perceptions and Influencing Factors. Education Intelligence.* https://ei.britishcouncil.org/sites/default/files/latinamericaresearch/English%20in%20Colombia.pdf

Byram, M. (1997) *Teaching and Assessing Intercultural Communicative Competence.* Clevedon: Multilingual Matters.

Byram, M. (2011) From foreign language education to education for intercultural citizenship. *Intercultural Communication Review* 9, 17–35.

Byram, M. (2012) Language awareness and (critical) cultural awareness – Relationships, comparisons and contrasts. *Language Awareness* 21 (1–2), 5–13.

Byram, M. (2013) Foreign language teaching and intercultural citizenship. *Iranian Journal of Language Teaching Research* 1 (3), 53–62. https://files.eric.ed.gov/fulltext/EJ1127400.pdf

Byram, M. (2021) *Teaching and Assessing Intercultural Communicative Competence: Revisited.* Bristol: Multilingual Matters.

Byram, M. and Guilherme, M. (2000) Human rights, cultures and language teaching. In A. Osler (ed.) *Citizenship and Democracy in Schools: Diversity, Identity, Equality* (pp. 63–78). Staffordshire, England: Trentham Books.

Byram, M. and Wagner, M. (2018) Making a difference: Language teaching for intercultural and international dialogue. *Foreign Language Annals* 51 (1), 140–151.

Byram, M., Gribkova, B. and Starkey, H. (2002) *Developing the Intercultural Dimension in Language Teaching: A Practical Introduction for Teachers.* Strasbourg, France: Council of Europe. https://rm.coe.int/16802fc1c3

Crozet, C. (2017) The intercultural foreign language teacher: Challenges and choices. In M. Dasli and A.R. Diaz (eds) *The Critical Turn in Language and Intercultural Communication Pedagogy: Theory, Research and Practice* (pp. 143–161). New York: Routledge.

Cuartas Álvarez, L.F. (2020) Intercultural communicative competence: In-service EFL teachers building understanding through study groups. *Profile: Issues in Teachers' Professional Development* 22 (1), 75–92.

Dasli, M. and Diaz, A.R. (2017) *The Critical Turn in Language and Intercultural Communication Pedagogy: Theory, Research and Practice.* London: Routledge.

De Leo, J. (2010) *Reorienting Teacher Education to Address Sustainable Development: Guidelines and Tools. Education for Intercultural Understanding.* Bangkok: UNESCO.

de Mejía, A.M. (2004) Bilingual education in Colombia: Towards an integrated perspective. *International Journal of Bilingual Education and Bilingualism* 7 (5), 381–397.

Deardorff, D.K. (2006) Identification and assessment of intercultural competence as a student overcome of internationalization. *Journal of Studies in International Education* 10 (3), 241–266.

Deardorff, D.K. (2009) Implementing intercultural competence assessment. In D. K. Deardorff (ed.) *The Sage Handbook of Intercultural Competence* (pp. 477–491). Thousand Oaks, CA: Sage Publications.

Deardorff, D.K. (2011) Assessing intercultural competence. *Special Issue: Assessing Complex General Education Student Learning Outcomes: New Directions for Institutional Research* 149, 65–79.

Dervin, F. (2016) *Interculturality in Education: A Theoretical and Methodological Toolbox.* London: Palgrave Macmillan.

Dervin, F. (2020) Creating and combining models for intercultural competence for teacher education/training: On the need to rethink IC frequently. In F. Dervin, R. Moloney and A. Simpson (eds) *Intercultural Competence in the Work of Teachers: Confronting Ideologies and Practices* (pp. 57–72). London: Routledge.

Fandiño-Parra, Y.J. (2011) Programas de formación de docentes de inglés centrados en la reflexión. *Educación Y Educadores* 14 (2), 269–285. https://educacionyeducadores. unisabana.edu.co/index.php/eye/article/view/1922

Fernández-Agüero, M. and Garrote, M. (2019) 'It's not my intercultural competence, it's me.' The intercultural identity of prospective foreign language teachers. *Educar* 55 (1), 159–182.

Fonseca-Greber, B. (2010) Social obstacles to intercultural competence in America's language classrooms. *Proceedings of Intercultural Competence Conference, Center for Educational Resources in Culture, Language and Literacy (CERCLL)* 1, 102–123. http://cercll.arizona.edu/ICConference2010

Guilherme, M. (2002) *Critical Citizens for an Intercultural World: Foreign Language Education as Cultural Politics.* Clevedon: Multilingual Matters.

Guilherme, M. (2007) English as a global language and education for cosmopolitan citizenship. *Language and Intercultural Communication* 7 (1), 72–90.

Henao, E., Gómez, J. and Murcia, J. (2019) Intercultural awareness and its misrepresentation in textbooks. *Colombian Applied Linguistic Journal* 21 (2), 179–193.

Jaime Osorio, M.F. and Insuasty, E.A. (2015) Analysis of the teaching practices at a Colombian foreign language institute and their effects on students' communicative competence. *HOW* 22 (1), 45–64.

King, P.M. and Baxter Magolda, M.B. (2005) A developmental model of intercultural maturity. *Journal of College Student Development* 46 571–592. https://eric. ed.gov/?id=EJ743902

Liddicoat, A.J. (2008) Pedagogical practice for integrating the intercultural in language teaching and learning. *Japanese Studies* 28 (3), 277–290.

Liddicoat, A. and Scarino, A. (2013) *Intercultural Language Teaching and Learning.* Chichester: Wiley-Blackwell.

McKinnon, S. (2012) *What Is Intercultural Competence?* Global perspectives project. Centre for Learning Enhancement and Academic Development, Glasgow Caledonian University. Glasgow, Scotland. http://www.gcu.ac.uk/media/gcalwebv2/theuniversity/centresprojects/globalperspectives/Definition_of_Intercultural_competence.pdf

Moya-Chaves, D.S., Moreno-García, N.P. and Núñez-Camacho, V. (2018) Interculturality and language teaching in Colombia: The case of three Teacher Education Programs. *Signo y Pensamiento* 37 (73), 53–69.

Nguyen, T.L. (2013) *Integrating Culture into Vietnamese University EFL Teaching: A Critical Ethnography Study. Electronic Theses and Dissertations.* Auckland University of Technology, New Zealand. http://hdl.handle.net/10292/5975

Nugent, K. and Catalano, T. (2015) Critical cultural awareness in the foreign language classroom. *Lincoln: Faculty Publications: Department of Teaching, Learning and Teacher Education.* https://digitalcommons.unl.edu/teachlearnfacpub/194/

Peña Dix, B. (2018) Developing Intercultural Competence in English Language Teachers: Towards Building Intercultural Language Education in Colombia. Doctoral theses, Durham University. Available at Durham E-Theses Online: http://etheses.dur. ac.uk/12619/

Pensky, Max (2009) *The Ends of Solidarity: Discourse Theory in Ethics and Politics.* New York: State University of New York Press.

Porto, M. and Byram, M. (2015) Developing intercultural citizenship education in the language classroom and beyond. *Argentinian Journal of Applied Linguistics* 3 (2), 9–29. http://www.faapi.org.ar/ajal/issues/302/PortoAJALVol3(2).pdf

Richards, J. and Lockhart C. (1994) *Reflective Teaching in Second Language Classrooms.* Cambridge: Cambridge University Press.

Sercu, L. (2006) The foreign language and intercultural competence teacher: The acquisition of a new professional identity. *Intercultural Education* 17 (1), 55–72.

Sercu, L. (2005) Teaching foreign languages in an intercultural world. In L. Sercu, E. Bandura, P. Castro, L. Davcheva, C. Laskaridou, U. Lundgren and P. Ryan (eds) *Foreign Language Teachers and Intercultural Competence: An International Investigation* (pp. 1–18). Clevedon: Multilingual Matters.

Sercu, L., Bandura, E., Castro, P., Davcheva, L., Laskaridou, C., Lundgren, U. and Ryan, P. (eds) (2005) *Foreign Language Teachers and Intercultural Competence: An International Investigation*. Clevedon: Multilingual Matters.

Skopinskaja, L. (2009) Assessing intercultural communicative competence: Test construction issues. *Synergies Pays Riverains de la Baltique* 6, 135–144. https://gerflint.fr/Base/Baltique6/liljana.pdf

Smakova, K. and Paulsrud, B. (2020) Intercultural communicative competence in English language teaching in Kazakhstan. *Issues in Educational Research* 30 (2), 691–708. http://www.iier.org.au/iier30/smakova.pdf

Soboleva, A.V. and Lomakina, A.J. (2018) Critical thinking as a premise for the intercultural competence development. *Language and Culture* 11, 104–111. https://cyberleninka.ru/article/n/critical-thinking-as-a-premise-for-the-intercultural-competence-development

Sobkowiak, P. (2016) Critical thinking in the intercultural context: Investigating EFL textbooks, *Studies in Second Language Learning and Teaching* 6 (4), 697–716. https://files.eric.ed.gov/fulltext/EJ1134499.pdf

Spitzberg, B.H. and Changnon, G. (2009) Conceptualizing intercultural competence. In D.K. Deardorff (ed.) *The Sage Handbook of Intercultural Competence* (pp. 2–52). Thousand Oaks, CA: Sage.

UNESCO (2013) *Intercultural Competence. Conceptual and Operational Framework*. Paris, France: UNESCO.

Velez–Rendon, G. (2003) English in Colombia: A sociolinguistic profile. *World Englishes* 22 (2), 185–198 https://onlinelibrary.wiley.com/doi/abs/10.1111/1467-971X.00287

11 Assessing Intercultural Capability: Insights from Processes of Eliciting and Judging Student Learning

Angela Scarino and Michelle Kohler

Introduction: The Need for and Ambivalence Towards Assessing Intercultural Competence/Capability

Byram's (1997) seminal book: *Teaching and Assessing Intercultural Communicative Competence* and his subsequent body of work has inspired a consideration of intercultural language learning for almost three decades. This work has influenced teachers, and through them, learners of foreign languages (maintaining Byram's own terminology) as well as teacher educators and researchers who have drawn upon diverse dimensions of his work to extend theorisation and practice in languages education. Working with Zarate in the context of framework development for the Council of Europe, he began a long-standing consideration of the question of the assessment (Byram & Zarate, 1994) of intercultural language learning, recently reconsidered in the revised edition of his work (Byram, 2021). Notably, they elaborated the notion of the 'intercultural speaker', thereby shifting the goal away from so-called native-speaker competence. His work has been applied in diverse contexts internationally and with diverse educational communities, often through collaboration, and it is for this reason that his work is presented with the voice of deep experience and reflection.

As Byram (2021) makes clear in Chapter 5 of his most recent volume, his interest in assessment is an interest in educational assessment in an expansive sense, rather than 'testing'; he sees assessment as an integral part of teaching and providing evidence of learning. Following the work of Gipps (1994) who argues for a paradigm shift in assessment, his focus is on the assessment of achievement, rather than proficiency. This is assessment that is related specifically to curricular or programme objectives. His priority in assessment is in promoting and valuing student learning above matters related to certification and institutional accountability.

In a 25-year review of foreign language learning, where Byram (2014) traces expansions in the learning of languages towards 'intercultural citizenship', he notes that the question of assessment, specifically in the context of intercultural language learning, remains insufficiently developed. This is so notwithstanding the expanded interest in interculturality both in languages education and in education in general (see for example OECD, 2017; Nussbaum, 2011).

There are divided views on whether or not a complex capability such as intercultural capability can or indeed should be assessed. Kramsch, who has elaborated a rich and complex theorisation of intercultural language learning from a post-structural perspective (see Kramsch, 2006, 2009b), and tracing over time a shift from communicative competence to interactional competence, to intercultural competence, to symbolic competence, has noted:

> [S]ymbolic competence based on discourse would be less a collection of ... stable knowledges and more a savviness i.e. a combination of knowledge, experience and judgment ... Trying to test symbolic competence with the structuralist tools employed by schools ... is bound to miss the mark. Instead symbolic competence should be seen as the educational horizon against which to measure all learners' achievements. (Kramsch, 2009a: 118)

Seeing assessment as traditional testing, conceived as measurement of knowledge that is depersonalised, decontextualised, standardised and objective, understandably, is not conducive to assessing a complex capability such as symbolic competence. She does not entertain an alternative to such a traditional view of assessment. Alternative assessment, and especially learning-oriented assessment (see Turner & Purpura, 2015) that opens up assessment to a consideration of learning and development rather than measurement and that recognises the personal, contextualised and subjective nature of assessment offers distinctive possibilities (Scarino, 2010, 2014). Kramsch's focus on knowledges that are not 'stable' and the *combination* of knowledge, experience and judgement characterise the very features of communication and intercultural exchange that are difficult to capture in assessment.

Borghetti (2017) has noted, reflectively, that if intercultural competence is *not* assessed, it may well be considered to be a less significant goal; on the other hand *not* assessing may well also convey an important message to students that not everything that *is* valuable needs to be assessed.

Assessment of intercultural capability is delicate precisely because it goes to learner subjectivity; it is sensitive not only to language but also to the person, relationship, perspectives and subjective knowledge and experience. It is not only a matter of assessing performance and achievement but also the capability to decentre from one's own situatedness in one's own language and culture of one's primary and subsequent socialisation. Furthermore, the assessment of dispositions and values raises important ethical questions in relation to learning and development to which teachers are particularly sensitive.

Having set the scene in relation to Byram's ongoing interest in the assessment of intercultural competence and the contested perspectives that pertain, we now turn to a brief discussion of the state of play with regard to assessing intercultural language learning. In this discussion, we foreground diverse conceptualisations of the intercultural capability itself, often intersecting with Byram's conceptual work, specifically in relation to the nature of the capability and how it is developed. We then describe briefly an ongoing programme of praxis-oriented research on assessing intercultural capability that we have sustained at the Research Centre for Languages and Cultures at the University of South Australia[1] to provide a characterisation of assessment within an alternative assessment paradigm, and we illustrate the discussion through a case study example that sought to capture evidence of intercultural language learning in an intermediate Indonesian language learning programme at a South Australian university. We conclude with a discussion of the value of assessment of the intercultural capability, not only for individual students and their teachers, but also as a means for gaining further insights on the nature of this capability.

A note on terminology is warranted here. When referring to Byram's work, we retain the term 'intercultural communicative competence'. In our work, we use the notion of 'capability' because it conveys, for us, a sense of ongoing potentiality; 'competence' has some connotations of referring to knowledge held in the mind of the individual, and knowledge that is fixed, which is counter to our conception.

Assessing Intercultural Capability in Language Learning

Describing the construct

Though modelled extensively, intercultural capability as a construct remains fuzzy (see Spitzberg & Changnon, 2009; Zotzmann, 2015, for a review of diverse conceptualisations). In the space of this chapter, it is not possible to discuss the full range of models. These vary in relation to dimensions such as the nature of the capability, whether or not language is included in the modelling and how language is understood, the view of culture, the extent to which it includes critical/political dimensions as well as ethical dispositions, the extent to which it addresses intra-cultural as well as inter-cultural perspectives, and the underlying view of development.

Byram's well known componential model of intercultural communicative competence combines (1) dimensions of communication as modelled by Canale and Swain (1980) and van Ek (1986), namely, linguistic competence, sociolinguistic competence and discourse competence, with (2) interrelated clusters of knowledge, skills and attitudes called *savoirs* which comprise intercultural competence: knowledge (*savoirs*), skills of interpreting/relating (*savoir comprendre*), skills of discovery/interaction (*savoir apprendre/faire*) attitudes-curiosity/openness (*savoir être*) and the cultural *savoir*, which is critical, cultural awareness (*savoir s'engager*) (see Byram, 2021: Chapter 2). While comprehensive in capturing a fuller range of dimensions that are well beyond traditional language learning and assessment, the model as it stands does not articulate the relationship between the *savoirs* and communication in the context of linguistic and cultural diversity.

Risager (2007) extends the modelling by including two additional dimensions: languacultural competences and resources, and transnational cooperation in order to foreground the plurilingual nature of communication. Sercu (2004) extends the construct through the inclusion of 'a metacognitive dimension', though this is intended as metacognition in relation to learning processes rather than metacognitive reflection on the mediating role of language and culture in communication and learning. Kramsch, as indicated above, has expanded the construct of interactional competence to include a focus on intersubjective meaning-making which she calls 'symbolic competence' and which she sees as 'embodied experiences, emotional resonances and moral imaginings' (Kramsch, 2006: 251) in the exchange of meanings with others in the negotiation of symbolic systems.

The extensive modelling to capture the construct of intercultural capability means that a range of dimensions that come into play in language learning, language use and language assessment have been largely captured. Any conceptualisation, however, particularly for the purposes of educational assessment, needs to capture not only framings of the nature of intercultural capability but also its development. This would allow for addressing the question of extent or depth of intercultural engagement that is also relevant to assessment.

A well-known 'developmental' model of intercultural competence, developed by Bennett (1986), posits the development as six stages: the first three are ethnocentric stages (denial → defense → minimisation); the second three are ethno-relative stages (acceptance → adaptation → integration). Although such a scale foregrounds development, it does so in a way that is generalised and decontextualised and ignores the context of situation and the context of culture (Halliday, 1993) of particular instances of intercultural exchange. It describes levels of competence leading to intercultural competence, with the implication that a particular level remains in preparation for movement to the next level regardless of particular instances. It does not appreciate that it is precisely the context of the particular instance of intercultural exchange that needs to be managed.

Byram's original conceptualising work was carried out alongside the development of the Common European Framework of Reference (CEFR) (Council of Europe, 2001), which has recently been extended (Council of Europe, 2018). The construct that is the driving force of the CEFR is conceived as plurilingual competence but in what is now a traditional understanding of functional language use, rather than as language use with meta-awareness and personal meaningfulness. The construct is operationalised in scales (that is, proficiency descriptions), and it is these scales that are the most influential part of the CEFR as its use extends globally. These scales represent hypothesised norms of proficiency, ordered to depict progression or increasing levels of sophistication, that are assumed to be common for all languages, contexts of use and learners. These norms, however, cannot do justice to the ways in which people, in diversity, mediate the exchange of meanings. These descriptions are necessarily reductive and elide individuals and their own personal goals and desires vis-à-vis additional language learning. They assume that meanings are given, rather than understanding meaning as a co-construction that relies on reciprocal interpretation and creation of meanings in situ. They assign students to the role of performers, doing or acting out communication, rather than being both performers and analysers who come to understand the exchange of meanings as effortful and ethical as it involves exchange across difference, a process that is complex and at times, conflictual. Though the CEFR provides richer descriptions of language learning than is captured in the scales, it is the scales that have come to define language learning. As McNamara (2019) states:

> Defining the goals and meaning of language learning in purely functional communicative terms ignores the role of language learning in the subjective experience of the learner as an individual with a history, both personal and cultural ... erases all historical and cultural differences among languages and learners in their specific socio-cultural and historical contexts as determining influences on the motivation to learn language. (2019: 116)

Byram does not incorporate these level descriptions in his operationalisation of the assessment of intercultural communicative competence. He focuses on achievement assessment through objectives described for each of the five *savoirs* of the model (Byram, 2021: Chapter 5). For each objective, he considers possible evidence in order to develop assessment criteria. This approach to operationalising the construct of intercultural competence for the purposes of assessment raises two observations that are worth signalling. First, each objective is presented as a separate entity, when in practice any holistic instance of intercultural exchange will necessitate several objectives operating together. Second, the systematic pre-specification of objectives, though important for the purposes of educational planning, tends not to leave sufficient space for the unpredictability and uncertainty of intercultural exchange. The outcomes of intercultural exchange are unpredictable precisely because of the exchange being an engagement with difference.

Byram recognises the challenge of capturing the holistic nature of engaging in intercultural exchange and the crucial need for developing the meta-awareness of learners towards their development of self-understanding in intercultural exchange. He also recognises the challenge of specifying criteria for judging performance and the impact of processes of certification. Regarding the issue of levels of achievement along a scale, he highlights rightly that the kinds of assessment envisaged for assessing intercultural competence 'require a shift in perspective, not a movement along a scale' (Byram, 2021: 146). Considering the ongoing efforts to develop frameworks and scales to 'measure' intercultural competence, he reiterates the limitations of traditional, objective, psychometric testing and the advantages of rich descriptions, self-assessments and portfolios of data collected over time (Byram, 2021: 50).

Understanding the Assessment of Intercultural Capability – An Interpretive Approach

In the praxis-oriented approach to understanding the assessment of intercultural capability in the context of language learning that we have developed at the Research Centre for Languages and Cultures at the University of South Australia, we have sought to address the challenges that the assessment of the intercultural capability presents to teachers.

We have worked with teams of teachers of diverse languages at primary, secondary and tertiary levels in cycles of conceptualising intercultural capabilities, designing language learning within an intercultural orientation, gathering classroom learning and assessment data, analysing and judging samples of student work in order to evidence and warrant the learning, and evaluating the process. We see the intercultural capability as a mutual, interpretive process of making sense of the subject matter being exchanged and the person (see Kohler, 2020; Liddicoat & Scarino, 2013; Scarino, 2014, 2020). We understand intercultural language learning as a hermeneutically inspired view of language learning that takes into account the linguistic and cultural profile of learners, their knowledge, beliefs, memories, desires, perspectives that come from their primary and subsequent socialisation (that is, their situatedness) and the mediating role of languages and cultures in the act of learning. Equally, we understand assessment as interpretive, with all aspects of the assessment process relying on interpretation: interpretation of the assessment experience/task on the part of learners; interpretation of student responses and reactions on the part of teachers; interpretation of the persons engaged in intercultural exchange (self and others) on the part of student-participants in intercultural exchange; interpretation of the learners on the part of the teachers and peers, and more. In assessing intercultural capability in language learning, it is necessary to capture:

- observation, description, analysis and interpretation of phenomena shared when communicating and interacting;
- active engagement with the interpretation of self (intraculturality) and 'other' (interculturality) in diverse contexts of exchange;
- understanding of the ways in which language and culture come into play in interpreting, creating and exchanging meaning;
- the recognition and integration into communication of an understanding of self (and others) as already situated in one's own language and culture when communicating with others. (Liddicoat & Scarino, 2013: 130–131)

It is the *integration* of these dimensions that provides the holistic orientation that best captures the intercultural capability. Within this view of the nature of assessment of the intercultural capability knowledge is understood as embodied in learners rather than as 'objective' knowledge. It values processes as much as products of learning (including for example, elaborating, explaining, comparing, translating, exemplifying, juxtaposing, relating, reformulating, mediating), and the development of students' performance and achievement over time. The aim is to understand what people mean and to locate these meanings within particular social, cultural, historical, institutional contexts.

More specifically, at a practical level, this understanding of assessment is operationalised through three facets that we consider to be integral to assessing intercultural capability: (1) participation/performance within an experience or task, understood as interpretive, evaluative moments of intercultural exchange; (2) analysis of the role of language and culture in shaping reality and the construction of knowledge and understanding and (3) reflection and reflexivity, both on the phenomena/ideas/concepts exchanged, and the persons, their reactions and responses.

It is also operationalised through concept-based units of work (as opposed to individual experiences or tasks) as this permits conceptual contextualisation of the learning, teaching and assessment as an holistic process and permits discussion of notions of multiplicity, perspective, positionality, criticality that are central to intercultural work. It also permits the development of creative ways of inviting students to externalise or make visible their reflection, for it is through commentary and explanation that intercultural capability is most likely to be evidenced.

Assessment of intercultural capability, then, is conceptualised in our work as a process of interpretation, within an understanding that all interpretation is governed by history and all interpretation itself is linguistic and cultural (see Gadamer (2004) for a discussion of the historicity and linguisticality of interpretation; see Gallagher (1992) for a discussion of hermeneutics and education; see Moss (2008) for a discussion of hermeneutics and assessment). Assessment is also seen as a process of *inquiry*, reflecting our interest in drawing systematic assessment information from defined assessment moments as well as from the teachers' ongoing work with students and recognising that the evidence of intercultural capability is emergent and developmental.

Finally, we understand that with respect to reporting on the assessment of intercultural capability, it is not a matter of *benchmarking* evidence of intercultural capability in relation to external, predetermined and ultimately vague standards, captured *a priori* in scales, but rather that it is a matter of *profiling*, capturing the qualitative characteristics or features of intercultural capability and students' *personal* responses and understandings, reflective of the variability that students represent and the diverse interpretations that they make, as revealed in their explanations of their understanding. Students will necessarily react in different ways to experiences that may be incongruent with their personal frames of reference. They will differ in terms of prior experiences and critical moments in that experience. Their response will also involve emotion as they engage with potentially altering to some extent their habitual practices and ways of understanding – and the different reasons they themselves have for seeing and valuing experiences and phenomena as they do. It is likely that ipsative-referenced assessment as proposed by Sadler (1987, 1989), through which students' understanding is judged based on their previous performance and linked to long-term progress, is likely to serve the assessment of intercultural capability well.

The sustained example elaborated below illustrates these features of assessment of intercultural capability that have emerged from our work.

Assessing intercultural capability: An example

The following example is drawn from a larger study of the development and assessment of intercultural language learning (Kohler, 2020). It was a sustained, self-study conducted over an academic year in an Australian tertiary institution. It is important to note how the context of the study shaped its design and enactment. At the university level, national standards prescribe aspects such as hours of instruction and number of assessments and generic standards, as set out in the Australian Qualifications Framework (AQF). At the local level, course aims and objectives/intended outcomes are approved typically through faculty-based teaching and learning committees. As such, there is some flexibility for academics to shape course content and assessment within approved course structures.

The larger study was designed as a longitudinal case study of 15, second language learners of Indonesian in their second (intermediate) year of a three-year language major. Students studying Indonesian in the Australian tertiary context are typically first language speakers of

English, and most in the second-year course had prior knowledge of Indonesian either through completing first year or having studied the language to Year 12 at secondary school. Some students had travelled to Indonesia for personal or study experiences, while others had no engagement with the community, either in Indonesia or locally. Students came from a range of disciplines including education, law, development studies, international studies and the arts. Many were drawn to Indonesian for personal reasons or for potential career or community service opportunities in future.

The study was strongly curriculum and achievement oriented, investigating how teachers' interrelated curriculum planning, teaching and assessment practices could support learners' development of intercultural capability in language learning. The teaching programme and assessment were systematically designed with reference to three facets of language learning that operationalise an intercultural orientation, as follows:

- participation in performance and experience of communication;
- analysis of aspects of language and culture involved in communication;
- reflection on the comparative, interlinguistic and intracultural dimensions of language learning and language use. (Liddicoat & Scarino, 2013)

These facets provided a basis for considering dimensions of language learning, subject positions, roles and perspectives that learners would take in their learning and assessments. Across the year, learners were required to be participants, analysers and reflective language learners. As intermediate learners, they were expected to become intercultural mediators, using their evolving repertoires to move between their existing language and culture, and Indonesian language and culture. This goal was reflected in the set of assessments across the course and in particular, the final assessment that drew on all of their learning.

Designing assessment to elicit intercultural capability

The programme was developed with respect to the learners, their needs, interests, prior experiences and aspirations. It comprised a series of sequential units based on concepts that formed an overarching 'narrative' that aimed to expand learners' conceptual frames derived largely from their primary socialisation, to that of the world of Indonesian language and culture (recognising that this is dynamic and multifaceted). Concepts were mapped across the programme, moving from concrete such as self and relationship, to more abstract ideas of faith, nationalism and adaptation. (See Kohler (2020) for a full discussion of the programme, units of work and concepts.)

The overarching goal of the intermediate programme was to develop students' capability to participate in intercultural exchanges and act as mediators, and the assessment was designed to elicit evidence of this across the year. The suite of assessments needed to increasingly allow students to show their learning, and thereby evidence their development of intercultural capability over time. The assessments took into account the three facets, and each assessment built on the previous one, developing learners' awareness and capacity for reflection with each assessment experience. Three assessments that had an explicit emphasis on eliciting intercultural capability were spread across the year, one in each semester and a further culminating one at the end of the course. Each of these comprised both 'language using' (communicating), and 'language and culture learning', and each incorporated some kind of 'gap' or disparity in knowledge or opinion, perspective or understanding that required learners to mediate in some way. Furthermore, each assessment included an element of reflection, both on the specific instance/experience, and on the process of intercultural exchange.

The first assessment was based on a unit exploring the concept of 'relationship'. Students were expected to read, translate and respond to an authentic email from a young woman seeking advice about whether to leave a polygamous marriage. Throughout the assessment, students were to record their thinking through an audio-recording/think-aloud process. The purpose was to elicit their processing of and reactions to the text in terms of both language use and ideational content. It was also intended to elicit their mediation processes, how they understood and expressed their meanings to someone operating within another language and culture framework. This required them to decentre; to notice how they were making sense of the text, and the kinds of reactions they were having, and considering and explaining why. It involved them standing back, recognising their assumptions and cultural situatedness, and considering how this impacted their communication in responding to the email. The planned criteria for judging students' learning that reflected these intentions were as follows: ability to comprehend the text and apply translation/mediation strategies to express own personal meaning; ability to construct meaning using new language for giving advice and solving problems; ability to reflect on and explain thinking, reactions and language choices in constructing a response. The think-aloud process enabled students to externalise their processing and affective reactions in relation to a potentially controversial phenomenon. A process, such as a think-aloud used in this open-ended way, provided an opportunity for intercultural capability to be elicited.

The second of the assessments was a recount based on an excursion to a local mosque as part of a 'faith'-based unit. The assessment was designed to elicit learners' ability to recount an experience in some detail, conveying their understandings and opinions about Islam in general and in their own community. They were also required to reflect on the role of language and culture in the interaction with members of the mosque congregation. The criteria for judging performance included students' ability to use the target language to express their opinions and knowledge about the phenomenon of Islam, and faith more broadly, and their ability to reflect on the experience and diverse perspectives encountered during the visit.

The third assessment related to the final unit around the concept of 'adaptation' and to the programme overall. The assessment involved students creating a bilingual and intercultural resource for prospective Indonesian peers or families intending to settle in Australia. To do this, students needed to situate/position themselves as mediators, decentring from their own linguistic and cultural worlds, and taking into account an 'outsider' perspective. The assessment required students to develop a bilingual resource designed to support an Indonesian person/family to learn to live in the local community. The resource was to include aspects covered across the programme including environment, lifestyle, attitudes and values that might be encountered, and advice about how these might be understood. In addition, students were required to reflect on the entirety of the year, and on their own language development and use in interaction, the role of language and culture in communication, and on their own sense of identity. The assessment was cumulative and open-ended in its design, inviting students to draw on their full language, culture and learning repertoires to show how they could act as intercultural mediators, and what they had learned about themselves and intercultural exchange in the process. The criteria focused on the quality of the resource, its suitability for an Indonesian audience (accommodating perspectives of others) and the depth of reflection and reflexivity (showing awareness of own enculturation and assumptions, and insights into the role of language and culture on intercultural mediation and identity formation). Responses were varied and included brochures, video clips, guides or blogs, exploring local environs, youth culture and university life, cultural norms and values.

The nature of the evidence

It is not possible within the scope of this chapter to discuss the full set of responses of all students. Instead, in order to consider how intercultural capability may be evidenced and judged, a selection of extracts from the responses of one student, referred to as Kim, is provided along with a translation of these to assist the reader. The extracts are presented in the sequence in which they occurred during the course, with comments on the different kinds of evidence (indicated in italics) and what these reveal overall.

Extract 1: Response to email about polygamy with explanatory commentary

Response

Begini ibu, pernikahan yang penuh dengan kepura-puraan tidak sehat untuk anda.

Kejujuran, kesetiaan dan kehormatan penting sekali untuk *hubungan yang hebat*. Juga, pernikahan yang berhasil berarti *komitmen dan kepedulian*. … saya menyarankan supaya kalian *berdiskusi bersama* anak-anak itu. Cobalah menjelaskan mereka masih ada ayah dan ibu yang sangat mencintai mereka. Saya kira ibu tidak harus *menyerahkan karir*. Ada banyak ibu janda yang masih bekerja. … *Apakah ibu kira* anda dan suami bisa memperoleh keputusan tentang anak-anak dan uang yang adil? Apakah anda bisa menjelaskan kepada dia yang *dia harus membiayai* anak-anaknya? Ada jalan keluar yang dapat anda ikuti *menurut pendapat saya*.

Translation

It's like this ma'am, a marriage full of pretense is not good for you. *Honesty, loyalty and respect* are very important for *a good relationship*. Also, a successful marriage takes *commitment and care*. I suggest you *discuss it* with your children. *Try to explain* to them that they still have a father and mother who love them. I think you shouldn't have to *give your career up*. There are lots of divorcees who still work. *Do you think* you and your husband can reach *a fair decision* about your children and money? Can you explain to him that he *must pay* child support? There is a way out that you can follow *in my view*. [Translation by Kohler]

Explanatory commentary

I decided to respond to Zia's problem *how I would to a friend or family member* who was in that position. I also really *enjoyed* being able to respond to a personal problem *with emotion* and include more of *my own values* as my Indonesian improves … I felt *sad* when Zia referred to her marriage as 'lifeless' and 'full of pretense' … *it made me wonder* whether people in arranged marriages 'learn' to love their partner or often end up in situations like Zia, feeling sad, lost and confused. I was *quite shocked* when Zia mentioned her husband's mistress and him not supporting her, as I *wasn't expecting that*. *In our society* divorce unfortunately is so common but it *would be hard* giving this advice to someone whose country does still consider divorce/divorcees as a negative status and a bad act. In my advice I also suggested that she *try and find a fair solution* regarding the custody of the children and their money. However, this advice *would be easier* to give to someone living in Australia.

Comment on Extract 1:

In this early stage of the programme, Kim primarily responds to the dilemma with reference to her own cultural framework, including values such as honesty, loyalty and care. In her response in Indonesian, she emphasises openness and direct dialogue about the issue, not recognising that this may not be the norm in Indonesia. Her use of questions suggests that she is aware of uncertainties and that values such as 'fairness' may not be shared. She assumes societal and legal expectations such as child support but concludes by acknowledging that it is a 'view', suggesting she may have some awareness of her cultural situatedness.

In her think-aloud, Kim explains her response with reference to her social context. She reflects, with satisfaction, on the experience of using the target language to express views that matter to her. She notes her affective reaction (sad, shocked, wasn't expecting that) and contemplates alternative realities (it made me wonder). She notes the impact of culture on expectations and communication and contrasts an Indonesian context with her own, 'would be hard/easier' ... 'in our society'. Kim recognises that her own advice is culturally bound and that different norms are likely to apply, 'try and find a fair solution'.

Extract 2: Recount and personal views about excursion to local mosque

Response

Lalu, kami pergi ke atas untuk melihat tempat doa yang khusus untuk perempuan. Sementara di mesjid *orang wanita dipisahkan dari laki laki*. Walaupun demikian pemandu kami *memberitahu alasannya* untuk mencegah gangguan, itu masih *sedikit membingungkan untuk saya*.

Kelihatan ada banyak *kesamaan* di antara agama Islam dan agama Kristen.

Kita semua berbeda tetapi *tidak ada kepercayaan* yang terbaik. Orang-orang semua *memilih untuk menginterpretasi* akhirat dengan cara yang berbeda. Juga, *hati saya senang* untuk melihat *gairah* pemandunya untuk *kepercayaan, agama dan nilainya*. Ini cukup berbeda dibandingkan dengan orang Australia karena *sering mereka lebih pendiam* tentang itu.

Translation

Then we went upstairs to see the prayer area specifically for women. While in the mosque, *women are separated from men*. Although this is the case, our guide told us *the reason is* to avoid distraction, it's still *a bit puzzling to me*.

There are many *similarities* between Islam and Christianity. *We are all different* but there *isn't one belief* that's best. People all *choose to interpret* the afterlife differently.

Also, I was *heartened* to see our guide's *enthusiasm for his beliefs, faith and values*. This is quite different to Australians who are *often more reserved* about this. [Translation by Kohler]

Comment on Extract 2:

In this response, there is evidence of increased cultural knowledge about Islam in particular, 'women separated from men in the mosque'.

Kim recognises that there is a good reason, from the perspective of her guide; however, she struggles to reconcile the fact with her own values. She shows greater control of the target language to express her views, interweaving factual details with her reactions and views, 'heartened'. She notices similarities and differences, and entertains commonality, using the inclusive 'we' (*kita*) form, and multiplicity and equality 'there isn't one belief that's best'. Kim explains variability as related to choice and interpretation. In her final comment, she expresses feeling 'heartened' by a way of being in relation to faith (enthusiastic) that contrasts with her own cultural norm, although she does qualify this with 'often' indicating that she is aware of variability within her own culture. She is noticing other ways of being, and through this, becoming more aware of her own and her cultural context.

Extract 3: Develop an artifact and provide an overall reflection

Kim produced a poster as her artifact, making it difficult to reproduce here. Hence, in the interests of brevity and illustrating different aspects of evidence, only part of the reflection is provided.

Response

Overall, this year has prompted me to *consider my life as a bilingual person* and how this impacts my identity, relationships, mindset and my plans for the future. I believe being submerged into learning Indonesian language and culture has *opened my mind, my views of the world and connected with other passions of mine* in ways I could never have predicted. The ability to *have an alternate bicultural identity*, being able to express yourself in another language, *truly connect* with people and develop your character is a thrilling and wonderful experience. I also believe *learning how to act* 'interculturally' is extremely mind opening. There have been moments in Indonesia where I have felt isolated and wondered if the people I am friends with *truly know who I am*, and times when cultural differences have been *overwhelming*. However, I feel it is important to remember that *I am still developing* the ability to *incorporate my personality into my 'Indonesian identity'*, which still expresses my individual attributes but *adapts to different* cultural values, beliefs and rituals. I believe that being a 'bicultural bilingual' person *requires a shift* in behaviour, reactions and values, rather than being a bilingual speaker who *just translates* from their native language to the language they are learning. Appreciating the language and *adopting certain ways* of speaking, even dependent on where you are in Indonesia, is far different to simply translating *word for word which lacks depth and understanding*.

Moreover, I have come to understand that *each language holds a worldview* that its speakers *identify with* when using it. I do not believe that people necessarily switch personalities but rather *adjust their behaviours and attitudes towards different contexts*, adapting to 'cultural accommodation'. *Incorporating two cultures within myself is quite fascinating* and I believe Indonesian language *triggers culture-specific values, thoughts and reactions within myself* different to English. Although I know I have a long way to go I do believe this year has significantly improved my process of becoming 'biculturally bilingual'.

Comment on Extract 3:

In her overall reflection on the concept of 'adaptation' and her own development, Kim draws a number of connections: between language and culture, between her studies of Indonesian and her 'other passions', between herself and others in interaction and between her 'personality' and 'Indonesian identity'. She recognises identity as dynamic and culturally situated, requiring 'shifts' including in herself, to accommodate the 'other'. Kim observes a relationship between language and culture, 'language holds a worldview', and the power of language in 'truly connect[ing]' with others, arguably showing signs of symbolic competence. Finally, Kim's reflection includes frequent references to identity, in general, and her own, with observations about how hers has expanded; 'more open-minded', 'an alternate identity', 'my Indonesian identity' as well as describing the process in more abstract terms, 'becoming biculturally bilingual', and acknowledging this as on-going.

Comment on the set of extracts

Each extract provides evidence of Kim's evolving intercultural capability and, taken together, reveal her overall development, from her reliance early on her own cultural framework, to an increasing comfort in the main with divergent views and practices, multiplicity and ultimately awareness of her own identity transformation.

The extracts also indicate that evidence takes many forms. Sometimes it is an observation, a declarative statement, a comparative comment or an item of cultural knowledge. Other times, the evidence is an explanation, a question, a wondering/musing or problematising, a connection or comparison/juxtaposition, a feeling or a realisation. At times, the evidence is expected, e.g. observing the relationship between language and culture, while other times, it is less so, e.g. expressing appreciation for another way of being. The evidence is both highly specific to the individual, their observations and interpretations, and often their emotions and stories. It is also abstracted, referring to the nature of language learning, intercultural exchange and identity development. The evidence is also messy, often with multiple aspects woven through a single sentence, and often emerging over time. Ultimately, evidence of learners' intercultural capability is itself manifested through language and therefore subject to interpretation by others, including the teacher.

Judging the evidence

Byram (2021) advocates the use of 'explicit and agreed criteria' as a basis for judging whether learning objectives have been achieved, and as a means for addressing reliability and scrutinising interpretations of evidence. Learning-oriented assessment recognises that the process of judging evidence is fundamentally one that involves interpretation, and therefore subjectivity. It does not mean, however, that anything goes. Nor does it mean doing away with criteria but rather, we would argue, developing criteria that reflect the learning intentions/objectives of the course, while recognising them as provisional, leaving room for learning that may emerge unexpectedly. While it is possible to develop criteria that reflect aspects of intercultural capability such as 'depth of reflection on self as communicator', these are meaningless in the absence of contextualisation in the particular instance in which the learning was demonstrated. Particularly as learners are encouraged through assessment to express the interpretations, reactions and connections that they are making, predetermined criteria are insufficient to account for the highly personalised nature of responses and evidence of learning. Evidence may take unexpected forms such as a personal anecdote, reflective question, affective response or a reaction that even surprises the learner themselves, and the process of judging needs to acknowledge this.

Furthermore, learning-oriented and ipsative-referenced assessment foregrounds the process of giving feedback as a means to further learning. Feedback can take various forms including descriptive comments, questions, scores and grades. These represent ways of valuing learning and need to be socialised with learners in order that they too understand the system for attributing value. In the example outlined above, a combination of scores, in-text comments and an overall descriptive comment were used. In this way, learners received a score that provided feedback about their achievement in relation to the objectives that also met institutional requirements. In addition, they received individualised feedback on specific aspects and areas for further reflection as well as more abstract ways of characterising their learning that could enhance 'deep learning' (Entwistle, 1992 in Gipps, 1994) and learning transfer. Both eliciting and judging, including providing feedback, need to take account of the individual and their particular learnings, and provide rich accounts of learning in order that this can be shared with individual learners as part of their on-going development.

Evidencing intercultural capability, through a set of assessments, yields a series of 'performances' that reflect how individual learners are developing over time. The example outlined here indicates that assessing intercultural capability needs to include processes that require learners to decentre from their own language and culture, and from their own learning in order to consider their learning trajectory. Such processes are not automatic, and assessment needs to be designed with deliberate attention to eliciting and valuing aspects such as personalisation and reflection. With each assessment, students are invited to consider their development, to recognise changes in their perspectives, understandings and capability to exchange meanings with diverse others. It is particularly helpful to have a cumulative assessment that elicits students' overall performance and meta-reflections. Through periodic and overall reflection, learners come to develop their own critical, intercultural stance that travels with them into new contexts, never static or complete, but always enriched and made more robust with each new experience, becoming part of who learners are.

Profiling permits the individual to be themselves as it invites variation and personalisation; encouraging learners to explain what sense they are making, and importantly, why and how. It is a process that captures evidence of greater sophistication of intercultural capability in exchange, including through 'less successful' moments when often deeper reflection occurs on why communication 'succeeded' or not. The value of the profile is that it is an account of what learners actually do by evidencing how their capability becomes more and more sophisticated, while recognising that it remains ever-evolving and unfinalisable.

Conclusion

Assessing intercultural competence (for us, capability) has been recognised as a challenging and complex area since Byram's (1997) seminal work set out a framework for it over 20 years ago. His work has given rise to many different approaches, across diverse contexts, aimed at addressing some of the challenges posed. In this chapter, we have offered an interpretive orientation within a paradigm of educational assessment. A hermeneutic view foregrounds the role of interpretation in teaching and learning, and in assessment, recognising the latter as an intersubjective process. This kind of view necessarily invites close attention to individual learners, to the specifics of their learning and development over time, acknowledging that no two learners will be the same. A learning-oriented view of assessment is particularly valuable for eliciting and judging intercultural capability as it offers the potential to incorporate evidence that is both planned and unforeseen. In this way, judging becomes a process of referencing evidence not to an external, generalised scale but to the learner's own development.

An orientation to assessing intercultural capability that is primarily designed to reinform teaching and learning may address some issues however is not without its own challenges. As Byram (2021: 127) notes, the 'purposes of assessment are determined by context' and especially the demands of certification. Providing evidence and judgements that are defensible and meaningful to learners and institutions are increasingly pressing matters for educators that often create tensions as they attempt to reconcile assessing complex capabilities with existing institutional requirements and assessment culture. Such requirements and processes will require change if they are to accommodate the interpretive kind of assessment that we have outlined and that takes seriously the first-person subjective relationship of students to their world.

It will be important to continue a programme of research, particularly praxis-oriented approaches, not only to strengthen processes of evidencing, judging and warranting the assessment of intercultural capability but also to better understand the nature of the capability itself. Such work is less an exercise in modelling and more a matter of conceptualisation and imagination, to explore complexities and the unpredictable dimensions of intercultural exchange, which can aid in realising the goal of developing open-minded, reflexive, ethical people, capable of engaging with diversity.

Note

(1) The research programme includes Anthony Liddicoat as well as the authors of this chapter.

References

Bennett, M.J. (1986) A developmental approach to training for intercultural sensitivity. *International Journal of Intercultural Relations* 10 (2), 179–196.

Borghetti, C. (2017) Is there really a need for assessing intercultural competence? Some ethical issues. *Journal of Intercultural Communication* 44, 1404–1634.

Byram, M. (1997) *Teaching and Assessing Intercultural Communicative Competence.* Clevedon: Multilingual Matters.

Byram, M. (2014) Twenty-five years on – from cultural studies to intercultural citizenship. *Language, Culture and Curriculum* 27 (3), 209–225.

Byram, M. (2021) *Teaching and Assessing Intercultural Communicative Competence: Revisited* (2nd edn). Bristol: Multilingual Matters.

Byram, M. and Zarate, G. (1994) *Definitions, Objectives and Assessment of Sociocultural Competence.* Strasbourg: Council of Europe.

Canale, G. and Swain, M. (1980) Theoretical bases of communicative approaches to second language teaching and learning. *Applied Linguistics* 1 (1), 1–47.

Council of Europe (2001) *Common European Framework of Reference for Languages (CEFR): Learning, Teaching, Assessment.* Cambridge: Cambridge University Press.

Council of Europe (2018) *Common European Framework of Reference for Languages: Learning, Teaching, Assessment: Companion Volume with New Descriptors.* Strasbourg: Council of Europe.

Gadamer, H.-G. (2004) *Truth and Method* (J. Weinsheimer and D.G. Marshall, trans., 2nd edn). New York: Continuum.

Gallagher, S. (1992) *Hermeneutics and Education.* New York: State University of New York Press.

Gipps, C. (1994) *Beyond Testing: Towards a Theory of Educational Assessment.* London: Falmer Press.

Halliday, M.A.K. (1993) Towards a language-based theory of learning. *Linguistics and Education* 5, 93–116.

Kohler, M. (2020) *Developing Intercultural Language Learning.* Cham: Springer Nature.

Kramsch, C. (2006) From communicative competence to symbolic competence. *Modern Language Journal* 90 (2), 249–252.

Kramsch, C. (2009a) Discourse, the symbolic dimensions of intercultural competence. In A. Hu and M. Byram (eds) *Interkulturelle Kompetenz und Fremdsprachliches Lernen. Modelle, Empirie, Evaluation. [Intercultural Competence and Foreign Language Learning: Models, Empiricism, Assessment]* (pp. 107–122). Tübingen: Gunter Narra Verlag.

Kramsch, C. (2009b) *The Multilingual Subject: What Foreign Language Learners Say about Their Experience and Why It Matters.* Oxford: Oxford University Press.

Liddicoat, A.J. and Scarino, A. (2013) *Intercultural Language Teaching and Learning.* Chichester: Wiley-Blackwell.

McNamara, T. (2019) *Language and Subjectivity.* Cambridge: Cambridge University Press.

Moss, P.A. (2008) Sociocultural implications for assessment: Classroom assessment. In P.A. Moss, D.C. Pullin, P.J. Gee, G.H. Haertel and L.J. Young (eds) *Assessment, Equity and Opportunity to Learn* (pp. 222–258). Cambridge: Cambridge University Press.

Nussbaum, M.C. (2011) Capabilities, entitlements, rights: Supplementation and critique. *Journal of Human Development and Capabilities* 12 (1), 23–37.

OECD (2017) *Global Competence Framework.* Retrieved from: https://www.oecd.org/pisa/Handbook-PISA-2018-Global-Competence.pdf

Risager, K. (2007) *Language and Culture Pedagogy: From a National to a Transnational Paradigm.* Clevedon: Multilingual Matters.

Sadler, D.R. (1987) Specifying and promulgating achievement standards. *Oxford Review of Education* 13 (2), 191–209.

Sadler, D.R. (1989) Formative assessment and the design of instructional systems. *Instructional Science* 18, 119–144.

Scarino, A. (2010) Assessing intercultural capability in learning languages: A renewed understanding of language, culture, learning and the nature of assessment. *The Modern Language Journal* 94 (2), 324.

Scarino, A. (2014) Learning as reciprocal, interpretive meaning-making. A view from collaborative research into the professional learning of teachers of languages. *The Modern Language Journal (Special Issue)* 98 (1), 386–401.

Scarino, A. (2020) Mediation in the assessment of language learning within an interlingual and intercultural orientation: The role of reciprocal interpretation. In M.E. Poehner and O. Inbar-Lourie (eds) *Toward a Reconceptualization of Second Language Classroom Assessment: Praxis and Researcher-Teacher Partnership* (pp. 43–60). Cham: Springer.

Sercu, L. (2004) Assessing intercultural competence: A framework for systematic test development in foreign language education and beyond. *Intercultural Education* 15 (1), 73–89.

Spitzberg, B.H. and Changnon, G. (2009) Conceptualising intercultural competence. In D. Deardorff (ed.) *The Sage Handbook of Intercultural Competence* (pp. 2–52). Thousand Oaks, CA: Sage Publications.

Turner, C.E. and Purpura, J. (2015) Learning-oriented assessment in second and foreign language classrooms. In D. Tsagari and J. Banerjee (eds) *Handbook of Second Language Assessment* (pp. 255–272). Boston, MA: De Gruyter Mouton.

van Ek, J.A. (1986) *Objectives for Modern Language Learning, Vol. 1: Scope.* Strasbourg: Council of Europe.

Zotzmann, K. (2015) The impossibility of defining and measuring intercultural competence. In D. Rivers (ed.) *Resistance to the Known – Counter-Conduct in Language Education* (pp. 168–191). New York: Palgrave Macmillan.

12 The NCSSFL-ACTFL Can-Do Statements for Intercultural Communication: Cultivating Sojourners in the Language Classroom

Aleidine J. Moeller

Introduction

With the introduction and explosion of digital media and expansive global migration and immigration, the world has become connected and diversified in ways unimaginable 30 years ago. As communities, schools and families seek ways to address these changes, the need for building and sustaining relationships with individuals whose language and culture are different from their own require intercultural skills that include traits such as openness, awareness, and curiosity in order to learn to live and work together. When such cultural shifts occur in societies and communities, it typically falls to educational institutions and organizations to take the lead in creating models and frameworks that guide the pathways to social change. In order to respond to the needs of multicultural and multilingual society, government agencies and professional organizations in Europe, the United States and Australia were among those that created policies and educational frameworks emphasizing the need to develop empathy and understanding between people from different cultural backgrounds who work and live together (Common European Framework of Reference for Languages, 2001 [CEFR]; World Readiness Standards for Learning Language, 2015 [WRSLL]; Developing Intercultural Competence in the Language [DICL]) (Dellit, 2005).

The CEFR, DICL and WRSLL reflected a growing awareness of the role that (language) education plays in developing the skills, attitudes, knowledge and critical awareness of self and other cultures necessary for effective communication with co-workers, neighbors and community members, as well as broader social engagement. In addition to linguistic skills, the ability to observe and interpret what is being seen, heard and experienced became seen as pivotal to successful interaction. This tasked language teachers with creating pedagogy that promotes and encourages inquiry, reflection, identity formation, democracy and social justice. Such a reconceptualization of the role of the language teacher had important implications for pedagogical skills.

However, while these documents established broad frameworks indicating what teachers should teach, they *did not tell them how to teach it*. Documents such as CEFR, CICL and WRSLL lacked specificity as regards to how language teaching approaches and teachers should integrate and achieve intercultural communicative competence in their learners. In the U.S. context, it was perceived that what was needed was a framework for language educators that promoted these skills, and more importantly, helped language instructors integrate intercultural communication goals and practices into their world language classrooms.

This chapter focuses on the role of the NCSSFL-ACTFL *Can-Do Statements for Intercultural Communication* (2017) in helping operationalize intercultural competence goals at a concrete level useful for language teachers. Based on ACTFL's 3 Ps model (Products, Practices and Perspectives) and Michael Byram's Intercultural Communicative Competence model (Byram, 1997), NCSSFL/ACTFL created the *Can-Do Statements for Intercultural Communication* (*ICC Can-Do Statements*) designed to guide learners to reflect critically upon their own cultural products, practices and perspectives as well as those of another culture through human interaction in the target language and interpretation of informational texts and media. The *ICC Can-Do Statements* provide performance goals with classroom examples that systematically promote critical reflection aimed at building a deeper understanding of cultural products and practices that produces a shift in perspectives of one's own culture as well as that of others.

The chapter traces the development of the *ICC Can-Do Statements* by considering important shifts in language education policy and pedagogical emphases, highlighting in particular the transformative impact of Michael Byram's ideas. It then presents a classroom ICC model that embodies Byram's emphasis on the skillset of the sojourner. It places the learner in the role of cultural anthropologist who investigates and discovers knowledge and understanding through experiential, discovery and inquiry-based learning tasks informed by research-based learning approaches (Moeller & Faltin-Osborn, 2014). These carefully pedagogically designed learning tasks aim to promote reflection, critical thinking and self-assessment, thereby creating 'sojourners' who can navigate between cultures, mediate misunderstandings and promote understanding, collaborations and empathy among individuals from different cultures.

The Language Classroom as Nexus for Promoting Intercultural Competence

Scholars in the past three decades have examined and written extensively about the role of foreign language learning in fostering intercultural understanding (Byram, 1997; Byram *et al.*, 2017; Garrett-Rucks, 2016; Kearney, 2016; Kohler, 2015; Kramsch, 1993; Liddicoat & Scarino, 2013; McConachy, 2018; Moeller & Nugent, 2014; Wagner *et al.*, 2018a, 2018b) These studies foreground the different ways that foreign language classrooms provide a fertile context for critically examining issues and challenges associated with integrating into a new cultural environment, particularly in formal schooling when learners find themselves collaborating with others, finding a sense of belonging, and forming an identity as they develop personally, cognitively and socially. While intercultural learning is not limited to the foreign language classroom, it is often seen as a natural context for engaging with difference in a structured and supportive way. As Byram (1997) noted, foreign language teaching (FLT):

> has the experience of otherness at the centre of its concern, as it requires learners to engage with both familiar and unfamiliar experiences through the medium of another language ... FLT has a central aim of enabling learners to use that language to interact with people for whom it is their preferred and 'natural' medium or experience. (1997: 3)

Such an intercultural approach to language teaching offered the opportunity to include 'intellectually, humanistically oriented, cultural "content"' (Kramsch, 1995: 83) that would engage learners cognitively in content across disciplines (Kramsch & Nolden, 1994). As will be discussed later, this is something very much supported and integrated in the World-readiness standards for learning languages (WRSLL) (The National Standards Collaborative Board, 2015) through their overarching goal areas of communication, cultures, connections, comparisons and communities.

Byram's perspectives on the role of culture in the language classroom have had a significant impact on the field internationally, particularly his model of intercultural communicative competence. Byram (1997) noted that many understandings of intercultural competence ignore the language component despite the fact that it is a core element of intercultural communication, as most interactions involve a second language. He distinguishes between intercultural competence (IC) and intercultural communicative competence (ICC) (1997, 2021). IC refers to the skills and ability individuals draw on to interact in their native language with people from another culture. ICC refers to the ability to interact successfully across cultures while using a second language. ICC focuses on 'establishing and maintaining relationships instead of merely communicating messages or exchanging information' (Byram, 1997: 3).

He uses the metaphor of a tourist and sojourner when explaining ICC. A tourist has preconceived notions and assumptions of what will be seen and experienced and basically remains unchanged in previously held beliefs and behaviors. An individual equipped with language, a sojourner, has the opportunity to learn and become educated through interaction with target-language speakers, texts, visuals and media. This promotes a deeper understanding of the how and why of what is observed and experienced. The potential for transformation of thoughts and, more importantly, behavior can only occur when equipped with language.

Byram described the aim of the intercultural dimension in language teaching to develop an 'intercultural speaker'. Intercultural speakers are described as competent communicators (Byram & Zarate, 1996) who engage with complexity and multiple identities and 'avoid stereotyping which accompanies perceiving someone through a single identity' (Byram et al., 2002: 5). In other words, the intercultural speaker is someone who is successful not only in communicating information but also in developing human relationships with people of other languages and cultures. Byram used this term to underscore the role of the intercultural speaker as mediator, represented in the Common European Framework of Reference (CEFR) as an individual who can 'act as an intermediary between interlocutors who are unable to understand each other directly—normally (but not exclusively) speakers of different language' (Council of Europe, 2001: 87). Further, he explains that the concept of the intercultural speaker aimed 'to distance the notion of intercultural competence from the cultural competences of a native speaker' (Byram, 2009: 326). Byram posits that the qualities of an intercultural speaker 'are seldom acquired without help, are seldom learnt without teaching' (Byram, 1997: 2), and there is thus an important role for the language teacher to incorporate intercultural learning into the classroom.

For many teachers, however, it is common to spend the majority of time in language classrooms on building language proficiency skills, predominately through vocabulary and grammatical structures (Kramsch, 1993; Moore, 1996). Asay et al. (2019) surveyed US language teachers about the integration of culture in their language classrooms and found that culture was not taught as an integral part of the curriculum. While teachers intended to include cultural dimensions, they did so only intermittently and in unplanned ways (Byram et al., 1991). In part, teachers attributed this to a lack of attention to cultural dimensions during teacher training (see also Byram & Risager, 1999; Garrett-Rucks, 2016). Teachers also expressed they did not know enough about the culture, how to teach culture, lacked the pedagogical tools and resources, and found it challenging to teach culture using the target language (Asay et al., 2019). They were also uneasy about the reaction to sensitive topics that may be controversial resulting in pushback from the learners. Another major concern that surfaced was how to assess intercultural competency. Measuring attitudes would require a rethinking of assessment approaches with which they were unfamiliar.

Such challenges and resistance to integrating culture further underscored the need for a model and exemplars that could be used at the classroom level to assist teachers in the intercultural integration process. As will be discussed below, this necessitated the development of a number of policy initiatives and curriculum frameworks.

Europe and the US: A Contrast in Language Policy and Practice

It is important to note that in the United States, unlike many other nations, a study of languages is not mandated, but is regarded as an elective. Many universities require two years of language study for admission resulting in languages being seen largely as a gatekeeper into higher education. According to a recent study conducted by the American Councils on International Education, ACTFL and the Center for Applied Linguistics, approximately 10,000,000 learners, or nearly 20% of the population of US students in grades K–12, are enrolled in world language programs, whereas, according to the Modern Language Association, approximately 1.7 million students, or just 7.5%, study a world language at the postsecondary level (Goldberg *et al.*, 2015). These enrollment numbers reflect the lack of value placed on the study of world languages in the US as compared to other world nations.

In Europe, language standards, curriculum, examinations and syllabi for language study established by the Council of Europe had a direct effect on national policies, resulting in specific recommendations for practice. Such a unified national policy indicates that the study of languages and cultures are highly valued and represent an essential part of the core curriculum of schooling. This perspective is not shared in the US, where monolingual ideologies can create a narrow learning environment for language study (Reagan & Osborn, 2001). Kramsch (1993) noted that most regard language education as the study of grammar, vocabulary and simple customs from other cultures. With a lack of national curriculum and leadership at the federal level, the responsibility for language education leadership was assumed by the professional world language associations and organizations. To further complicate matters, a national policy about curriculum, examinations and syllabi as seen in Europe does not exist; rather, policy is determined by states and local school districts.

A Standards Task Force established through collaboration of professional language organizations was tasked with the development of World Language Standards, one that has undergone several iterations, the most recent being the *World-Readiness Standards for Learning Languages* (WRSLL, 2014). In order to facilitate alignment with local state standards, the WRSLL were organized around five broad interconnected goals of Communication, Communities, Culture, Connections and Comparisons that underscored direct connection with cultures. While aligned with WRSLL, the individual state frameworks specifically determine the goals for instruction, the content and structure of the content. The school district curriculum determines the local goals for instruction, specifies the specific unit content, sequence, methods and resources and finally, the lesson, or unit plan, identifies the specific objectives for learning – what should be learned and demonstrated.

The first iteration of language standards (*Standards for Foreign Language Learning,* 1999) that provided a model for teaching culture dubbed the 3 Ps described desired endpoints of an inquiry-based approach to the teaching of culture for achieving cultural competence as follows:

2.1 Students demonstrate an understanding of the relationship between the practices and perspectives of the culture studied

2.2 Students demonstrate an understanding of the relationship between the products and perspectives of the culture studied (1999: 4)

This model represented a reconceptualized approach to culture that shifted the focus of teaching culture to a study of underlying values, attitudes and beliefs, rather than simply learning about cultural products and practices. Such a shift defined ICC to be an essential goal for the achievement of proficiency in a foreign language. As Lange (1999) reported, the 3 Ps approach avoided 'the common, overworked conflict between C and c by interweaving the formal and informal aspects of daily life, as one normally lives it in any culture' (1999: 60). This helped teachers 'tie together the disparate knowledge about products and practices, while helping students begin to relate products and practices to perspectives and acquire a deeper understanding of culture overall' (Dema & Moeller, 2012: 29). What was lacking, however, was how to teach culture in the language classroom in a way that promoted effective communication (Dema & Moeller, 2012).

Learning of the progress made by the Council of Europe, the National Council of State Supervisors of Foreign Languages (NCSSFL) in 2003 met with the Council of Europe in Germany and were introduced to the Common European Framework of Reference and the Can-Do descriptors used in the European Language Portfolio (ELP) to describe language functions at various stages of language development and learning. The ELP was of particular interest to these state supervisors of world language programs as they saw the enormous potential and impact this self-assessment tool could have for language teaching and learning in the United States (Van Houten, 2004, 2007). Upon returning to the United States, NCSSFL launched an initiative to build on and adapt the European Language Portfolio developed by the CEFR. Making transparent to teachers and learners the language skills in the form of language functions and descriptors that aligned with the ACTFL Proficiency Guidelines allowed learners to self-assess their language performance based on clear short and long-term learning goals. These *Can-Do Statements* seamlessly link classroom learning tasks with benchmarked learning objectives, state and national standards and with broad proficiency outcomes for life-long learning. This held the promise of motivating learners to persist in their language study. Unlike in Europe, language study is not mandated in K-12 schools; however, it is a gatekeeper for entry into higher education.

The National Council of State Supervisors for Foreign Language (NCSSFL) and the American Council on the Teaching of Foreign Languages (ACTFL) collaborated to develop the *Can-Do Statements* to assess what learners 'can do' with language in the Interpersonal, Interpretive, and Presentational modes of communication. These progress indicators for language learners, strategically aligned with the ACTFL Proficiency Guidelines (2012), provided learning targets for curriculum and unit design and a way to chart learners' language progress from Novice through Distinguished levels of language proficiency. These statements described specific language tasks that learners are likely to perform at various levels of proficiency. The statements describe in the form of language functions what language learners can actually do with language. For example, at the intermediate mid-level in the interpersonal mode of communication a Can-Do Statement is 'I can ask for information, details, and explanations during a conversation'. These *Can-Do Statements* make transparent to learners a clear performance-based learning target and allow them to self-assess their own performance (Moeller & Yu, 2015). By reflecting on how well they are able to accomplish the task, they see the gap in their performance and can put in the extra effort to fill that gap. This involves the learner more directly in the learning process itself as the learning and assessment is being done by the learner, not unto the learner. Too often learners are seen as subjects of assessment, not users of assessments. To become the primary users of assessment information, learners must make what they learn part of themselves.

One important means for involving learners in their own learning process is by having them participate in a goal-setting process to determine how well they are accomplishing their learning targets. Learning goals, such as the *Can-Do Statements* form the foundation for motivation in an instructional setting and determine where working memory is being allocated (Wegge *et al.*, 2001). Motivation is critical to learning because, 'without sufficient motivation even the brightest learners are unlikely to persist long enough to attain any really useful language' (Dörnyei, 2009: 74). It is vital to understand motivation in order to promote learner autonomy which is key to building language proficiency and intercultural competence. As the levels of language proficiency increase, key terms and descriptors in the *Can-Do Statements* evolve from more concrete to more abstract skills (identity, describe, compare, analyze, evaluate) that promote critical thinking and reflection.

In order to determine the validity of the intervention of the US version of the ELP, named LinguaFolio, Moeller *et al.* (2012) conducted a five-year longitudinal study in 23 high school districts to determine the impact of short- and long-term goal setting (*Can-Do Statements*) on language achievement (in this case, Spanish). The findings in this mixed methods research study indicated significant gains in all language skills including speaking, reading, writing and listening. A replication study conducted at the university level confirmed these results as did a study conducted on the ELP in German schools (Ziegler, 2014; Ziegler & Moeller, 2012).

While CEFR and ACTFL had created levels of language proficiency (A1-C2; Novice-Distinguished) and identified learning targets in the form of *Can-Do Statements* aimed at guiding the teacher and learners to assess growth in language, there was nothing similar in place for intercultural communicative competence. In light of the strong evidence supporting significant increase in language achievement when integrating the NCSSFL-ACTFL *Can-Do Statements* at the classroom level, NCSSFL-ACTFL commissioned an ICC Task Force to investigate ICC theoretical frameworks aimed at providing a unified approach to integrating interculturality into the language classroom. The ICC Task Force determined to adapt and build on Michael Byram's *Multidimensional Model of Intercultural Communicative Competence* in the creation of the NCSSFL-ACTFL *Can-Do Statements* for Intercultural Communication.

Toward NCSSFL-ACTFL Can-Do Statements for Intercultural Communication

Byram's model for teaching intercultural competence adapted in the WRSLL required a reconceptualization of the role of the language teacher as a teacher of both language and intercultural competence. The NCSSFL-ACTFL *Can-Do Statements* for Intercultural Communication are a first step in the process to simplify the complexities of ICC and provide guidance for educators and learners. Rather than a linear process, ICC is more iterative and interactive as each individual begins at different cognitive, cultural and linguistic stages and progresses at various rates. As noted in the introductory narrative to the ICC Can-Do Statements, ICC is a complex non-linear process, one that results from acquiring cultural knowledge, practices and social encounters within a variety of cultural contexts. An individual can possess strong cultural competence but demonstrate a low level of language proficiency. Another individual may display high language proficiency but minimal cultural competence (ACTFL, 2017).

The *Can-Do Statements* depict the linguistic competency from Novice to Distinguished levels of language proficiency across the modes of communication. The *Can-Do Statements* of Intercultural Communication

PROFICIENCY BENCHMARKS

Identify the overarching features of language performance, i.e., context, text type and function, in each of the three modes of communication to describe learner's progress along the ACTFL Proficiency continuum. Benchmarks support learners in setting long-term goals and inform program and course outcomes.

PERFORMANCE INDICATORS

Deconstruct the Benchmark by focusing on certain aspects of language performance, i.e., context, text type, and function. Indicators describe the steps toward reaching the overarching Benchmark goal. Indicators support learners in charting progress toward meeting language learning goals and inform unit design.

EXAMPLES

Illustrate language performance in a variety of learning contexts (e.g., social, academic across PK-20, immersion, adult) and inform instruction at the lesson or learning activity level.

Figure 12.1 Proficiency benchmarks, performance indicators and learning examples of NCSSFL-ACTFL Can-Do Statements: https://www.actfl.org/resources/ncssfl-actfl-can-do-statements. Used with permission of ACTFL

explicitly provide benchmarks (investigate and interact), learning indicators (products, practices and language) and learning examples, which can systematically guide classroom teachers in the ICC integration process (see Figure 12.1). The purpose of these learning objectives, formulated in the form of *Can-Do Statements*, is to assist teachers to more intentionally include intercultural competency in their pedagogical aims.

For example, the Benchmark for intermediate IC for Investigate reads 'In my own and other cultures I can make comparisons between products and practices to help me understand perspectives'. The Learning Indicator for Products is 'In my own and other cultures I can compare products related to everyday life and personal interests or studies', and for Practices 'In my own and other cultures I can compare practices related to everyday life and personal interest or studies'. A Learning Example for Investigate reads 'In my own and other culture I can compare how and why houses, buildings and towns affect lifestyles' and for Interact 'I can show respect when visiting an historical site by dressing appropriately, adjusting the volume of my voice, and acting with consideration for others'. For language, the learning indicator reads 'I can converse with peers from the target culture in familiar situations at school, work, or play and show interest in basic cultural similarities and differences'.

HOW TO USE THE NCSSFL-ACTFL CAN-DO STATEMENTS

EDUCATORS set daily learning targets and incorporate the Statements in lesson, assessment and rubric design to make learning transparent. Educators assist learners to realize what learners can do with language, how to set goals, and what to do to improve.

STATES set proficiency target expectations within their course codes for different levels and sequences of language study, to guide districts in organizing their programs and in setting policy for performance-based granting of credit

LEARNERS set learning goals and regularly chart their own progress. Through reflection, they identify what it takes to advance

SCHOOLS provide time for professional learning communities for language educators to review and analyze evidence of learning and collaborate on assessment design. Schools set policies to determine criteria for performance-based credit.

UNIVERSITIES develop entrance and exit requirements based on proficiency levels and set proficiency targets for language courses; encourage learners to set learning goals, and grant credit for consistent demonstration. Teacher preparation courses show educators how to use the Statements to set learning targets, design units, plan lessons, and create assessments and rubrics for evaluating learners' performance

DISTRICTS & SCHOOLS set proficiency targets for graduation, design curriculum and units based on Benchmarks and Indicators and provide professional learning for educators on how to move learners up the proficiency levels. Educators collaborate to design end-of-unit or end-of-course assessments to provide evidence of learners independently and consistently demonstrating the targeted level of proficiency

NCSSFL
National Council of State Supervisors for Languages

© ACTFL-NCSSFL 2017

ACTFL
Language Connects

Figure 12.2 Overview of how to use the NCSSFL-ACTFL Can-Do Statements: https://www.actfl.org/resources/ncssfl-actfl-can-do-statements. Used with permission of ACTFL

The graphic above provides an overview of how the NCSSFL-ACTFL *Can-Do Statements* can be used in schools, school districts, universities and states as learners gain language proficiency and intercultural communicative competence (see Figure 12.2).

The NCSSFL-ACTFL *Can-Do Statements for Intercultural Communication* broaden the scope of the *Language Can-Do Statements* to show how language can be used to lead learners toward developing intercultural communicative competence at the classroom level. The cultural goals expand on ACTFL's 3 Ps approach by incorporating Byram's (1997) emphasis on the importance of skills of 'discovery and interaction' and 'interpreting and relating' (1997: 33). By building skills, knowledge and attitudes to interpret and interact in culturally appropriate ways, individuals are empowered to build and sustain relationships with others and can serve as mediators between and among cultures. Using Byram's terms of 'investigate' and 'interact', the NCSSFL-ACTFL Intercultural Communication Proficiency Benchmark is organized into two broad categories of Investigate and Interact.

Cultural Goal: Interact with cultural competence and understanding

Standard 1:   Learners use the language to investigate, explain and reflect on the relationship between practices and perspectives of the cultures studied

Standard 2:   Learners use the language to investigate, explain and reflect on the relationship between products and perspectives of the cultures studied

(NCSSFL-ACTFL Can-Do Statements for Intercultural Communication, 2017).

The *ICC Can-Do Statements* were developed to show the intersection of language proficiency and cultural competence, which do not always align as individuals who possess high ICC skills may not necessarily possess a high level of language proficiency and vice versa. The ICC Can-Do Statements provide sample performance tasks through which learners can demonstrate their intercultural competence from Novice to Distinguished levels of language proficiency across the modes of communication (Interpretive, Interpersonal, Presentational). The statements incorporated an emphasis on examining and reflecting on one's own cultural beliefs, values and behavior prior to introducing the target language culture, thereby exposing one's own hidden cultural biases. Each sample ICC learning task begins with the wording of 'in my own and other cultures'. For example, a Can-Do Statement for IC Communication states:

In my own and other cultures I can compare how and why houses, buildings, and towns affect lifestyles.

Because intercultural growth involves elements in the affective domain, it can be challenging to evaluate learner progress. For that reason, the NCSSFL-ACTFL *Can-Do Statements for Intercultural Communication* suggest learning activities that allow for and support opportunities for intercultural encounters. This allows teachers to evaluate how well learners' language use demonstrates intercultural competence to the extent that an individual can fully understand and participate in a culture as related to the level of language proficiency. These *Can-Do Statements* serve a dual purpose. They provide examples of carefully sequenced performance tasks that allow teachers to see exemplars of potential performance activities and learners to see what they can actually do with language as well as identify gaps in their performance. The statements can be used by the teacher to assess students' knowledge and performance, while learners use these to self-assess and reflect how well they are able to demonstrate intercultural communicative competence. When learners can demonstrate intercultural communicative competence through a performance task, their motivation and self-efficacy is enhanced (Ziegler, 2014; Ziegler & Moeller, 2012).

As described above, Byram provided the building blocks that served as the foundation for formulating the *Can-Do Statements for Intercultural Communication*. For language teachers, the statements provide a very useful orienting basis for bringing an intercultural focus to classroom teaching, but it can still at times be challenging to convert learning goals into pedagogical practices. The next section of the chapter will give an example of a model for classroom application that shows how learning oriented toward the Can-Do Statements above could be enacted. This model takes into account shifts that have occurred within the teaching profession in the US toward a learner-centered classroom where the intercultural teacher assumes the role of assisting rather than presenting and where learners develop the skills to inquire about culture using relevant research tools and collaborative activities. Such a model guides teachers through learning tasks designed to build curiosity, openness, knowledge and understanding that could reduce the hesitation for integrating IC expressed by teachers who were queried about culture teaching.

Observe, State, Explore, Evaluate, Resources (OSEER): From Theory to Practice

Michael Byram had stated the need for clear models of implementation available to teachers (Byram *et al.*, 2002: 12) to resolve the gap between theory and practice to move the integration of IC in classrooms forward. With this need in mind, Moeller (2015) proposed a methodological approach which took insights from Byram (1997) and built on Deardorff's (2004, 2009) work on intercultural competence to guide teachers in the development of ICC through learning tasks guided by the NCSSFL-ACTFL *Can-Do Statements*. Byram's tenets are most evident in the emphasis on investigation as a means to develop the attitudes, knowledge, skills and critical awareness (*savoirs*) that support the linguistic competencies and allow learners to interact and see relationships between cultures and mediate them. The OSEER model I present below incorporates from Deardorff's (2006) Pyramid Model of Intercultural Competence the importance of developing the attitudinal dimension as a condition for increasing knowledge and skills. Knowledge of one's own and the other's products and practices lays the foundation from which one's understanding of perspectives is built and strengthened. Skills of observing, comparing, analyzing, evaluating and mediating are carefully structured to promote effective and appropriate communicative and behavioral interactions.

Helping students interpret cultural input from multiple perspectives requires carefully structured learning tasks that place the learner in the role of a cultural anthropologist with the purpose of building skills of noticing and observation within the context of self and other. Such intentional learning tasks would enable teachers to assume the role of guide and place the learner in the role of actively engaged learner. Inspired by Byram (1997) and Deardorff (2004), the OSEER model makes use of authentic cultural images as the starting point for engagement in learning to develop the attitudinal dimension in terms of curiosity, openness, noticing and non-judgmental observation.

Products ⟷ Perspectives
Practices ⟷ Perspectives

Figure 12.3 Image as authentic resource: https://www.thebeijinger.com/
blog/2017/02/21/cost-marrying-one-chinas-outnumbered-women-continues-sky-
rocket (Used by permission of the *Beijinger*)

The first step is to identify the short-term learning goals in the form
of *Can-Do Statements* that underscore the learner's active role in the
learning process (Moeller & Yu, 2015). In the following learning task,
possible *Can-Do Statements* could be stated as follows: *I can describe the
importance of the red envelope; I can explain when, how and why red
envelopes are exchanged; I can compare this event to one in my own
culture.*

The OSEER model begins with having the learners simply *observe* an
authentic image/photo without comment such as the one depicted in
Figure 12.3 that reveals a Chinese wedding ritual (developing observational skills).

After learners *observe* the image for a few minutes, they are asked to
state, or record on paper what they see without talking. Once all have
documented their observations, learners are asked to explore possible
explanations of what they see and share with a small group of peers (interaction, negotiation of meaning, realizing varied interpretations). The students might comment on the decorative clothing and hypothesize that this
is a celebration of sorts, such as a birthday, or perhaps a wedding. They
will guess what may be in the envelope, note the color red as prominent
and notice that the red envelope is being received with both hands. They
may notice that the woman giving the envelope is older and note the differences in the hands. Once the discussion among peers has ended, the
learners *evaluate* which of the ideas about what was seen seems the most
plausible. This builds curiosity and motivation as learners want to know
what the 'answer' is to confirm the accuracy of their evaluation. Developing
an attitude of curiosity and openness is a core tenet of Byram's model
aimed at suspending 'disbelief about other cultures and belief about one's
own' (Byram, 1997: 50).

After the students have completed sharing their observations, the teacher can promote deeper noticing skills by posing probing questions that focus them on additional details in the photo. At this point, the teacher provides each group a variety of *resources* that may include a link to a video, a text, a podcast, an interview with a target-language speaker, or web links. The learners are placed in the role of 'discovering and interpreting' knowledge as each member of the group explores a different resource, followed by a sharing of their findings (interactive). The role of discovery is one Byram emphasized to promote interest in 'other perspectives on interpretations of familiar and unfamiliar phenomena both in one's own and in other cultures and cultural practices' (Byram, 1997: 50). As a group, they create a digital poster in which they use images, text and graphics to summarize what they learned and present the results to their peers. This task places the learners in the role of cultural anthropologists who observe, explore, and evaluate an aspect of another culture.

This model minimizes judgment on the part of the learner as they are observing and stating what they see without comparison to other cultural practices. As they negotiate possible explanations for what they are seeing with peers, they recognize a variety of explanations and perceptions highlighting the diversity of interpretations which is 'conducive to developing intercultural competence' (Byram, 1997: 50). This form of deeper learning sparks curiosity, develops observational skills and motivates learners to put in the effort to find the information needed to fully understand the significance of the image. When learners are engaged in task-based discovery learning, the achievement is higher, motivation is greater and the level of cognitive engagement is enhanced (Alfieri *et al.*, 2011; Bruner, 1961; Dean & Kuhn, 2006).

Implementing Intercultural Learning Tasks

While authentic images communicate meaning and cultural knowledge, images also promote visual literacy, the ability to read visual aspects of one's surroundings. As Genelle Morain (1997: 13) so beautifully articulated, 'Someone who is visually literate is able to recognize the natural and manmade symbols around one and interpret their meanings in the same way as those who live in that environment would interpret them'. As discussed by Kramsch (1993), language learners necessarily bring their own background cultural knowledge into play in interpreting foreign cultural symbols and images. For example, if a US student hears that a person in France has stopped for bread on the way home, the student is likely to imagine stopping at a supermarket, picking up a loaf of bread wrapped in cellophane containing a bar code used to scan the price at the check-out counter. Meanwhile, a person in France may be more likely to associate picking up bread with a visit to the bakery and the image of a wide variety of fresh baked breads purchased and then carried home in a shopping bag brought by the purchaser. Introducing culturally authentic images can be a powerful way of challenging students' preconceived mindset and helping them decenter from their familiar reality (Byram, 1997). Such images can be used to promote 'knowledge of social groups and their products and practices in one's own and in one's interlocutor's country' (Byram, 1997: 51) and also stimulate students' cultural imagination in new directions. These learning scenarios are designed for novice and intermediate proficiency language learners at the middle/high school and college levels. They can be adapted for higher levels of proficiency by adjusting the texts, documents, and materials as well as the products and performances required of the learners.

Another scenario may be as follows: an American learner of German might tell friends in Germany that they are stopping for coffee – the learner pictures a quick stop at a drive through at Starbucks, but the German individual is picturing a cup of coffee and dessert at an outdoor café with a friend. By using authentic cultural images, the learner sees how things are perceived from the local perspective. Such images are a great venue for employing the 3 Ps approach to cultural teaching. The teacher poses the following questions of her learners: what are the products, what are the practices and what are the perspectives gained about the culture? Students explore responses with peers and identify coffee as the product, compare the practices of drive through versus sitting in a café and critically examine the why of these two practices. As they explore the underlying societal values, or perspectives, they learn much about their own culture, namely the US values of efficiency and convenience, as well as that of the German culture, that values enjoying a cup of coffee as social time with friends and an opportunity to relax. In order to underscore that such values vary within each culture, videos of interviews with both US and German individuals can serve to illustrate a lack of uniformity of practices within and outside these cultures.

Another learning task aimed at building cultural knowledge and language skills places learners in groups of three or four. Group members are provided a large poster sheet containing a single phrase, or topic related to a theme being studied in the classroom. The words 'Berlin Wall' may serve as an example. All students equipped with a marker write everything they know on the poster sheet about the Berlin Wall. Having completed this task without benefit of talking with one another, the teacher distributes four texts in the target language: one for each participant that provides different aspects of information about the Berlin Wall (personal story, historical events, role of the allies, Berlin Airlift). The students read the text individually and then interact with one another as they share what they learned. They return to the poster and add the new information gleaned from the texts and cross out any misinformation that they have recorded at the onset of the learning task. Once they have added all the information, they create a summary in the target language about the

Berlin Wall using a Google Doc to collaborate. This task combines language and cultural learning in a collaborative, social learning setting where students are actively and cognitively engaged in using the target language in the learning process. Such a task illustrates the important aspect of linking language and cultural learning underscored by Byram and actualized through the *Can-Do Statements* that closes the gap between theory and practice of how to integrate ICC in the classroom.

Affective traits of curiosity, suspension of judgment, and open-mindedness are critical components of intercultural competence. The following learning task aims to develop attitudes, knowledge, language skills and critical awareness in order to avoid the distraction of obvious surface differences of another culture and overcome the limitations of one's own perceptions. Learners begin by investigating their own individual culture to recognize the diversity within their own culture before addressing a second culture. Graphic organizers are effective tools to promote deeper inquiry and learning that can be used to compare and contrast two cultures through language (e.g. see Figure 12.4).

Students individually record all things they typically do to celebrate New Year's in their families in the upper left-hand square. Once finished, in groups of four, students compare responses. They realize the very different ways their peers celebrate New Year's – this crucial first step alerts students that there are myriad ways of celebrating this holiday within their own community. To further emphasize the diversity within US culture, students are provided short readings highlighting traditional regional practices related to New Year's traditions that underscore the varied products, practices and perspectives. These activities build an attitude of open-mindedness before learning about another culture. Turning to the upper right square containing the words Chinese New Year, individual students record

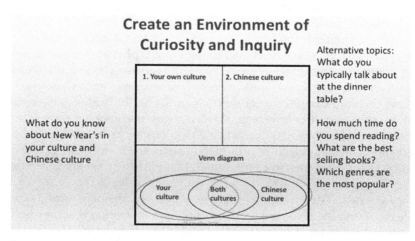

Figure 12.4 Promoting learner inquiry through graphic organizers (Moeller, 2015)

what they know about Chinese New Year celebrations. They share results and fill in additional information. The teacher provides materials that may include media, documents and images to the group, each one containing information about a different aspect of Chinese New Year traditions. The students review these materials, summarize orally what they learned with peers and record the new information and cross out the misinformation. They compare and contrast the New Year's celebrations between China and the US using a Venn diagram. Alternatively, they could summarize the results via PowerPoint, podcast, video or text, allowing them to choose how they wish to demonstrate their learning. Tasks, such as these bring cultural biases to a conscious level, lessening the likelihood of misinterpreting the practices and behaviors of culturally different individuals.

To maximize learning when creating IC learning strategies, it is important to intentionally build in researched-informed pedagogical practices. Research-based pedagogical approaches, as demonstrated in the preceding tasks, enhance learner achievement. Some of these strategies include allowing students personal options for how they will demonstrate learning. This provides an important motivational factor that cultivates learner investment and responsibility. Research in neuroscience has revealed important learning gains through social interaction that promotes a sense of community and belonging. Cozolino (2013: 17) noted that the 'curriculum and social environment of a classroom have a synergistic impact on learning. Supportive, encouraging, and caring relationships stimulate students' neural circuitry to learning, priming their brains for neuroplastic processes'. Providing pair and small group work that requires interaction and collaboration lowers anxiety, builds community and promotes negotiation as learners exchange information, critically examine and navigate varied perspectives.

Conclusion

A crucial responsibility for language educators in the 21st century is to create sojourners equipped with skills, knowledge, attitudes and critical awareness of their own and other cultures. The NCSSFL-ACTFL *Can-Do Statements for Intercultural Communication* are the culmination of foundational work initiated by Michael Byram and his colleagues which ultimately led to the important step of pedagogical application at the language classroom level. The ICC *Can-Do Statements* serve as a framework for teachers to systematically integrate interculturality and target language use at the classroom level, making clear the inextricable link between language and culture. Learners guided by the carefully structured performance-based learning tasks and equipped with language as a tool to gain more of an insider's perspective, can begin to assume the role of a sojourner, a mediator in a third space that can build connections and enables movement between different worlds.

It is important to note that this is the first iteration of the NCSSFL-ACTFL ICC Can-Do Statements and much like the NCSSFL-ACTFL Language Can-Do Statements will undergo multiple modifications as research informs practice. The ICC Can-Do Statements are intended as a guide to assist language educators and learners to deconstruct the complexities of ICC and to assist language educators and learners to evaluate how well language use demonstrates intercultural competence given that the extent to which one can fully understand and participate in a culture is related to the level of language proficiency (ACTFL, 2017).

References

ACTFL (2012) *ACTFL Proficiency Guidelines*. Alexandria, VA: American Council on the Teaching of Foreign Languages (www. actfl. org).

ACTFL (2017) *Can-Do Statements for Intercultural Communication*. https://www.actfl.org/sites/default/files/can-dos/Can-Do%20Introduction%202020.pdf

Alfieri, L., Brooks, P.J., Aldrich, N.J. and Tenenbaum, H.R. (2011) Does discovery-based instruction enhance learning? *Journal of Educational Psychology* 103 (1), 1–18.

Asay, D.T., Martinsen, R.A., Bateman, B.E. and Erickson, R.G. (2019) A survey of teachers' integration of culture in secondary foreign language classrooms. *NECTFL Review* 83, 9–39.

Bruner, J.S. (1961) The act of discovery. *Harvard Educational Review* 3(1), 21–32.

Byram, M. (1997) *Teaching and Assessing Intercultural Communicative Competence*. Clevedon: Multilingual Matters.

Byram, M. (2003) On being 'bicultural' and 'intercultural'. In G. Alred, M. Byram and M. Fleming (eds) *Intercultural Experience and Education* (pp. 50–66). Clevedon: Multilingual Matters.

Byram, M. and Risager, K. (1999) *Language Teachers, Politics and Cultures*. Clevedon: Multilingual Matters.

Byram, M. and Zarate, G. (1996) Defining and assessing intercultural competence: Some principles and proposals for the European context. *Language Teaching* 29 (4), 239–243.

Byram, M., Esarte-Sarries, V. and Taylor, S. (1991) *Cultural Studies and Language Learning: A Research Report*. Clevedon: Multilingual Matters.

Byram, M., Gribkova, B. and Starkey, H. (2002) *Developing the Intercultural Dimension in Language Teaching: A Practical Introduction for Teachers*. Language Policy Division, Directorate of School, Out-of-School and Higher Education, Council of Europe.

Byram, M., Golubeva, I., Han, H. and Wagner, M. (eds) (2017) *From Principles to Practice in Education for Intercultural Citizenship*. Bristol: Multilingual Matters.

Council of Europe (2001) *Common European Framework of Reference for Language: Learning, Teaching, Assessment*. Strasbourg/Cambridge: Council of Europe: Cambridge University Press.

Cozolino, L. (2013) *The Social Neuroscience of Education: Optimizing Attachment in and Learning in the Classroom*. New York, NY: Norton.

Dean, D. Jr. and Kuhn, D. (2006) Direct instruction vs. discovery: The long view. *Science Education* 91 (3), 384–397. doi: 10.1002/sce.20194.

Deardorff, D.K. (2004) The identification and assessment of intercultural competence as a student outcome of international education at institutions of higher education in the United States. Unpublished dissertation, North Carolina State University, Raleigh, 8.

Deardorff, D.K. (2006) Identification and assessments of intercultural competence as a student outcome of internationalization. *Journal Studies in International Education* 10 (3), 241–266.

Deardorff, D.K. (ed.) (2009) *The Sage Handbook of Intercultural Competence.* London: Sage.

Dellit, J. (2005) *Getting Started with Intercultural Language Learning: A Resource for Schools.* Melbourne: Asian Languages Professional Learning Project, Asia Education Foundation.

Dema, O. and Moeller, A. (2012) Teaching culture in the 21st century language classroom. In T. Sildus (ed.) *Touch the World* (pp. 75–91). Eau Claire, WI: Crown Prints.

Dörnyei, Z. (2009) Researching motivation: From integrativeness to the ideal L2 self. In S. Hunston and D. Oakey (eds) *Introducing Applied Linguistics: Concepts and Skills* (pp. 74–86). New York and Oxon: Routledge.

Garrett-Rucks, P. (2016) *Intercultural Competence in Instructed Language Learning. Bridging Theory and Practice.* Charlotte, NC: Information Age Publishing, Inc.

Goldberg, D., Looney, D. and Lusin, N. (2015, February) *Enrollments in Languages Other Than English in United States Institutions of Higher Education, Fall 2013.* Retrieved 13 March 2021, from https://apps.mla.org/pdf/2013_enrollment_survey. pdf

Kearney, E. (2016) *Intercultural Learning in Modern Language Education.* Bristol: Multilingual Matters.

Kohler, M. (2015) *Teachers as Mediators in the Foreign Language Classroom.* Bristol: Multilingual Matters.

Kramsch, C. (1993) *Context and Culture in Language Teaching.* Oxford: Oxford University Press.

Kramsch, C. (1995) The cultural component of language teaching. *Language, Culture and Curriculum* 8 (12), 83–92.

Kramsch, C. and Nolden, T. (1994) Redefining literacy in a foreign language. *Die Unterrichtspraxis/Teaching German* 27 (1), 28–35.

Lange, D.L. (1999) Planning for using the new national culture standards. In J. Phillips and R.M. Terry (eds) *Foreign Language Standards: Linking Research, Theories, and Practices* (pp. 57–120). Lincolnwood, IL: National Textbook and Alexandria, VA: American Council on the Teaching of Foreign Languages.

Liddicoat, A.J. and Scarino, A. (2013) *Intercultural Language Teaching and Learning.* Hoboken, NJ: John Wiley & Sons.

McConachy, T. (2018) *Developing Intercultural Perspectives on Language Use: Exploring Pragmatics and Culture in Foreign Language Learning.* Bristol: Multilingual Matters.

Moeller, A.J. (2015, November 20–22) *Interculturality: Where Language Meets Culture* (Conference session). American Council on the Teaching of Foreign Languages. San Diego, CA.

Moeller, A.J. and Faltin Osborn, S.R. (2014) A pragmatist perspective on building intercultural communicative competency: From theory to classroom practice. *Foreign Language Annals* 47 (4), 669–683.

Moeller, A.J. and Nugent, K. (2014) Building intercultural competence in the language classroom. In S. Dhonau (ed.) *Unlock the Gateway to Communication* (pp. 1–18). Eau Claire, WI: Crown Prints.

Moeller, A.J., Theiler, J. and Wu, C. (2012) Goal setting and student achievement: A longitudinal study. *Modern Language Journal* 96 (2), 153–169.

Moeller, A.J. and Yu, F. (2015) NCSSFL-ACTFL can-do statements: An effective tool for improving language learning within and outside the classroom. In P. Swanson (ed.) *Dimension* (pp. 31–50). Norwalk, CT: Crown Prints.

Morain, G. (1997) Perspective on the cultural perspectives. *Learning Languages* 3 (1), 12–14.

Moore, Z. (1996) Culture: How do teachers teach it? In Z. Moore (ed.) *Foreign Language Teacher Education: Multiple Perspectives* (pp. 269–286). Lanham, MD: University Press of America.

National Standards in Foreign Language Education Project (2014) *World Readiness Standards for Learning Languages*. Alexandria, VA: ACTFL.

NCSSFL–ACTFL Can-Do Statements (2015) *American Council on the Teaching of Foreign Languages*. Alexandria, VA: ACTFL.

NCSSFL-ACTFL Can-Do Statements for Intercultural Communication (2017) *American Council on the Teaching of Foreign Languages*. Alexandria, VA: ACTFL.

Reagan, T.G. and Osborn, T.A. (2001) *The Foreign Language Educator in Society: Toward a Critical Pedagogy*. New York: Routledge.

The National Standards Collaborative Board (2014) *World-Readiness Standards for Learning Languages* (4th ed). Alexandria, VA.

Van Houten, J. (2004) *A Look at the European Language Portfolio: Its Implications for Use in the U.S.* In R. DiDonato and N. Humbach (eds) *Making Connections: From the Classroom to the World Beyond* (pp. 19–30). Eau Claire, WI: Crown Prints.

Van Houten, J. (2007) NCSSFL's LinguaFolio project. In C. Cherry and L. Bradley (eds) *Dimension: Proceedings of the Southern Conference on Language Teaching* (pp. 1–12). Winston-Salem: SCOLT Publications.

Wagner, M., Cardetti, F. and Byram, M. (2018a) The humble linguist: Enriching education for intercultural citizenship and intellectual humility. In E.M. Luef and M.M. Marin (eds) *The Talking Species: Perspectives on the Evolutionary, Neuronal and Cultural Foundations of Language* (pp. 419–443). Graz, AT: Unipress.

Wagner, M., Perugini, D.C. and Byram, M. (2018b) *Teaching Intercultural Competence Across the Age Range: From Theory to Practice*. Bristol: Multilingual Matters.

Wegge, J., Kleinbeck, U. and Schmidt, K.-H. (2001) Goal setting and performance in working memory and short-term-memory tasks. In M. Erez, U. Kleinbeck and H. Thierry (eds) *Work Motivation in the Context of a Globalizing Economy* (pp. 49–72). Mahwah, NJ: Lawrence Erlbaum Associates Publishers.

Ziegler, N. (2014) Fostering self-regulating learning through the European language portfolio: An embedded mixed methods study. *The Modern Language Journal* 98 (4), 921–936. doi: 10.111/mol.12147.

Ziegler, N. and Moeller, A.J. (2012) Increasing self-regulated learning through the LinguaFolio. *Foreign Language Annals* 43 (3), 330–348.

13 Exploring a Pedagogy for Understanding and Developing Chinese EFL Students' Intercultural Communicative Competence

Shuoqian Qin and Prue Holmes

Introduction

This chapter explores how Byram's (1997) intercultural communicative competence (ICC) framework can inform the development of an intercultural communication course delivered within English language education in a Chinese university. The theoretical concept of ICC represents a comprehensive set of criteria that provides a useful basis for designing intercultural language learning curricula and associated learning objectives in a systematic way. At the same time, the incorporation of such a theoretical concept into the language curriculum within the Chinese EFL context also presents a challenge to teachers, particularly given the exam-oriented education system and the traditional focus on grammatical knowledge and skills.

In this chapter, we report on an exploratory action research study which aimed to investigate how the integration of intercultural dimensions into an English as Foreign Language (EFL) syllabus can provide Chinese university students with opportunities to develop their ICC. This involved the first author, Qin, in the development and implementation of a six-week sequence of intercultural teaching for undergraduate English language students across multiple majors in a Chinese university. The study reveals the emergence of complementary themes to the five *savoirs* in Byram's (1997) ICC framework and recommends further development and implementation of contextualised intercultural pedagogies that integrate culturally appropriate teaching materials, and creative student-centred learning strategies.

In the next sections, we first provide an overview of ICC in English language teaching in the Chinese context, and then present the details of the study and the Intercultural English Course (IEC).

An Intercultural Approach in the Chinese EFL Context

In the field of foreign language education in China, an intercultural language teaching approach is seen, in a general sense, as an expanded and more fully developed language pedagogy that increases opportunities for language students to develop their intercultural communicative competence (Gu, 2017; Wang *et al.*, 2017; Xu & Sun, 2013). The value of an intercultural approach centres on a shift from a view of language learning as merely acquiring linguistic skills accompanied by some factual knowledge about countries where the language is spoken, to the development of more comprehensive abilities for engaging with difference and cultivating relationships across cultural boundaries (Byram, 1997). In China, this idea of relating to otherness is understood both through the notion of 'intercultural communicative competence' (跨文化交际能力) (Sun *et al.*, 2021) and also through the notion of 'interculturality' – where people meet each other in different cultural spaces or contexts, learn about shared and unshared experiences and negotiate different perspectives (e.g. Dai & Chen, 2015). From a pedagogical perspective, adopting an intercultural approach entails designing learning experiences in a way that students have opportunities to reflect on cultural differences and consider the consequences of these differences for themselves and others (Lu & Corbett, 2012).

English as a Foreign Language (EFL) teachers in China, especially in higher education, have shown an increasing interest in introducing intercultural dimensions in their classes (Yang & Li, 2017; Zheng & Li, 2016). Their attempts are often impelled by their own desire to innovate and improve their teaching practices, and more specifically, by the guidelines related to improving College English students' ICC proposed in the *College English Teaching Guidelines* (2020) and *Teaching Guidelines for College English Language Majors* (2020).

The teaching objectives, curriculum and standards for foreign language and intercultural education in the Chinese context are affected by China's diverse social and cultural environment, and the political economy (Jin *et al.*, 2017), and yet are expected to conform to China's national circumstances, as exemplified in Jia *et al.*'s (2019) textbook designed to develop the ICC of English language students in Chinese higher education. Throughout the English teaching guidelines, articulated in the *English Teaching Syllabus for College English Majors* (2000), learning the 'target culture' is clearly mentioned for courses aimed at

English-major students, and those who must study English as a compulsory course in their first two years at university (called 'College English'). Furthermore, 'intercultural communication ability' is also a teaching objective of students majoring in English in social and cultural courses. However, the concept of 'culture' has not been clearly defined and was mostly replaced by 'cultural knowledge' (Qian & Garner, 2019). The recent *College English Teaching Guidelines* (2020) has seen a modification of the teaching objectives, emphasising 'enhancing intercultural communication awareness and communication skills' and 'improving comprehensive cultural literacy' (which means developing English learners' ICC) (Wang, 2016: 5). Meanwhile, the *National Standards for the Quality of Foreign Language and Literature Education* (2018) also incorporated the training goal of improving students' ICC into the guidance for planning undergraduate courses for foreign language majors.[1]

Despite the increasing impetus for taking an intercultural approach, there are barriers to implementation within English language classrooms in higher education in China. First, like higher education generally, English language education is examination-oriented. Thus, teachers generally attach greater importance to teaching knowledge about language itself than to the cultural aspects. Furthermore, teachers are not necessarily familiar with theoretical conceptions of ICC and may view cultural content in terms of traditions and customs, history, geography or political conditions (Han, 2011; Zhang, 2009; Yan, 2014). This situation can be traced to the relative lack of relevant empirical studies on intercultural language teaching in the Chinese context, and the limited opportunities for systematic pedagogical training in ICC for EFL teachers (Han, 2014; Zhang, 2012). Despite their enthusiasm, teachers are often uncertain about which teaching approaches they should apply to develop their students' ICC (Sun *et al.*, 2021).

In order to establish an intercultural approach that can be smoothly implemented into Chinese EFL classrooms and a College English language syllabus, Qin devised and carried out an action research study to explore students' intercultural learning from the viewpoint of ICC. As explained in the next section, both the design of the syllabus and the analysis of students' learning were largely informed by Byram's (1997) model of ICC.

Next, we present the action research project designed to address the research question, followed by the findings that emerged from its implementation.

Integrating Intercultural Dimensions into English Language Learning: The Study

The study, guided by the standpoint of Qin's own observation and teaching experience, was informed by action research (Kemmis &

McTaggart, 1988; McNiff *et al.*, 2003) which starts with a problem or concern, then leads to planning, action, evaluation and critical reflection. The planning consisted of the development of a specifically designed course, namely, the Intercultural English Course (IEC), followed by its implementation and evaluation. Qin, as teacher-researcher, taught the course to her students, tracked their ICC development and gathered feedback from them on their experiences of the course. She also recorded her own reflections of the course – the students' experiences of and reactions to the content – in her researcher journal. From this analysis, implications for course revision and the development of learners' ICC in similar foreign language educational contexts emerged.

Unlike other undergraduate English courses at the university concerned, the IEC integrated linguistic and intercultural communication skills, and intercultural elements into its curriculum. In developing the curriculum for the IEC, Qin was guided conceptually by Byram's (1997) ICC framework since it was considered the most suitable in her teaching-researching context, influential in the Ministry of Education documents, and well-represented in foreign language education internationally. It also provides a guide to foreign language teachers to design their syllabus and plan their teaching.

The five *savoirs*

The ICC framework consists of five separate but interdependent components or *savoirs*: knowledge, attitudes, skills of interpreting and relating, and skills of discovery and interaction, accompanied by critical cultural awareness. The objectives Byram (1997) set for the five *savoirs* serve as guiding criteria to develop and evaluate learners' intercultural competence particularly in the foreign language education context. Accordingly, Corbett (2003: 31) argues that the five *savoirs* are a 'fully worked-out specification of intercultural competence, which involves the kinds of knowledge and skills needed to mediate between cultures'. The framework's emphasis on becoming an 'intercultural speaker' (Byram, 1997: 32) makes it different from models that are solely based on communicative competence.

Among the five *savoirs*, Byram (1997) distinguishes *savoir s'engager* – 'critical cultural awareness' (CCA) or 'political education' – as central. This dimension intentionally emphasises the 'social' and 'political' domains in language awareness (James & Garrett, 1992), particularly important for critically analyzing and evaluating cultural viewpoints. *Savoir s'engager* is regarded as the core of ICC and the developed outcome of the other four *savoirs*. In addition to relating, interpreting and analyzing cultural differences, intercultural speakers should also be competent to generate their own critical opinions based on logical criteria from their own and other cultures. According to Byram (1997: 103), CCA not only enhances the transferability of skills and attitudes but also functions as 'a basis for study of other cultures and languages or for coping with interaction in other culture and linguistic environments'. CCA also incorporates the idea of 'taking action' (Byram, 2008) and responsibility and ethical and moral action/communication as in the citizenship literature, and in more recent critiques of the terms 'competence' and 'intercultural competence' (e.g. Ferri, 2018; Guilherme, 2002).

Key Considerations in Integrating Byram's ICC into EFL in the Chinese Context

Any attempt to incorporate a model of ICC into classroom pedagogy in a new context needs to consider the model's theoretical 'fit' for that context and take into account any relevant critiques or limitations. In this vein, it was important to consider issues that have been raised in relation to Byram's ICC model.

First, Coperías-Aguilar (2002) suggests that teachers may face challenges in how to apply the ICC model to actual teaching, because some aspects of ICC cannot be taught in the classroom. For example, in developing the IEC, Qin found that some dimensions of the *savoirs* are abstract and may not be achievable in the timeframe of the IEC. So, in being purposeful in her syllabus design, she decided to incorporate the *savoirs* into the construction of the learning objectives, clarifying and simplifying them for students to understand (see the following section).

Another consideration is that the concept of culture embedded in Byram's ICC model has been suggested as based on 'essentialist' and 'nationalist' views (Belz, 2007). However, if sufficient attention is paid to the fundamental purpose of the 1997 book, this doubt can be removed (see Byram, 2021; Introduction, this volume). In Qin's view, both teachers and curriculum designers in the Chinese context could benefit from a concise framework and a systematic pedagogy and method of evaluation with illustrations.

In approaching pedagogical design, a further issue to consider is local contextualisation. As Byram (1997) has emphasised, successful teaching and assessing of ICC requires sufficient contextualisation, which means considering local factors such as the 'learners' origins, as well as the languages, cultures they are learning' (1997: 4). In this view, when applying Byram's ICC approach to the Chinese tertiary EFL context, context-sensitive points should be noted and reviewed purposefully and extensively before and after the study. It is impossible to define a general syllabus to teach ICC by listing only the guidelines to design a specific syllabus (Byram, 1997). Rather, evaluation and teaching should be closely interrelated and supported by detailed objectives. For Chinese teachers, unfamiliar with how to incorporate ICC objectives into the EFL classroom, the model, with its specific ICC objectives, offers a starting point. Given the focus in this study on developing Chinese students' ICC through language education in the Chinese context, Byram's model was considered useful as a comprehensive framework to design the IEC syllabus, inform the research question and teaching practice and scaffold the data analysis. Next, the IEC course is introduced.

The Intercultural English Course (IEC): Approach and Learning Objectives

The teaching sessions in the IEC endeavoured to present learners with current sociocultural issues in some English-speaking cultures such as the UK by using authentic examples and case studies. The purpose of this approach was to arouse learners' interest in conducting critical analysis of the examples and eventually provide learners with transferable intercultural attitudes and skills when encountering otherness. The course involved various types of assignments, including: implementing analysis of texts after reading, reflecting on videos and discussion of intercultural topics.

Learners who attended the IEC had studied English for at least eight years, having matriculated in English from secondary school, and were considered upper-intermediate or advanced language speakers (at university level). The primary teaching objectives sought to engage learners in ICC development. In constructing the course objectives, Qin simplified Byram's savoirs to facilitate learners' understandings and accommodate the purposes of the IEC. The course objectives were as follows:

(a) to gain knowledge of English-speaking cultures via reading authentic texts addressing different English-speaking cultures, and discuss issues in different disciplines;
(b) to find information about English-speaking cultures, compare or/and contrast them with similar aspects in Chinese culture, and explain the perspective and/or sources of misunderstanding;
(c) to gain curiosity and openness, via reflecting on their attitudes towards members of English-speaking countries;
(d) to acquire new knowledge of an English-speaking culture and cultural practices in various ways available;
(e) to achieve 'critical cultural awareness', an ability to evaluate critically, and on the basis of explicit criteria, perspectives, practices and products in one's own and other cultures and countries (based on Byram, 1997: 63).

Next, the course materials and instruction methods directed towards developing students' ICC are outlined.

Intercultural English Course Content

When choosing language teaching materials, most Chinese EFL teachers place a high priority on matching the language level of the students and there is normally little concern about the sociocultural facets of the materials or the students' intercultural level. Byram *et al.* (2002: 4) claimed that an intercultural speaker will succeed not only in 'communicating information but also in developing a human relationship with people of other languages and cultures'. Sociocultural knowledge can also be drawn from many resources such as surveys, television programs and films.

Qin therefore considered materials that enabled students to find sociocultural perspectives embedded both in the text and in their own sociocultural context. She wanted to include topics that addressed elements of Byram's (1997) model, i.e. topics that would encourage students to consider their own sociocultural knowledge and intercultural attitudes. Therefore, readings, pictures and video clips were used as the teaching materials, and the topics were chosen mainly based on students' preferences, elicited through discussion with the students of their feedback given in the pre-course questionnaires.

Instruction Methods in Accordance with the ICC Model

The IEC included varying instructional techniques to arouse learners' interest, such as task-based group work, individual presentations and group discussion.

The six teaching sessions engaged students with sociocultural issues (e.g. dining habits, greeting customs and education systems) in some English-speaking cultures, using authentic examples and case studies. The course involved various types of assignments, such as reading and analysing texts, reflecting on video clips and discussion of intercultural topics. For example, the readings for the first teaching session (five sojourner students' diary entries) revolved around 'culture shock'. Students discussed evidence of difficulties, or 'cultural bumps' in groups and then reported their interpretations to the whole class, which the teacher then responded to. The purpose of this approach was closely interrelated with ICC savoirs and aimed to arouse students' interest in conducting critical analysis of some sociocultural issues in intercultural communication, and eventually provide students with transferable intercultural attitudes and skills when encountering otherness, whether in China or beyond.

Data Collection and Analysis

The data collection instruments (see Table 13.1) used in this study contained students' pre-course and post-course questionnaires, students' learning process worksheets (LPWs) and the teacher's reflective journal based on her teaching reflection. These were used to look for indicators of intercultural development and to shape and evaluate the IEC.

Table 13.1 Data collection stages

Stages	Data collection activities	Materials
1 Preparation	Syllabus design Ethical matters Induction session for the study Students' pre-questionnaire	Lesson plans Consent forms Fine-tuning topics for lessons
2 Intercultural English Course	The six teaching sessions: Teaching Session 1 Culture shock (critical incidents) Teaching Session 2 International greetings Teaching Session 3 Food and eating habits Teaching Session 4 Study in the UK Teaching Session 5 Festivals Teaching Session 6 Developing intercultural skills	Video-taping teaching sessions; Teacher's class observation field notes; Teaching reflective journal Students' learning process worksheets
3 Post-course	Students' post-questionnaire Focus group interviews	Gathering and presenting the data; undertaking the analysis

Questionnaires

Two sets of structured questionnaires (pre- and post-course) with open questions (see Appendix 13.1) were implemented in the project to elicit students' views. The pre-course questionnaire, taken by the students prior to the course, was important in establishing learners' positions and perspectives before starting the course and shaping the content. The questionnaire focused on the following topics: previous learning experiences; expectations of the IEC and suggestions for cultural topics to be included in the teaching sessions; and a self-evaluation of previous intercultural knowledge and skills. Results revealed that learners' expectations towards the IEC related to four main areas: curiosity in cultural knowledge, linguistic proficiency, practical purposes and personal development. Qin took these factors into account when designing the course syllabus, especially the teaching content and instructional methods. The pre-course questionnaire also revealed that sociocultural aspects learners had covered in their previous language learning experiences were mainly limited to general cultural facts and different cultural values or beliefs, though these tended to be expressed stereotypically in questionnaire responses.

The purpose of the post-course questionnaire was to understand, rather than assess, whether the students' expectations for the IEC were met and identify how students perceived any potential development in their intercultural knowledge and skills, or change of attitudes, having undertaken the course (see Appendix 13.2). Students were generally greatly satisfied with the course and their attainment.

Students' learning process worksheets

Students completed LPWs before and after each teaching session of the IEC. The LPWs were embedded in every IEC teaching step within each of the six teaching sessions. (See Appendix 13.3 for an illustration of the indicative questions that the students were required to answer, which is taken from a teaching step in Session 2.)

The LPWs had three functions: (1) check students' reflections on their intercultural communicative knowledge, attitudes, skills and critical cultural awareness both before and after the teaching session; (2) record their evaluation of the IEC teaching contents and instructional methods and (3) record any changes students perceived in their own ICC development. Therefore, as well as showing students' self-reflections and self-evaluations of perceived ICC development during the course, the worksheets also had a pedagogical and a research function for the teacher-researcher.

The questions in the first part addressed functions one and three above. These questions were purposefully designed to guide students' reflection on whether their ICC knowledge, skills and attitudes had been enhanced, for example: cultural knowledge of English-speaking cultures; stereotypes of English speakers and how students felt about discussing these stereotypes; identification of the similarities and differences between their own culture and English-speaking cultures; explanation of misunderstandings across cultures; and suggestions to improve interaction with English-language speakers. As the questions were closely related to the teaching content and included repeated questions before and after the teaching session, the teacher-researcher was able to make sense of students' progress through their different or changed answers to the same question.

The questions in the second part concerned the second function (the IEC evaluation) and aimed to analyse the teacher's course design in more detail, and specifically, to detect particular content and instructional methods that were effective in arousing students' interest and/or enabling the achievement of the programme's learning outcomes.

Data analysis

Borghetti (2017) highlights the ethical dilemmas and other difficulties associated with assessing ICC and recommends self-report/reflection, peer and expert evaluations. To this end, the teacher-researcher combined students' self-evaluations and self-reflections provided in their responses in the pre- and post-questionnaires, LPWs and focus group interviews, as well as her observations and reflections (recorded in her researcher journal) to analyse and make sense of students' engagement in learning and their perceptions of their own ICC development. For example, students' responses in the post-questionnaire (specifically Questions 4–9) were analysed together with their individual responses in their pre-questionnaires and LPWs. Furthermore, when reflecting on their own ICC development, students were specifically asked to provide examples or 'instances' which they believe illustrate their sense of growth in terms of knowledge, skills and attitudes. Thus, the aim was not to generate a linear picture of ICC development but rather to capture evidence of engagement in learning that corresponded to the learning objectives established for the course, as informed by Byram's model of ICC. As will be presented below, this involved drawing on the five *savoirs* to locate understandings of students' ICC development, as well as looking out for other emergent themes that represented notions of intercultural learning outside this main framework.

Students' ICC Development (Following Byram's *savoirs*)

Altogether, 194 instances were identified which corresponded to Byram's (1997) five *savoirs* (see Table 13.2 for details). The *skills of discovery and interaction* (S2) dimension has the largest number of instances with 78 (40%), while *critical cultural awareness* showed no evidence. The dimensions of *knowledge* and *attitudes* contain similar amounts of instances, 55 (29%) and 53 (27%), respectively. The *skills of interpreting and relating* (S1) and *skills of discovery and interaction* (S2) were analysed separately according to Byram's (1997) original *savoir* categorisation, but if combined into the *skills* dimension, there were 86 instances in total (44%).

The following table (Table 13.3) presents indicative data showing how learners' comments were mapped onto the five *savoirs* (Byram, 1997) to demonstrate their engagement in learning.

Table 13.2 Instances of ICC learning objectives in students' feedback

ICC learning objectives	Number of instances	Percentage
Knowledge	55	29%
Attitude	53	27%
Skills of interpreting and relating (S1)	8	4%
Skills of discovery and interaction (S2)	78	40%
Critical cultural awareness	0	0
Total	194	

Table 13.3 Indicative data mapping onto the *savoirs*

Savoirs	Overview of analysis	Evidence
KNOWLEDGE: Of social groups and their products and practices in one's own and in one's interlocutor's country, and of the general processes of societal and individual interaction.	Students' responses demonstrate features in more than one dimension of the *Knowledge* objective. Approximately one third of students' feedback is concerned with knowledge about 'non-verbal behaviour of interaction', like shaking hands when greeting. While students may have already had this knowledge, their feedback suggests that they understood the differences more clearly after the course. Another most commonly addressed aspect is 'conventions of behaviour and beliefs and taboos in routine situations'.	'Different country has **different greeting culture**'. (TS2, G1-3-FB) 'I like to study in the UK. First, I think it has an **advanced higher education system. It stresses on improving students' creativity.** In addition, it helps students to find a way to solve tomorrow's problems'. (TS4, G3-3-FE)
ATTITUDES: Curiosity and openness, readiness to suspend disbelief about other cultures and belief about one's own. a) Willingness to seek out or take up opportunities to **engage with otherness** in a **relationship of equality, distinct from seeking out the exotic** or the profitable e) Readiness to engage with the **conventions and rites** of verbal and non-verbal communication and interaction	Both *Attitude e)* and *Attitude a)* (66% in total) are the most frequently identified dimensions. Learners are potentially open to interactions with culturally different others, and ready for change while encountering differences. However, in terms of initiating interactions with culturally different others involving suspending one's original cultural beliefs and discovering different perspectives, there is less clear evidence of learners' development.	'Every culture has their own beliefs or values. We cannot ignore it or push others accept us. We should be open to them'. (TS1, G4-3-ME)
SKILLS of INTERPRETING and RELATING (S1): Ability to interpret a document or event from another culture, to explain it and relate it to documents or events from one's own.	Students' responses are concentrated on 'identify[ing] **ethnocentric perspectives** in a document or event and **explain[ing]** their origins' and 'mediate[ing]' between **conflicting interpretations** of phenomena'. While confronting different cultural perspectives, they were active in identifying the common ground and trying to solve conflicting understandings.	'Different country has their different culture, for example, a country love a thing, but another country all hate it. … **Through some stories (Hong Kong students' diary, i.e. critical incidents), I know the differences between China's <Chinese> culture and other cultures.** And I know how to do when I meet that situation (conflict/cultural differences)'. (TS1, G1-5-FB)

(Continued)

Table 13.3 (Continued)

Savoirs	Overview of analysis	Evidence
SKILLS of DISCOVERY and INTERACTION (S2): Ability to acquire new knowledge of a culture and cultural practices and the ability to operate knowledge, attitudes and skills under the constraints of real-time communication and interaction. c) identify **similar and dissimilar processes of interaction, verbal and non-verbal**, and **negotiate an appropriate use** of them in specific circumstances e) identify **contemporary and past relationships** between one's own and the other culture and society	The S2 *savoir* was most evidenced with 78 instances, which mainly focused on students' ability to identify similar and dissimilar cultural interactional forms and negotiate a proper reaction. S2 instances were concentrated in two dimensions. They tended to acquire knowledge of a new culture by 'reading a document or watching an event', rather than 'conducting an inquiry through the interlocutor'. The latter may be difficult to achieve given the limited 'face-to-face' interactional opportunities with non-Chinese during the course. These outcomes suggest that the simulation scenarios and other imagined real-time interaction processes employed in the IEC may have supported this development. S2c indicates two phases in achieving a successful intercultural interaction: recognising the similarities and differences between cultural conventions; and being aware of the need to 'change' and 'accept' the differences, or negotiate a 'compromise'. The examples in S2e indicate students' capability of 'identify[ing] contemporary and past relationships between one's own and the other culture and society'.	'Don't be shy and afraid when communicate with others <English speakers>. … We should accept the different cultures based on the different environment'. (TS1, G2-2-FB) 'In my view it is not enough to talk about western culture. It is better to recognise western values from their histories such as Revival of Learning in which individualism occurred. These factors influence their behaviours and in this way we can better comprehend the differences between Eastern cultures and Western cultures'. (TS1, G3-5-ME)
CRITICAL CULTURAL AWARENESS (CCA): Ability to evaluate, critically and on the basis of explicit criteria, perspectives, practices and products in one's own and other cultures and countries.	CCA is indispensable to an intercultural interaction and is a consequence of using 'one's knowledge, skills and attitudes' in collaboration. Unfortunately, no clear evidence of this *savoir* was identified from IEC students' responses. The reasons for this outcome are uncertain, but may be due to the short nature of the course, the nature of the materials students worked with, or the lack of opportunity for prolonged real-time intercultural communication.	

Additional Emergent Themes Related to Intercultural Learning

In this section, we illustrate additional themes in students' intercultural learning which emerged in the students' feedback, which shed further light, in the Chinese EFL context, on Byram's (1997) five *savoirs*.

Knowledge

Two additional themes linked to the *Knowledge savoir* emerged: *Knowledge of Cultural Facts* and *Knowledge of Intercultural Communication*. These represent students' understandings of general types of knowledge considered useful for intercultural communication.

In relation to the former, students' responses showed their belief that gaining knowledge and understanding of other cultures is essential for further understanding of otherness and implementing intercultural interaction. For example: 'I have **known foreign culture more**, this is **useful** in my communication with foreigners' (PQ-4, G1-10-MB). Yet very few students referred to deeper understandings of cultural knowledge that addressed values and beliefs. For students who are only beginning to learn about culture within English language learning, there may be a tendency to think that cultural knowledge is the initial step for successful communication with English-speakers, and only when they understand the different cultures well can they engage in intercultural dialogue.

Students also emphasised the importance of acquiring *Knowledge of Intercultural Communication*, which they considered useful in promoting their successful intercultural communication. For example, '... this course helped me to know **the most essential information for me to make good communication with people outside China,** especially people in the UK' (PQ-1, G3-2-FT). Overall, their responses seemed to indicate that they appreciated having the chance to go beyond their previous intercultural learning, which had been limited to knowledge from a traditional perspective, mainly revolving around knowledge about food, customary clothing, holidays and cultural stereotypes, rather than knowledge for future intercultural understanding and communication when interacting with people from other cultures.

Attitudes

In addition to instances corresponding to Byram's (1997) *Attitudes savoir*, three additional *Attitudes* themes emerged: *More 'openness' than 'curiosity'*, *Chinese spiritual essence of 'harmonious society'* and *Chinese students' learning concept*.

First, students' responses indicated that they were more inclined to show 'openness' rather than 'curiosity'. On one hand, openness manifested in their eagerness to initiate and develop interactions with culturally different others. However, because they do not have opportunities to implement real-time interactions with English-speakers, their feedback was mainly concerned with their speculations to initiate and develop interactions. For example, 'I will try to find more materials to improve my skills and communicate more with foreigners' (PQ-8&9, G2-4-MB). However, concerning 'curiosity', students were only able to ask simple or surface questions about other cultures. Thus, while they were open to engaging with otherness, they often did not seem to have clear areas of interest or curiosity. This finding contrasts with Byram's (1997) model where openness and curiosity are presented in parallel. In line with the ICC model, this would mean that there is a gap between their current position and the objective, which expects them to seek out and articulate answers to complex questions about other cultures and reflect multiple cultural perspectives.

A second feature of students' *Attitudes* concerned the *Chinese spiritual essence of harmonious society*, linked to the principle of 'harmony' in interpersonal relations within the Confucian philosophical system (Xiao & Chen, 2009). Students' responses conspicuously showed their reluctance to break from this communicative integrity, seen in their frequent use of words such as 'positively', 'in a right way' and 'enthusiastic', demonstrating their efforts to implement a peaceful and smooth communication process.

For example: 'We should accept the difference of foreign culture **positively**' (TS1, G1-4-FB).

Concerning the third emergent *Attitude, Chinese students' learning concept*, students highlighted 'determined effort' as a core element for successful interaction and to accomplish successful learning outcomes. They recognised their progress but kept in view how they wanted to go further. For example:

I **can** perform better in communicating with members of English-speaking cultures **now**, and **will be better in the future**. I will keep attention on information of different cultures, and try to get more chances communicating with natives speakers of English. (PQ-8&9, G1-10-MB)

I feel **a little more comfortable** speaking with native English speakers. I think [it] **will be better** [in the future]. I will get more culture books and try to communicate with others [English speakers]. (PQ-8&9, G2-5-MB)

I also **feel nervous** [when I perform communication with members of English-speaking cultures]. **But if I practice more, I can change [develop] more**. I will try to find more materials to improve my skills and communicate more with foreigners. (PQ-8&9, G2-4-MB)

While all three students revealed their attitudes towards communicating with native English speakers – from being 'considerably comfortable' ('can', G1-10-MB), to 'moderately comfortable' ('a little more', G2-5-MB), and to 'not sufficiently comfortable' ('feel nervous': G2-4-MB) – all of them added supplementary explanations indicating future action and effort towards developing their intercultural competence.

Skills of interpreting and relating (S1)

Although the analysis did not reveal strong evidence of engagement which corresponded to the dimension 'identify areas of misunderstanding and dysfunction in an interaction and explain them in terms of each of the cultural systems present' (S1b, Byram, 1997: 61), a number of related themes did emerge: *'ethnorelative reflection'* and *'keeping neutral'*.

Developing an ethno-relative view via reflection. While pre-course questionnaires revealed that students had some stereotypical views of foreigners, students' responses after the whole course indicated recognition that their own stereotypes of others may play a role in intercultural communication and the adoption of a more ethnorelative view. For example, 'I always think foreigners have stereotype of Chinese, however, we should not have this thought' (PQ-3, G2-9-FA). Supported by IEC teaching methods (e.g. critical incident analysis), they modified their preconceived ideas through continuous reflection and realised that to 'have stereotyping views on others by the first impression' may limit understandings of that other. In Byram's terms, they have made some progress towards 'identify[ing] causes of misunderstanding and dysfunction' (1997: 61) which illustrates their potential development in *Skills of interpreting and relating* (S1).

'Keeping neutral' as the foundational stage of mediation. Although four instances illustrated students' development in S1c, which is the ability to 'mediate between conflicting interpretations of phenomena' (Byram, 1997: 61), student comments reveal a tendency of 'keeping neutral', which is the starting point of 'learning to mediate between conflicting interpretations of phenomena' (Byram, 1997: 61) when they are asked to respond while encountering misunderstandings of their own culture. The neutral attitudes represented in students' feedback while confronting misunderstandings may be linked to the 'harmony' orientation within interpersonal relations mentioned earlier. However, 'keeping neutral' is merely a passive way for mediation, and there is still a gap between 'neutrality' and 'successful mediation'. The students' responses within this dimension suggested that it had been a comparatively demanding task for them to interpret the sources of misunderstanding, analyse the differences and solve the problem.

Skills of discovery and interaction (S2)

The student feedback in this *savoir* coalesced around three major themes: *the underdeveloped ability to acquire new knowledge of a culture, speculated reactions in an imagined real-time interaction* and *broadening the domain in searching for knowledge of a new culture.*

The underdeveloped ability to acquire new knowledge of a culture. Students' absence of the two dimensions in S2 is closely related to the ability to 'acquire new knowledge of a culture and cultural practice'. One dimension emphasises the method of 'conducting an inquiry through the *interlocutor*' in search of implications, whereas the other underlines 'reading a document or watching an event' for hidden references. To achieve the former, 'conducting an inquiry with an interlocutor' is the precondition, which is easier and more accessible for students who have various opportunities to interact with people from other cultures. In many College English classrooms, it may be difficult for language students to obtain such opportunities, particularly via real-time interactions. By comparison, the latter, which highlights 'reading a document or watching an event' for implicit references, is more easily attainable, e.g. via the internet.

Speculated reactions in an imagined real-time interaction. 'Real-time interaction' is emphasised in two S2 dimensions, and the ability to practice 'knowledge, attitudes and skills in real-time interactions' requires extensive real-time communication. Since IEC students did not obtain opportunities to interact with English language speakers, unsurprisingly, no convincing examples were identified within students' responses. However, there were instances indicating reflection on how they would react in an imagined real-time interaction, together with some consideration of potential strategies. For example: 'If they talk with me about weather, I think I will respond enthusiastically, although it is a boring topic in China' (PQ-8, G1-3-FB). Such imagined scenarios provide a way of allowing students to consider their own responses to cultural differences.

Broadening the domain in searching for knowledge of a new culture. According to Byram (1997: 63), an important skill within the S2 *savoir* is 'to acquire new knowledge of a culture and cultural practices'. Regarding 'identify contemporary and past relationships between one's own and the other culture and society', Byram states that the intercultural speaker is expected to 'use sources (e.g. reference books, newspapers, histories, experts, lay informants)' to understand and analyse the relationships between cultures. The students' responses demonstrated a broadening of the domain of these sources, indicating their strong intention to continuously acquire new knowledge about a foreign culture via diverse kinds of routes and procedures. In searching for the information, they showed more interest in strategies such as surfing the internet, watching films or TV plays, listening to radio broadcasts or travelling abroad.

Similarly, learners are supposed to 'identify and make use of public and private institutions which facilitate contact with other countries and cultures' (Byram, 1997: 63), e.g. the British Council and Confucius Institutes (personal communication). Byram expects intercultural speakers to 'use knowledge of these institutions ... to establish and maintain contacts' with another culture. Again, IEC students' feedback indicates a broadened range of strategies used to 'establish and maintain contacts' with another culture, e.g. 'search the Internet', 'communicate with English speakers', 'keep in contact with foreign friends', 'watch films/listen to radio broadcast' and 'travel abroad'. These strategies complement the original domains in Byram's model and thus provide a valuable supplement to ICC framework construction, particularly in the Chinese educational context.

Critical cultural awareness

The IEC students' feedback gave no identifiable evidence of instances of Critical Cultural Awareness (CCA), which, as a consequence of utilising 'one's knowledge, skills and attitudes' in collaboration, is a key dimension among the five savoirs in intercultural interaction.

The three dimensions of CCA consist of three progressive steps, the third being 'the ability to interact and mediate in intercultural exchanges' (Byram, 1997: 63) as the final outcome. Although the students' feedback demonstrated no clear evidence recognised as CCA instances, their feedback did evidence learners' development of CCA 'a) identify and interpret explicit or implicit values in documents and events in one's own and other cultures' and 'b) make an evaluative analysis of the documents and events which refer to an explicit perspective and criteria'. For example, in Teaching Session 3 'Food and Dining Habits', students' discussions on Western fast food as an aspect of globalisation and their evaluation of the issue in the context of China's current development reveal their capability in a) and b). 'It is a way of globalization. We cannot avoid it. Maybe we can combine our traditional Chinese food with western food and create a new kind of cuisine' (G3-3-FE). However, there was no evidence of students having achieved the final step.

The lack of clear evidence of CCA suggests that it may be challenging to bring about development in this area within a short course like IEC, or without well-structured intentional guidance from teachers and appropriate materials conducive to deeper analysis and reflection.

Conclusions

In this chapter, we have reported on an exploratory action research study which sought to investigate ICC development in Chinese students who are studying College English in higher education in China. Byram's (1997) ICC framework informed the materials construction of the six-week intercultural English course (IEC) delivered by the teacher-researcher Qin and provided the theoretical basis for analysing students' feedback through and after the course. The study has shown the utility of Byram's

(1997) framework in identifying and supporting this group of Chinese College English language learners' ICC development in this specific Chinese EFL context. The focus on Byram's (1997) ICC learning objectives had four outcomes in this study: (1) providing guidance to the EFL teacher (Qin) in shaping the construction of methods and content in the IEC; (2) helping to make the teaching and learning more purposeful through the inclusion of specific ICC objectives; (3) providing specific and focused learning outcomes for students and (4) enabling the teacher to understand elements of students' ICC development, supported by the LPWs.

Three pedagogical implications emerge from this study. First, the development of certain intercultural skills, for instance, CCA will, ideally, require real-time interaction opportunities with people from other cultures. Since this was not feasible in this IEC course, we recommend offering examples of 'imagined real-time interaction' or creating possibilities for 'virtual exchange' in contexts where students do not have the opportunity for face-to-face or virtual intercultural communication, and creating opportunities for perspective taking and simulation through carefully designed activities (Cunico, 2005; Timlin *et al.*, 2021) or through the interpretation of cultural narratives (Kearney, 2012). Second, achieving a comprehensive range of objectives, exemplified in Byram's model, was demanding in this study as not all objectives were easily achievable or transferable to the Chinese EFL context. Our findings have illustrated that certain aspects of the *savoirs* were considered abstract and difficult to directly implement into English language teaching and learning. And third, while the desirability of programmes that enable students to achieve all aspects of ICC, and especially critical cultural awareness, is not in doubt, the practical limitations of time and resources need consideration (e.g. the IEC programme was two hours per week over six weeks). A future iteration of the IEC course design would need to be aware of and account for the challenges posed above, for example: by focusing the topics of the IEC around a singular theme that supports the development of CCA; or by designing activities that allow for perspective-taking within a global simulation or real-time intercultural communication project; or through inclusion of consistent simulations and debriefs, and critical incident analysis of case studies. Above all, care should be taken to match IEC course objectives with well-aligned curricular choices and instructional activities from which student learning and development can be analysed.

Currently, there is a growing interest in researching cultural and intercultural teaching pedagogy in the Chinese EFL context, as evidenced in the *College English Teaching Guidelines* (2020). For example, the three-year Chinese-European capacity building project 'Resources for Chinese Higher Education' (RICH-Ed)[2] has developed modules for the teaching of ICC accompanied by teacher training. Language courses that promote ICC should find a place in the university curriculum, but training is needed to support teachers in learning how to integrate intercultural communication into the EFL syllabus, and to prepare teachers to effectively facilitate students' ICC development (Sun *et al.*, 2021). While many teachers are willing to implement intercultural aspects in their language classrooms, their teaching practices tend to be based on incidental or limited experiential learning. This exploratory study, supported by Byram's (1997) ICC framework, provides a specific and local understanding of how an intercultural approach in English language teaching could be implemented into an EFL programme. With a particular focus on College English, it offers a possible theoretical perspective and pedagogy for the language curriculum that aims to facilitate and understand students' ICC development. However, caution is advised when transferring the outcomes from this small-scale exploratory study conducted in one university in Eastern China to other EFL programmes and classrooms. Further exploration of the IEC and the emergent ICC themes linked to Byram's *savoirs* is required in other EFL contexts in China.

Acknowledgements

We thank the editors and reviewer for their careful reading of our chapter and very helpful suggestions, which (word count permitting) we have adopted.

Notes

(1) Byram was influential in the inclusion of ICC into the Standards through invitations by the National College English Teaching Advisory Board and the Beijing Education Committee to give lectures and workshops on his ICC model between 2015 and 2020, which included a short course on ICC in foreign language education in 2015.
(2) See www.rich-ed.com for further information on this project.

References

Belz, J. (2007) The development of intercultural communicative competence in telecollaborative partnerships. In R. O'Dowd (ed.) *Online Intercultural Exchange: An Introduction for Foreign Language Teachers* (pp. 127–166). Clevedon: Multilingual Matters.
Borghetti, C. (2017) Is there really a need for assessing intercultural competence?: Some ethical issues. *Journal of Intercultural Communication* 44, 1–18. ISSN 1404-1634. Retrieved from https://immi.se/intercultural/nr44/borghetti.html
Byram, M. (1997) *Teaching and Assessing Intercultural Communicative Competence.* Clevedon: Multilingual Matters.
Byram, M. (2008) *From Foreign Language Education to Education for Intercultural Citizenship: Essays and Reflections.* Clevedon: Multilingual Matters.
Byram, M. (2021) *Teaching and Assessing Intercultural Communicative Competence: Revisited.* Bristol: Multilingual Matters.
Byram, M., Gribkova, B. and Starkey, H. (2002) *Developing the Intercultural Dimension in Language Teaching. A Practical Introduction for Teachers.* Strasbourg: Council of Europe.

Coperías-Aguilar, M.J. (2002) Intercultural communicative competence: A step beyond communicative competence. *ELIA* 3, 85–102.

Cunico, S. (2005) Teaching language and intercultural competence through drama: Some suggestions for a neglected resource. *The Language Learning Journal* 31 (1), 21–29.

Dai, X.D. and Chen, G.M. (2015) On interculturality and intercultural communication competence. *China Media Research* 11 (3), 100–113.

Ferri, J. (2018) *Intercultural Communication: Critical Approaches and Future Challenges*. London: Palgrave Macmillan.

Guilherme, M. (2002) *Critical Citizens for an Intercultural World: Foreign Language Education as Cultural Politics*. Clevedon: Multilingual Matters.

Han, H. (2010) An Investigation of Teachers' Perceptions of Culture Teaching in Secondary Schools in Xinjiang, China, Durham theses, Durham University. Available at Durham E-Theses Online: http://etheses.dur.ac.uk/109/

Han, X.H. (2014) Cultivating college students' intercultural communicative competence: From the perspective of college English teachers. *Foreign Language Research* 3, 106–110 (in Chinese).

James, C. and Garrett, P. (1992) *Language Awareness in the Classroom*. New York: Longman.

Jia, Y.X., Byram, M., Jia, X.R., Song, L. and Jia, X.L. (2019) *Experiencing Global Intercultural Communication: Preparing for a Community of Shared Future for Mankind and Global Citizenship*. Beijing: Foreign Language Teaching and Research Press.

Jin, Y., Wu, Z., Alderson, C. and Song, W. (2017) Developing the China standards of English: Challenges at the macropolitical and micropolitical levels. *Language Testing in Asia* 7 (1), 1–19.

Kearney, E. (2012) Perspective-taking and meaning-making through engagement with cultural narratives: Bringing history to life in a foreign language classroom. *L2 Journal* 4 (1), 58–82.

Kemmis, S. and McTaggart, R. (1988) *The Action Research Planner* (3rd edn). Geelong: Deakin University.

Lu, P.Y. and Corbett, J. (2012) An intercultural approach to second language education and citizenship. In J. Jackson (ed.) *The Routledge Handbook of Language and Intercultural Communication* (pp. 325–329). London: Routledge.

McNiff, J., Lomax, P. and Whitehead, J. (2003) *You and Your Action Research Project*. London: Routledge Falmer.

National College English Teaching Advisory Board 高等学校大学外语教学指导委员会 (2020), 《大学英语教学指南》 (*College English Teaching Guidelines*), 高等教育出版社。

National Foreign Language Teaching Advisory Board 高等学校外语专业教学指导委员会 (2000), 《高等学校英语专业英语教学大纲》 (*English Teaching Syllabus for College English Majors*), 上海外语教育出版社。

National Foreign Language Teaching Advisory Board 高等学校外语专业教学指导委员会 (2018), 《普通高等学校本科专业类教学质量国家标准（外国语言文学类）》(*National Standards for the Quality of Foreign Language and Literature Education*), 高等教育出版社。

National Foreign Language Teaching Advisory Board 高等学校外语专业教学指导委员会 (2020), 《普通高等学校本科外国语言文学类专业教学指南（上）——英语类专业教学指南》 (*Teaching Guidelines for College English Language Majors*), 上海外语教育出版社。

Qian, L. and Garner, M. (2019) A literature survey of conceptions of the role of culture in foreign language education in China (1980–2014). *Intercultural Education* 30 (2), 159–179.

Sun, Y.Z., Liao, H.J., Zheng, X. and Qin, S.Q. (2021) 《跨文化外语教学研究》 (*Research on Intercultural Foreign Language Teaching and Learning*). 外语教学与研究出版社。 Beijing: Foreign Language Teaching and Research Press.

Timlin, C., Warner, C., Clark, L. and Ploschnitzki, P. (2021) Living literacies in a *Märchenwelt*: World building and perspective taking in a fairy-tale simulation project. *Die Unterrichtspraxis/Teaching German* 54 (1), 5–19.

Wang, S.R. 王守仁 (2016) 《大学英语教学指南》要点解读.外语界 (03), 2-10. doi:CNKI: SUN:WYJY.0.2016-03-001.

Wang, Y.A., Deardorff, D.K. and Kulich, S.J. (2017) Chinese perspectives on intercultural competence in international higher education. In D. Deardorff and L. Arasaratnam (eds) *Intercultural Competence in International Higher Education* (pp. 95–108). New York: Routledge.

Xiao, X.S. and Chen, G.M. (2009) Communication competence and moral competence: A Confucian perspective. *Journal of Multicultural Discourses* 4 (1), 61–74.

Yan, J.L. 颜静兰 (2014) 外语教师跨文化交际能力的"缺口"与"补漏". 上海师范大学学报 (哲学社会科学版) 01, 138-145.

Yang, H. and Li, L. W. (2017) An action research on the integration of intercultural competence with College English teaching. *Foreign Languages and Their Teachings* 2, 9–17 (in Chinese).

Zhang, H.L. (2012) Foreign language teaching guided by intercultural education: Past, present and future. *Foreign Language World* 2, 2–7 (in Chinese).

Zheng, X. and Li, M.Y. (2016) Exploring reflective intercultural teaching: An action research in a College English class. *Foreign Languages in China* 3, 4–11 (in Chinese).

Appendix 13.1

Pre-questionnaire for course learners

Thank you for your precious time. Your responses are very valuable to this investigation. It won't take you more than 20 minutes to complete this form. Please feel free to use as much space as necessary.

Pseudonym (choose any English name you like)_____

Gender: _____

English entrance result: _____

1. What aspects of English-speaking cultures are you familiar with? Please give some examples.
2. Have you had any English classes where the discussed cultural aspects that are different from your culture (e.g. values, beliefs system, etc.) If yes, what topics were addressed?
   Yes: ____ No: ____
   Explain:_____
3. Have you been taught in your previous English classes how to interact with English speakers (for example, use of gestures or facial expressions when talking with them)?
   Yes: ____ No: ____
   Explain:_____
4. What aspects of the language do you feel you need to improve?

5. Do you practice English with native speakers? Yes: _____ No: _____
   When? _____
   Who with? _____
   How often? _____
6. Do you find you have difficulties when you interact with native English speakers?
   If so, what types of difficulties?
7. Besides the formal language classes, what do you do to improve your English?
8. Why are you taking this course?
9. What are your expectations of this course?
10. What culture-related topics would you suggest to discuss in this course?
11. Give an example of a situation in which you experienced a misunderstanding when you interacted with a native speaker:
    – Misunderstanding:
    – How you solved the problem:
12. Do you know the term intercultural communicative competence? Whether yes or no, what does the term mean to you?

Appendix 13.2

Post-questionnaire for course learners

Thank you for your precious time. Your responses are very valuable to this investigation. It won't take you more than 20 minutes to complete this form. Please feel free to use as much space as necessary.

Pseudonym
(please ensure you give the same name with your pre-questionnaire)

_____

Gender: _____

1. Has the Intercultural English Course met your expectations? Why? Explain and give specific examples.
2. What was the most interesting part of it? Explain
3. What did you find lacking in the course? Explain
4. What new knowledge have you gained? Explain
5. What new skills have you developed? Explain
6. Are you more aware now of how culture impact communication than you were at the beginning of the course? Explain
7. Do you feel more comfortable speaking with native speakers of English?
8. Do you think you can perform effectively and appropriately with members of English-speaking cultures? Explain your response and give examples.

9. What do you intend to do to continue developing your intercultural skills?

Appendix 13.3

Excerpt from Student Learning Process Worksheet (partial questions from Teaching Session Two)

Before Class
1. Suppose you meet your foreign teacher, a 50-year-old gentleman for the first time and his name is Thomas Smith, what is the exact way you call him?
2. If he tells you that he doesn't like others call him Mr. Smith, what will you do when you meet him again?
3. Are you curious to know more about different styles of international greetings? Why or why not?
4. If you are in a foreign country and people treat you with their social greeting custom (for example, in France, they hug and kiss on your cheeks), what will you do?
5. If you don't like others' (especially foreigners') greeting style or body language, what will you do?

After Class
After you have learned from this class, please answer the following questions (there are some questions you have encountered already, but you might provide different answers this time):

6. Suppose you meet your foreign teacher, a 50-year-old gentleman for the first time and his name is Thomas Smith, what is the exact way you call him?
7. If he tells you that he doesn't like others call him Mr. Smith, what will you do when you meet him again?
8. Are you curious to know more about different styles of international greetings? Why or why not? If you want to investigate deeper on this topic, what will you do?
9. If you are in a foreign country and people treat you with their social greeting custom (for example, in France, they hug and kiss on your cheeks), what will you do?
10. If you don't like others' (especially foreigners') greeting style or body language, what will you do?

14 Engaging Educators: Facilitating Interdisciplinary Communities of Practice in the USA

Rita A. Oleksak and Fabiana Cardetti

Introduction

Coming together to share a passion, interacting regularly in collaborative work and enhancing learning that empowers others to grow along with you are key components to building a Community of Practice (CoP). For educators, CoPs provide opportunities to learn from and with one another in a learning community focused on teachers' needs (Grossman *et al.*, 2001; Tannehill & MacPhail, 2017). They enable us to develop individually and collectively, engaging in a process of mutual learning through social interaction and collaboration (Wenger-Trayner & Wenger-Trayner, 2015). Hadar and Brody (2010) assert that CoPs do not occur randomly, but they are actually intentionally initiated and promoted by facilitators who are connected and responsive to the needs of members. For eight years, we have been involved in two projects bringing together teachers and graduate students as CoPs focused on improving the K-12 educational experience. Participants in our CoPs have come from a variety of disciplines: World languages (e.g. Spanish, German), education (e.g. Curriculum and Instruction), Unified Arts (e.g. Health and Wellness) and Sciences (e.g. Mathematics) all sharing a passion for developing students' Intercultural Communicative Competence (ICC) and Intercultural Citizenship (ICit). Throughout these projects, we have relied on Michael Byram's model of ICC (1997) and on his subsequent work in ICit (2008) because his presentation of these complex concepts and theories resonates with us as well as with our colleagues and university students in ways that no other resources do. Byram directs our aim toward developing school students' critical cultural awareness while positioning them as agents of change who use this awareness to analyze problematic societal conditions relevant to them in order to pursue actionable solutions. These fundamental experiences are unfortunately not universally present in K-12 classrooms. However, in our experience, once our groups had the opportunity to explore them, they could see the value and importance of working collaboratively to re-design curriculum guided by these foundations to improve education. This point was highlighted in a personal communication from Patricia Silvey, a member of one of our CoPs, who stated:

> As teachers of languages, I feel we all understood Mike's desire and endeavor to challenge ourselves to see how and where we could facilitate [ICC] through our respective languages. For many, it was most likely the first time thinking in this way: that Critical Cultural Awareness must be the backbone of all that we present to our students. ... I saw the proverbial wheels turning within each teacher to figure out how to make it happen not only in the collaborative lesson, but in all subsequent lessons. (6 October 2020)

We would be remiss if we did not mention the significance of this type of work at this moment in history where there is an urgent need to attend to vital educational and societal issues. In particular, teaching for ICC and ICit with its focus on knowing one's own perspective, considering and inviting the perspectives of others, helping each other understand their origins and implications and ensuring all voices are heard are just some ways that allow us to address critical classroom issues around bias, privilege, discrimination, inequity – to name a few. The focus on having students think critically about issues in their local community, together with the exploration of similar issues on larger scales (statewide, nationwide, worldwide), to consider possible solutions or actionable items, make it possible to bring to the forefront current societal problems for analysis, reflection and action. The development of interculturally competent citizens starts with a strong educational foundation. Beginning in pre-kindergarten and continuing throughout learners' educational experience and beyond, it nourishes mutual understanding and consideration of cultural and linguistic diversity, forming the basis for a healthy and prosperous development.

In this chapter, we bring theory to practice by highlighting the impact of Byram's scholarly contributions which helped deepen the work between language teachers and educators across disciplines. In particular, we focus on advancing understanding of the work of facilitators who engage, support and sustain CoPs working together on ICC and ICit. We offer our perspectives, interpretations and insights based on our personal experiences serving as facilitators. Consequently, before continuing, we include here a brief description of our professional backgrounds which have shaped and influenced our writing of this chapter.

Rita is the Director of World Languages/English Language Learning in the Glastonbury Public School District in Connecticut, USA. In this position, she is responsible for the direct supervision of the World Language and English Language Learning Departments, which includes hiring and maintaining highly skilled staff, targeted teacher professional development and implementation of curriculum development. In Glastonbury, Rita has supported a strong focus on Backwards Design and the use of Essential Questions to guide learning and is a strong proponent for teaching languages for ICC. Rita serves on numerous national boards with impact on K-16, presents regularly on district initiatives to colleagues around the world and has authored several articles and chapters about language education. She worked in collaboration with other members of the Glastonbury community to develop a statement for ICC which reads:

> Intercultural competence is not about knowing everything about another culture but rather recognizing cultural nuances and being able to adapt/ understand without judgment. It is understanding that culture is a very complex and changing concept and you cannot look at it just from the surface. It is not about answers, but rather the questions that are generated by curiosity and observation. (Comenale & Campbell, 2013)

Fabiana is a professor in the Department of Mathematics at the University of Connecticut, USA. Her research focuses on investigating methods to help learners acquire more flexible mathematical knowledge for improving their problem-solving skills, strategies to enhance learners' capacity to communicate their mathematical thinking and opportunities to integrate mathematical proficiency and communication skills to move students from learners to critical thinkers. Building from her work on mathematical argumentation and communication, she has concentrated on advancing the study of interdisciplinary curriculum development using the foundational theories of ICC and ICit in collaboration with experts in the field. This ongoing work has resulted in the development of courses, workshops, seminars and long-term projects for teachers and graduate students of different disciplines engaging them in the creation and implementation of ICC and ICit curriculum materials. She has disseminated this work through multiple presentations, articles and a co-authored book (Wagner *et al.*, 2019).

After much reflection and dialogue between us, we decided to tell the story of our journey. We base our writing on two separate projects working with CoPs consisting of K-12 teachers and graduate students of multiple subjects (mentioned above), with at least one member with language expertise. In one of them, Dr Manuela Wagner, Dorie Perugini and Rita were co-facilitators (see Wagner *et al.*, 2018), in the other the co-facilitators were Dr Manuela Wagner, Tara Vazquez and Fabiana (see Cardetti *et al.*, 2015). In this chapter, we begin with CoP's foundational background and defining characteristics, and we synthesize important points from the existing literature and also discuss major challenges that relate to our context. Then, we work through different stages that shaped our facilitators' work, each one paving the way for the next and setting the groundwork for successfully engaging educators in CoPs. Though our experiences were unique to our settings and projects, the groundwork of facilitating CoPs remained the same. Giving consideration to the interrelationship among theory, experience and practice, we incorporate throughout our discussion concrete examples of what we did, as well as excerpts from personal communications with members of these communities (started above).

Through this chapter, it is our hope that our story will help advance the understanding of facilitating the development of interdisciplinary CoPs particularly when educators are engaged in promoting and cultivating ICC and ICit.

Communities of Practice

A CoP is a well-known framework for collaborative learning that has been implemented in a wide range of educational and institutional settings to contribute to individual, organizational and social development (Churchman & Stehlik, 2007). Lave and Wenger (1991) first proposed the concept of CoPs as part of situated learning theory, which emphasizes that learning and forming who we are occurs in the process of engagement in social practice in a social setting with a network of people that reflects authentic activity, context, and culture. Wenger and colleagues (2002) broadened the original definition to include sharing in the network of a common concern, set of problems, or passion about a topic, and the deepening of knowledge and expertise through ongoing interaction. Participants are committed to share information and ideas, discuss common issues, produce tools and documents, which commonly results in the development of personal relationships. As trust and relationships build within the group, members become increasingly engaged and are more likely to share their knowledge and challenges with each other (Crosby, 2014). Burk (2000) posited that CoPs act as learning spaces which accelerate the sharing of knowledge and experiences, thus fostering innovation and creative problem-solving. The process of sharing information and experiences with the group helps the members to learn from each other and gives them the opportunity to develop themselves personally and professionally. Recently, Wenger-Trayner and Wenger-Trayner (2015: 3) presented three defining elements of a CoP that is summarized as follows:

Domain: The CoP's identity is defined by a shared domain of interest. Membership implies a commitment to the domain, a value for their collective competence and a motivation to learn from each other to grow in their understanding of the domain.

Community: In pursuing their interest in their domain, CoP members engage in collaborative activities and discussions, help each other and share what they know. They build relationships that enable them to learn from each other and care about their standing with each other.

Practice: Members of a CoP are practitioners. With time and sustained interaction, they develop a shared repertoire of resources: experiences, strategies, approaches to addressing recurring problems, lessons learned – a shared practice.

The combination of these three elements constitutes a CoP. And it is by developing these components in parallel that one cultivates a community. It is key for participants to interact on a regular basis and develop a shared repertoire of resources: experiences, stories, tools and ways of addressing recurring problems. In other words, the community creates a shared practice. Wenger (2002) maintains that becoming a more effective participant in society involves not only acquiring knowledge and skills but also becoming a member of a CoP. In our context, teaching and learning are major activities; therefore, the CoP must function as a community of learners, in which members participate in teaching and learning with other involved members. We use this approach to stimulate professional development among educators who are committed to learn how to infuse ICC and ICit into their curriculum.

Multiple studies have shown that teaching and learning improves when teachers collectively question their practice, examine new paradigms, find generative means to acknowledge and respond to difference and conflict and engage actively in mutually supporting their professional growth (Achinstein, 2002; Grossman *et al.*, 2001; Witziers *et al.*, 1999). A supportive CoP empowers educators' identities and strong collaboration increases their sense of personal responsibility for effective instruction (Louis, 1992). While these results are encouraging, barriers to collaborative work exist. These include a strong conception that teaching is a highly individualized practice; a marginalization of collaborative work based on the impression that working collaboratively results in washed out content; a belief that collaborations are a one-and-done effort that has no long-term effects; this is compounded by a feeling that collaboration is simply too hard, too time consuming and with no guarantees of success. In addition, for educators working within a school or university setting, challenges for collaboration include conflicting schedules and limited time, lack of institutional recognition, apprehension to, or fear of, innovation, as well as conflicting or divergent views of teaching purpose, objectives, and goals. For participants working at different educational levels (e.g. teachers, graduate students), the challenges are magnified by apparent detachment in mindsets, professional purpose and educational goals in spite of many clear and strong bonds in the type of work in which they are engaged. Often there is a lack of common professional norms and language; no (apparent) shared goals and sometimes the absence of a space to bring the participants together. These barriers resound and are heightened for participants working across disciplines where there are marked differences in terms of disciplinary and pedagogical practices, habits of mind, curriculum content and organizational cultures (Brown *et al.*, 2010). The institutional systems are generally not conducive to interdisciplinary collaboration, but rather reinforce the idea that people in different disciplines operate in 'silos' with little awareness of practices outside their own. These pose particular challenges for our students who are left to make sense of the important connections across their learning experiences on their own. This is especially concerning since the world outside school walls is faced with complex problems on which many different disciplines converge, each with an important contribution to offer.

Research has shown that some of these barriers can be overcome successfully (McDermott, 2004). We argue that many of these challenges can be mitigated when strong partnerships across different educational levels and disciplines are built to support the work of CoPs. In our case, Rita in her role of school administrator and expert in World Languages and Fabiana as a university faculty and expert in Mathematics, we represent different sides of these partnerships and can attest to their value. Research on successful CoPs also recognizes the crucial role of facilitators. For example, Ortquist-Ahrens and Torosyan (2008) assert that facilitators play 'an essential role in helping to create and sustain not only the structures but also the ethos that can foster genuine community, deep learning, and projects of significance' (2008: 32). The scholarly work that we have mentioned has been fundamental in clarifying the importance of CoPs and the critical elements that contribute to their success, yet the existing literature provides little in terms of the work of facilitators to successfully engage educators in CoPs that cross the boundaries of educational levels and disciplines. In this chapter, we aim to increase the understanding of the practices involved in facilitating CoPs who work to foster ICC and ICit. In making our results public, we aim to contribute to a public knowledgebase of this area within teacher education.

Engaging Educators Successfully at Every Phase

Even though we work in different organizations and at different educational systems, our work has important intersections. In general terms, we are both involved in supporting teachers' professional learning, development and growth, but more specifically, we see our roles in the facilitation of CoPs as complementary and dependent on each other. For this chapter, we engaged in a self-study of practice to unpack and understand the specific details and nuances of engaging educators in successful CoPs. According to Loughran and colleagues, self-study research is self-initiated and focused on intentionally and systematically investigating practices in order to improve them, and it is interactive, requiring the collaboration with others who could help challenge long-held assumptions or reveal potential blind spots (Loughran *et al.*, 2004).

Self-study research can be messy and complex; therefore, to help uncover the different components that characterize our work, we gathered data in different ways. We engaged in dialogue because, 'it often includes storytelling ... it allows for the social construction of knowledge, [it] can capture the distributed and dynamic nature of teacher cognition, [and it] provides opportunities to confront misconceptions' (LaBoskey, 2004: 851). Dialogue allowed us to engage in inquiry to help us better understand important aspects of our work, in our different venues, with different people, across different levels of the educational spectrum. This dialogue took place at weekly meetings over a period of five months. At every meeting, we both took notes to keep an account of the ideas and discussion points that surfaced. As the study evolved and the characteristics of our practice started to unfold, we created a document with the emerging findings that we polished based on our discussions. Moreover, between meetings, we independently reflected on our experiences addressing questions such as (a) Were there specifics about my work as a facilitator of CoPs that I would attribute to their success? (b) What is the role of ICC in the success of the CoPs? (c) How have CoPs influenced my experiences? Where is the crossover and what would we identify as our mutual understanding of CoPs? These reflections helped us trace our steps back to capture our different perspectives about the work of facilitating successful CoPs. As mentioned, we also consulted several colleagues who were members of our CoPs to share with us their takeaways from participating in these experiences, helping us ensure that important aspects of the work were not overlooked. This turned out to provide us with significant opportunities for further reflection and a shift in the story we wanted to share with our readers. Bringing their voices into our report of the findings enabled us to offer a more comprehensive picture that goes beyond our personal experiences and incorporates a hint of the impact that the CoPs had on the participants.

As a result of our self-study, we identified a series of facilitators' actions that, in our experience, lead to successfully engaging, supporting and sustaining the work of CoPs on ICC and ICit.

These actions follow sequentially from one another and can be categorized under six stages that form a cycle (Figure 14.1). That is, when the last stage is completed, new ideas and connections are made that serve as a bridge to start the cycle anew. Each stage in the cycle is described in detail in the subsequent sections where we elaborate on the identified different actions. Our discussions of the findings are further complemented with excerpts taken from our consultation described above. We identified and dated them to acknowledge participants' thoughtful insights that provide an invaluable dimension to our results.

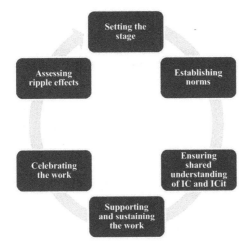

Figure 14.1 Six-stage cycle used to categorize facilitators' actions

(1) Setting the stage

As we analyzed our experiences with CoPs, a key finding emerged: the importance of a strong liaison from the school administration, specifically teacher leaders such as the curriculum coordinators or program directors as points of contact for planning and general endorsement of the work within the CoPs. Without their determination and drive, it is difficult to move projects forward and bring about any change. Their expertise in, and understanding of, the district goals, school dynamics and teacher interests as well as individual and collective needs help build the foundation on which the CoPs can form and flourish – recognizing that this cannot be realized without meaningful relationships between university faculty and teacher leaders. We also found that it was important that we understood our role to empower our group members, to help them find their voice, recognize each other's expertise and take ownership of their own learning and final products. In other words, regardless of our positions as school administrator or university faculty, we shared the view that 'facilitation is a way of providing leadership without taking the reins. As a facilitator, your job is to get others to assume responsibility and take the lead' (Bens, 2000: 7). In our examples, the leadership team consisted of the facilitators and Michael Byram.

Thinking about ways to provide professional opportunities to teachers and graduate students, we worked to remove any possible barriers that might impede participation. At the school level, this involved identifying areas for growth and bringing the professional learning experiences into the district for staff. This allowed for better participation and greater buy in and engagement. We worked collaboratively between school and university partners in order to support teachers' growth in current pedagogical theory while remaining in their home district as part of a professional learning initiative – a win-win experience. At both the school and the university level, securing funding to provide such experiences, without out-of-pocket expenses to the participants, also allowed for a more diverse audience.

We agreed that an important part of our work involved setting a welcoming environment with a low affective filter and assurances that all team members would grow in this work together, including the leaders. This really starts to build the foundational work of a CoP where we have opportunities to learn and grow from each other. One of our experiences involved offering the opportunity to participate in a graduate course on ICC, in-district, which set the groundwork for all that followed. As part of the ICC course, Glastonbury teachers selected the units they wished to work on, and students joined them in the effort. This is where the real learning began. Across all experiences, we took into account that teacher learning could occur while working on revisions of existing units they already earmarked as part of their work. With this in mind, mutually beneficial opportunities for teachers and graduate students can be offered through graduate courses, workshops or seminars around a topic of high interest, such as ICC and ICit, with the goal of using Byram's model to guide the modification or creation of the units. We consider it is important to provide an open invitation for teachers and graduate students to engage in these opportunities because it empowers participants to make a personal commitment to learning. We believe that this process ensures that everyone involved has shared intentions; a common purpose on which the CoPs are built.

We agreed that, as facilitators of CoPs, it was imperative for us to keep a pulse on the work of the participants, offering support for individuals and for the group in order to best maintain continued movement forward. Flexible grouping: graduate students, K-12 classroom teachers or a mixture of both, provided not only opportunities for each participant, but also challenges within each group or pair. Finding time to work together with academic schedules that were not aligned (university vs. K-12 education), as well as time to dedicate to the different courses and particular units of study were the most significant hurdles. Conflicts between the varying schedules and different personal commitments can be frustrating especially when deadlines are looming. On the other hand, the opportunity to learn from each other and see the work through different lenses provides stimulus for growth for each group, personally and professionally, especially when trying to unite around a common goal of deepening the understanding of ICC through shared work. This is where the members of the CoP need to feel comfortable to reach out, not only to the group mates but also to others for guidance and assistance. Talking through complicated work and embracing the thoughts of others has great value, but there needs to be a sense of safety and openness to admit vulnerabilities – elaborated more in the next section. Working with the facilitators and team members develops bonds and forms a strong CoP that unfolds as the team grows in their understanding of ICC and how to address the different components of Byram's model. Each group met with different levels of success, but everyone deepened their commitment to a goal and a belief that they could make a valuable contribution to the profession.

(2) Establishing norms

Effective collaboration requires a lot from everyone involved, and this is intensified by the fact that collaboration across groups can be challenging. As facilitators, we put these issues on the table for everyone to consider from the start, even before our large groups separated to form smaller groups where they would delve into the work of developing units. We made sure to foster a collaborative environment for the entire group and bring forth the message that for each CoP to be successful, all of us needed to pay attention to the conditions that would allow all members to thrive. Our approach for this has been to establish group norms; sometimes implicitly and other times explicitly depending on what would flow more naturally for the group. This work is not straightforward and requires determination as expressed by Steven LeMay, a Math member of one of our CoPs, who said:

> It took a not insignificant amount of effort for our group to unpack and make explicit the norms and methods of communication that various communities subconsciously implement. These ways of belonging in a community sometimes misalign when working interdependently. ... effort had to be made to ensure effective communication and mutual understanding. (personal communication, 10 October 2020)

It is important to highlight that when the work of the CoPs is focused on ICC and ICit, the team needs to be able, and comfortable, to share their understanding and ideas, even when these may expose misunderstandings or involve conflicting views. Thus, our work as facilitators included making sure group norms were in place to promote supportive yet challenging conversations. Our teacher participants welcomed the opportunity to discuss ideas and materials related to their work with others in the group, making the initial conversations easy to foster. Yet, discussions that support critical examination of teaching are more challenging. Such conversations must occur, however, if CoP members are to collectively explore ways of improving school students' experiences and support one another as they work to develop new teaching materials. To foster such discussions, we found that we needed to help CoP members develop communication norms that would enable critical dialogue while respecting individual community members yet critically analyzing possibilities and contributions. Achieving this was done in part by modeling it ourselves, creating opportunities for discussions that called for dissenting views or opinions or where the topic of discussion would be struggles or difficulties, and making the center of attention our (the facilitators') personal experiences. Putting our own vulnerabilities on the table and guiding the discussion toward a generative dialogue, rather than allowing it to drown our conversation or turn to it to blame toward ourselves or our students, helped demonstrate how to engage in productive discussions about sensitive issues. In addition, because our work revolved around ICC, where othering, essentialism and stereotyping are critically explored, this modeling naturally had a positive influence in the attitudes, behaviors and dispositions within the CoPs that implicitly informed the groups' norms.

We also made sure to build in time for members to get to know each other in informal settings. Prior to beginning the substantive work of each project, we created opportunities for them to exchange ideas, food, experiences and knowledge, all of which assisted with building rapport and trust within our communities and with us. In fact, developing these relationships with participants provided us with an additional layer of understanding of what they knew and how they were thinking that allowed us to better support and champion their work. The benefit is mutual, as participants got to know us at a deeper level, encouraging them to approach us openly to resolve difficulties and feed off our excitement to push past initial hesitation as expressed by Patricia when she was reflecting about Michael Byram's passion and the effect it had on the group:

> That came through loud and clear each time ... I could feel [Byram's] strength of passion as he spoke about his theoretical models and how they could and should be implemented across all grade levels. It is due to his passion that all tiers of collaborators were so willing to work together on the creation of the IC lessons. (personal communication, 6 October 2020)

(3) Ensuring a shared understanding of ICC and ICit

> ... what makes Byram's model particularly powerful is its emphasis on reflecting upon experiences and backgrounds. This leads to finding, germinating, and maintaining sustainable pathways of understanding. (Steve Lemay, personal communication, 10 October 2020)

Developing a shared understanding is crucial for the success of any opportunities presented to the CoPs and possible only when partnerships are made with school districts where there is an understanding of the importance of ICC and ICit for the improvement of learning and a commitment to learning more about the theories for the creation of learning experiences that can be implemented in the classrooms.

Whether members of the CoP were attending graduate ICC courses as teachers or graduate students, or joining as members of a funded project, all had different background knowledge of ICC. Some had prior knowledge from previous coursework or training, while others were learning about it for the first time. Consequently, before sending CoPs to start working on their independent projects, we created opportunities to achieve common ground for everyone to develop a more profound understanding of ICC and ICit. This was achieved, for example, through extended discussions, unpacking the nuances of the theory and analysis of several models, attending to what they are, how they originated, what they are intended for, which gaps they help fill, how they are important for each subject, and also how we nourish agency in students, in which ways can students engage with their communities and take action in the world, among others. Ultimately, we focused on Byram's model since it has been developed purposefully for education, it is comprehensive yet straightforward, and its components are clear. His ICit theory is powerful and helpful in attending to students' agency and taking action. We do not want to give the wrong impression that this is an easy task to accomplish, the richness and complexity in ICC and ICit cannot be understated. This sentiment was echoed by Patricia, who commented that '[it] *takes a great deal of dedication and perseverance to work with diverse groups, teaching styles and districts to accomplish an understanding and implementation of [the] model*' (personal communication, 6 October 2020).

Through multiple group discussions about curricular cases, uncovering the potential of the theories and the model, and how these connect to practice and specifically to their own practice, allowed us to achieve a shared understanding. Then, we could move to considering the practical applications that involved identifying specific teaching goals that could be fulfilled with achievable and realistic learning objectives. Participants' newly-formed understandings of ICC, especially the model's focus on understanding different perspectives, predisposed the members to work together to enact what they were hoping the students would learn. Critical thinking and creativity were challenged as the participants took risks to go deeper in their understanding of ICC as they developed the units.

While ICC has been present as an underlying concept in world languages, its actual realization in curriculum and classroom instruction has remained latent (Kearney, 2019). Teachers are not regularly teaching for ICC in ways that are reflected in the curriculum and instruction. In this regard, ICC remains in its infancy in K-12 classrooms. Relatedly, over the past decade, the curriculum standards for content and practice in Science, Mathematics and Social Studies, among other subjects are calling for classrooms where students engage in authentic exploration of problems that affect their lives and communities. These changes reflect the need for students to learn to handle and evaluate the emergent, ambiguous, contradictory and context-dependent nature of problems through which they can learn to make informed, reasoned decisions. Subject teachers are called to support their students' development of critical thinking and robust communication skills that are seen as essential for students' active participation in society. These calls are ambitious and require a great deal from teachers who have not been prepared for this type of work. CoP's look to world languages as a place where empathy and multicultural understanding affords opportunities for deepening understanding of the knowledge, attitudes and skills that are inherently needed today. Reaching out to world languages offers CoPs the opportunity to collaborate in inter-disciplinary work which deepens understanding across subjects. The work that takes place in these classrooms is challenging, takes time and involves a process that never ends. Establishing ICC and ICit as the core of the work binds all the subjects together to overcome challenges and address new demands. Madelyn Colonnese, whose expertise is in Curriculum and Instruction, commented on the impact that having participated in our CoP's work with ICC has had in her current work. She explained that

> ... the idea of critical cultural awareness is an important concept in understanding the multiple mathematical funds of knowledge children bring into the classroom. ... the work in [the CoP] has helped me to better understand the concept of cultural and linguistic funds of knowledge, so I can more effectively provide my preservice teachers with experiences to help them learn this too. (personal communication, 12 October 2020)

(4) Supporting and sustaining the work

Because our groups were a mix of graduate students and teachers who came from different contexts with different backgrounds, we learned that communities are more robust when CoPs form spontaneously, based on their compatible interests and commitment to the work; thus, we argue holding back on suggestions for grouping unless requested by them. As facilitators, we acknowledge that it is also important to be flexible regarding the decisions groups make about how they prefer to work together, their day-to-day dynamics and also what they choose for their 'final' product. The 'buy in' on the part of the participants is imperative to the success of their work. The rigor is in following Byram's model which offers a systematic guideline to address the needs of the students. We admittedly dedicated a significant amount of time to uncover the most favorable conditions and opportunities in order to be able to address the needs and strengths within each CoP as well as to obtain a solid understanding about how each of us could help support and sustain the momentum as work progressed.

We found that an important part of supporting the work of CoPs is to provide them with logistical and subject-matter support. Selecting a place and time for us to work together regularly, respecting the participants' availability, brings a layer of accountability that the team needs and values. We also provided structure to the meetings to help advance the work. In whole group meetings, these can vary from organized whole-group discussions of readings and ideas to CoP's brainstorm sessions.

We also found we need to build structures for the sustainability of the work of our groups. To address this, specific times are also built in for regular check-in points where CoPs describe their progress, their plans or any changes/struggles. When struggles arise due to barriers across educational levels or disciplinary boundaries, we help them overcome these by facilitating and mediating negotiations to find common ground and ultimately bring their ideas to fruition (Ortquist-Ahrens & Torosyan, 2008). At other points in the work, adjustments are necessary to help them strike a balance between missed opportunities or ideas that are too grandiose. During these check-in points, critical feedback is essential to move forward with the work, which community norms and collegial atmosphere make possible. As time progresses, these check-in points become more focused with finer grains of specificity. Aside from feedback and encouragement from the facilitators, we organize the CoPs into feedback partners, where groups take turns to update each other and request/provide feedback to move forward. If time allows, several pairing rounds can be organized. This continues until products are ready for classroom implementation.

While teachers hold the expertise and knowledge about implementation of lessons in their classrooms, decisions on how to do it are made collaboratively in the CoPs, resulting in co-teaching, or a member as a classroom aid, or running the class independently. The support of school administrators is invaluable for reaching this point, and in our experiences, having one as facilitator has proven to be an important component of success. Whether or not everyone in the CoP is involved in the classroom implementation, we create opportunities for all team members to reflect on it. We provide guiding questions for them to consider and discuss, that allow them to focus on how it went, so they can make informed decisions about adjustments or modifications for future implementations or consider new directions or ideas. We have found that this reflective work can be reinforced and enriched when this work includes concrete products they need to create to bring their work outside of our own community: writing proposals for presentations at conferences, drafting articles that can be submitted for publication and/or preparing slide presentations. Our work focuses on structuring and coordinating collaborations, which address challenges and barriers we have mentioned earlier in this chapter, so that CoPs can flourish and endure.

(5) Celebrating the work

At this stage of the CoPs' development, a central goal for us is to help bring public visibility to the exceptional outcomes of the work. Through this study, we have come to understand that in doing this, we have been addressing one of the challenges of engaging in collaborations. People hesitate to go through the tremendous efforts which might go unnoticed outside of the collaborative groups and which seldom receive recognition at institutional or professional levels.

As facilitators, we look for ways to build the momentum that has been created to celebrate the work already completed while also expanding participants' networking connections for potential professional opportunities. With encouragement and support a CoP can deepen experiences through contributions to a broader community of learners in many different ways. Joan Campbell, Curriculum Director of German Studies and CoP member, commented on the power of extending the work beyond the personal experience saying, 'For my colleagues, participation in a research study suddenly went from being something complicated that can only take place on campus at a university to action research that can help us all in our everyday lives as teachers' (emphasis added, personal communication, 12 October 2020).

We arranged for CoP members to give presentations in school meetings or in seminars at the university. We sought funding opportunities to hold special events, where participants could disseminate their work to a wide audience. Many times, their proposals were successful, allowing our participants to present at professional conferences or publishing articles showcasing the results of the CoP experience. We also offered the opportunity to collaborate on co-authoring chapters that captured participants' work on their curriculum units as well as their personal and professional growth over time in ICC (Wagner et al., 2018). As always, this professional opportunity was offered to anyone who was interested, committed and open to collaborating with CoP partners on such work. Engagement in any of these opportunities needs to be encouraged and supported by the facilitators as it can be exciting yet daunting to take the first steps forward.

(6) Assessing the ripple effects

We have seen and experienced the transformative power of the collective work for ICC and ICit, not only on specific curricular changes, but also in how it nourishes individual ICC growth. We have noticed significant ripple effects among participants, students and ourselves. It is important not to lose sight of the continuing and expanding results of the work. Assessing these ripple effects helps us better understand the broader influence of the work which in turn serves to uncover new opportunities. Probing new ideas and exploring potential opportunities from these ripple effects prompts us to restart the cycle.

One cannot underestimate the impact that these learning experiences, infused with ICC and ICit, have on a school student. Taking a deep dive into the knowledge, skills and attitudes of a person or culture opens doors to develop a deeper appreciation for and understanding of 'the other'. This was evidenced on multiple occasions by our CoPs and specifically by Spanish teacher Jocelyn Tamborello-Noble, who commented:

> *This impacted me as an educator, students still talk about the projects, I ran into a student who is now a World Language teacher, who told me that project led to her understanding of how important the role of a World Language teacher is. World Language teachers change the world, and open communities and bring the world to a classroom.* (personal communication, 28 September 2020)

As we have noted in the stages above, each CoP member grew as a result of the foundational work we did. The lens through which they view the world is very different now and continues to evolve, sometimes presenting frustrations where opportunities are not heeded as quickly as one would hope. The work is intense, and time is needed to embrace all the possibilities. For others, the ICC work becomes a springboard for personal and professional opportunities as Dorie Conlon Perugini explained,

> *this experience has impacted me professionally the most. ... [it] led me to begin a PhD in Applied Linguistics and Discourse Studies with Manuela Wagner as my advisor so I could continue research in this area. I now work with districts around the country helping them implement Mike Byram's model in K-12 contexts. ... my students are encouraged to reflect deeply about intercultural topics both in school and beyond.* (personal communication, 2 October 2020)

As facilitators, we feel a sense of urgency to keep the momentum going and a sense of responsibility to ensure that this is not a one and done experience. We look for new opportunities to work with the CoPs to further the initial work or explore other possibilities within their curriculum. The ripple effects have resulted in new partnerships within the same schools or with other schools/districts. In schools, we have provided a sample Student Learning Objective for ICC as part of the teacher evaluation plan to help them incorporate ICC into units and lessons with more fidelity and purpose, identify action steps and anticipate evidence into the yearlong goal. At the university level, we have created new courses, workshops and seminars for ICC and ICit, and it has inspired us to explore connections with related lines of research including Intellectual Humility, Human Rights education and Service Learning.

Conclusion

In this chapter, we have elaborated on our experience facilitating CoPs anchored around the themes of ICC and ICit, suggesting and elucidating many complex areas of this work. Drawing on our different backgrounds, we examined our roles to help us unpack the practices that support the work of CoPs for the professional development of educators across different educational levels and disciplines. Concentrating on what we believe helped make our CoPs successful, we have highlighted the importance of strong partnerships between facilitators who represent both the practical and the theoretical perspectives, in our case curriculum developers and university faculty. Our self-study rendered a detailed description of practices that capture how we enact our roles through a cycle of stages that follow our journey. Through this work, we have added to the body of literature about engaging, managing and guiding educators in fruitful CoP work. There is work still to be done in all areas of what we have presented, insights gained from design and research efforts in one area will undoubtedly lead to ideas for new projects in other areas. We have provided practical ideas for readers who would like to take on this fulfilling work that incorporates Byram's model and theories of ICC and citizenship in our efforts to better prepare our students to navigate the complexities of life.

Acknowledgements

We would like to thank all participants for their dedication to the work in the CoPs, particularly Joan Campbell, Madelyn Colonnese, Dorie Conlon Perugini, Kyle Evans, Steven LeMay, Patrica Silvey, Jocelyn Tamborello-Noble and Deane Wallace for sharing their thoughtful insights with us. Because of space limitations, we could not include everything they shared. Thanks to Manuela for encouraging us to write this piece and providing the opportunity to get to know Michael Byram, whose life's work has had an immense impact on education and whose positive attitude, clarity of thought and humble demeanor inspire us to continue this transformative work for ourselves and our teachers, ultimately bettering the future of our students.

References

Achinstein, B. (2002) *Community, Diversity, and Conflict Among Schoolteachers: The Ties That Blind*. New York, NY: Teachers College Press.
Bens, I. (2000) *Facilitating with Ease! A Step-by-Step Guidebook*. San Francisco, CA: Jossey-Bass.
Brown, V.A., Deane, P.M., Harris, J.A. and Russell, J.Y. (2010) Towards a sustainable future. In J.A. Harris, V.A. Brown and J.Y. Russell (eds) *Tackling Wicked Problems: Through the Transdisciplinary Imagination* (pp. 16–30). London: Earthscan.
Burk, M. (2000) Communities of practice. *Public Roads* 63 (6), 18–22.
Byram, M. (1997) *Teaching and Assessing Intercultural Communicative Competence*. Clevedon: Multilingual Matters.
Byram, M. (2008) *From Foreign Language Education to Education for Intercultural Citizenship: Essays and Reflection*. Clevedon: Multilingual Matters.

Cardetti, F., Wagner, M. and Byram, M. (2015) Interdisciplinary collaboration to develop intercultural competence by integrating math, languages, and social studies. *NERA Proceedings* 2015, 7.

Churchman, D. and Stehlik, T. (2007) Transforming academic work: Communities of practice in Australian universities. *Journal of Organisational Transformation and Social Change* 4 (3), 263–278.

Comenale, R. and Campbell, L. (2013) Unpublished official Glastonbury Public Schools Foreign Language Department Position Statement on Intercultural Competence, developed during ICC Workshop with Manuela Wagner.

Crosby, C. (2014) Communities in the workplace. In U. de Stricker (ed.) *Knowledge Management Practice in Organizations: The View from Inside* (pp. 98–112). Toronto: Information Science Reference.

Grossman, P., Wineburg, S. and Woolworth, S. (2001) Toward a theory of teacher community. *The Teachers College Record* 103, 942–1012.

Hadar, L. and Brody, D. (2010) From isolation to symphonic harmony: Building a professional development community among teacher educators. *Teaching and Teacher Education* 26 (8), 1641–1651.

Kearney, E. (2019) Professional (re)visions of language teaching for interculturality. In B. Dupuy and K. Michelson (eds) *Pathways to Paradigm Change: Critical Examinations of Prevailing Discourses and Ideologies in Second Language Education. AAUSC Issues in Language Program Direction* (pp. 248–281). Boston, MA: Heinle Cengage.

LaBoskey, V.K. (2004) The methodology of self-study and its theoretical underpinnings. In J.J. Loughran, M.L. Hamilton, V.K. LaBoskey and T. Russell (eds) *International Handbook of Self-study of Teaching and Teacher Education Practices* (pp. 817–869). Dordrecht, the Netherlands: Kluwer.

Lave, J. and Wenger, E. (1991) *Situated Learning: Legitimate Peripheral Participation.* Cambridge: Cambridge University Press.

Loughran, J., Hamilton, M.L., LaBoskey, V. and Russell, T. (eds) (2004) *International Handbook of Self-study of Teaching and Teacher Education Practices.* Dordrecht, the Netherlands: Kluwer.

Louis, K.S. (1992) Restructuring and the problem of teachers' work. In A. Lieberman (ed.) *The Changing Contexts of Teaching* (Vol. 1, pp. 138–156). Chicago, IL: University of Chicago Press.

McDermott, R. (2004) How to avoid a mid-life crisis in your CoPs: Uncovering six keys to sustaining communities. *Knowledge Management Review* 4 (2), 10–13.

Ortquist-Ahrens, L. and Torosyan, R. (2008) The role of the facilitator in faculty learning communities: Paving the way for growth, productivity, and collegiality. *Learning Communities Journal* 1 (1), 1–34.

Tannehill, D. and MacPhail, A. (2017) Teacher empowerment through engagement in a learning community in Ireland: Working across disadvantaged schools. *Professional Development in Education* 43 (3), 334–352.

Wagner, M., Cardetti, F. and Byram, M. (2019) *Teaching Intercultural Citizenship Across the Curriculum: The Role of Language Education.* Alexandria, VA: ACTFL.

Wagner, M., Conlon Perugini, D. and Byram, M. (eds) (2018) *Teaching Intercultural Competence Across the Age Range: From Theory to Practice.* Bristol: Multilingual Matters.

Wenger, E., McDermott, R. and Snyder, W. C. (2002) *Cultivating Communities of Practice.* Boston, MA: Harvard Business School Press.

Wenger-Trayner, E. and Wenger-Trayner, B. (2015) *Communities of Practice: A Brief Introduction.* Retrieved from http://wenger-trayner.com/wp-content/uploads/2015/04/07-Brief-introduction-to-communities-of-practice.pdf

Witziers, B., Sleegers, P. and Imants, J. (1999) Departments as teams: Functioning, variations and alternatives. *School Leadership and Management* 19 (3), 293–304.

15 Developing Intercultural Citizenship and Intellectual Humility in High School German

Manuela Wagner and
José Aldemar Álvarez Valencia

Introduction

As the current global pandemic surrounding Covid-19 has made abundantly clear, we live in an interconnected world in which we need to solve problems together to survive. Intercultural competence (IC) has received attention in recent years as a crucial asset for students to engage in dialogue – and solve problems – with people from different cultural backgrounds. Various organizations such as the Council of Europe (CoE) and the American Council on the Teaching of Foreign Languages (ACTFL) advocate for the teaching and learning of languages from an intercultural orientation as a way to promote cultural and social equity, diversity and inclusion (see Chapters 4 and 13, this volume). A growing body of educational research reports on projects in which the model of Intercultural Communicative Competence (ICC) (Byram, 1997) has been applied to teach intercultural knowledge, skills and attitudes (e.g. for book-length collections of projects see Byram *et al.*, 2001; Wagner *et al.*, 2018b). Other work has focused on Intercultural Citizenship (ICit) (Byram, 2008), which includes an action component to address a societal problem in the here and now, requiring students to have an impact in local, national and international communities (see, for example, projects presented in Byram *et al.*, 2017; Wagner *et al.*, 2019). Although the work on intercultural competence began in world language education, it has been extended to other subjects such as mathematics and social studies to foster students' collaborative skills and enhance specific content knowledge in these subject areas while also advancing students' development of ICit (see Cardetti *et al.*, 2015, 2019; Wagner *et al.*, 2019).

At the same time, concerns are accumulating about an increase in xenophobic rhetoric (e.g. Lee, 2021), a resistance to facts and a tendency towards arrogance, and people on social media spending time in echo chambers rather than engaging with each other, resulting in what Lynch (2019) calls the 'know-it-all society'. Due to the potential of intellectual humility (IH) and ICit to be supportive of public deliberation and collaborative problem-solving, Wagner *et al.* (2018a) started unpacking the relationship between the theory of ICC (e.g. Byram, 1997) and the notion of IH. They found that IH, which can be described as owning the limitations of one's knowledge (e.g. Whitcomb *et al.*, 2017), shared similarities with ICC with respect to its essence, as well as attention to processes of facilitating communication among members from different groups and/or about divisive issues. Given that the two theories share basic characteristics, the integration of IH in ICC offers the promise of a deeper understanding of ICC and vice versa. With this in mind, this chapter intends to explore how the teaching and learning of ICC and ICit can be supported through applications of IH in an L2 (German language) classroom. Below we present a case study in which we worked with one teacher to integrate aspects of IH into an ICit unit developed for a high school German class in the Northeast of the USA. We draw on an interview with this teacher to explore how she experienced the implementation of aspects of ICC and IH and how she perceived students' learning engagement.

Intercultural Citizenship and Intellectual Humility: Points of Convergence

The concept of ICit (Byram, 2008) emerges as a complement to Byram's ICC model, which consists of attitudes, such as openness and curiosity, knowledge, skills of interpreting and relating, skills of discovery and interaction, and critical cultural awareness (Byram, 2021). In Byram's model of ICC, these dimensions of intercultural competence combine with linguistic, sociolinguistic and discourse competences to provide learners with tools to mediate interaction with speakers of other languages or other social groups transnationally or intranationally. ICit draws on principles of language and political education and provides a basis for curriculum planning and outcomes in schools and higher education. Although learners usually receive education to become active citizens within their own countries, Byram (2008) emphasizes that the role of language education is to develop students' knowledge, skills and attitudes to become intercultural citizens who can negotiate meaning and solve problems together with those from different backgrounds.

The role of the language teacher is central in ICit education since teachers are expected to help learners develop the communicative and intercultural resources that they will require to engage in intercultural activities. Essentially, education for ICit implies:

- causing/facilitating intercultural citizenship experience, which includes activities of working with others to achieve an agreed end;

- analysis and reflection on the experience and on the possibility of further social and/or political activity;
- thereby creating learning that is cognitive, attitudinal, behavioral change in the individual;
- and a change in self-perception, in relationships with people of different social groups. (Wagner & Byram, 2017: 3–4)

As mentioned above, at the theoretical level, some initial work has established connections between ICC/ICit and IH. IH has its roots in Philosophy (e.g. Tanesini, 2016) and has since been investigated in a variety of fields, including Psychology (e.g. Deffler *et al.*, 2016) and Education (e.g. Kidd, 2016; Paul & Elder, 2002). In the philosophical literature, some conceptualize IH as one unified trait while others consider it a collection of related traits (Johnson *et al.*, 2017). Another way of conceptualizing IH, according with Roberts and Wood (2003: 258), is 'in connection with their vice-counterparts', in specific opposite to a number of vices, including arrogance, vanity, conceit, egotism, grandiosity, pretentiousness, snobbishness, impertinence (presumption), haughtiness, self-righteousness, domination, selfish ambition and self-complacency (2003: 257–258). Several researchers in education, who have conducted research in the field of educational psychology, have also emphasized the importance of IH in education (Baehr, 2016; Hazlett, 2016; Kidd, 2016; Paul & Elder, 2002).

Whitcomb *et al.* (2017: 520) indicate that 'IH consists in proper attentiveness to, and owning of, one's intellectual limitations'. They emphasize that IH can only be considered an intellectual virtue when 'one is appropriately motivated to pursue epistemic goods, e.g. truth, knowledge, and understanding' (2017: 520) and make 19 'predictions related to a variety of activities, motivations, and feelings' of a person who is intellectually humble. Many of these predictions align with ICC descriptors, such as Prediction 2 which states that 'IH reduces both a person's propensity to pretend to know something when he doesn't and his confidently answering a question whether or not he knows the answer' (2017: 522). In terms of ICC, it relates with Attitudes: individuals' 'willingness to question their taken for granted cultural knowledge, values and presuppositions and the capacity to take up 'other's perspectives in order to contrast and compare with the dominant evaluations in their own society' (Byram, 2021: 63). Other predictions connect directly with ICC and critical intercultural awareness. As an illustration, Prediction 14 posits that 'IH increases a person's propensity to have a clearer picture of what he knows and justifiedly believes and what he neither knows nor justifiedly believes' (Whitcomb *et al.*, 2017: 525). By pointing at the need for a justified criterion to sustain a person's source of knowledge and beliefs, this prediction relates to Byram's descriptor that intends learners to 'evaluate, critically and on the basis of an explicit, systematic process of reasoning, values present in one's own and other cultures and countries' (Byram, 2021: 66). In short, at the theoretical level, the connection between ICC/ICit and IH has been established

(Wagner *et al.*, 2018a); however, this connection needs to be explored at the pedagogical level, which is the focus of the current case study.

Overview of the Case Study

The exploratory case study presented here is part of a larger study entitled 'Intellectual Humility and Intercultural Citizenship across the disciplines' aimed at investigating the relationship between ICit and IH which was made possible through the support funding from Humility and Conviction in Public Life (https://humilityandconviction.uconn.edu/). Institutional Review Board approval to conduct the study was obtained. One of the Principal Investigators (PI), Manuela, has a long-standing relationship with the public school district in which the study was conducted. The teacher of German, for whom we use the pseudonym Joan, and, Manuela, had collaborated in prior projects related to ICC and ICit. Therefore, Joan was already familiar with the concepts related to ICC and ICit. When we asked Joan if she was interested in integrating IH, she agreed to be part of the study. She decided, together with the research team, that a visit by 14 students from their partner school in Bavaria, Germany, which would happen around the time of the study, would be an excellent opportunity to implement a unit that fostered the skills of ICC that integrated IH in an intentional manner.

The PIs then modified a unit on sports to integrate components of ICC and IH throughout the unit. Two consultants for the grant, Michael Byram and Heather Battaly, provided input along the way. Joan indicated that she was excited about implementing the prepared unit and felt that she had enough material to do so. The PIs and Michael also visited the school and gave a presentation on ICC, ICit and IH to teachers in the World Languages Department before the unit implementation. Joan then implemented the unit that had curricular components in German, Health, and Mathematics and extracurricular components, such as a soccer game and diverse events that were part of the exchange. Unit implementation lasted about five weeks. After the implementation, Joan (J) participated in a semi-structured interview with the PIs Manuela (M) and Fabiana (F) to shed light on the perceived impact of the unit on the students' development of ICC and IH. The interview was about 40 minutes long.

Below we share the unit that was designed for implementation. We prepared the ICit unit separately from the IH components to give Joan the choice to integrate activities to foster IH as she saw fit.

Unit prepared for implementation with German students and visitors from Germany

Context: The unit was developed for a second-year German class which consisted of 24 students (primarily 10th graders) and their 18 student visitors from Germany. The enrollment by race and ethnicity in the school district in America over the past years has consisted of about 77% to 80% White, around 5% each African American and Asian and between 7% and 8% Multi Race, Non-Hispanic. The school scores above average in student achievement data in the state.

Description of the unit: The unit dealt with sports and leisure activities. This coincided with both the Sport / Freizeit (leisure activities) chapter of Prima 2.2, the textbook that Joan used in this course, and the visit of exchange partners from Germany with whom they engaged in various sports activities both inside and outside of the classroom. The unit included presentations by the German students on the Bundesliga (the German soccer championship), an explanation of baseball by the American students, and it usually culminated in an authentic Bavarian sports competition.

Based on this unit, the PIs prepared the following ICit unit.

(1) In the first step, the American students read a webpage (in German) on challenges in sports in Germany. The students visiting from Germany read a webpage in English that provided interesting facts about sports in America.

(2) The students were asked to reflect on the following questions in their homework:

Does anything strike you as odd/weird?
Which are the three things you found most interesting/surprising?
Which of these interesting facts are specific to the culture (American or German)?
Can you identify one or two things that you would not find in your own country?

The American students were also asked to prepare two to three questions in German that they would ask their German classmates to get more information about the specific topic. The German students did the same in English. In German classes, all students generally spoke German. Outside of class, both languages were used.

This was planned as the knowledge discovery phase in which students had to interpret information from a different context and relate it to their own. The first question was used to elicit any preconceived notions and to help the teacher understand where students might need more information to make a judgment based on specific evidence later on in the unit.

(3) In the next step, students asked each other their prepared questions, treating their informants as experts.

Students were also asked to complete a table like the one below with their own beliefs. Here, we elicited stereotypes students might have had about the other or their own cultures. We provided only some examples

Table 15.1 Exploring students' stereotypes about sports

About USA	About Germany
Americans are the best at all sports	Soccer is not a real sport/is boring
Cheerleading is not a sport	The Germans are not good at baseball
In sports we do not discriminate against others. OR There is no racial discrimination in sports	

and asked students to prepare their own tables. As can be seen in the table, we presented an example of looking at societal issues related to sports and asked about racial discrimination. We signaled to students that they could address more serious topics. This step still was planned to foster the skills of 'interpreting and relating' in the model of ICC.

(4) In the next step, students were 'detectives of facts' (Faktendetektive) and needed to confirm or disconfirm the statements in their tables by interviewing their German classmates. They made conclusions based on their interviews of at least five students and the information they had found out in different ways. This encouraged students to use their critical cultural awareness to make judgments about products, practices and perspectives, based on specific criteria. Students received input representing different perspectives, for example, for the different documents they researched, the interviews with their peers visiting from Germany and from the teachers. Students then represented their information/data so that their conclusions could be understood from these representations.

For their data analysis, we recommended that they look at findings from the interviews. How often was their opinion confirmed or disconfirmed? In this step, Joan collaborated with a Mathematics teacher. The students represented their data mathematically with the help of the Mathematics teacher. At the end, the question that elicited their critical cultural awareness and judgment about 'the other' was 'Was ist nun deine Meinung?' ('What is your opinion now?')

(5) Now that students used their skills of interpreting and relating (Steps 1 and 2), discovery and interaction (Step 3), and their critical cultural awareness to make a judgment based on specific evidence (Step 4), they were asked how they could present their conclusions to each other and how they could perhaps share these within their respective communities.

(6) The next step entailed action in the community, a crucial component of ICit (Byram, 2008). We suggested that, in mixed groups, students could prepare (in German) posters about sports in the USA as part of the report/exhibition the German group will present to their school. They also could prepare posters in English for the American school

reporting on the visit of the German students. One idea was to invite members of the school community and have some food available. This could become the basis of a critical discussion: e.g. If we found there is discrimination in sports 'in the other country' does that happen here as well?

Joan shared later that she had to modify the activities described in Point 6 due to time constraints. Joan's students and the visitors interacted with other students in several curricular events (Mathematics class, Health class) and extracurricular events (farewell party, sports events, etc.) and engaged in critical discussions with the community outside the German class that way.

Activities suggested for discussing and integrating Intellectual Humility

Joan also received a handout with explanations of IH and activities supporting a choice of predictions proposed by Whitcomb and colleagues (2017) that seemed most closely related to and supportive of components of ICC. For example, for Prediction 2 mentioned above related to 'a person's propensity to pretend to know something when he doesn't' (Whitcomb *et al.*, 2017: 522), we suggested an activity based on a modified KWL chart in which K refers to what students know about the topic, W refers to what they would like to know (e.g. Who? What? Where? When? Why? How?), and L refers to what the students learned. The modification consisted of an added 'S' for including sources so that students are nudged to back up their findings and analyze the reliability of the information. As a next step, we suggested that teachers debrief with the students what their findings were. Sample reflection questions included, 'What did other people know that you did not know and vice versa?' and 'How will you go about learning what you need to know?'

The next four characteristics of IH have to do with taking into account different perspectives and critically analyzing information based on specific evidence. These features of IH clearly relate with developing critical cultural awareness. For example, listening to the views of others can help students gain insights into different perspectives and gain new knowledge; critically analyzing one's own beliefs and comparing them to beliefs held by others, especially, those who disagree, could help correct one's false beliefs.

IH increases a person's propensity:

- *to revise a cherished belief or reduce confidence in it, when she learns of defeaters (i.e. reasons to think her belief is false or reasons to be suspicious of her grounds for it).*

- to consider alternative ideas, to listen to the views of others, and to spend more time trying to understand someone with whom he disagrees.
- to have a clearer picture of what he knows and justifiedly believes and what he neither knows nor justifiedly believes.
- to hold a belief with the confidence that her evidence merits.

(Whitcomb *et al.*, 2017: 524–525)

We addressed these points with the 'fact detective' activity below. Additionally, we suggested that students could write a journal entry at home or, with sufficient scaffolding, in class. The questions below served as guiding questions for the students' inquiry about their beliefs.

(1) You investigated several statements about sports in _____. Were there statements you believed before but changed your mind about after your investigation? Please explain.
(2) What were the reasons for you changing your mind?
(3) Do you think you have all the evidence you need to know the 'correct' answer to your question now? In other words, do you know for sure you know whether the statement is true or not? If so, how and why? If not, what else would you need to do to find out?
(4) What was the most important lesson for you in this activity? Did you learn something you consider important? If so, what was that? Is there something you would now like to share with your friends who have not completed this activity?

We also suggested a mind map activity aimed at creating awareness of what is already known about a topic and where more information is needed to address the prediction linked to 'a person's propensity to defer to others who don't have her intellectual limitations, in situations that call upon those limitations' (Whitcomb *et al.*, 2017: 522). Joan reported that she completed all suggested activities.

Joan's Reflections on Unit Implementation

Here, we provide our interpretation of the interview with Joan in which we wanted to understand how she perceived the implementation of aspects of ICC and IH, the students' reactions, and the effects of the unit on the students' behaviors. We also share verbatim excerpts of the interview as transliterations below each theme we identified in the interview data, each followed by a short discussion of connections between ICC and IH.

Learning about sports and revisiting values and beliefs

The first question we asked was what happened in the implementation with regard to the students' development of IC and how Joan felt about how the unit implementation went. Joan emphasized that compared to prior visits by their partners from Germany when the students also talked about sports, this time their conversations went deeper and included cultural analyses rather than, as in prior years, being more focused on learning mostly vocabulary surrounding sports in their own and their partners' cultures. Students made comparisons between the Bundesliga (soccer) and Major League Baseball (MLB) as the World Series was in full swing during the visit. One point of comparison was how it was decided when there was a foul. The students from Germany mentioned that in soccer, the game is videotaped and there are instant evaluations of calls by the referee while that is not the case in the MLB.

J: Ya. Ahm, No, what was definitely, you know, we've talked with the exchange kids in the past, we've done things around sports and lived and played soccer with them. Ahm but this time I felt like because of the way you helped us frame the project, I felt the kids went a lot deeper and really started to understand rather than oh, the German word for goal is 'Tor'. And, you know, the German word for referee is 'Schieri' and things like that, you know they, they certainly benefited from being conversant about the sports that they played in another language. But I felt like they were way beyond this time and started to really understand what, what culturally sports, sports mean. And especially it was interesting too, like a whole sort of school sports connection was, I felt where it came out most prevalently. Ahm because we talked about, we talked about the Bundesliga. It was interesting because when the German kids were here it was the time of the World Series. So baseball was certainly in the forefront and they made a lot of comparisons to the Bundesliga into major league baseball. And ahm they did have a very interesting conversation about the video assistants because ahm it works so differently than in the US than in Germany.

Joan indicates that the prepared ICit unit helped her students discuss cultural products, practices and perspectives related to sports rather than staying mostly at the level of discussing vocabulary related to sports. In a later part of the interview, Joan mentions that the unit 'led to some interesting discussions culturally like what does this say about the American psyche?' which points to critical cultural awareness and deep reflections about different ways of thinking and doing things (Byram, 1997).

Joan explained that it seemed interesting for students to understand the role of sports in their respective contexts, for example, that in the USA often the whole school schedule is planned around sports. She said: '… it blew their mind that school sports were such a driver in the school of even the time that the school day ends is driven by sports'. This is one example showing that students tried to wrap their minds around their partners' cultures requiring attitudes of curiosity, open-mindedness, and tolerance of ambiguity.

Joan shared that this year, students seemed a bit more open to sports with which they had less familiarity in their own contexts. While in prior years the word 'weird' as a judgment was uttered rather often, students seemed more curious and open-minded during the implementation of the unit. Joan collaborated with the Health teacher and took the students to the climbing gym in their school. Students worked on vocabulary related to climbing in German and English:

> J: So that was that was interesting. And I also think in terms of some sports activities that our kids in the past when we've done the sports thing; I think I mentioned to you the whole handball thing that our kids, obviously 'Oh it's weird'. Like the handball thing I don't get it, I think it's fun, but it's a really weird game. It's weird. And nobody used that term this time.

Here, Joan clearly states that students in the past judged some sports as 'weird'. Later on, we get a glimpse of the role that IH might have played in this. While this cannot be confirmed with the data in this study, this raises the question if when we are open-minded and when we are in an environment in which it is okay not to know something, we might be less inclined to make premature judgments.

When asked whether in Joan's opinion the students' understanding went beyond talking about the topic perhaps more superficially, Joan confirmed that this time the students indeed seemed to be more inquisitive. The students from Germany were especially first surprised by, and then interested in, the notion that being good at sports could provide university scholarship opportunities. As Joan recalls in the excerpt below, eventually both groups, the students visiting from Germany and those in the US, appeared to change their opinion and 'flip-flopped'.

> M: And you said in the beginning that the kids went deeper and understood more, went beyond being conserv being conversant and in this topic but thought about it as well?
>
> J: They did, they did, they thought about. I think some kids really thought about school sports and for, and for the first time because one thing that blew the German kids' minds was the notion of sport scholarships.
> M&F: aha.
>
> J: And they're like, what do you mean they pay for you to go to the University because you can play football? What? Like they … just that seemed so bizarre. And that was one of our survey questions that we did. So we had the stats, and it was interesting then some of the American kids really started to think about that.
> M: mhm.
>
> J: And they came down on the side of, well, maybe there shouldn't be sport scholarships. And then the Germans all of a sudden thought it was great.

Laughter.

J: Because I think like they see American universities being so expensive and, 'what do you mean? Like, I can play tennis, so it'd be cheaper for me cuz I can play tennis. That's kinda cool'.
F laughs.

J: So both sides, it was really interesting there was just like this little flip-flop.

The excerpt above sheds light on the question whether students were able to start seeing their partners' perspectives as can be inferred from Joan's comments that the students changed their opinions and 'flip-flopped'. Joan stated at the beginning of the quote above and in another part of the interview that her students and their visitors had a hard time seeing 'the other side at the beginning'. The visiting students found it unimaginable that you would and should receive an academic scholarship because you are good at sport. After they discussed these issues in the interviews and in conversations in and outside of class, they reportedly changed their mind. Similarly, Joan shares that the students in the American school started seeing the point that it might not make as much sense as they thought to link sports and academics. While we cannot make a link to the intervention, students show IH, as they are willing to change their beliefs in light of receiving new information. This relates to Whitcomb and colleagues' (2017) predictions: '11. IH increases a person's propensity to consider alternative ideas, to listen to the views of others, and to spend more time trying to understand someone with whom he disagrees' (Whitcomb et al., 2017: 524). This change in perspective relates to the goal of using ICit and IH to help students become informed citizens capable of evaluating evidence critically and making them less susceptible to participate in the 'know-it-all society' (Lynch, 2019).

Implementing IH: From what is 'weird' to what is different

When Joan is prompted to think about the impact of the addition of IH, she shares that perhaps the biggest change, as mentioned above, was that students did not use the word 'weird' although we even prompted the use in a reflection question, and instead admitted that they did not know much about a specific sport.

F: So just freshen up our minds. So what did you do in introducing the intercultural ah intellectual humility into your ahm unit?

J: Well, ahm we had a conversation about you know some of the sports with which the kids were far less familiar, like climbing, like Handball. And let's think about, like what don't you know?

M: Mhm.

J: What don't you know about this? And how do you feel about what you don't know?

F: Mhm.

J: And that was, you know, I keep coming back to this word weird. But that was to me kind of the part that was striking when we had those conversations about like what doesn't make sense to you. They never said it's weird.

J: They just said like 'I don't know. Like I don't understand'. And then it was good to them that they had the German kids there as a resource like they imme, they went to the, they went to the German kids to try to find out ...

F: On their own or that you have a ...

J: I had kind of a framework. And they said, you know, like let's figure out what you don't know and like what resources could you use to figure it out? But I ask first, is kind of the fundamental questions like do you want to know more?

F: ah.

J: I like, maybe I don't.

M: yeah. Yeah.

J: Like maybe this is enough and there were some things like about the rules of handball, like no no that we're good, we don't need to do that.

In Joan's perception, evaluating something as 'weird' the way the students did in prior years precluded them from further being curious and investigating a certain issue. On the other hand, admitting that they didn't know something could easily lead to curiosity and further questions, which in turn could lead students to engage in skills of interpreting and relating, discovery and interaction, and ultimately to making a critical judgment. Of course, students could also decide (as they did in some cases) that they did not want to know more about a certain topic for specific reasons. The excerpt above hints at connections between the intervention and students' IH in that they went and got help from their visitors when they did not know an answer to a question related to their partners' perceived expertise as related to '12. IH increases a person's propensity to seek help from other sources about intellectual matters' (Whitcomb et al., 2017: 524).

It is interesting to note that students considered the German students experts on those sports that were unknown to them. They did so to a degree that they thought all students needed to know details about the sport, such as how much professional players of handball earn. The students needed to learn that not all people in a particular country know the ins and outs about sports that are popular in that country. However, the students then googled the question together and were able to find an answer. Furthermore, Joan helped students understand what they wanted to know and what they might not want to investigate in more detail. This is an aspect that has to do with IH in that we learn more about what we know and what we don't, and in so doing that we own the limitations of our knowledge.

Being fine with not knowing at times

Reflecting on the relationship of ICC and IH, and whether the additional focus in her class had a specific impact, Joan mentions that she felt relieved that she could have the focus on IH. She referred to 'the way the world is going' and that it was wonderful that students were able to be fine with not knowing at times. It is important to note that she emphasizes the importance of having the vehicle of teaching IH and the relationship of this to the students' ability to be citizens of the world regardless of where they were.

J: … I have to say just kind of because of the way like the world is going, I felt really good and really confident like having a vehicle. You know, teaching German is great. But there were days when I felt wonderful, it was almost more important to me to have this vehicle to get kids to recognize what they don't know and for them to be okay with that. Like you're not gonna know, you're not gonna know everything. And if you start making assumptions about languages and about cultures, you're gonna A) probably really get yourself into trouble and embarrass yourself and make some sort of faux pas or in a B, you're never gonna learn it because you're going to be basing everything on your assumption. So I think giving kids the tools to recognize what they don't know, and having those really good moments of like, 'well, I don't know, but I'm gonna go ask Magdalena cause she's German' and then going to her and she doesn't know either. That it's okay not to know things and to sort out like, 'okay, these rules of handball are sure complicated and I don't want to, I don't want to do it. It's too much and just to let that go'. 'But I really do want to find out about like, how much do they earn?'. To be able to sort out the things I don't know into those I want to explore and those 'I'm just I'm done. I don't need to know all that'.

Here, Joan shows her own relief at the fact that her students could develop IH. She connects IH to her students engaging in intercultural dialogue and evidencing ICC attitudes and skills, such as 'discovery and interaction' when students consulted their peers, and 'interpreting and relating' when they together investigated remaining questions by googling them and then interpreting them together. She further reports that students seemed to have the ability to evaluate what they knew, what they wanted to know and what they might not want to know, which are important aspects of IH.

General Discussion

In this case study, we drew on an interview with a high school teacher of German to explore how she experienced the implementation of aspects of ICC and IH and how she perceived students' learning engagement. It is important to note that this is not a comparison study as was originally planned. Therefore, we cannot conclude that the addition of IH *per se*, or the combination of ICit and IH, were responsible for the differences that Joan observed in her students when she compared behaviors and learning of students the year of the implementation with those of students from prior years. However, it was clear that Joan felt that both the ICit unit on sports and the integration of IH were beneficial for her students. First, she indicated that students appeared to go deeper in their understanding of their own and each other's cultures. Joan also mentioned that her students during that year, and in stark contrast to other years, seemed willing to admit when they did not know something. The admission that they did not know something, rather than being embarrassed about their lack of knowledge, which could have caused them to judge something as weird and leave it at that, might have caused them to be more curious and go to the 'experts' and find out more even by googling the questions together with their visitors which was also something Joan reported her students did. These behaviors have consequences in that students listened to other perspectives, had more opportunities to interpret what they learned and related it to their own contexts. It is also logical that they would gain more knowledge this way and be able to be more critically culturally aware.

The various components of intercultural competence (Byram, 1997) seem to benefit from students' growing awareness of their IH as observed by Joan in the case study. As shown above, Joan reported that students did not only develop knowledge about sports in the US and Germany but also reflected upon the values and practices associated with them such as how central sports are in schools and US colleges. In the interview, Joan also stated that students showed attitudes of openness and critical cultural awareness by being able to evaluate their own practices and beliefs about sports and those of the German group. Joan seemed surprised that American students went as far as to question the sports scholarship system in the US. While all of these learning opportunities were important, one central achievement for students was to be aware of the limitations of their knowledge. Joan pointed out that it was 'wonderful' that students were able to admit when they did not know something. She made the link to the political climate at that time that was characterized by controversy and a lack of dialogue. The project 'Humility and Conviction in Public Life' mentioned in the introduction, addressed a question related to Joan's comment 'How can we balance our most deeply held convictions with humility and open-mindedness in order to repair public discourse?' (Humility and Conviction in Public Discourse, n.d., ¶1). While we did not examine students' convictions, the study can shed some light on students' behaviors surrounding their willingness to gain new knowledge and examine that knowledge in the light of new findings. In an educational culture in which standardized assessments often require students to have answers rather than questions, and what can display an attitude Watson (2020) calls 'winning by knowing' in an 'answer-oriented education', creating an atmosphere in which students are more comfortable with not having all the answers could be an important step to support dialogue and deliberation. Indeed Watson (2020) argues that an 'answer-oriented education' model might well be a barrier to the students' development of IH. The relatively short intervention shown in this case study therefore opens up the question of a combination of IH and ICit could indeed help students investigate their beliefs and perhaps even convictions.

Conclusions

The main goal of the current study was to determine how the teaching and learning of ICC and ICit can be supported through applications of IH in an L2 German classroom. The results of the teacher interview presented hint at the fact that IH indeed complements and supports the development of ICC/ICit evidenced through behaviors and attitudes of openness and curiosity of students who were less likely to be dismissive of new information by stating that something was weird, an attitude that was the case in prior years or in the group of students who did not participate in the IH implementation. It is important to note that this is an exploratory study which relies on the perceptions of a teacher. Nonetheless, the teacher's responses provide some insight into approaches that can help students understand their beliefs, adopt humble attitudes toward the unknown and perhaps revise beliefs that were held because of missing or wrong information. As we prepare learners to engage in intercultural dialogue, develop critical thinking and become active citizens of their local communities and the world, we realize that at the core is how humans relate with what they know or don't know and how it affects their relations with the world and people. IH has the potential to impact in a positive way how learners relate to their inner world but also how they relate with and approach intercultural relations. Future studies could investigate in more detail how IH strengthens and enriches the implementation of ICit pedagogy in education because as Pritchard (2020: 406) concludes 'more than ever before, it is vitally important to develop citizens who have both the courage of their convictions, when epistemically appropriate, while also exhibiting the intellectual respect for others that we have seen to be characteristic of intellectual humility'.

Acknowledgements

This project was made possible through the support of a grant from the John Templeton Foundation. Thanks are due to Fabiana Cardetti, Mike Byram, Heather Battaly and Joan Campbell for their active engagement in various phases of this study.

References

Baehr, J.S. (ed.) (2016) *Intellectual Virtues and Education: Essays in Applied Virtue Epistemology.* London: Routledge.

Byram, M. (1997) *Teaching and Assessing Intercultural Communicative Competence.* Clevedon: Multilingual Matters.

Byram, M. (2008) *From Foreign Language Education to Education for Intercultural Citizenship: Essays and Reflections.* Clevedon: Multilingual Matters.

Byram, M. (2021) *Teaching and Assessing Intercultural Communicative Competence: Revisited.* Bristol: Multilingual Matters. https://doi.org/10.21832/BYRAM0244

Byram, M., Nichols, A. and Stevens, D. (2001) *Developing Intercultural Competence in Practice.* Clevedon: Multilingual Matters.

Byram, M., Golubeva, I., Han, H. and Wagner, M. (eds) (2017) *From Principles to Practice in Education for Intercultural Citizenship.* Bristol: Multilingual Matters.

Cardetti, F., Wagner, M. and Byram, M. (2015) *Interdisciplinary Collaboration to Develop Intercultural Competence by Integrating Math, Languages, and Social Studies.* Northeastern Educational Research Association Conference Proceedings, Paper 7.

Cardetti, F., Wagner, M. and Byram, M. (2019) Intercultural citizenship as a framework for advancing quantitative literacy across disciplinary boundaries. In L. Tunstall, V. Piercey and G. Karaali (eds) *Shifting Contexts, Stable Core: Advancing Quantitative Literacy in Higher Education* (pp. 27–36). Washington, DC: Mathematical Association of America.

Deffler, S.A., Leary, M.R. and Hoyle, R.H. (2016) Knowing what you know: Intellectual humility and judgments of recognition memory. *Personality and Individual Differences* 96, 255–259.

Hazlett, A. (2016) The civic virtues of skepticism, intellectual humility, and intellectual criticism. In J. Baehr (ed.) *Intellectual Virtues and Education: Essays in Applied Virtue Epistemology* (pp. 71–94). London: Routledge.

Humility and Conviction in Public Discourse (n.d.) https://humilityandconviction.uconn.edu/blank/mission/.

Johnson, C., Gunn, H., Lynch, M. and Sheff, N. (2017) Intellectual humility. In *Oxford Bibliographies.* https://www.oxfordbibliographies.com/view/document/obo-9780195396577/obo-9780195396577-0347.xml

Kidd, I.J. (2016) Educating for intellectual humility. In J. Baehr (ed.) *Intellectual Virtues and Education: Essays in Applied Virtue Epistemology* (pp. 54–71). London: Routledge.

Lee, C. (2021) #HateIsAVirus: Talking about COVID-19 'Hate'. In R. Jones (ed.) *Viral Discourse* (pp. 61–68). Cambridge: Cambridge University Press.

Lynch, M.P. (2019) *Know-It-All Society: Truth and Arrogance in Political Culture.* New York: Liveright Publishing.

Paul, R. and Elder, L. (2002) *Critical Thinking: Tools for Taking Charge of Your Professional and Personal Life.* London: Pearson Education.

Pritchard, D. (2020) Educating for intellectual humility and conviction. *Journal of Philosophy of Education* 54 (2), 398–409.

Roberts, R.C. and Wood, W. (2003) Humility and epistemic goods. In M. DePaul and L. Zagzebski (eds) *Intellectual Virtue: Perspectives from Ethics and Epistemology* (pp. 203–226). Oxford: Clarendon Press.

Tanesini, A. (2016) Intellectual humility as attitude. *Philosophy and Phenomenological Research* 96 (2), 399–420.

Wagner, M. and Byram, M. (2017) Intercultural citizenship. In Y. Yun Kim and K.L. McKay (eds) *The International Encyclopedia of Intercultural Communication* (pp. 1–6). Hoboken, NJ: John Wiley & Sons.

Wagner, M., Cardetti, F. and Byram, M. (2018a) The humble linguist: Enriching education for intercultural citizenship and intellectual humility. In E.M. Luef and M.M. Marin (eds) *The Talking Species: Perspectives on the Evolutionary, Neuronal and Cultural Foundations of Language* (pp. 419–443). Graz: Unipress.

Wagner, M., Conlon Perugini, D. and Byram, M. (eds) (2018b) *Teaching Intercultural Competence Across the Age Range: From Theory to Practice.* Bristol: Multilingual Matters.

Wagner, M., Cardetti, F. and Byram, M. (2019) *Teaching Intercultural Citizenship Across the Curriculum.* Alexandria, VA: American Council on the Teaching of Foreign Languages.

Watson, L. (2020) 'Knowledge is power': Barriers to intellectual humility in the classroom. In M. Alfano, M.P. Lynch and A. Tanesini (eds) *The Routledge Handbook of Philosophy of Humility* (pp. 439–449). London: Routledge.

Whitcomb, D., Battaly, H., Baehr, J. and Howard-Snyder, D. (2017) Intellectual humility: Owning our limitations. *Philosophy and Phenomenological Research* 94, 509–539. https://doi.org/10.1111/phpr.12228

16 When the Axiom of Supranational Communication in Intercultural Citizenship Theory is not Met: Enriching Theory and Pedagogy

Melina Porto and Verónica Di Bin

Introduction

Motivated by Byram's (2008) concept of Intercultural Citizenship (ICit) for foreign language education, this chapter locates its starting point in an analysis of its axioms (Byram *et al.*, 2017). The way they are conceived is in terms of people acting together, where the premise is that people act differently as 'intercultural citizens' than they would as 'national citizens'. One axiom is that 'intercultural experience takes place when people from different social groups with different cultures (values, beliefs and behaviors) meet' (Byram *et al.*, 2017: xxiv); one characteristic is the creation of 'a community of action and communication which is supranational' (Byram *et al.*, 2017: xxv); and one criteria is that 'learners … create and cooperate in groups of several nationalities' (Byram *et al.*, 2017: xxvi) using the foreign languages they are learning. But what happens when this supranational communication is not possible and when the people who interact do not belong to different social groups with different cultures and native languages? Aiming to investigate whether intercultural citizenship is possible pedagogically in classrooms where this axiom, characteristic and criteria are not feasible, this chapter describes a case study carried out in the English classroom in a secondary school in Argentina that challenged nationalist thinking in a way not identified in

285

the theory. It addressed the theme 'the world we want' using the UN sustainable development goals as foundation, with particular attention to environmental issues, and no transnational communication. Our findings indicate that internationalist thinking as opposed to nationalist thinking (Byram, 2018) became central in our case, as the outcome was more important than the one possible process of engaging in supranational communication identified as an axiom in the theory. On this basis, we argue that our study challenges ICit theory and pedagogy in their current form and suggest they could be enriched by drawing on the notions of internationalism, imagined communities and ecological citizenship.

Intercultural Citizenship Theory

Intercultural citizenship combines foreign language education, in particular its international perspective (communication with other people with different languages, cultures, backgrounds, worldviews) and citizenship education, in particular its action orientation (social or civic engagement with the local, regional and/or global community) (Byram, 2008). The ultimate goal is to develop learners as intercultural citizens by equipping them with the competences needed to act as citizens in their local communities, or more broadly, for instance, regionally or globally. These competences which are often described in documents for education for citizenship (Crick Report in the UK, 1996; Ley Nacional de Educación in Argentina, 2006) are enhanced by new concepts and ways of seeing the world which are enabled by the contact with another language and context. While citizenship education develops a national identity, intercultural citizenship fosters contact with new worldviews and develops a new sense of identification beyond the nation (Byram, 2008). This is a temporary identification with an international perspective on social issues and how they can be addressed.

The evolution of ICit theory took place in several stages over more than a decade. The main contribution is the move from the concept of 'intercultural speaker' to 'intercultural citizen'. Byram *et al.* (2017) and Byram and Golubeva (2020) summarize this historical development. It comprised a move from intercultural competence (interaction of people of different social groups with different cultures using the same language) to intercultural communicative competence (interaction involving at least one partner using a foreign language). The learners' attention is directed to otherness, in particular toward those who speak the foreign language being learned or used, with an international focus beyond the nation. The combination of linguistic and intercultural competences enables students to take the perspective of their interlocutors, understand their own preconceptions as well as their interlocutors' and find a common basis to make communication possible (Byram, 1997/2021). ICit adds the competences needed to be and act as a democratic citizen (Alred *et al.*, 2006;

Byram, 2008), not as a final outcome of their education but as a goal to be achieved *simultaneously* with the language learning that takes place in schools and universities. For this to happen, learners need to be encouraged to engage in social or civic action in their communities during their language learning. Byram (2008) argues that this community engagement, or action in the world, could be fostered through foreign language teaching in transnational communities. Empirical research applying and developing the theory is described in edited works such as Byram *et al.* (2017) and Porto *et al.* (2018).

This focus on activity has recently been emphasized in language and intercultural communication education and research, as well as in applied linguistics. For example, Phipps and Ladegaard (2020: 219) make a call to the field to 'engage in action, advocacy and activism', and Ladegaard and Phipps (2020: 75) promote 'an ethically responsible social activism agenda, which encourages intervention at the socio-cultural and political levels'. Zhu (2020) suggests the need to conceptualize research in the field as social action and Kramsch (2020: 473) speaks of the 'use of language as political action in a situational and cultural context'. Yet little is said about what such 'action' actually involves, and Ladegaard and Phipps (2020) note that there are few attempts to bridge theory/research and social and political action, recognizing Byram *et al.*'s (2017) work on intercultural citizenship as one of those.

Internationalism, Imagined Communities and Ecological Citizenship

The issue of transnational communication and transnational identification is at the core of this chapter. The premise in ICit is that people act differently as intercultural citizens than they would as national citizens. Byram (2018) formulates this as the difference between national and internationalist thinking and calls it 'internationalism', defined as 'a sense of identification beyond national identification and a willingness to work together with people of other countries' (Byram *et al.*, 2017: 251). More specifically, an internationalist perspective 'means addressing issues which are "too big" for nations' [it is] 'an Archimedean point from which to view the world, and their [learners'] own nation and country within it, a point from which they can see what they have never seen before' (Byram, 2018: 72). As foreign language education directs learners' attention to users of the foreign language they are learning, and consequently confronts them with otherness (linguistic, cultural or otherwise), it plays a significant role in the development of internationalist perspectives.

Furthermore, internationalism emphasizes a common humanity based on humanism and the understanding of others, and it provides a moral direction that foregrounds mutual responsibility. It involves criticality and reflection on one's values and beliefs and those of others and fosters civic engagement contributing to the development of democratic and peaceful societies. While at face value internationalism may resonate with global citizenship (e.g. Myers & Zaman, 2009) and cosmopolitan citizenship (e.g. Osler & Starkey, 2018), according to Byram (2018: 77):

> they both lack a moral direction. Internationalism is a way of thinking and acting which is grounded in historical events and philosophies. Liberal internationalism has a vision of the world which goes beyond the national and is based on promoting a change for the better both in terms of the moral position taken and with respect to the actions which follow.

Internationalism is realized pedagogically in ICit with projects that:

- create a sense of international identification with learners *in the international project*;
- challenge the 'common sense' of *each national group* within the international project;
- develop a new 'international' way of thinking and acting (a new way which may be either a modification of what is usually done OR a radically new way);
- apply that new way to 'knowledge', to 'self' and to 'the world'. (Byram *et al.*, 2017: xxviii, emphasis added)

It should be noted that in related work, Byram and Wagner (2018) state that ICit can occur in one's own country and community, not necessarily at a transnational level, although collaboration is assumed to take place across linguistic and cultural boundaries. Considering that ICit theory was developed for foreign language education contexts, what happens when supranational communication involving students from two or more countries who speak different native languages (Byram *et al.*, 2017) is not possible? Does this mean they will not be able to analyze and challenge their naturalized assumptions (usually with a national basis) and develop a new way of thinking and acting, i.e. an international/transnational identification? If the theory is to be applied to other cases such as the one described in this chapter, which is different from those the authors had in mind at the time, does the theory need to be modified? The question is whether it remains a theory which is for use only in language teaching contexts where different languages and transnational communication are involved, or can be extended to other foreign language teaching situations.

We suggest that the notions of imagined communities and ecological citizenship can be useful here. We draw on Risager (2006) who takes the concept of imagined communities (Anderson, 1983) to distinguish between 'experienced' and 'imagined' communities. Experienced communities are small, and members interact with one another. By contrast, in imagined communities:

the 'members' are so many that they do not have a chance of knowing each other, and therefore do not have the possibility either of acting together in personal interaction (...) It is precisely a community that is only imagined first and foremost. Imagined communities can vary in extent and do not have to be territorialized. (Risager, 2006: 190)

Members of imagined communities develop a sense of belonging, group identity or social identification (Ellemers, 2012; Tajfel, 1982) even when they have never met each other. Considering the strong environmental and ecological focus of this investigation, the element of internationalism in ICit theory and the concept of imagined communities are related to the notion of ecological citizenship in environmental politics and green political theory. Dobson (2007), Dobson and Bell (2006) and Valencia Sáiz (2005), among others, propose that it is 'a new kind of citizenship' (Valencia Sáiz, 2005: 164) because it breaks with other conceptions of citizenship in several ways:

- it is not only related to rights but fundamentally to obligations and collective responsibilities (the moral direction of internationalism);
- activity in the private sphere is as important as activity in the public domain;
- it is not restricted to the nation but is de-territorialized or 'non-territorial' (Dobson, 2003: 89); consequently, there is no political entity sustaining it (such as the nation-state);
- no specific status is required to 'belong' (Valencia Sáiz, 2003);
- because it is de-territorialized, its scope in terms of space is 'anywhere' (Valencia Sáiz, 2003: 292). Territorial contiguity is irrelevant, and the effects of ecological citizenship are better understood in terms of 'action at a distance' (Dobson, 2005: 52). The territorial contiguity that supports the notion of 'one world' in global and cosmopolitan citizenship and the transnational requirement of ICit are not adequate;
- it addresses 'key internationalist themes' (Dobson, 2007: 285) that allow students to think of creative and contextualized responses to issues they observe in their immediate surroundings, which have international scope and impact.

Dobson (2007) explains:

A further characteristic of environmental citizenship is the recognition that rights and responsibilities transcend national boundaries (...) [they] are genuinely international. In a very obvious way, my ecological footprint is not confined to the UK. I constantly draw on environmental resources from beyond my national boundaries – and most of us in so-called advanced countries do so, so it follows that my responsibilities as an environmental citizen are international (and almost certainly intergenerational) responsibilities. Therefore, unlike any other type of citizenship (...), environmental citizenship is both international and intergenerational. (2007: 282)

Furthermore, ecological citizens operate on the basis of justice (fairness), care and compassion (Dobson, 2007; Dobson & Bell, 2006), feel responsibility toward the planet and fellow human beings they do not know and will never know, and have a sense of commitment and moral obligation to contribute to the common good and to solving local problems with a global impact on future generations (Dobson, 2007; Valencia Sáiz, 2003; Vives Rego, 2013). As Dobson (2000: 59) states, 'these obligations are owed primarily to strangers, distant in both space and time'. It is therefore a 'citizenship of strangers (...) we are strangers not only among ourselves, but also our places and even our times are' (Dobson, 2005: 53). For this reason, it is based on an ethics of care and compassion for these strangers (Dobson, 2003, 2005, 2007; Valencia Sáiz, 2003) who belong to an imagined community (Risager, 2006). Finally, ecological citizens feel morally obliged to the common good out of justice. There is 'an explicitly transnational and duty- or responsibility-oriented component (...) [with] international, and perhaps intergenerational, and even interspecies, obligations' (Dobson, 2007: 283). In this chapter, we show how the notions of imagined community and ecological citizenship enrich ICit.

The Project

The research was carried out between September and December 2019 during 14 weeks in *Colegio Nacional Rafael Hernandez*, a public secondary school belonging to Universidad de La Plata in Argentina. There were 111 students from four courses taught by two teachers: 58 students, aged 15–16, were in two fourth-year groups and had A2-B1 level of English according to the CEFR; 53 students, aged 16–17, were in two fifth-year groups and had B1 level. Each group had three compulsory 40-minute English lessons a week. The teachers worked with a set course book, which they supplemented with extra material developed by themselves addressing topics such as culture and identity, globalization, Latin American art and environmental issues. The four courses implemented the same teaching sequence whose general theme was 'the world we want', developed using the UN sustainable development goals as foundation.

The project had the following steps:

(1) Awareness-raising stage: In each language course, the teacher introduced the topic 'the world we want' with the trigger question 'what are the biggest problems in the world today?' The discussion led to the introduction of the concept 'sustainable development goals' and involved reflection on the reasons why they were proposed by the UN. Students carried out several tasks. For instance, they analyzed the

UN's description of each goal, ordered them in terms of priority, explored possible links between them and related them to the initial trigger question.

(2) Research stage: In small groups, still in their course, students chose one goal, identified a local problem related to it and researched it (e.g. they examined its main causes).

(3) Action-stage: In the same groups, they considered ways of coping with the problem and raising awareness about it in society. With this aim, they created an icon to represent their chosen goal and local problem visually.

(4) Collective action plan: The students in the four language courses got together to design a collective action, in this case an environmental campaign on Instagram, where they shared their newly designed icons (UN goal + local problem) with others in Argentina and also around the world. Using their icons as a basis and different artistic techniques, they designed their own infographics on a piece of cloth to convey their messages. They gathered all the infographics in a quilt which was exhibited at the school, and they created a video compiling all the posts from the Instagram account which was shown at the main entrance hall.

Research Methodology

Designed as a case study (Yin, 2018), our research question is as follows: Is intercultural citizenship possible in classrooms where supranational communication with out-groups with different cultural and linguistic backgrounds is not feasible?

Data comprise:

(a) Instagram publications (in video, text and a variety of semiotic resources);

(b) Instagram comments;

(c) student artefacts created in class (graphs, charts, tables, visual representations);

(d) 21 infographics sewed together to make a quilt;

(e) a project video created by the 111 students; and

(f) 85 Autobiography of Intercultural Encounters (AIE) (Byram et al., 2009) (a resource intended to guide users to reflect upon an intercultural encounter) completed by the students in English.

Parents signed informed consent forms, and we followed the ethical research guidelines in Cohen et al. (2018).

We looked for data which confirmed or otherwise the presence of the axiom in ICit theory and from the theory of internationalism related to transnational communication in cycles of deductive analysis (Popper, 2005/1935). To do so, we took a dual approach. We first analyzed the linguistic evidence in our data, for instance, by observing, discovering and describing particular features of the students' Instagram posts, infographics and the use of AIE productions. In so doing, we engaged in a form of discourse analysis as we treated language as situated discursive practice (Cohen *et al.*, 2018). We then complemented this linguistic and discourse perspective with analysis of non-verbal, visual and other semiotic elements in the data (Kress, 2015), for instance, in the infographics, videos and Instagram posts.

We address two main findings: (a) students developed an internationalist way of thinking and acting without engaging in supranational communication and (b) students developed a transnational identification with unknown others as ecological citizens, leading to individual and collective responsibility and action. We italicize the evidence for our arguments in the multiple data extracts we use as illustration.

Findings

Students developed an internationalist way of thinking and acting without engaging in supranational communication.

Here, we present findings in two groups: first, internationalist thinking and acting as conceptualized by teachers (in learning aims and teaching plans) and by students (in their written descriptions of the project in their Autobiography of Intercultural Encounters – Byram *et al.*, 2009); second, internationalist thinking and acting 'in action', i.e. during project implementation.

(a) Teachers' and students' conceptualizations of internationalist thinking and acting

Internationalist thinking and acting were initially materialized in the learning aims the teachers had for the project:

THINKING

- explore, analyze, reflect on and discuss environmental issues locally and globally;
- challenge taken-for-granted representations of and conceptions about the environment.

ACTING

- devise an action plan intended to raise awareness in society about the UN sustainable development goals and implement it.

The teaching sequence was also devised to foster internationalism. For instance, to begin to address the guiding question 'what are the biggest problems in the world today?', students analyzed and discussed the UN 2030 Agenda for Sustainable Development. They identified the lexical chain indicating the basis of internationalism as problems that are too big for nations (Byram, 2018) and class discussion followed.

> [The Agenda] provides a *shared blueprint for peace and prosperity for people and the planet, now and into the future.* At its heart are the 17 Sustainable Development Goals (SDGs), which are an urgent *call for action by all countries* – developed and developing – *in a global partnership.* They recognize that ending poverty and other deprivations must go hand-in-hand with strategies that *improve health and education, reduce inequality, and spur economic growth – all while tackling climate change and working to preserve our oceans and forests.*
>
> (https://unosd.un.org/content/sustainable-development-goals-sdgs, emphasis added)

Students then conceptualized the project in writing in the Autobiography of Intercultural Encounters (Byram *et al.*, 2009). The autobiographies show that they embraced this internationalist thinking. The expressions 'protect and change our world', 'in our world', 'all the people who watch the video get to know', 'save the world' and 'the world is in danger' indicate they were not thinking of their city or country but rather of the world as a whole. The expressions 'make people conscious', 'inspire them to make a change', 'I share lots of pictures', 'we have to stop the pollution', 'show people about the problems in the world' and 'sharing information on Instagram' are indicative of internationalist acting.

> This is a project to *protect and change our world.* Then, the objective of the project is to *make people conscious of the problems in our world* and *inspire them to make a change and help.* (Course 3, Student 2)
>
> The video we posted *made me aware how terrible is this problem* and after that I'm trying to take care of water. *I hope that all the people who watch the video get to know the gravity of the problem.* (C4S9)
>
> During the project I realized I'm not doing things to *save the world* all the time but I do some things that I thought. For example, *every time I use Instagram, I share lots of pictures and post in my profile* because *it's important to me people realize the world is in danger and we have to stop the pollution we started, the waste of our resources.* (C3S6)
>
> We are trying to *show people about the problems in the world* doing this project and *sharing information on Instagram.* (C1S7)
>
> It is a project that served us to understand and to investigate a lot of *problems in the world.* (C2S15)

(b) Internationalist thinking and acting 'in action' during project implementation

This internationalist perspective present in teachers' aims and plans and in students' general reflections was also identified in the students'

Figure 16.1 Internationalist thinking in students' infographics

infographics representing the whole world (Figure 16.1) instead of their city, country or region.

Reflecting on the aims and audience of their infographics in the auto-biographies, students explicitly mentioned an international focus:

> The aim of the infographic is to inform the *people around the world* and to raise awareness. *The audience is real people from different parts of the world, people in general, anyone that can be interested in this.* (C3S6)

> [The audience is] To *all the society.* (C1S7)

The aim is (...) to *reach people from different places* and to make them be together for *a unique global aim*. (C4S13)

... thinking to *reach people from different parts of the world* (through Instagram). (C3S22)

The same problems are shared by different countries so, *the same actions must be taken by everybody in the world*. (C2S19)

... we know that *most problems are international*. (C3S13)

Through engagement with texts of all kinds, students started thinking in an internationalist way. They examined the national basis of their own views and values by researching, discovering and critically comparing and contrasting worldviews, knowledge and perspectives. For instance, after a research and enquiry stage, one group designed a visual representation showing two maps of Argentina in a colored scale indicating the percentage of households without drinking water and sewers in each province in the country and used the maps to compare and contrast the information with the situation in other countries. This critical analysis brought about surprising revelations: While only 6 provinces out of 24 have almost full provision of drinking water (97%), Argentina is ranked at the top together with Uruguay in water provision in South America.

Figure 16.2 shows how another group addressed the current state of global renewable energy in 13 countries including Argentina using statistical information from the International Renewable Energy Agency. The research stage ('learned a lot', 'read a lot about') led to awareness of different perspectives on the topic ('but then we discovered some bad points') and the adoption of a critical stance ('we decided to inform on that: advantages and disadvantages') with an international focus (13 countries). One section in the infographic included a call to take action: 'we can all help to live in a better world'.

I *learned a lot, and read a lot about* renewable energy. *I was very satisfied with our findings but then we discovered some bad points* about it (very little ones). *So, we decided to inform on that: advantages and disadvantages* of renewable energy *illustrated with 13 countries*. (C4S5, AIE)

Another group connected two themes – floods and deforestation – in Argentina and Brazil, and through research and discussion, discovered the root causes of recurrent floods in Northern Argentina, strongly linked to deforestation practices in the neighboring country. By exploring links with the situation concerning each UN theme in other parts of their country (Misiones province) and beyond, i.e. in the region (Brazil) and the world ('not only locally but internationally'), students dug into the root causes of current problems and their consequences on people ('for people',

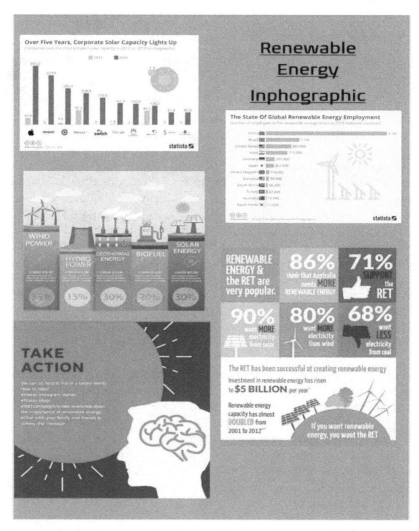

Figure 16.2 Visual representation: Renewable energy internationally

'every person in the world'). They were tracing ecological footprints ('caused in the south of Brazil') and were guided by moral obligations to a community of strangers ('dangerous and terrible for people') (Dobson, 2007) – internationalism's moral direction (Byram, 2018).

> More local problems are the floods in the north of Misiones [an Argentinian province]. *Floods main cause is the deforestation caused in the south of Brazil.* Authorities or local government from Brazil aren't doing different things to cope with the problem. Authorities from Misiones design different plans. *Also, the people in Argentina try to raise awareness in people here and in Brazil about the problem* (…) We mustn't

cut the trees, they are the lungs of the planet, they give us oxygen, fresh air, and a beautiful place to live. Also, if we cut the trees, we cause floods and that's dangerous and terrible *for people. And these things have effects not only locally but internationally. We live in the same world, every person in the world and every government must help.* (C3S6, AIE)

Yet another group addressed a related goal, Number 14, life beneath water (Figure 16.3), and structured their visual representation around three questions: 'What are we aiming for?', 'How does it affect us locally?' (connecting the topic to the 'Matanza-Riachuelo river' and its pollution), and 'What can we do to help?' The research stage led to discovery ('I learned', 'one of the most contaminated rivers'), awareness ('made me realize') and a sense of concern ('highly concerned me'):

> Because of the project, *I learned that* the Riachuelo is *one of the most contaminated rivers in the world*, which *highly concerned me and made me realize* how close these problems are to us. (C3S22, AIE)

It also led to changes in perspective ('shocking numbers of contamination', 'made me change the way I look at things') and in actions ('It changed a lot of things about my daily life decisions'):

> In the area that I worked 'Life below water', *I had the chance to learn the shocking numbers of contamination* in the world's most big resource: water. *It changed a lot of things about my daily life decisions* and *made me change the way I look at things.* (C3S4, AIE)

The group concluded:

> *Action needs to be taken* and quickly. The contaminated waters not only affect marine species but also the people living around it. Although there have been some projects funded by the government in the past, none have been effective. *Sadly, it is a problem beyond our reach since major changes need to be made but it is* **our duty** *as citizens to step up and insist regulations are put in place.* **Altogether we** *can sign a petition and make history* **ourselves** (from Figure 16.3).

The use of passive voice in the first sentence is to be noted as it reveals that these students did not apparently feel responsible for this identified need to take action. However, after a brief description of the state of affairs ('contaminated waters affect marine species and people'), the tone changes. They showed awareness of the basis of internationalism ('it is a problem beyond our reach'), recognized feeling emotionally involved ('sadly'), distanced themselves from the responsibility using passive voice again ('major changes need to be made') (and the major nature of the problem needing solutions beyond the national level is another

Figure 16.3 Visual representation: Life below water

characteristic of internationalism), and finally took responsibility and made a call to take action ('it is our duty as citizens', 'insist regulations are put in place', 'sign a petition', 'make history'). In short, this visual representation illustrates an internationalist way of thinking and acting. A strong identification with others they did not know, a finding we discuss in the next section, is evident here in the use of first-person plural pronouns and expressions (in bold in the extract): 'our duty', 'we', 'ourselves', 'altogether'.

The collective action of the 111 participating students consisted in going public by creating an Instagram account (@takeactioncnlp) to share their visual representations with others in Argentina with attention to local problems ('developed the problem in our Río de La Plata') and also with others around the world as a global concern ('this is a problem in many places', '#savetheworld', '#climateaction', '#gointernational'). This global action stage was an environmental campaign on Instagram ('in "takeactioncnlp" where you can find') with transnational focus and reach.

> Our goal was life below water. *This is a problem in many places* but we *developed the problem in our Río de La Plata.* We made a video and painted an infographic. (C3S13, AIE)

> My group and I talked about the goal 14 'life below water'. *We made an informative video about 'El Río de La Plata' that you can see Instagram, in 'takeactioncnlp' where you can find more informative videos* about other goals. *We made patch to make a quilt later.* The quilt is going to have patches about all the goals. (C4S15, AIE)

> Takeaction: Are you ready to save the planet? We want to help foster environmental awareness. (Instagram post)

> #globalwarming *#savetheworld* #climateaction *#gointernational*

The video they created compiling all the posts from the Instagram account contained a call to unknown others to take action: 'If we don't do anything ... who will?' (video 5:05min).
https://drive.google.com/file/d/1Aeca_GcbDNQlb48iQtxvZMegH2Y5W2Jb/view?usp=sharing

Figure 16.4 is a collage of several infographics about goal 14, life beneath water, each one made by a different group of students, which shows the ways in which they made a call to others to take action, in other words, an internationalist way of acting.

The first two infographics are purely visual, painted by hand on canvas, with no use of language. The third one shows one fish ironically trapped in what should be its natural habitat and a direct address to the global community with which students identified by means of imperatives: 'clean the shores', 'don't waste plastic'. Similar uses of imperatives to make a call to unknown others to take action, or an internationalist way of acting, can also be observed in the other infographics ('be clean', 'make a blue world', 'don't pollute', 'save our waters', 'save the oceans', 'stop pollution' and 'stop dropping trash into the splash').

Finally, an important element in the development of internationalist thinking and acting involves 'an Archimedean point from which to view the world ... from which they [learners] can see what they have never seen before' (Byram, 2018: 72). In the following AIE extracts and Instagram comments and posts, expressions of surprise (including exclamation marks) and disbelief are indicative of this Archimedean point ('I had never imagined', 'I couldn't believe that', 'Wow', 'I can't believe my eyes!', 'it is incredible'), which led to awareness ('now I realize') and change both at a personal level in the private sphere ('I will unplug my charger') as well as collectively in the public domain ('we have to do something now!', 'we

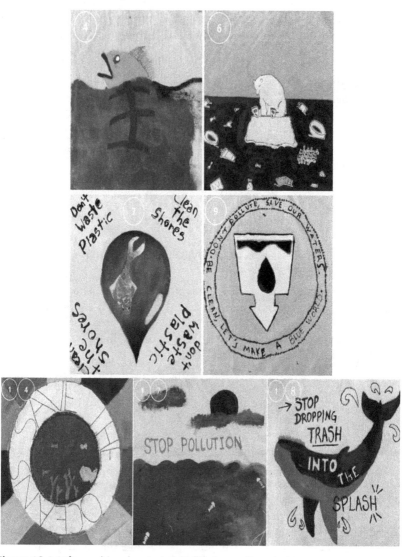

Figure 16.4 Infographics about goal 14 (life beneath water)

have to stop this', 'keep fighting!') (awareness and change highlighted in bold). The examples also illustrate students' moral position beyond the nation to promote change and actions leading to a better world, characteristic of internationalism (Byram, 2018) and ecological citizenship (Dobson, 2007).

> The information and photos I saw *had a huge impact on me*, they *were really strong* since *I had never imagined* the problems were so serious despite being **sometimes aware of them.** (C4S6, AIE)

… the problems of not renewable energy that we use. *It was new to me* and *I couldn't believe that* 4 million Argentinians live in areas with contaminated water. (C1S5, AIE)

@xxxxx: *Wow, that picture impact me. I can't believe my eyes!* **We have to do something now!** (Instagram comment)

@xxxxx: I charge my phone every night. *I didn't know that* if you unplug your charger you save energy, *but* **now I realize how important this is. Now I will unplug my charger when I stop using it.** (Instagram comment)

@xxxxx: *Wow!* **Now I realize how serious this is. We need to do something to save the planet now!!** (Instagram comment)

@ xxxxx: *Wow!* This is so sad!! *Look at those images! I can't believe this is true.* What are we going to do? **It's time to change.** (Instagram comment)

@ xxxxx: *I can' t believe it.* We are destroying our world. **Now I realizing how serious is this. We have to stop this. Keep fighting!** (Instagram comment)

Overall, despite the fact that the characteristic of supranational communication did not happen, students encountered different perspectives through interaction with people from the same social group and with similar linguistic and cultural backgrounds; and also in and through texts of all kinds using the internet. In this way, they developed an internationalist way of thinking and acting.

Students developed a transnational identification with unknown others as ecological citizens, leading to individual and collective responsibility and action.
One axiom in ICit is the emergence of a temporary supranational (international, transnational) group identity which develops through interaction between people with different languages and cultures and Byram *et al.* (2017) have provided empirical evidence of this identification in several studies. Here, our point is that in our study there was no transnational identification in this sense simply because there was no interaction with an out-group. Our findings show, however, that a transnational identification did develop, not with transnational peers but with unknown others where the identification involved a sense of belonging to an imagined community (Anderson, 1983; Risager, 2006) of ecological citizens as revealed in the Autobiography of Intercultural Encounters ('our world', 'ourselves and the place we're living', 'a better future for all of us'). This transnational identification is also a characteristic of ecological citizenship (Dobson, 2000, 2007). The autobiographies show that the basis for this identification was that students were committed to and cultivated sustainable, long-lasting and world-friendly perspectives and behaviors – another characteristic of ecological citizens who operate on the basis of justice, care, compassion and responsibility

(Dobson, 2007; Dobson & Bell, 2006) ('the main cares that we should have', 'take care of species in danger and ourselves', 'watch over the future', 'being aware about the things that we throw up', 'help the world to be better', 'veganism'). This identification and committed spirit are revealed linguistically in the use of first-person plural pronouns and expressions ('we', 'our world', 'ourselves', 'all of us') and modality respectively ('should', 'have to') (in bold). Because of the international basis of the UN goals and the evidence in the previous section, our understanding is that these first-person plural instances could not be referring only to Argentinians. Furthermore, and importantly, in eco-logical citizenship all local problems and actions, and all private actions, have an environmental impact on others, other places and the planet, and consequently the focus is always international, intergenerational and interspecies (Dobson, 2007).

> We were doing a project involved on *the main cares that* **we** should *have to protect* **our** **world** and *take care of species in danger and* **ourselves** to *watch over the future to have a better one.* (C4S23, AIE)

> The importance of *being aware about the things that* **we** *throw up, because it can affect not only animals, but* **ourselves** *and the place we're living,* **we** **have to** *take care of* **our** **world**. The *same problems are shared by different countries* so, the *same actions must be taken by* **everybody** **in the world**. (C2S23, AIE)

> I actually get really interested when it comes about *be aware of the things* **we** *do to help the world to be better. Veganism it's one of them* **we** **can** increase *a better future for* **all** **of** **us** *if more people is aware of the problem with meat.* (C2S19, AIE)

The ecological citizen operates on a moral dimension that compels individuals to form part of, and identify with, an imagined community of people, living species, places and the Earth and has ethical responsibilities toward it ('we have to take care of our world') (Dobson, 2000, 2007). These ethical responsibilities and their commitment triggered students to work cooperatively to build a better future together on the basis of justice, care and compassion (Dobson, 2003, 2005, 2007; Valencia Sáiz, 2003), in other words, to enact social transformation by identifying and challenging inequalities, oppression and human rights abuses. This 'moral direction' is also a characteristic of internationalism (Byram, 2018: 77). For instance, a group of students created a visual representation to denounce the unequal access to drinking water and sewage in Argentinian provinces. Inequalities based on this theme were disclosed through reflection in the autobiographies as well as in Instagram comments:

> Con los distintos objetivos que nos dieron, vos ayudas a *tomar conciencia sobre las desigualdades que hay en nuestro planeta* como por ejemplo

que *no en todos los hogares haya agua potable*. Me parece que *es algo que no hay que olvidar*. (C1S13, AIE)

With all the objectives we were given, you help *raise awareness as regards inequalities present in our planet*, such as the fact that *there is no running water in all homes*. I think *this is something not to forget*. (our translation)

@xxxxx: Oh! That's so worrying *we should capt the attention of the government to solve this problem*. For example, *do a manifestation. The topic of the manifestation can be 'Drinking water and sewers for everyone!'* (Instagram comment)

In this way, students enacted change, however piecemeal and modest, in their social milieu. In the process of working to build a better future together, students communicated with their peers and conveyed their messages to their imagined audience, i.e. the global community they identified with. Figure 16.4 shows some of the messages they conveyed using imperatives as a means to involve others in their environmental campaign ('be clean', 'don't pollute', 'save the oceans', 'stop pollution'). In all cases, these messages were complemented by pictorial means, many times reinforcing their awareness raising aims in society by triggering the audience's emotional engagement with the theme artistically: a fish half body and half skeleton (Infographic 4), polluted waters (Infographics 6 and 7), polluted waters with fish skeletons (Infographic 17). As the project moved forward, students developed a bond and a sense of identification with the unknown members of this imagined community. In the data, this transnational identification became evident in the use of first-person plural forms and expressions of communion in their infographics such as 'save **our** waters' and '**let's** make a blue world' (Figure 16.4), 'If **we** don't take action, **we** won't survive' (Figure 16.5) and '**WE**'re destroying **US**' (Figure 16.6, the capitals belong to the students). To be noted in Figure 16.6 is the play between the globe and its message to people in the world ('You're destroying me') and this group of students' call to their imagined community by changing the pronouns 'you' and 'me' to 'we' and 'us'.

Evidence of this transnational identification was also observed in the autobiographies and Instagram comments as can be gleaned from the following extracts ('let's', 'together', 'WE', 'US', 'we', 'our'):

We're damaging **our** planet, and *if* **our** planet *is in danger,* we're too. (C4S15, AIE)

Do you care about the environment? I do. **Let's** *be the change! Together* **WE** *can transform the world. Saving the planet is not an individual thing, it needs* **US**. (C4S2, AIE)

@xxxxx: it is very sad to see how the number of damage and global pollution are increasing day by day. **We** *have to do something!* (Instagram comment)

Figure 16.5 Students' infographic: 'We won't survive'

Figure 16.6 Students' infographic: 'We're destroying us'

@xxxxx: it's a pity that the world is like that. I think that **we** *can do something to improve this situation if* **we** *act* **together. We** *could compost in our houses, stop buying plastic bottles, control* **our** *water use (try not to use more than necessary). There's a lot* **we** *can do! Start at home!* (Instagram comment)

@takeactioncnlp: Why **should we** *stop using plastic*? (Instagram message)

This identification became the basis of concrete individual action ('compost in our houses', 'stop buying plastic bottles', 'control our water use', 'start at home') as well as collective action ('we have to do something', 'act together', 'saving the planet is not an individual thing') to protect the environment. The combination of activity in the private and public domains is a characteristic of ecological citizenship (Dobson, 2005, 2007). Linguistically, students used varied means to engage the imagined audience with which they identified, for instance direct addresses ('do you care about the environment?', 'why should we stop using plastic?'), invitations ('let's be the change!'), suggestions ('together WE can transform the world'), specific calls, many times with exclamation marks ('we have to do something!', 'there's a lot we can do!), conditionals ('if our planet is in danger', 'if we act together') and imperatives ('start at home').

Overall, students were united with their imagined audience, with their peers and with others they met on Instagram by shared environmental goals and concerns:

> … despite differences our contexts may have in relation to the same global problem, *we share the same aim or goal.* (C3S22, AIE)

> My classmates and I took part in a project that was for make people aware about *what is happening in our planet.* (C4S15, AIE)

> @takeactioncnlp: We invite you to share in the comments your tips about *what you actually do to take care of water.* (project Instagram)

These shared goals and concerns fostered individual as well as collective responsibility and action, and such responsibility is a characteristic of the ecological citizen:

> *I felt responsible because* there are a lot of things *people must change to save the world that we don't do.* In my position, *I think I have to make people aware of the situation,* for example *when someone cut some plant or leave the tap open, I should say to that person they are putting the world in danger* even with a simple thing. (C3S6, AIE)

> *I'm going to change the things that I consume. I'll stop using plastic items,* like bottles, straws, cutlery. (C3S4, AIE)

> With my family *we started a recycling project to make fertilizers for our plants*. (C3S15, AIE)

Finally, this drive toward individual and collective responsibility and action fostered interaction with unknown others about the UN goals addressed in the project using English on Instagram at @takeactioncnlp. For instance:

> Later, we created an Instagram account to reach many people and *we got followers from other parts of the world too*. It is great to *inform that people about* problems we have here and *share information about their problems*. (C4S15, AIE)

> WE HAVE TO MAKE A CHANGE
> @xxxxx: We should take action.
> @xxxxx: Sabe the World.
> @xxxxx: It's not too late.
> @xxxxx: Chance the World for a better place.
> .
>
> CLEAN WATER AND SANITATION:
> @xxxxx: What are our polititians
> doing to protect our rivers?
> .
>
> THE RIACHUELO RIVER
> @xxxxx: This is a very sad notice.
> @xxxxx: Save it, it's possible.
> @xxxxx: Something must be done.
> .
>
> 4 MILLIONS OF ARGENTINIANS LIVE IN AREAS WITH CONTAMINATED WATER:
> @xxxxx: We have to protect the fishes and water animals.
> @xxxxx: Together we can change our country.
> .
>
> RUNNING WATER:
> @xxxxx: This is so bad we should work all together to get a better future.
> @xxxxx: I didnt know that.
> .
>
> THE EARTH IS IN DANGER:
> @xxxxx: We need start to use more bikes to reduce cars fumes.
> @xxxxx: The global warming it's making animals unable to live un their habitats
> (Instagram)

In sum, although there was no transnational identification in the sense of identification with a group arising from interaction with people from another country, our findings show another kind of transnational identification involving a sense of belonging to an imagined community (Anderson, 1983; Risager, 2006) of ecological citizens (Dobson, 2000,

2007). This identification became the basis of concrete individual and collective responsibility and action, motivated by shared environmental goals and concerns. It also fostered interaction with unknown others on Instagram using English.

Conclusion and Ways Forward

In ICit theory and pedagogy (Byram *et al.*, 2017), peer transnational communication using foreign languages and a shared collaborative community-oriented task are essential characteristics. The joint endeavor of needing and wanting to solve a particular problem in the community through a collaborative outcome, using the foreign languages both groups of students are learning, assures that participants develop a strong sense of communion and bonding among themselves called 'transnational identification'. Our research challenges ICit theory as it disproves the requirement of transnational communication between groups of people from different countries with different native languages. We have shown that similar outcomes in terms of action and transnational identification can happen with pedagogic projects that do not meet this axiom and characteristic of ICit stated in the theory. The question is whether the theory is for use only in language teaching contexts where different languages and transnational communication are involved, or can be extended to other foreign language teaching situations. More work is necessary to investigate this issue.

A brief comment is in order at this point regarding the interaction with international others that occurred on Instagram as students received comments and posts from unknown people about their project and responded to them. This is a potentially interesting finding, worth taking note of. It was, however, incidental, as it was not planned by teachers and occurred spontaneously toward the end of the project when the students engaged in action. We do not think it undermines our argument that supranational communication did not occur, because such communication was not substantial, nor part of the planning or the classroom implementation itself.

Our research suggests that students can 'meet others' and start thinking and acting in an internationalist way through engagement with texts of all kinds and interaction with peers in their social milieu instead of people from a different country. In terms of ICit theory and pedagogy, the outcome seems to be more important than the process involving transnational communication. It is possible that ICit experience in and of itself, in its original characterization in the theory, is not what ultimately matters but rather the change in mindset that ICit pedagogy fosters through collaborative work with others, whether they are international peers or peers from the same social group and backgrounds, which leads to a new sense of bonding, identification and communion with unknown and imagined others as 'ecological citizens'. This contact with peers, even those from the same social group, encourages interaction with different perspectives, awareness of the national basis of one's views, identification of ethical responsibilities and commitment to global problems (shared with those peers and unknown others) and shared goals and joint actions to build peaceful and sustainable societies. Furthermore, and importantly, we are also suggesting that all students' engagements with difference and communities of all kinds (real, imagined) are valuable and that this can happen in a range of configurations – supranational communication, international perspectives and action-taking without supranational communication (as described in this chapter). Going one step further, learner engagements with real or imagined communities can happen through other pedagogies different from ICit, yet to be explored and investigated. Many approaches and configurations may become transformative experiences for learners in terms of mindset and action.

Finally, we suggest that ICit theory and pedagogy could be enriched by drawing on the notions of internationalism, imagined communities and ecological citizenship. The fact that students focused mainly on environmental themes developed from the UN goals clean water and sanitation, affordable and clean energy, climate action, life below water, life on land and responsible production and consumption may have contributed to the kind of transnational identification that emerged without any supranational communication and may have fostered students' motivation and commitment to take action. Students deployed internationalist thinking and acting on the basis of local problems with an international, intergenerational and interspecies impact. These problems required their action in collaboration with unknown others as part of a big imagined community. Their ethical commitment, responsibility, care and sense of justice was a driving force in our project which led them to develop a sense of bonding with unknown others as members of a worldwide imagined community and to take action at the local and global levels, as well as privately (in their homes) and publicly (environmental campaign). These are characteristics of the ecological citizen reported in the literature. We suggest that the connections between intercultural and ecological citizenship deserve further exploration.

References

Alred, G., Byram, M. and Fleming, M. (2006) *Education for Intercultural Citizenship: Concepts and Comparisons.* Clevedon: Multilingual Matters.

Anderson, B. (1983) *Imagined Communities.* London: Verso.

Byram, M. (1997) *Teaching and Assessing Intercultural Communicative Competence.* Clevedon: Multilingual Matters.

Byram, M. (2008) *From Foreign Language Education to Education for Intercultural Citizenship.* Clevedon: Multilingual Matters.

Byram, M. (2018) An essay on internationalism in foreign language education. *Intercultural Communication Education* 1 (2), 64–82.

Byram, M. (2021) *Teaching and Assessing Intercultural Communicative Competence: Revisited*. Bristol: Multilingual Matters. https://doi.org/10.21832/BYRAM0244

Byram, M., Barrett, M., Ipgrave, J., Jackson, R., Méndez García, M.C., Buchanan-Barrow, E. and Leclercq, J.M. (2009) *Autobiography of Intercultural Encounters. Context, Concepts and Theories*. Strasbourg: Council of Europe.

Byram, M. and Golubeva, I. (2020) Conceptualizing intercultural (communicative) competence and intercultural citizenship. In J. Jackson (ed.) *The Routledge Handbook of Language and Intercultural Communication. Second Edition* (pp. 70–85). London: Routledge.

Byram, M., Golubeva, I. Han, H. and Wagner, M. (eds) (2017) *From Principles to Practice in Education for Intercultural Citizenship*. Bristol: Multilingual Matters.

Byram, M. and Wagner, M. (2018) Making a difference: Language teaching for intercultural and international dialogue. *Foreign Language Annals* 51, 140–151.

Cohen, L., Manion, L. and Morrison, K. (2018) *Research Methods in Education* (8th edn). Bristol London: Routledge.

Dobson, A. (2000) Ecological citizenship: A disruptive influence? In C. Pierson and S. Torney (eds) *Politics at the Edge* (pp. 40–62). Basingstoke: MacMillan.

Dobson, A. (2003) *Citizenship and the Environment*. Oxford: Oxford University Press.

Dobson, A. (2005) Ciudadanía ecológica. *Isegoría* 32, 47–62.

Dobson, A. (2007) Environmental citizenship: Towards sustainable development. *Sustainable Development* 15 (5), 276–285.

Dobson, A. and Bell, D. (eds) (2006) *Environmental Citizenship*. Cambridge, MA: MIT Press.

Ellemers, N. (2012) The group self. *Science* 336, 848–852.

Kramsch, C. (2020) Educating the global citizen or the global consumer? *Language Teaching* 53 (4), 462–476.

Kress, G. (2015) Semiotic work. Applied linguistics and a social semiotic account of multimodality. *AILA Review* 28, 49–71.

Ladegaard, H. and Phipps, A. (2020) Intercultural research and social activism. *Language and Intercultural Communication* 20 (2), 67–80. doi: 10.1080/14708477.2020.1729786

Ley Nacional de Educación 26.206 (2006) Ministerio de Educación de la Nación Argentina.

Myers, J.P. and Zaman, H.A. (2009) Negotiating the global and national: Immigrant and dominant culture adolescents' vocabularies of citizenship in a transnational world. *Teachers College Record* 111, 2589–2625 (unpaginated).

Osler, A. and Starkey, H. (2018) Extending the theory and practice of education for cosmopolitan citizenship. *Educational Review* 70 (1), 31–40.

Phipps, A. and Ladegaard, H. (2020) Notes towards a socially engaged LAIC. *Language and Intercultural Communication* 20 (2), 218–219.

Popper, K. (2005/1935) *The Logic of Scientific Discovery*. Abingdon: Taylor & Francis.

Porto, M., Houghton, S.A. and Byram, M. (2018) Guest editorial: Intercultural citizenship in the (foreign) language classroom. *Language Teaching Research* [Special issue] 22 (5), 484–498.

Qualifications and Curriculum Authority (The Crick Report) (1996) *Education for Citizenship and the Teaching of Democracy in Schools*. London: Qualifications and Curriculum Authority.

Risager, K. (2006) *Language and Culture: Global Flows and Local Complexity*. Clevedon: Multilingual Matters.

Tajfel, H. (1982) Social psychology of intergroup relations. *Annual Review of Psychology* 33 (1), 1–39.

Valencia Sáiz, A. (2003) Ciudadanía ecológica: una noción subversiva dentro de una política global. *Revista de Estudios Políticos (Nueva Época)* 120, 269–300.

Valencia Sáiz, A. (2005) Globalisation, cosmopolitanism and ecological citizenship. *Environmental Politics* 14 (2), 163–178.

Vives Rego, J. (2013) El ciudadano ecológico: reflexiones sobre algunos contextos sociales y elementos cosmovisionales. *Sociología y tecnociencia* 3 (1), 83–104.

Yin, R.K. (2018) *Case Study Research: Design and Methods* (6th edn). London: Sage.

Zhu, H. (2020) Making a stance: Social action for language and intercultural communication research. *Language and Intercultural Communication* 20 (2), 206–212.

17 Towards a Shared Future: Michael Byram's Engagement with the Chinese Academic Community

Lihong Wang

Introduction

I was thrilled to join others in applauding the contributions that Mike – please allow me to use this affectionate address – has made to the cause of intercultural teaching and learning worldwide on the occasion of the 25th anniversary of his *Teaching and Assessing Intercultural Communicative Competence* (1997) and the publication of *Teaching and Assessing Intercultural Communicative Competence: Revisited* (2021). Though a prominent scholar based in Europe, Mike's influence and the impact of his intercultural communicative competence model (ICC) and his framework of intercultural citizenship education have traveled far beyond Europe and reached well to China. For the past decades, Mike has been in extensive contact with the Chinese academic community and helped Chinese languages teachers develop intercultural dimensions in their language classroom through co-authoring books, giving lectures and webinars and offering onsite workshops. For example, more than a decade ago, Mike's article 'Developing a concept of intercultural citizenship' appeared in the first volume of *Intercultural Communication Research*, published by Higher Education Press in 2009 in China. The volume was co-edited by two Chinese scholars, Yuxin Jia and Guo-Ming Chen, who were the Chairman of China Association for Intercultural Communication (CAFIC) and the Executive President of International Association of Intercultural Communication Studies (IAICS), respectively, at that time, so the volume includes articles by both renowned international and Chinese scholars, who study intercultural dialogue to address the issues posed by globalization and advocate for the idea '和而不同', that is, 'unity within diversity' (Jia & Chen, 2009: 3) for the new century.

During the past decades, Mike was regularly invited to deliver keynote speeches at conferences in China. On 9 June 2018 at the annual conference of China Association for Intercultural Communication (CAFIC) held in Shandong University, Mike presented the Reference Framework of Competences for Democratic Culture (RFCDC) for the first time in China in his plenary keynote speech titled 'Intercultural Education and a Shared Future – from a European Perspective'. This thoughtful title shows much of his intercultural sensitivity to the sociocultural context of China, where the catchphrase 'a community of shared future for mankind' has become a socio-political mantra in China, appearing in multiple Chinese discourses, political, economic, social and cultural, with the connotations of building a harmonious world. My titling this chapter 'Towards a Shared Future' is inspired by his speech as well as by his recent book subtitled *Preparing for a Community of Shared Future for Mankind and Global Citizenship*, co-authored with Prof. Yuxin Jia, former Chairman of China Association of Intercultural Communication (CAFIC), and his Chinese colleagues (see Jia *et al.*, 2019).

Owing to his generous contribution to Chinese academic communities, Mike was awarded various honorary titles and guest professorships from Chinese universities and institutions, such as Harbin Institute of Technology (HIT), Beijing Foreign Studies University (BFSU), Beijing Language and Culture University (BLCU), Beihang University, Shanghai International Studies University (SISU), Shanghai Normal University (SNU), etc. He also provides consultancy for some Chinese higher educational institutions, serving as 'State Language Commission High Level Language Expert' and advisor for the Beijing Advanced Innovation Centre for Language Resources, just to give a few examples. Nonetheless, his sincere concern and active engagement with language teaching and language teacher education in China may be less known outside China, and thus it is worth bringing attention to this. In the following sections, I will, first, review some of his collaborations with Chinese scholars by focusing on Mike's engagement with Chinese indigenous concepts out of his concern with linguistic and conceptual relativism in intercultural communication; second, I will give a report on his series of workshops tailored to the needs of Chinese language teachers, as well as how his intercultural learning theories are localized and thriving in Chinese contexts; Lastly, I gave a brief introduction to his essay 'How do/should Interculturalists respond to the Corona/Covid 19 crisis?', which was published only in its Chinese version in China (see Byram, 2021), to show his engagement as an interculturalist with the world in the crisis of Covid-19.

Engagement with Chinese Indigenous Concepts

Here, I use 'Chinese indigenous concepts' to refer to those culture-specific concepts in Chinese philosophy and cultural tradition that can hardly find their equivalent counterparts in other languages without losing their embedded rich meanings. To address the complexities of the lifeworld of other cultures, Geertz, when introducing his book *The Interpretation of Cultures* (1973), borrowed the term 'thick description' from Ryle's (1971) essays, to characterize ethnographers' work and to avoid the imposition of the category deriving from one tradition on another. Later, 'thick translation' was introduced into translation studies by Appiah (2000) to counteract the illusion of equivalence theories as well as the inadequacy of interlingual renderings by using footnotes, annotations, explications, etc.

As a polyglot, Mike shows constant vigilant attentiveness to the exactness of words in different languages when translating a culture-loaded concept from one language into another and especially when there is no equivalent in the target language. He holds the view that linguistic and conceptual relativism should not be overlooked in any intercultural discussion, and these nuances not only present difficulties of translation in intercultural communication, but also contain conceptual complexities, which reveal potential problems in public debate, especially for less widely taught and spoken languages. Therefore, using indigenous concepts with 'thick description' (Geertz, 1973: 6–7; Ryle, 1971) and 'thick translation' (Appiah, 2000) is one of his ways not only to show his genuine interest and respect for other cultures but also to be wary of the tendency of cultural reductionism.

In their book *Preparing for a Community of Shared Future for Mankind and Global Citizenship*, the authors employ the framework of intercultural citizenship education to promote ideas of intercultural education by adopting Chinese indigenous concepts to develop arguments for cultivating a young generation morally and ethically for a community of shared future. The book is written in English and is intended to be used as an intercultural communication course textbook for Chinese college students. In view of the multilingual and multiethnic sociocultural context in China, both the terms 'citizenship' and 'citizenship education' are contested notions (Feng, 2006), while 'global citizenship' seems to be more lucid in the title than the concept of 'intercultural citizenship', but regardless of the labels, as Mike emphasizes, both focus on competence education rather than identities (Byram, 2003, 2008).

The authors localize global citizenship education in the Chinese context through engaging the cultural core concept 道/dao of Chinese philosophy and drawing on Confucian humanism, where humanity is perceived as in unity with Heaven, Earth and the myriad things; the future of the global human life community in the 21st century is predicated on intercultural dialogue on an equal footing as the ideal form of intercultural communication. As a Chinese philosophical concept, no single word in English or in many other languages could convey the multifaceted meanings of 道/*dao*. Literally, it means 'way', 'road', 'path' or 'course', but also 'word', 'speech' or even 'truth'. Robert G. Henricks translated it as 'the Way', but pointed out even Lao-tzu, the author of the word *dao* 'does not know its *true* name, he simply "calls" it the Way' and all things (Heaven and Earth) emerge from the *dao* in creation (Henrick, 1989: xviii–xix). Drawing upon the etymological interpretation of the cosmic *dao*, which pictographically has the meaning of 'walk' and 'to lead', the authors argue for *dao* giving directions towards a community of shared future for mankind. Besides, '道/dao', other indigenous Confucian ethical concepts, such as 仁/*ren*, (humanness/co-humanity), 义/*yi* (righteousness), 和/*he* (harmony), 恕/*shu*, (reciprocity), are also adopted as key concepts to offer insights into the nature of intercultural communication. The character 仁/*ren* (benevolence) itself consists of 'two people' pictographically, so this 'benevolence' is interpreted as plural, between and among humans; 义/yi ('righteousness') connotes a moral sense or a moral disposition to do good, but without any religious or disapproving tone associated with 'righteousness'; likewise, 和/*he* is an ethical concept denoting the harmonious state of the relationship in a much broader sense than the English word 'harmony'. The importing of these conceptualizations obviously disturbs the assumption of transparent translation of concepts from other cultures.

In contrast to 'anthropocentrism', the authors proposed an 'anthropocosmic vision' as an alternative perspective on the future world:

> [T]his anthropocosmic vision proposes the principle of 'being for both self and other' as global communicative ethics and criteria for criticality in contexts of interculturality and serves as a perspective on intercultural communication and global citizenship education for a community of shared future for mankind. (Jia *et al.*, 2019: 3)

This anthropocosmic vision foregrounds Confucian ethics of 'how to be a human', emphasizing *ren, shu* and *he* among ethical relationships and the ideal way, i.e. *dao* to co-create core values through intercultural dialogue on an equal footing for a community of a shared future.

As a textbook for college students to learn to conduct intercultural communication, it may not be as academic as expected in nature, and some concepts are used without rigorous examination, which is not uncommon in such a high context culture as in China. However, this accommodating or localized approach will help Chinese students to be more self-reflective and gain a better understanding of their own culture. Furthermore, these indigenous ethical concepts will certainly help intercultural dialogue and enrich existing intercultural communication theories, which are more often created from an Anglo or Eurocentric perspective. As sinologist Roger Ames lamented in his book *Confucian Role Ethics – A Vocabulary*, there is a long-lasting and harmful asymmetric relationship between Chinese and Western cultures partly because

Western scholars simply use Western words to talk about Chinese indigenous concepts (Ames, 2011).

In our paper (Wang & Byram, 2011) on Chinese postgraduate students' learning beliefs and experiences encountering British culture of teaching, we focused on concepts and vocabulary that Chinese students use to talk about their learning, such as 苦心 *kuxin,* 虚心 *xuxin,* 用心 *yongxin,* and keep these original Chinese characters presented in *pinyin* (Chinese phonetics) with 'thick translation', such as providing notes, commentary or explications, since the implied 'affective' connotations of the term may not be captured by a neat English translation. In this way, the themes of the 'heart and mind' and person or virtue orientation of learning conceptions are all grounded in the data, showing the affective and moral dimensions of conceptions of learning in Chinese culture, which have not received due attention in earlier research where teaching and learning is more cognitive-oriented. Besides, the participants' indigenous words and their practice of translanguaging and code-switching (between English and Chinese) can be a significant analytical tool to understand their conceptualization of their newly acquired concepts and the process of their learning in a new cultural context. We also argue, this code-switching practice deserves more attention in analyzing the process and dynamism of intercultural encounters.

Invited to lead an EU-funded project on 'New European Young Researchers' Identities, Exchanges and Doctoral Students – an international study of processes and outcomes in the EU, Mike was also thinking of expanding this Euro-focused approach to include a non-European case study to provide a comparative angle and perspective. Since my university Beijing Language and Culture University (BLCU) has arguably the largest number of international students studying Chinese language, I happily joined the project group. In the summer of 2016 when Mike happened to be in Beijing, he joined me in interviewing two Malaysian doctoral students who were studying at my university at that time. Although he had the prepared interview questions at hand, Mike was very patiently listening to the students talking about various aspects of their doctoral experiences in China. The interview lasted for 1 hour and 40 minutes, during which the girls mentioned a couple of times the help in both academic study and everyday life from their *tongmen* brothers and sisters. Mike was sagaciously aware that this term *tongmen* denoting a strong sense of disciplinary unity and solidarity seemingly similar to 'the cliques within departments' (Parry, 2007: 58) but might not mean the same as the common disciplinary community or the general support from 'others' in the previous literature, such as 'community of practice' (Wenger, 1998). Later, through analyzing seven international doctoral students' experiences of supervisions, the concept of *'tongmen'* emerged from these data as a kind of unique aspect of supervision in the Chinese context of doctoral education, where both explicit rules, practices of the discipline, tacit values and norms are passed from the old timers, i.e. senior doctoral researchers, to the novice doctoral researchers (see Wang & Byram, 2019).

The literal translation of the Chinese word 'tongmen' 同门 is 'of the same door', referring to the graduate students supervised by the same supervisor. They form such a community or 'clique' where novices and juniors are mentored and socialized through this established hierarchy of tongmen to acquire the traditions and conventions of their discipline as through the socialization process provided by formal doctoral programs. The difference is this 'clique' is not just for specialism or disciplinary solidarity but is also a social network providing both academic and emotional support. The significance of this finding lies in its potential in changing the unquestioned realities of other university systems and intellectual traditions in the process of internationalization of higher education. Tongmen network can be 'a major factor in overcoming the loneliness, the challenges of a different academic tradition, and the problems of working in a foreign language, which Elliot et al. (2016) identified as peculiar to international students' (Wang & Byram, 2019: 269). Furthermore, despite obvious advantages of 'tongmen' community practice, the limiting influence or disadvantage of this family-like bond supervisor-student relationship on creativity and academic ethos are worth further study.

Methodologically, Mike emphasizes such emic research design to reveal the linguistic and cultural complexities and suggested that we take a combination of a naturalistic approach, which emphasizes 'insider' status, and a positivistic approach, which maximally standardizes research instruments and procedures to approach our study on the students' intercultural sojourning experience. He had the foresight to advocate for a bilingual native ethnographer's betwixt-and-between speaking position in fusing the etic and the emic, and in probing the hybridity as a result of cultural interactions. And this 'native ethnography' methodology, or 'the native study the native', did prove to be advantageous for understanding the nuances of the meaning attached to the words and concepts of the studied.

Mike always emphasizes the rigorous standardization of research procedures and instruments by reminding me and his other students that 'we all write theses (and books) about ourselves' (Wang, 2015: ix); the writing, even if it appears to be in an academic and objective style, is a personal and subjective experience shared with others. He warns us of the subjectivity and intersubjectivities of any writing and reading experience and that an author has to be aware that they are influenced by their own traditions and practices. A reader has to be aware that their own traditions and practices influence how they understand what they are reading. The author, furthermore, has to be careful not to suggest or imply that what they are saying is valid for every context and tradition, and the reader has to understand that they cannot simply transfer ideas from one tradition to another and expect them to flourish and be useful.

Engagement with Chinese Language Teacher Community

Mike's ICC model is widely spread and embraced in the intercultural communication field in China. He was invited to deliver keynote addresses at various conferences and CAFIC annual intercultural communication conferences in China, usually attended by hundreds of language teachers, most of whom teach English at different levels of education in China. In his talks, Mike would remind his audience of the importance of considering cultural contexts when applying any theories or models by straightforward declarations such as 'the notion of intercultural dialogue is closely related to the "European idea" of social cohesion and living together' or 'from a Euro-centric perspective'. Mike's work served as inspiration for myself and colleagues to work on such challenging and unresolved issues of language education as linguistic assimilation and ideological tensions around protecting, preserving and developing ethnic minority languages and cultures (Feng & Wang, 2022). Importantly, Mike stresses that language education needs to locate all education in its social, economic and political context. He would use his namesake Michael Sadler's gardening metaphor (Bereday, 1964) of different foreign systems of education to illustrate his point of teaching values and teachers' responsibilities in a language teaching garden:

> On the one hand, all gardens have common features, being places where gardeners/teachers tend their plants/learners and want them to grow and realise their full potential. On the other hand, gardens lie in different climates and gardeners have different conceptions of what a garden is – a Japanese garden is different from a French garden which is different from an English garden, and so on – and we can learn to appreciate all of them in their own way. (Byram, 2020: 84)

Therefore, Mike was fully aware of the different cultures of teaching and learning in a different country and made appropriate accommodations and 'localizations' in his lectures delivered to his Chinese audience. Between 2015 and 2018, Mike received invitations from Chinese universities and the Foreign Language Teaching and Research Press (FLTRP) to give lectures and workshops for foreign language teachers, which consisted of both the Chinese teachers teaching English language in China and teachers teaching Chinese language to speakers of other languages (TCSOL), either inside China or abroad at overseas Confucius Institutes.

Foreign language teaching and learning, or English teaching and learning, to be specific, has been instrumental in orientation in China for taking high stake tests and getting jobs. In Chinese universities, non-English majors, regardless of their disciplines, are all required to take College English Test Level 4 (CET-4) or CET-6 (usually for graduate students). The phrases of 'to cultivate intercultural communicative competence' or 'to broaden students' international horizon' were just lip service in the discourse and documents, because intercultural competence was not imperatively taught nor evaluated in the syllabus.

To my knowledge, Mike's lectures and speeches at various conferences on teaching ICC have been highly appreciated by both teachers and influential figures in foreign language education disciplines in China, such as the head of the steering committee for foreign language teaching and Chairman of CAFIC. This led to the reformulation of the statement about 'both instrumental and humanistic features' of English education in the national document, i.e. College English Teaching Guideline in 2015. According to this new guideline, an 'intercultural communication course' is added to the College English Syllabus for the first time, 'which aims at intercultural education, helps students to understand the different outlooks, values, thinking modes between China and other countries, cultivates students' intercultural awareness, and improves their sociolinguistic and intercultural communication competence' (College English Teaching Guideline by College Foreign Language Teaching Steering Committee of Ministry of Education, 2015). This is a milestone document in English language teaching in China.

Since his engagement with Chinese language teachers of TCSOL is less recorded in literature outside China, I will now review his series of lectures organized by Beijing Foreign Studies University (BFSU) and FLTRP in the summer of 2016 in Beijing.

In July of 2016, at the request of the Vice President of BFSU, Mike designed a series of tailored workshops which were attended by about 500 Chinese language teachers across the country. He delivered four lecture series titled:

(1) Fundamental issues in intercultural communicative language teaching (ICLT).
(2) Curriculum and lesson planning.
(3) Assessment and evaluation.
(4) Critical thinking and the humanistic purpose of ICLT-the way forward.

These lectures were transcribed and translated into Chinese and published as a book titled *Intercultural Communicative Language Teaching and TCSOL* by FLTRP in 2017.

In his preliminary remarks, Mike pointed out the two aims of foreign language teaching: the instrumental aim, i.e. using language for communication; and the humanistic aim, which is not adequately recognized, i.e. using language teaching to understand others and ourselves. He used the official College English Teaching Syllabus to contextualize his model and theories and expounded that humanistic and instrumental rationales are not mutually exclusive.

Addressing issues of teaching culture in TCSOL, Mike used examples to pose the question what kind of culture the language teacher should teach the learner: surface culture and/or deep culture? That is relevant to international Chinese language education which has been promoted vigorously across the globe by the Chinese government via Confucius Institutes and other initiatives for the past two decades. He emphasized that 'culture is a verb', a matter of behavior, value and belief. He would raise heuristic questions for trainee teachers to think about: Should you as Chinese teachers teach, for example, your Vietnamese students to see themselves as Chinese people see them? To know China like the Chinese, or to know how to think and act in a Chinese way with Chinese values?

Mike invited me to his second lecture 'Curriculum and Lesson Planning', where we gave a double presentation on how to change curriculum textbooks from cultural to intercultural. We selected one lesson from a popular Chinese textbook about 'using chopsticks' to show the difference between what is cultural teaching and what is intercultural teaching and how to design a lesson to develop the students' skills of discovery and interaction and their critical cultural awareness instead of just cultural knowledge of 'do's and don'ts' about chopsticks. During the Q & A session, the trainee teachers were very actively interacting with us. Some Chinese teachers may not be very proficient in using English, but Mike could always understand their concerns and answered their questions patiently. One question was about the difference between an intercultural communicative approach and the popular/familiar communicative language teaching approach. Mike explained that the shift from traditional language teaching to the communicative approach did not change the idea that 'learners are implicitly, sometimes explicitly, learning to imitate native speakers. The move from communicative to intercultural is to emphasise the point ... that the identity of the learner is not to imitate the speaker but to become something in between, an intercultural speaker, a mediator ...' (Byram, 2017: 83). This concept of intercultural speaker or mediator was unfamiliar to most TCSOL teachers, but the feedback from the participant teachers indicated that they embraced this idea and started to reflect on their teaching beliefs about language and culture.

As an extension of 'intercultural speaker' (Byram, 1997), Mike developed his concept of 'intercultural citizenship' (Byram, 2008, 2009) to encourage language teachers and learners not only to critique and challenge but also to become involved in action in their community and to take action in a changing society and the world. The main arguments are, first, foreign language teaching can play a major role in the development of intercultural competence and, furthermore, foreign language teaching needs to be allied with citizenship education, which means the objectives of foreign language teaching need to engage not just cultural and educational dimensions but also ethical and political dimensions and to be further augmented with an emphasis upon action in the world.

In his last lecture on humanistic and critical approaches to language teaching, Mike emphasized the two concepts 'criticality' and 'action in the community'. He was fully aware of, but did not avoid, the challenges and dilemmas with which teachers were confronted, particularly in the Chinese context, in implementing these approaches in their classroom. He invited the teachers to think 'what are the teachers' aims here' and cited Confucius's words 'we want our learners to think', to explore, analyze and reflect on a topic or an issue. Mike explained that critical cultural awareness means making cultural comparisons and judgments against explicit criteria. He used the example of a project (see Byram *et al.*, 2017, for more information about the project) done between a British university and an Argentinian university on the event of the 30th anniversary of the war called Falkland War in the UK and the Malvinas in Argentina, to show how language teachers combine teaching of languaculture with some aspects of citizenship education, that is, to take 'action in the community' to develop intercultural competence, and to acquire a third space or mediating perspective. Considering his Chinese audience, he made a point of demystifying critical thinking skills to show that the teacher's job was not to tell learners what to think, but to help them be critical and think for themselves, from a national perspective but also an international perspective. Obviously, that is relevant to the Chinese educational context, which has long been criticized for lacking criticality or a critical approach in its culture of teaching and learning. He concluded his lecture with the following:

> My belief as a languaculture teacher is that this is what we should be doing. As languaculture teachers, we should be part of how education improves and changes society. But as I said before, this is a dilemma which we all have to consider as teachers for ourselves. Everyone has to think for themselves. It is not for me to tell other teachers what to think. Teachers should have their responsibilities and must make their own decisions. (Byram, 2017: 161)

This agency stance certainly has implications for teacher education, and for the professional identities of language teachers. Traditionally, teachers in China are endowed with the double responsibility of 'teaching (via) the book and cultivating the person' ('教书育人'); therefore, this ideology or approach is not alien to Chinese teachers, and the workshops provided the language teachers with concrete hands-on methods as to how to integrate this dimension into foreign language classroom teaching. As argued in his book co-authored with the Chinese scholars mentioned above, 'a community of shared future is inherently embedded in the process of intercultural communication' (Jia *et al.*, 2019: 10) and to build a harmonious community of shared future for mankind takes on the most urgency for intercultural education in the 21st century. Currently, Chinese teachers of all levels are required by the Ministry of Education to incorporate political-ideological content into their daily teaching to cultivate socialism builders and successors. Mike's intercultural citizenship education to prepare young generations to learn to be 'active citizens' has the potential to be a valuable theoretical underpinning for Chinese educational theory and practice to produce a new generation interdependent and committed/'engagé' in a community of a shared future.

In 2018, Mike was invited by FLTRP again to deliver two webinars: 'English Language Teaching and a Community of a Shared Future for Humankind' and 'Interpreting the Humanistic Features of Foreign Language Education from an Intercultural Perspective' (together with his doctoral student Qin Shuoqian) at Unipus. Unipus is a large learning and teaching platform created by the FLTRP, affiliated with Beijing Foreign Studies University. Both internationally and domestically renowned experts and scholars in the field of foreign language education are regularly invited to offer live webinars and share teaching and learning resources via Unipus, which could reach up to 50,000 teachers. These lectures and webinars exerted a great impact on the Chinese teachers' teaching beliefs, either teaching Chinese language to the speakers of other languages or teaching English language to the Chinese learners. It might be a fruitful endeavor to keep track of these Chinese language teachers to see how this intercultural approach is implemented in their classrooms.

Furthermore, Mike's theories and works have inspired Chinese teachers and scholars to explore the field of teaching intercultural competence and developing intercultural education theories locally (see Dai, 2011; Gao, 1998; Sun et al., 2016; Zhang, 2012; Zheng, 2018). For example, Zheng (2018) conducted an interview with Mike during her visit to Durham University, and later she published the interview account and her evaluation of intercultural content in the textbooks published in China. From the interview, we can also see the importance that Mike attached to the localization of intercultural communication theories and formative assessment of intercultural learning. Professor Sun Youzhong and his colleagues drew upon Mike's ICC model and compiled a set of English language textbooks, published in 2016 by FLTRP, with the English word 'Think' on the cover, explicitly foregrounding the importance of training the learners' critical thinking and intercultural competence in cultivating international and global talents. These textbooks are widely used in Chinese universities and have greatly advanced the intercultural dimension in English education in China. In Shanghai International Studies University (SISU), Professor Steve Kulich and Professor Zhang Hongling have been actively promoting an online intercultural communication course. As a dedicated researcher and scholar in intercultural communicative competence in China, Professor Dai Xiaodong from Shanghai Normal University (SNU) has been comparing various ICC theories of both home and abroad and told me that he read Mike's monograph of 1997 *Teaching and Assessing Intercultural Communicative Competence* four times!

It may not be exaggerated to say that Mike's intercultural teaching and learning theories have reshaped the landscape of the research in this field in China. When I searched the China National Knowledge Infrastructure (CNKI) website with the keywords 'intercultural communicative competence', 'intercultural competence' and 'intercultural education and intercultural teaching', there were more than 60 papers for the past decade, and about two thirds of them cited or referred to Mike's ICC model. After 2018, about 12 articles focus on intercultural teaching specifically, and the emerging trend indicates that more empirical studies have appeared.

This is a great step forward, because, from 2011 to 2015, few empirical studies were done in this field. The most recently published book by FLTRP *Research on Intercultural Foreign Language Teaching and Learning* (in Chinese, see Sun *et al.*, 2021) systematically reviews the key intercultural theories and the development of foreign language teaching research and provides a comprehensive description of the purpose, principles and methods of intercultural foreign language teaching, as well as the research on foreign language teachers, teaching materials and assessment issues in the field of intercultural foreign language teaching and learning. Moreover, more and more Chinese language specialists and trainers start to adopt an intercultural approach to teaching Chinese languages to the speakers of other languages. For instance, in a recent online seminar organized by the Faculty of International Chinese Language Education of BLCU for Chinese language teachers abroad, two out of the three specialists invited cited Mike's ICC model in their presentations and strongly advocated for teaching intercultural communicative competence in Chinese language classrooms.

Coda: Engagement with the World in Crisis: Towards a Shared Future

In April of 2020 when the Covid-19 pandemic was raging all over the world and internationalism was challenged by a rising nationalism, my university, BLCU, invited Mike and some other world-renowned scholars to contribute their thoughts on the current perplexing issues posed by the pandemic crisis. Mike wrote an essay 'How do/should Interculturalists respond to the Corona/Covid 19 crisis?' The essay (translated by me) was recently published in its Chinese version in China.

The essay starts with the depressing experience of his French colleague Catherine who has lived in Germany for many years but was denied by German authorities boarding a chartered plane leaving Costa Rica (due to the Covid-19 epidemic) for Germany with her French passport. The French authorities would not accept her on their plane either – despite her French passport – because she resided in Germany. Mike lamented the disappearance of the European ideal in these moments of stress and the reappearance of nationalism and national borders. Through revisiting intercultural theories and models which claim to 'prepare young people – and perhaps older ones too – for the "post-modern" world', he pointed out that 'the re-appearance of national boundaries and nationalist ideologies and identities' means that 'models of intercultural competence must pay renewed attention to communication across national boundaries'. He called upon language teachers and interculturalists to respond beyond the walls of their institutions and choose to become 'engagé' both in their theoretical and experiential practice, and encourage their students to take 'action in the community' to become 'active citizens'.

This active stance coordinates with his unequivocal statement in the last chapter of his book on education for intercultural citizenship: '[i]t is the notion of taking action that links the concept of intercultural communicative competence with education for citizenship'. He calls for the teachers of foreign languages 'not only to combine utility and educational values, but also show learners how they can and should engage with the international globalized world in which they participate', or 'engagement in action'. Mike admitted that this is a new step, a movement 'from' and 'to', a new agenda for 'things to be done' (Byram, 2008: 229).

Again, Mike was concerned that something might be lost in translation when I told him that his essay was to be published only in Chinese. We had detailed discussions about the proper translation of the culturally loaded words such as 'engagé' into Chinese. I shared with him my rendition '责任当担' (*zeren dandang*) based on my understanding of 'engagé' as 'active participant with commitment', and he thought that was appropriate.

As an active and committed educator and interculturalist, subscribing to W.B. Yeats' saying that 'Education is not the filling of a pail, but the lighting of a fire', Mike has been engaging himself addressing the critical issues that threaten world peace and humanity, and unremittingly working towards a shared future of light, warmth and hope.

Conclusion

I have tried to present a profile of Mike's engagement with the Chinese academic community in an area of foreign language teaching and intercultural education in China. These less-known academic involvements on part of Mike deserve attention and appreciation. Not only as a distinguished scholar, but also as a superb teacher, supervisor and mentor for his colleagues and students, Mike has certainly touched many peoples' lives, most of whom are language teachers in all parts of the world. I consider myself extremely fortunate in having Mike as my supervisor and mentor, who illuminated my doctoral journey with his brilliant thinking and uncanny wisdom. I am and will always be proud of being Mike's student and live up to his educational ideals as a committed language educator and an optimistic interculturalist. Whenever I feel disheartened at the current dismal world, his warm words always bring me light and hope:

> *Today we have rain but we have a stove and plenty of wood to make a fire. Better weather is promised for tomorrow.* (Personal communication, 20 April 2020)

References

Ames, R.T. (2011) *Confucian Role Ethics—A Vocabulary*. Cambridge, MA: Harvard University Press.

Appiah, K.A. (2000) 'Thick translation'. In L. Venuti (ed.) *The Translation Studies Reader* (pp. 417–429). London: Routledge.

Bereday, G.Z.F. (1964) Sir Michael Sadler's 'Study of Foreign Systems of Education'. *Comparative Education Review* 7 (3), 307–314.

Byram, M. (1997) *Teaching and Assessing Intercultural Communicative Competence*. Clevedon: Multilingual Matters.

Byram, M. (2003) On being 'bicultural' and 'intercultural'. In G. Alred, M. Byram and M. Fleming (eds) *Intercultural Experience and Education* (pp. 50–66). Clevedon: Multilingual Matters.

Byram, M. (2009) Developing a concept of intercultural citizenship. In Y.X Jia and G.M. Chen (eds) 《跨文化交际研究》 (*Intercultural Communication Research*) (Vol. 1, pp. 16–29). Beijing, China: Higher Education Press.

Byram, M. (2017) *Intercultural Communicative Language Teaching and TCSOL*. Beijing: Foreign Language Teaching and Research Press.

Byram, M. (2020) The responsibilities of language teachers when teaching intercultural competence and citizenship – An essay. *China Media Research* 16 (2), 77–84.

Byram, M. (2021) How do/should interculturalists respond to the Corona/Covid 19 crisis? In L. Liu (ed.) 《全球战"疫", 天下一家》 (*Together in the Fight Against COVID- 19*) (pp. 87–92). Beijing: Sinolingua.

Byram, M. (2021) *Teaching and Assessing Intercultural Communicative Competence: Revisited*. Bristol: Multilingual Matters.

Byram, M., Golubeva, I., Han, H. and Wagner, M. (eds) (2017) *From Principles to Practice in Education for Intercultural Citizenship*. Bristol: Multilingual Matters.

Council of Europe (2018) *Reference Framework of Competences for Democratic Culture*. Strasbourg: Council of Europe.

Dai, X. (2011) 《跨文化交际理论》 (*Intercultural Communication Theories*). Shanghai: Shanghai Foreign Language Press.

Elliot, D.L., Vivienne, B. and Kate, R. (2016) Searching for 'a third space': A creative pathway towards international PhD students' academic acculturation. *Higher Education Research & Development* 35 (6), 1180–1195.

Gao, Y. (1998) 跨文化交际能力的"道"与"器" (*Dao* and *Qi* in Intercultural Communicative Competence) 《语言教学与研究》 (*Language Teaching and Research*) 3, 39–53.

Geertz, C. (1973) *The Interpretation of Cultures: Selected Essays*. New York: Basic Books.

Feng, A. (2006) Contested notions of citizenship and citizenship education: The Chinese case. In G. Alred, M. Byram and M. Fleming (eds) *Education for Intercultural Citizenship: Concepts and Comparisons* (pp. 86–108). Clevedon: Multilingual Matters.

Feng, A. and Wang, L. (2022) Towards an empowerment model for multilingual education at Minzu universities in China. In B. Adamson and A. Feng (eds) *Multilingual China: National, Minority, and Foreign Languages* (pp. 139–149). London: Routledge.

Henricks, R.G. (1989) *Lao Tzu Te-Tao Ching*. New York: Ballantine Books.

Jia, Y.X., Byram, M., Jia, X.R., Song, L. and Jia, X.L. (2019) *Experiencing Global Intercultural Communication: Preparing for a Community of Shared Future for Mankind and Global Citizenship*. Beijing, China: Foreign Language Teaching and Research Press.

Jia, Y.X and Chen, G.M. (eds) (2009) 《跨文化交际研究》 (*Intercultural Communication Research)* (Vol. 1). Beijing, China: Higher Education Press.

Parry, S. (2007) *Disciplines and Doctorates*. Dordrecht: Springer.

Ryle, G. (1971) *Collected Papers*. Volume II: *Collected Essays 1929–1968*. London: Hutchinson.

Sun, Y. (2016) (edited) 《大学思辨英语教程》 (*Think-College English Course Book*), Foreign Language Teaching and Research Press, Beijing, China.

Sun, Y., Liao, H., Zheng, X. and Qin, S. (2021) 《跨文化外语教学研究》 (*Research on Intercultural Foreign Language Teaching and Learning)*. Beijing: Foreign Language Teaching and Research Press.

Wang, L. (2015) *Chinese Students, Learning Cultures, and Overseas Study*. London: Palgrave MacMillan.

Wang, L. and Byram, M. (2011) "But when you are doing your exams it is the same as in China"—Chinese students adjusting to western approaches to teaching and learning. *Cambridge Journal of Education* 41 (4), 407–424.

Wang, L. and Byram, M. (2019) International doctoral students' experience of supervision: A case-study in a Chinese University. *Cambridge Journal of Education* 49 (3), 255–274.

Wenger, E. (1998) *Communities of Practice: Learning, Meaning, and Identity*. Cambridge: Cambridge University Press.

Zhang, H. (2012) 以跨文化教育为导向的外语教学: 历史、现状与未来 (Foreign language teaching oriented towards intercultural education: History, current situation and future) 《外语界》 (*Foreign Language World*) 2, 2–7.

Zheng, X. (2018) 跨文化视角下的教材评价研究 (Evaluation of teaching materials from intercultural perspective—Revelation from a dialogue with Professor Michael Byram). 《外语界》 (*Foreign Language World*) 2, 80–86.

Looking Back and Looking Forward

Mike Byram and Multilingual Matters: A 40-Year Partnership

We (my late husband, Mike Grover, and I) met Mike Byram in the early 1980s when Multilingual Matters Publishing Company was formed. Mike was one of our first authors, who believed in our mission to bring well-researched information on multilingualism and multiculturalism to a wider audience. At that time, there was very little information available on the subject despite a large part of the world population speaking more than one language and different ethnic groups and nationalities living side by side. Our aim was to publish research studies from different countries on the subject and dispel the myth that monolingualism is the norm. In monolingual countries, bilingualism was often seen as a problem, and immigrants were expected to assimilate to the majority culture as far and as fast as possible. Publication of Mike's book *Minority Education and Ethnic Survival* in 1986 was one of the early books in our Multilingual Matters series, and it was the start of a very successful author/publisher relationship. Mike being at Durham University gave an interesting addition to that relationship as my husband was a Durham graduate (although his degree, physics, was nothing to do with languages).

Bringing up children bilingually in the 1980s was not as easily accepted as now, and information for parents was scarce. 'The Bilingual Family Newsletter' was born from our own need to understand how we could best bring up our two sons speaking my mother tongue, Finnish, in England when English was not only the language of the society and school but also the world language. We looked for academics who could 'translate' research findings into a language that parents would understand, and who also had personal experience bringing up children bilingually. Mike Byram was an obvious choice for the advisory board, as Mike and Marie-Therese were keen to bring up their children to speak French, Marie-Therese's mother tongue. I vividly remember how comforting it was to hear that even a professional linguist had to work hard to make sure that the minority language was not drowned under an influx of English. Mike and his family's contributions to the Newsletter were much appreciated.

Not long ago, I met Mike and Marie-Therese in Brighton for a cup of coffee. Our bilingual children have flown their nests a long time ago, and we are now retired. Sadly, my husband died in 2013 after only five years of retirement, but I think Mike Byram, being an academic, will never completely retire as the world of academia needs people with an abundance of experience. Mike and Marie-Therese have moved from Durham to Brighton, an easy distance from their house in France. I still live in Clevedon but travel to Finland and America (where my grandchildren are) regularly. Our children, being born into bicultural families, are all living quite international lives, the Byram children even more so than the Grover children – Alice living in Spain and Ian in Pakistan. We agreed that grandparenting from a distance was not our choice, but thanks to modern communication and travel, it is probably easier than it was for our parents 40+ years ago.

Thanks to researchers like Mike Byram, we now have a much better understanding of multilingualism and multiculturalism. He has definitely smoothed the road for future generations, and I am very grateful for it.

Marjukka Grover, Clevedon
Co-founder of Channel View Publications and Multilingual Matters

Mike Byram's Commitment to Council of Europe Values

Those of us who have had the good fortune to collaborate with Mike Byram in Council of Europe (CoE) projects or elsewhere will have been struck by his deep commitment to quality and equity in education. The promotion of plurilingual and intercultural education (PIE), intercultural understanding and citizenship in democratic societies were central to Mike's broad vision that enriched not only CoE language work but also its education programme in general. This was particularly the case during his time as Adviser to the Language Policy Division in Strasbourg, alongside Jean-Claude Beacco, a period of dynamic development at the Council of Europe following the steady accession of countries in Central and Eastern Europe.

Mike Byram's impact had already been apparent in a pioneering 1994 study on sociocultural competence (with Geneviève Zarate) commissioned for the CEFR process, which introduced the key concepts 'cultural intermediary' and 'social actor', focusing attention on the action of mediation by an 'intercultural speaker'. His seminal savoirs model of intercultural communicative competence subsequently underpinned CEFR Chapter 5.1 'General Competences'. The inclusion of attitudes and personality factors in his *savoir-être* component brings to mind Mike's openness to different perspectives, his democratic approach and mediation skills, attributes widely appreciated in his many contributions in Strasbourg and further afield, including in sensitive political contexts.

During the preliminary stages of the CEFR development process, we imposed tight deadlines on authors, which inevitably prevented a more in-depth treatment of intercultural competence at that time. Thankfully, Mike subsequently accepted the challenge to develop this crucial transversal dimension further as the Council of Europe intensified its activities to promote democratic citizenship and intercultural dialogue. With his and Jean-Claude Beacco's guidance, intergovernmental language programmes were developed to support the implementation of its values through PIE.

This broad concept, or 'vision' as Mike has described it, promotes a coherent learner-centred perspective, encompassing all languages and varieties present in the school and in the learner's repertoire, whether formally acknowledged or not: foreign, minority, migrant, classical and, crucially, language(s) of schooling. As an experienced teacher educator, Mike Byram was sensitive to the implementation challenges posed by this transversal approach to the curriculum. In typically pragmatic fashion, he worked with Jean-Claude Beacco, Daniel Coste, Mike Fleming and many others in developing an open, dynamic 'Platform of Resources and References for Plurilingual and Intercultural Education' in order to assist member states in the implementation of PIE in schools, in an approach centred on the learner as a developing social actor with an existing repertoire to enrich and diversify through educational processes: https://www. coe.int/en/web/language-policy/platform.

While CoE programmes had been focused mainly on foreign language education, Mike Byram's abiding concern to ensure effective implementation of the right to education in practice, to promote quality and equity in education, led to a major project on the language(s) of schooling (LoS) – language taught as a subject and the academic language competences essential for successful learning across the full curriculum. As to be expected, Mike ensured a strong focus on inclusive education, taking into account the rights and needs of disadvantaged learners and children of migration.

Member states received assistance with policy renewal through on-the-spot CoE assistance with self-assessment of policy, complemented with values-oriented policy and curriculum guides by Byram, Beacco and others. This rolling project made many demands on Mike's time, and we always looked forward to seeing him in Strasbourg, although we no doubt took advantage of his generous nature at times, as occasional notes scribbled on paper napkins while sharing a *tarte flambée* might suggest.....

The outcomes of the LoS project provided the basis for a Recommendation of the Committee of Ministers 'on the importance of competences in the language(s) of schooling for equity and quality in education and for educational success'. The critical role of language competence in learning and teaching democratic citizenship and for facilitating full participation in democratic and culturally diverse societies has been convincingly demonstrated by Byram and Fleming with regard to the Reference Framework of Competences for Democratic Culture (RFCDC).

Mike Byram's support for a cross-disciplinary approach to CoE values is particularly evident in his follow-up to the CoE White Paper on Intercultural Dialogue. He brought together specialists from languages, history, education for democratic citizenship, religious education and other relevant disciplines, including Martyn Barrett and Robert Jackson, to develop an 'Autobiography of Intercultural Encounters' designed to help young people reflect on and understand better their own responses and feelings when confronted with Otherness in their national context or in an international one. In a similar vein, Mike has recently pointed to increased opportunities for supporting learners to be intercultural citizens in their own and in international communities by exploiting the 'political' relevance of CoE reference instruments such as RFCDC, CEFR and its associated documents, including the Companion Volume.

Mike Byram's unique contribution has developed and enriched the foundational work of John Trim, his distinguished predecessor in CoE projects. In the recent Revisited edition of his seminal book, Mike generously acknowledges the intellectual stimulation and friendship he enjoyed in Strasbourg. This was fully reciprocated by all who had the privilege of collaborating with him in the promotion of our shared values.

I am grateful to Mike for his friendship, for his guidance and support and for so willingly and generously putting his remarkable *savoirs*, not least his *savoir-être*, at the service of quality and equity in education.

Joe Sheils, Dublin
Former Head of the Language Policy Division,
Council of Europe, Strasbourg

Working with Mike Byram

I first met Mike Byram in Cambridge in 2004. We had both been invited to act as external examiners for a PhD thesis. Before the viva, Mike and I were taken out for lunch by the candidate's supervisor, and over the course of the meal, we discovered how much our research interests overlapped, despite our very different disciplinary and theoretical perspectives. I did not realise at the time that our meeting would have a profound impact on my own research trajectory and that it would also be the starting point for a lasting friendship.

Two years later, in 2006, Mike, in his role as adviser to the Language Policy Division of the Council of Europe, was helping Joe Sheils set up an expert group for the purposes of developing a new educational tool to support learners' reflections on their intercultural encounters and promote their intercultural competence – the Autobiography of Intercultural Encounters (for details, see Chapter 4 in the present volume). I was invited to join the activity. From the outset, there were several features of the expert group that made a strong impression on me. Most notable were the working method that was adopted and the warmth of the personal relationships that rapidly developed between the members of the group. These features were not unconnected. Mike chaired the meetings of the group in a spirit of openness, inclusiveness and sensitivity to the different perspectives of the various group members. And as one might expect, the meetings were always highly respectful of the linguistic diversity of the group – while French and English are the two official languages of the Council of Europe, participants in projects are always drawn from a number of member states and have a variety of different languages as their first language. Mike's chairmanship skills meant that the meetings were not only intellectually stimulating but also very productive. Furthermore, the generous and convivial spirit of the meetings continued during the coffee breaks and at mealtimes, with evening meals together in a restaurant somewhere in the centre of Strasbourg always being a particularly enjoyable event. Inevitably, close friendships developed among the members of the group. I have subsequently participated in several further projects at the Council of Europe. These have included follow-on Autobiography projects that were also chaired by Mike, as well as other projects that have been chaired by other people. And it has become abundantly clear to me that the open and genuinely inclusive working method developed by the Autobiography team was unique and characteristic only of the groups chaired by Mike.

The other context in which I have witnessed the interplay of Mike's personal, intellectual, professional and intercultural skills is Cultnet. I started to attend the annual Cultnet meetings because I had heard a great deal on the grapevine about how rewarding these meetings are. I soon discovered that one of the most striking features of these meetings (in addition to the pervasive sense of affection for Mike himself) is Mike's focus on nurturing and encouraging younger colleagues in their research endeavours. He has a fascinating ability to combine intellectual rigour with sensitive and supportive questioning to stimulate critical reflection and generate new avenues for thought without creating any sense of threat.

Having now worked closely with Mike for a decade and a half, there is no question that I owe him an enormous debt. As a consequence of him drawing me into the work of the Council of Europe – which is the ideal institutional context for anyone who is passionate about human dignity and human rights – my own research interests soon moved away from developmental and social psychology towards the application of theories and findings from across the social sciences to theory and practice in inter-cultural education and citizenship education. Along the way, and through our very fertile collaboration, I have learned an enormous amount from Mike about all sorts of issues, not only in the field of education, and I have also been deeply inspired by his rigorous yet accessible style of reasoning.

It is also through Mike that I have learned about a fascinating figure in Danish literature – Tom Kristensen. Not many colleagues will be aware of the fact that Mike is the global expert on the work of Kristensen, having conducted his PhD thesis on 'The Novels of Tom Kristensen – Livets Arabesk, En Anden and Hærværk in their original context'. He has also authored the definitive book on Kristensen's literary output that includes not only novels but also some startling poetry. I can certainly recommend Hærværk very strongly indeed to anyone who enjoys reading substantial modernist novels (it is available in English translation under the title Havoc).

Looking back on our years of friendship, I know that I have been extremely privileged to work with Mike. He is not only an outstanding and innovative scholar but also a modest, deeply respectful and inspiring individual.

Martyn Barrett
Emeritus Professor of Psychology,
University of Surrey

Tribute to Mike Byram

Down time. I check my emails. There's one from Professor Michael Byram. (No, he's 'Mike' to everyone, everywhere, except in keynote introductions.) The email is an update on yet another new project he is embarking on – doctoral assessment. At the end of his email, I notice something new – a YouTube video link to his newly published book *Teaching and Assessing Intercultural Communicative Competence: Revisited* (Byram, 2021). I open the link to the video – a conversation between Mike and Karen Risager (see https://www.youtube.com/watch?v=IDbpRNStfPc). I watch and listen with interest. I'm eager to learn how Mike and Karen work together to discuss the book's contribution. Suddenly, I am overwhelmed. I find myself smiling, so widely – right down to my heart and lungs; there is something so familiar in seeing Mike there on the screen.

As I watch the video, my pleasure increases. Mike, as always, is spontaneous and natural. I'm reminded, whenever we start video calls with colleagues across our interconnected activities that Mike has invited me into, that we – not Mike – begin by lamenting our lot in these COVID times. And Mike's usual response is to defer to his Yorkshire roots, 'Oh well, as we say in Yorkshire, "mustn't grumble"'. Mike never does! After all, we are here to enjoy our work, and he makes it so.

In the video, Mike is himself. In fact, he's always himself. Never ruffled, always composed, ever ready and willing to listen and help. I feel privileged. But no, I should not! I'm but one of the many scholars, researchers, teachers whom Mike includes in his work routines, tirelessly. This is how Mike is. Ever willing to support others, wherever they are, sharing his knowledge and experience in researching and publishing. Ever willing to give his time and support to help others succeed! Retirement for Mike has released him to expand further his academic interests and networks. While many others would be 'slowing down', lessening their academic roles, Mike has continued to grow his – giving keynotes around the world, co-publishing with established and also emerging scholars – that's his way – to support scholars and scholarship, to make academia a better place, and academic endeavour worthwhile, and in doing so, to create enjoyment for us all. Mike is, after all, a leading world academic in every sense of the word.

My initial meeting with Mike goes back to 2005 when I first came to Durham from New Zealand, funded by a scholarship resulting from some left-over money that Mike had from a previous project. During this time, I got a taste of the activities and research Mike was engaged in, and the vibrant community of doctoral researchers under his supervision in the School of Education. On 1st July, 2010, my academic life changed as I came to work at Durham University. Unfortunately, Mike had not long retired. I wondered if I'd have to 'carry the mantle' alone. I needn't have worried. I was never alone as Mike never retired; he supported me through my three-year probation as research mentor, which he has remained. On the second day of my arrival, I was inducted into a research seminar Mike had set up, and so emerged my research trajectory on 'researching multi-lingually'; my connections with Mike have continued from this propitious start. Since coming to Durham, I've seen Cultnet expand exponentially through Mike's networks and involvement. The annual Cultnet meeting at Durham, established in 1997 and which Mike has missed only once, has maintained its original ethos of nurturing and supporting researchers and their research into language and intercultural communication education and teaching. I've been fortunate to co-supervise three doctoral students alongside Mike and engage in research projects (e.g. the Jean-Monet funded EUROMEC on doctoral supervision, and now a doctoral assess-ment project). The enjoyment and pleasure of learning alongside Mike means organisation, structure and rigour in thinking: There is no room for slippage (evidenced in his daily afternoon walks, once along the Wear River in Durham, and now along the Brighton foreshore)!

While the video for Multilingual Matters shines a light on Mike's new Revisited book, it does much more than that. It offers a glimpse into the ethical world Mike inhabits in and through his scholarship. He has worked tirelessly and worldwide to support interculturality in language education, and scholars and teachers involved in its research and delivery. There is always something inspiring and motivating about Mike's scholar-ship, his ideas and his approach to academic work. It fills me with confi-dence to go on with my own work. It fills me with pleasure that he has invited me, too, into his world. I smile with gratitude, admiration and, above all, respect. I smile, and in smiling, I feel honoured to be a part of Mike's world.

I wondered where I might start with this tribute. There are so many starting points, so many leads and entries. The video provided that entrée. The video marks Mike's lifelong endeavour. The timely publication of Revisited is perhaps fitting as we all write our contributions to Mike in and through this book. He has given so much to us all tirelessly and self-lessly. (Thank you, Marie-Thérèse, for sharing Mike with us.) Mike has made me a better academic, a better person. I am humbled. Although I speak for myself, I know that I am also speaking for so many others whom he has gathered up along the way and supported in their development, scholarship, mentoring, through co-publication, through engaging them in his many research projects, and in launching them into developing their own projects. It is with pleasure that we give our work back to you, Mike, in this book, so much of it is inspired by your scholarship and support over decades. We are all truly grateful. I am truly grateful for your help and friendship and to have been included in your scholarly world. A heartfelt thank you!

Prue Holmes
Professor in the School of Education
Durham University

References

Byram, M. (2021) *Teaching and Assessing Intercultural Communicative Competence: Revisited*. Bristol: Multilingual Matters.

Multilingual Matters (2021, March 17) *Behind the Books: Michael Byram, author of Teaching and Assessing Intercultural Communicative Competence, in conversation with Karen Risager* [Video]. YouTube. https://www.youtube.com/watch?v=IDbpRNStfPc

Index

CPSIA information can be obtained
at www.ICGtesting.com
Printed in the USA
JSHW021809090522
25754JS00003B/200